Death Work

A Study of the Modern Execution Process

Second Edition

ROBERT JOHNSON
American University

West / Wadsworth
I(T)P® An International Thomson Publishing Company

Belmont, CA • Albany, NY • Bonn • Boston • Cincinnati • Detroit • Johannesburg • London
Los Angeles • Madrid • Melbourne • Mexico City • Minneapolis/St. Paul • New York • Paris
Singapore • Tokyo • Toronto • Washington

Criminal Justice Editor: Sabra Horne
Assistant Editor: Claire Masson
Editorial Assistant: Kate Barrett
Marketing Manager: Mike Dew
Project Editor: Dianne Jensis
Print Buyer: Karen Hunt
Permissions Editor: Peggy Meehan
Copy Editor: Peter S. Toop
Cover Designer: Sandra Kelch
Cover Photo: Kevin Candland
Compositor: Thompson Type
Printer: Maple-Vail Book Manufacturing Group/Vail-Ballou Press

Printed in the United States of America
1 2 3 4 5 6 7 8 9 10

For more information, contact Wadsworth Publishing Company, 10 Davis Drive, Belmont, CA
94002, or electronically at http://www.thomson.com/wadsworth.html

International Thomson Publishing Europe
Berkshire House 168-173
High Holborn
London, WC1V 7AA, England

International Thomson Editores
Campos Eliseos 385, Piso 7
Col. Polanco
11560 México D.F. México

Thomas Nelson Australia
102 Dodds Street
South Melbourne 3205
Victoria, Australia

International Thomson Publishing Asia
221 Henderson Road
#05-10 Henderson Building
Singapore 0315

Nelson Canada
1120 Birchmount Road
Scarborough, Ontario
Canada M1K 5G4

International Thomson Publishing Japan
Hirakawacho Kyowa Building, 3F
2-2-1 Hirakawacho
Chiyoda-ku, Tokyo 102, Japan

International Thomson Publishing GmbH
Königswinterer Strasse 418
53227 Bonn, Germany

International Thomson Publishing Southern Africa
Building 18, Constantia Park
240 Old Pretoria Road
Halfway House, 1685 South Africa

Library of Congress Cataloging-in-Publication Data

Johnson, Robert, 1948–
    Death work : a study of the modern execution process / Robert Johnson.—2nd ed.
      p. cm.
    Includes bibliographical references and index.
    ISBN 0-534-52155-X
    1. Executions and executioners—United States.   2. Death row—United States.   3. Executions
and executioners—History.
    I. Title.
    HV8699.U5J643   1997   97-16577
    364.66'0973—dc21   CIP

For Deirdra, Brian, and Patrick
who keep me ever in touch with how good life can be
and, by implication, with how tragically awry things can go
for the victims of violent crimes and violent punishments.

Contents

FOREWORD   x i i

PREFACE   x i v

I   EXECUTIONS PAST   **1**

**1   EXECUTIONS PAST: EXECUTIONS IN THE
     WEST FROM ANTIQUITY TO THE
     TWENTIETH CENTURY**   **3**

Executions in Historical Perspective: An Overview   8
Executions Past   10
   Ancient Executions: Public, Passionate Violence   10
   Medieval Executions: Ceremonial Violence   12
   *Early Modern Executions: Refined Ritual,
   Subdued Ceremony*   16
The Threshold of Accepted Violence   20
Notes   21

2 EXECUTIONS IN AMERICA   **27**
The End of Public Ritual   27
Public Executions—Legal and Illegal—in the American South   31
Prison Executions: Private, Bureaucratic Procedure   40
Modern Executions and the Illusion of Humaneness   43
Modern Executions and the Ordeal of Dehumanization   47
Civilization and the Death Penalty   53
Notes   55

II WAITING TO DIE: A STUDY OF MODERN DEATH ROWS   **61**

3 DEATH ROW: CONDITIONS OF CONFINEMENT   **63**
Death Row Confinement in Historical Perspective   64
Current Conditions on Death Row   70
Death Row Reforms: The Illusion of Change   74
Case Study of a Failed Reform   76
Back to the Future: High-Tech Solitary Confinement on Modern Death Rows   80
A Death Row by Any Other Name...   84
Women on Death Row   86
Notes   87

4 LIVING AND WORKING ON DEATH ROW   **92**
Living on Death Row: The Psychology of Human Warehousing   94
Powerlessness   95
Loneliness   98
Vulnerability   101
Coping and the Crucible of Deterioration   104
A Living Death   106
Working on Death Row   109
Tension and Fear   109

Human Services   113
Us and Them: The Divisive Role of Executions   114
Notes   116

III IN COLD BLOOD: A STUDY OF MODERN EXECUTIONS   121

5 DEATH WORK A MODERN EXECUTION TEAM   123

Death Work and Death Workers: Defining Parameters   125
The Deathwatch Team   128
Executions by the Book   131
On-the-Job Training   133
Team Cohesion   134
"We're a Family"   134
The Private World of the Execution Team   136
An Elite Unit   137
A Modern Execution Team   139
Notes   139

6 DEATHWATCH: THE FINAL HOURS   142

Social Control   143
Keeping the Prisoner Calm   143
Maintaining Emotional Distance   145
Calculated Camaraderie   148
Unintentional Collusion   149
The Final Hours: Critical Junctures in an Execution   151
Defeated Men   155
Behind-the-Scenes Preparation   158
Psyching Up   159
Administrative Concerns and Chronic Uncertainty   160
Holding Up under Pressure   162
Notes   163

7 AN EXECUTION AND ITS AFTERMATH 167

Witness to an Execution 169

The Prisoner's Decline 171

The View from the Cell 171

The Executioners' Perspective 174

The Execution 175

The Morning After 178

Executions and American Society 183

Notes 189

IV MORAL AND LEGAL CONSIDERATIONS 193

8 A MODERN INSTANCE OF TORTURE 195

Defining Torture 196

Distinguishing Torture from Punishment 199

Death Row as Torturous Confinement 201

Dehumanization 204

Human Nature Defined 204

Human Nature Defiled 206

The Benefits of Torture 210

The Limits of Reform 213

Humane Death Rows 213

Closing Death Rows: Humaneness at a Safe Distance? 216

Implications 218

Summary 223

Notes 224

9 PUNISHING MURDERERS: CHOOSING LIFE OVER DEATH 230

Retribution and the Death Penalty 231

The Finality of Death 234

A Civil Death Penalty 239

Obstacles to Reform 243

Economic Objections   243

Public Safety Questions   245

Moral Objections   247

Conclusion   249

Notes   249

INDEX   **257**

Foreword

In Florida's death row, there is concern about "Old Sparky"—the sarcastic name used to refer to the electric chair. The last time it was used, Old Sparky did not work so well. Upon the pulling of the switch, the head of the prisoner being executed caught fire under the skullcap. Observers of this gruesome death described the smell of burning flesh and the shock of a body in flame. Other reactions to the incident varied: from the ironic assurances of medical officials that the decedent felt nothing, having already been dead before he caught fire, to the distressing display of occasional public delight about the agony that perhaps the prisoner had suffered in such an undignified death. The target of the execution was one Pedro Medina, a former Cuban national who had himself been convicted of a particularly grisly murder. A group of opponents of his execution thought he was being killed unjustly; a number of advocates of capital punishment were also uncomfortable with the way this episode went. The governor of Florida, Lawton Chiles—a man who may have signed more death warrants than any other elected state official in the country—decided to postpone any further executions until Old Sparky got back into proper working order.

The simple telling of this story highlights for us our immense national discomfort with capital punishment. Most advocates of the penalty want it used fairly, without cruelty or bias, and with a proper, somber appreciation for the gravity of this public act. Most opponents find themselves disquieted by the suffering of the victims of the crimes and their families, and look for some way other than execution to give symbolic meaning to that suffering. In our profound ambivalence about official killing, we stand as an extreme nation. No other Western democracy is as willing as America to end the lives of its citizens because of their criminal acts.

Professor Robert Johnson's second edition of *Death Work: A Study of the Modern Execution Process* deals with capital punishment in a way unique in criminology. He investigates modern executions by exploring the psychology of executioner and prisoner alike. He produced this book after lengthy, excruciating study on death row—talking to prisoners and their attendants, watching them each go about their daily tasks. It is hard to imagine a more compelling, riveting story. I welcome the second edition and commend it to the reader: student, advocate, opponent, or mere onlooker. After reading this book, your view of the death penalty will never be the same.

Johnson begins by telling us about death row—what it's like to be there as a prisoner and a worker. He shows us how simply being sent to death row is like suffering a small death, and how the awesome omnipresence of the potential cold-blooded execution permeates every aspect of the place. We are all familiar with the evidentiary argument about capital punishment: Do the existence and use of the death penalty prevent crimes? We know, too, the moral argument very well: Does the state have the right to take a life? Johnson shows us a completely new angle on these issues by presenting a phenomenology of execution practices. This is more than a social policy debate. Johnson is concerned with the question, "What does it mean for the lives of those involved to have and use a death penalty system of justice?"

His answer will surprise many and stimulate us all. After his long months visiting and documenting life on death row—and after wading through the voluminous evidence on all sides of the issue—Johnson can see the basis by which killers might themselves deserve to die. Yet he fails to see today's execution system as meeting the obligation of a "civil" society to provide for humane death. He says he would "rather be wrong without killing fellow human beings than be right in the stillness of the death house."

In its Contemporary Issues in Crime and Justice Series, Wadsworth Publishing Company offers students of crime and justice a chance to explore in depth and with excellence issues and controversies that dominate our field but receive insufficient treatment in most standard texts. This book is a superb illustration of the powerful insights that are stimulated by the writings in this Series.

Todd R. Clear, Series Editor
Florida State University

Preface

*D*eath Work is about executions. I've studied this grim topic for almost two decades now. My first concern was with the character of life on death row, where condemned prisoners await the outcome of their legal appeals. In this book I build on my earlier research, studying the executions that for more and more prisoners end the long, lonely wait on death row. It is in the death chamber that the condemned and their executioners make capital punishment a social reality. My aim is to place that fatal connection in historical perspective and to probe its psychological and moral significance.

In a perverse sort of way, this is a timely topic; more timely, even, than when the first edition of *Death Work* was published in 1990. For roughly a decade, from the late sixties to the late seventies, there was a moratorium on executions, backed by the authority of the Supreme Court. This was the culmination of a gradual but persistent decline in the use of the death penalty in the Western world during the twentieth century. It appeared at the time that executions would forever pass from the American scene. Nothing could have been further from the truth.

In 1977, the moratorium on the death penalty ended with the well-publicized execution of Gary Gilmore. Strapped to a chair, with a target affixed to his chest, Gilmore was shot through the heart by a firing squad whose rifle reports were heard 'round the world and in each and every condemned cell in our nation's prisons. As of April 3, 1997, some three hundred seventy-three prisoners have been put to death, most by the more modern and perhaps less intimidating methods of lethal injection and electrocution. (The tally for the different methods of execution since Gilmore's demise is as follows: lethal injection, 228; electrocution, 130; gas chamber, 10; hanging, 3; firing squad, 2.) Execution rates are high these days and are likely to stay high. Fifty-six prisoners were executed in 1995; another forty-five were put to death in 1996. For 1997, early indications are that we will have somewhere in the neighborhood of fifty executions.

Over the last five years (1992–96), the annual number of executions has remained higher than in *any* year between 1977 and 1991. In modern America as of today, more than twice as many prisoners have been put to death than when the first edition of this book was published in 1990, a mere six years ago. The backlog of condemned prisoners, moreover, remains high and growing. Some thirty-two hundred prisoners are presently confined on death rows across the nation, an increase of about nine hundred prisoners—40 percent—over the twenty-three hundred condemned prisoners held captive in 1990. Most of our condemned prisoners have lived under sentence of death for years, often a decade or more; a few prisoners have passed the two decade mark. Many death row prisoners are coming to the end of their legal appeals process. It is fair to say that executions will be with us for the foreseeable future, at a rate that would have been inconceivable only ten years ago.

For better or worse, the modern death penalty is a man's affair. Of the prisoners executed recently, only one, less than 1 percent, was a woman; there are forty-nine women on death row, a mere 1.6 percent of America's condemned prisoners. More women were executed in the past, especially during the infamous witch hunts, but so far as I can determine, in every historical period women have been executed for crimes at substantially lower rates than men. I am aware of no instance, at any time in history, of a woman serving as an executioner. Certainly none of today's executioners are women. To be sure, female staff members may take on supporting roles, particularly when the condemned prisoner is a woman, but their involvement stops at that point. Accordingly, my narration maintains a generic male perspective except where it is obviously inappropriate to do so.

The execution process today is distinctively mechanical, impersonal, and ultimately dehumanizing. This procedure may be routine, but it can never be mundane. Killing and dying under color of law always reflect a remarkable, elemental exercise of power. We cannot be complacent about the plight of those who wait to die on our nation's death rows. Nor can we be indifferent to the experiences of the prison staff who do our death work—who guard the condemned or carry out executions. The death penalty is, at bottom, a tragic social institution that matches the tragedy of violent crime with a punishment that is itself tragic and violent. We minimize or ignore the death penalty at our peril. To do so is to acquiesce, thoughtlessly, to a profound and irrevocable sanction that is imposed in our names. My hope is that, upon finishing this book, readers can give or withdraw their consent to executions with a better understanding of the human issues that lie at the root of this, our ultimate penal sanction.

I have revised *Death Work* in a number of ways. All statistics and sources have of course been reviewed and, where appropriate, updated. Relevant new research on the death penalty, including work done by myself as a follow-up to the original study, has been woven into the text, allowing me to refine and in some cases extend many of the observations and conclusions about the modern execution process spelled out in the first edition. The second edition offers, as well, a fuller examination of the history and evolution of the death penalty in America, covering execution rituals from colonial times to the present. Our history, regrettably, includes a robust pattern of illegal executions—lynchings—which in this edition have been carefully examined in relation to legal executions, especially in the South. (Readers will no doubt find the parallels disturbing.) The key issue of race—crucial in both historical and contemporary terms, in the South and indeed throughout the United States—is considered in some depth. Race has played a role in both the rate and the ritual of legal and illegal executions. A focus on race helps us to understand who gets executed and why certain patterns of execution persisted or evolved in the ways they did. The effects of executions on contemporary American society—particularly if executions were to be televised, so that all of us became witnesses to the violence—are also considered. Finally, the death penalty is reviewed in the light of newly developing international human rights case law. This emerging body of law portrays the death penalty, particularly after lengthy death row confinement (the norm in America), as an instance of "cruel treatment and torture." These holdings are grounded in a thoughtful consideration of the human dimensions of the modern execution process, and it is entirely possible (and, in my view, desirable) that they may one day influence developments in law and policy as they relate to capital punishment in America.

Acknowledgments

I owe a debt of thanks to the many people who helped me with this book in each of its incarnations. Staff and students associated with the Department of Justice, Law and Society have been quite generous with their time and effort. Thomas Stevenson, a former graduate assistant, and Michele M. Provost, a former administrative assistant, were kind enough to transcribe the research interviews that inform much of the first edition. Interviews for the second edition of the book were transcribed by myself and a host of graduate and undergraduate student volunteers. (I regret that I did not keep an up-to-date log so that I might thank each of them individually.) Lynn Taylor and Nicole Brooks Gerarden provided timely administrative support and even more timely help in negotiating the Internet. For diligently tracking down hard-to-find sources and statistics, I extend my thanks to Kellie Auman and Karen Moran, two top-flight graduate assistants. I have been most fortunate to work with administrators and colleagues—notably Richard Bennett, our department chair, and Neil Kerwin, dean of the School of Public Affairs, in which our department is housed—who prize scholarship and encourage and support it at every opportunity.

I also wish to thank those who made my work possible by participating in the research. This includes the prison warden and the execution team, the inmates of death row, and a host of prison reformers, all of whom spoke with me openly—in some cases, on two and even three separate occasions—about the personal and sometimes painful ways in which death work has impinged on their lives. I offer a special thanks to Marie Deans, whose insights were invaluable.

The text of this book benefited from thoughtful reviews. Paul S. Leighton, formerly my graduate assistant, now an assistant professor at Eastern Michigan University, and Jeffrey H. Reiman, who holds a distinguished chair in our philosophy department, reviewed not one but two separate drafts of the first edition, each time making detailed, constructive comments. (Leighton was kind enough to review the second edition in its entirety, as well.) The book is noticeably better for their efforts. I am also indebted to the reviewers selected by Brooks/Cole and subsequently by Wadsworth, whose comments enriched the book (and in some instances adorn the back cover of one or both editions). Similarly, I have been well-served by the production staff at each publishing house. For this edition, I received superb editorial and production support from Sabre Horne, Claire Masson, Jennie Redwitz, and Dianne Jensis. I also wish to thank Peter S. Toop, who edits with a light touch and a heavy appreciation—for better or worse—of the author's style.

I reserve my deepest thanks for my wife, Deirdra, and our two sons, Brian and Patrick. This book is lovingly dedicated to them.

Robert Johnson
April 1997

About the Author

Robert Johnson is Professor of Justice, Law and Society in the School of Public Affairs at American University in Washington, D.C. He holds a bachelor's degree in psychology from Fairfield University, and master's and doctoral degrees in criminal justice from the University at Albany, State University of New York. Dr. Johnson's books include *Culture and Crisis in Confinement, Condemned to Die: Life under Sentence of Death,* and *Hard Time: Understanding and Reforming the Prison* (now in its second edition). He also coedited and contributed to *The Pains of Imprisonment,* and has published numerous articles in professional journals and anthologies. Professor Johnson has testified and/or provided expert affidavits before state and federal courts, the U.S. Congress, and the European Commission on Human Rights. He received the American University Award for Outstanding Scholarship and the American University Teacher/Scholar of the Year Award. Dr. Johnson is a faculty member (Honora Causa) of Phi Kappa Phi, and has been formally honored as a Distinguished Alumnus of the Nelson A. Rockefeller College of Public Affairs and Policy, University at Albany, State University of New York.

PART I

Executions Past

The scaffold, indeed, when it is prepared and set up, has the effect
of a hallucination. . . . The scaffold is vision. The scaffold is not a
mere frame, the scaffold is not a machine, the scaffold is not an
inert piece of mechanism made of wood, of iron, and of ropes. It
seems a sort of being which had some sombre origin of which we
can have no idea; one would say that this frame sees, that this
machine understands, that this mechanism comprehends; that this
wood, this iron, and these ropes have a will. In the fearful reverie
into which its presence casts the soul, the awful apparition of the
scaffold confounds itself with its horrid work. The scaffold becomes
the accomplice of the executioner; it devours, it eats flesh, and it
drinks blood. The scaffold is a sort of monster created by the judge
and the workman, a spectre which seems to live with a kind of
unspeakable life, drawn from all the death which it has wrought.

VICTOR HUGO

The electric chair is a fearsome object. It's the end, no questions asked.
It's a machine of total destruction. It's the biggest chair you'll ever see.

PRISON WARDEN

The lethal injection setup ain't much to look at. A needle
is a needle. Gurney's nothing special. 'Cept maybe the
straps. The straps are thick. But the room is small, cold.
You walk in there and the whole business is cold as death.

EXECUTION TEAM MEMBER

1

Executions Past

Executions in the West from Antiquity to the Twentieth Century

There is an old joke, one I've told before, about a shipwrecked sailor. Adrift for days, he is washed ashore on an uncharted island. He looks about apprehensively. Presently his gaze falls on a gallows, whereupon he is visibly relieved. "At last," he sighs, "I've reached civilization!" The point of the joke is that only a comparatively settled, and hence civilized, society has the need for a permanent gallows and possesses the means, including skilled labor, to construct one. There is truth in that observation, though the earliest form of the death penalty involved stoning, which did not require a gallows or any other man-made instrument of execution.

The joke is funny, however, because the linking of civilization and the death penalty is, at least in the modern world, only half true and more than a little ironic. Civilized societies may execute some of their criminals, but executions are normally considered regrettable lapses from civilization. Executions today are necessary evils, surely, rather than hallmarks of a civilized way of life. No one, not even the staunchest supporter of the death penalty, would use the electric chair to symbolize the civilized quality of life in twentieth-century America or the lethal injection device, with its battery of mechanized syringes, as a harbinger of a great nation in the twenty-first century. More to the point, civilized societies are less likely to execute criminals than are uncivilized ones. And when civilized societies do execute criminals, they are likely to use less harsh means than are uncivilized societies. In historical terms, the gallows ranks as a primitive mode of execution. Perhaps the joke is on the sailor, after all.

Yet the death penalty is alive and well in contemporary America. Since we consider ours a highly civilized society, that would seem to belie my thesis (and perhaps comfort our sailor). My response, in brief, is that the death penalty is an anachronism that survives today because we hide it from our awareness and deny its violence. When we recognize the real nature of the death penalty, which in part means placing it in historical and comparative perspective, we will, I believe, do the right thing and abolish this sanction altogether. We as a society may then be free to grow up and away from the death penalty, which in turn may grow foreign to us. If the experience of Western Europe is a guide, the death penalty, a mere generation or two after its abolition, would be "no longer a political issue at all" and little more than "a barbaric relic, like slavery or branding."[1] Certainly this would offer a heartening contrast to today, where we find ourselves the bedfellows of—take your choice—nineteenth-century Western democracies or such twentieth-century repressive regimes as Iraq, Iran, and China, which flaunt their commitment to execution and the suppression of human rights.

For much of recorded history, executions were public "spectacles of suffering"[2] inflicted upon hapless offenders in the throes of terror.[3] (These spectacles, in their manifold forms, are discussed in this chapter and the next, which comprise Part I of the book.) Often, gross bodily torture was inflicted upon the condemned. Offenders would be executed soon after their crimes, with much of the community directly or indirectly involved. By contemporary standards, some of the crimes that were punished by death were decidedly trivial. The executions of petty thieves, for example—some of them children—strike us as primitive, bloodthirsty affairs. In America, minority children—Native-American and African-American boys and girls—have been put to death for crimes committed when they were as young as ten years old! In America, and indeed around the world, members of poor and otherwise marginal groups have been selected for the gallows with disturbing regularity.

Things are different today, though not as different as we might wish to believe. Executions are preceded by years of confinement on death row; prisoners are no longer subjected to the indignity and pain of physical torture. The condemned are merely held captive until they have depleted their legal appeals, then they are killed with much dispatch and (we hope) little pain. Executions today are removed from the public view; they are somber, restrained, professional undertakings reserved almost exclusively for adult men who have committed aggravated murder and been sentenced pursuant to legal guidelines designed to minimize racial and other forms of discrimination and to maximize accuracy in judicial deliberations. All of this produces an appearance of justice and humanity. Yet the reality of the modern death penalty is profoundly unjust. Too often, the death penalty entails the killing of moral innocents—the young and the retarded—as well as adults who are in fact legally innocent of the crimes for which their lives are taken. As always, there is an overrepresentation of the poor, especially the black poor, for whom the injustice of racism shapes the administration of capital justice.[4]

As of this writing, there are forty-six death row inmates who were sentenced to death as juveniles. Since 1976, nine persons have been executed for crimes committed when they were juveniles. These are children, some heartbreakingly immature, who were marked for death before they reached or even approached any meaningful notion of adulthood. A parallel injustice operates in the case of retarded adults, people whose reduced intelligence makes them children in adult bodies. Some have the mental age of a six-year-old child. To put this in perspective, imagine executing a first-grader! At least twenty-nine retarded offenders have been executed since 1976.[5] These offenders had little or no understanding of the meaning of their crimes or their punishments; some went to the death chamber fully expecting to wake up again the next day, to resume their lives.[6] While trite, the notion that these are lambs led willingly to slaughter comes readily to mind.

By all accounts, more offenders young in body or mind will be sentenced to death in the coming years. Youth and reduced intelligence were once mitigating factors in the eyes of the public and, derivatively, their elected representatives. Now, in these days of hardening attitudes toward the death penalty, this is much less likely to be true.[7] Only eleven of the thirty-eight death penalty states forbid the execution of the retarded. Youth may sometimes even work against the offender, on the premise that a young criminal has a long criminal career ahead of him that we might best stop now by executing him! Perhaps in line with this logic, twelve states have no minimum age of eligibility for the death penalty. Prosecutors have recently sought death for children as young as thirteen; in the state of Indiana, ten-year-old children are technically eligible for the death penalty.[8] One cannot help but be deeply troubled that these young offenders face death for behavior that occurred when they were little more than children, and in the vast majority of cases, children brutalized in homes marred by neglect and abuse.[9]

Errors in capital sentencing, often final and irrevocable, are remarkably common, legal safeguards notwithstanding. Between 1900 and 1985, some 350 people were wrongfully sentenced to death. There have been at least sixty-six people wrongfully sent to death row from 1977 to the present, the period covered by modern legal safeguards. Twenty-three legally innocent people have been executed in this century as of 1992.[10] The tally of the wrongfully executed continues to mount and indeed may escalate rapidly. The reason: Legal innocence is no bar to execution if evidence of innocence is found too late; that is, after so-called "discovery" statutes have run out. "Thus, even a compelling claim of innocence, such as a videotape of someone else committing the crime . . . does not guarantee a review in state or federal court."[11] This paradoxical situation affected one Leonel Herrera, who was executed (in Texas) even though substantial evidence of innocence was uncovered while he was still alive but after the period of legal discovery had expired. The politically popular notion that we should streamline the capital appeals process—shorten discovery periods and limit the number of appeals—will almost certainly land yet more legally innocent people in the death chamber.

Another name that must be added to the list of the wrongfully executed is that of Jesse Dewayne Jacobs. Jacobs was executed in Texas on January 4, 1996, even though prosecutors "actually acknowledged that Jacobs didn't kill the victim." His sister had. Further, prosecutors acknowledged that Jacobs "wasn't aware that his sister had a gun and was planning the murder." Jacobs's testimony was used to convict his sister of the murder but not to throw out his prior wrongful conviction for that same crime. At least one legal observer has argued that Texas, far and away the leader in executions over the last twenty years, if not indeed in America's history, "is so eager to convict, imprison, and execute as many people as possible that the fact of innocence is no longer a concern." An exaggeration, perhaps, but Jacobs's last words ring chillingly true: "I have news for you. There is not going to be an execution. This is premeditated murder." These sentiments have been echoed by former Supreme Court Justice Blackmun, who came to oppose capital punishment at the end of his legal career.[12]

Racism is perhaps the most salient social injustice associated with the death penalty in America, at least post–Civil War America, following the emancipation of millions of slaves. (During slavery, blacks were punished by means of the "domestic discipline" that ruled on slave plantations; only rarely were slaves vulnerable to the criminal courts or to mob violence because they were the protected, if poorly treated, property of their masters, in whom great financial hopes rested.)[13] Once former slaves became freedmen, they were routinely subjected to a racist criminal justice system and to the "popular justice" of lynch law meted out by local mobs and vigilante groups such as the Ku Klux Klan. It is hard to know which source of punishment—the criminal justice system or the lynch mob—was worse. For some sixty years, from roughly 1870 to 1930, African-Americans were the primary, and indeed almost the *exclusive*, targets of lynchings in the South. So, too, were blacks the primary target of *technically* lawful executions; that is, racism was so pervasive during this period that *legal* executions, which occurred at roughly the same frequency as lynchings and with not much more deliberation or due process, were little more than "legal lynchings."[14]

Lynchings, legal and illegal, are a thing of the past, at least as matters of regular practice, but these egregious injustices reflect an enduring legacy of racism in the use of executions. Overt and sometimes pronounced discrimination in the use of the death penalty in the South endured at least into the 1960s if not the early 1970s; a less severe but persistent racial bias existed in the North as well over this period.[15] A recent public opinion survey reveals that, even today, "support for capital punishment is associated with prejudice against blacks."[16] For many whites, violent crime is perceived as a black problem; hence, they see the death penalty as a black punishment. In a sense they are right: Blacks have been overrepresented among condemned prisoners throughout America's history, but the primary reason is bias—in society at large and in the justice system—rather than any natural proclivity for crime.[17]

Racial bias in the administration of the death penalty takes a number of forms. One relates to the race of the victim: Upwards of 85% of those who are executed in America today have killed a white man or woman, though fully 50% of all murder victims are black.[18] When a black man kills a white man or woman, his chances of being sentenced to death are anywhere from four to seven or even eleven times greater than the killer of a black victim.[19] In contrast, whites have only rarely been executed for capital crimes against blacks. Radelet reports that of the roughly sixteen thousand executions carried out in America since 1608, only thirty whites (spread over twenty-six cases) have been executed for crimes against blacks. This represents "about two-tenths of 1% of known American executions." Only two white offenders have been executed for killing black victims in the last twenty years.[20] The conclusion is inescapable that the lives protected by our death penalty have been and remain today white lives; the lives sacrificed are those of persons of color, and more specifically, young African-American males. It should come as no surprise that among those wrongfully put to death in this century, the majority were black.[21]

The death penalty has been and remains a poor man's punishment. As an old saying puts it, "only those without capital get capital punishment." There are no rich men or women on death row, and no rich person has ever been executed in America. The reasons are many. The rich can avail themselves of good lawyers who help their privileged clients avoid death sentences by artful plea bargaining or skillful courtroom tactics. The poor often get a shoddy legal defense. "If you're poor, your attorney is liable to be either young and inexperienced, or old and incompetent." Class and race bias often converge. It has been reported in the *National Law Journal* that "Indigent defendants on trial for their lives are being frequently represented by ill-trained, unprepared court-appointed lawyers. One death case in Georgia was tried (and lost) by a third-year law student, and in four other trials that led to death row, the defense attorneys referred to their clients in open court as 'niggers.'"[22]

More profound biases are also at work. White-collar crimes, most of which are committed by wealthy white offenders, sometimes result in death and destruction on a scale far greater than the typical capital murder. Take the case of negligently maintained work environments—coal mines or factories, for example—that pose life-threatening hazards to workers, sometimes resulting in mass deaths. These offenses are treated as tragedies, as civil matters, or as minor criminal matters but never as capital criminal matters, even though cold-blooded premeditation—the willingness to risk lives to save money—can be and has been readily established in a number of these cases.[23] If anyone deserves the death penalty, is it not a person of privilege—a *beneficiary* of class and race bias—acting with due deliberation and yet displaying complete disregard for the welfare of others?

Against this backdrop, we can appreciate the claim of Jesse Jackson and his son that the modern death penalty is so riddled with injustice as to be seen, even today, as a form of legal lynching.[24] They are speaking metaphorically—and focusing on extreme cases rather than, as in times past, widespread social practices—but they have a powerful point. At one time legal executions in the South were regularly and routinely comparable to lynchings, a point noted previously and developed at some length in the next chapter. Those days are in the past yet substantial injustices remain, resulting from the arbitrariness of the legal rules that apply to the death penalty and from residual biases relating to race and class. These injustices strain our faith in the death penalty process, not to mention the legal process in general. We have to be troubled, as Jackson and son are, that a penalty so readily embraced by lynch mobs lives on today. Remnants of injustices that marked the death penalty, then and now, as a primitive form of violence should be relegated to the dust bin of history.

Even if the modern death penalty were administered even-handedly to young and old, rich and poor, and black and white alike, it would *still* be unjust because the modern execution process is itself profoundly inhumane. Executions today involve nothing less than a slow death by psychological torture, which no offender deserves. No criminal, no matter how heinous or cruel the crime he or she commits, should ever be tortured as punishment. Torture is a violation of our most basic human right—the right to remain a person, which is to say, a human being with a distinct personality. Yet today's condemned prisoners are often completely dehumanized. They are reduced to the status of objects—bodies and not persons—then put to death following an impersonal bureaucratic routine. The executioners are dehumanized as well, though only partially and symbolically, in the specific context of carrying out executions. This dehumanization allows prison officials to function as impersonal agents of violence while remaining largely unaffected in their personal lives.

The modern execution process, broadly conceived, is assessed in the central sections of this book. The nature of life and work on death row are examined in Part II; the killing and dying that constitute executions are considered in Part III. The main argument of the book, formally explicated in Part IV (Chapter 8), is that the modern execution process strips prisoner and executioner alike of their humanity and, hence, is an actual and not merely a metaphorical instance of torture. Since torture can never be just, the death penalty is rejected as an unjust punishment. Also rejected is the notion, popular in some circles, that executions should be televised. We may have a legal right to know about punishments inflicted in our name, but not a right to be entertained by the degradation of our fellow citizens, however brutal their crimes and however devalued their lives may be in the eyes of the larger society. The book closes with an examination of alternatives to the death penalty, including true or natural life sentences.

EXECUTIONS IN HISTORICAL PERSPECTIVE: AN OVERVIEW

Sensibilities about violence—especially about the killing and dying that are at the heart of the death penalty—have evolved considerably over the ages. In general, these sensibilities impart a different form and significance to the death penalty at different stages of history. There was, first, the raw, passionate, largely unfettered rage that underlaid stonings in antiquity (3000 B.C.–A.D. 500). In that era, the violence was face-to-face and the entire community was involved as spectators or executioners.

Later, the rage of communal stoning, softened but not tamed, came to be expressed in the primitive marketplace hangings of the early medieval village (A.D. 500–1000). These hangings were rough-and-ready affairs, featuring the aggrieved party as the executioner. During the late Middle Ages (1000–1500), executions still took place in the marketplace or in the village square, but by then they had become more formal, dignified, even ceremonial undertakings. Procedures were more elaborate; rage was blunted by formalities. For the grievous offenders of this time—a category including heretics—executions were elaborate, highly planned exhibitions orchestrated by high officials. Rage was absent altogether in these pageants, but other strong emotions reigned. Most notably, there was excitement and awe, especially before the might and majesty of the Inquisition.

Executions marked by a restrained ceremony were the norm during the early modern period (1500–1800). Crowds of spectators might have lapsed into unseemly behavior, but such behavior was sharply at odds with the formal execution script. These executions featured ritual and etiquette, as in the late Middle Ages, but little pomp or circumstance. Milder feelings, such as those of devotion, were given an outlet in ceremony; excitement or awe was deemed inappropriately expressive. Officials and spectators were instead expected to show a quiet reverence, tinged by sadness.

In the modern period (from 1800 on), ceremony gradually gave way to bureaucratic procedure played out behind prison walls, in isolation from the community. Feelings are absent, or at least suppressed, in bureaucratically administered executions. With bureaucratic procedure, there is a functional routine dominated by hierarchy and task. Officials perform mechanically before a small, silent gathering of authorized witnesses who behave with marked restraint. Executions have come to be seen as "dirty work." Hence, there is no communal involvement of any sort. The proceedings are antiseptically arranged; few of us get our hands soiled.

The general trend in the conduct of executions is to remove ourselves from the violence. First, physically—we no longer throw stones. Then, existentially—we are no longer engaged in the process in any meaningful way, individually or as a society. This trend reflects our growing awareness of the humanity of others, which makes it harder for us to kill criminals—particularly in public, with bloody hands—even when we believe they deserve to die. Gradually but inexorably, executions have become more formal undertakings that are detached from community life. Ultimately, what was once a public, communal act has become the private preserve of prison officials, who approach the task of execution with the consummate impersonality of the modern bureaucrat. Capital punishment has thus become a commodity dispensed without any redeeming social or communal purpose.

Executions today are isolated acts carried out impersonally—in cold blood—to the detriment of us all. This is not violent justice, as was arguably true of the death penalty in times past, but violence pure and simple. We must recognize this violence for what it is and reject it out of hand. In the process, we will discover that we can live with our worst offenders—though some, perhaps even many, must spend their remaining days behind prison walls.

EXECUTIONS PAST

Ancient Executions: Public, Passionate Violence

Executions were once public, passionate events. The earliest executions were acts of spontaneous, explosive violence. Stonings, no doubt, had a savage character to them even as they united the community against the criminal. Later executions primarily featured hanging and took a more formal, restrained cast, though the crowds at hangings could be quite festive. The word *gala*, for instance, derives from *gallows*, an association that evokes the scene at many hangings in times past. The death penalty was both a confirmation and a celebration of community values and community life. One might weep for some of the condemned, but in general they were seen as demonic figures, already consigned to Hell, beyond the care or compassion of the community against which they had offended. The violence inflicted on them met with little or no repugnance.

Executions in antiquity, particularly during biblical times, served largely religious ends. People lived in fear of provoking God's wrath, which was thought to take the form of natural catastrophes ranging from plagues to famines and droughts. The offender sinned against God; through punishment, especially capital punishment, people sought to expiate the sin and thus appease God. In the words of the authoritative *Encyclopedia Judaica*, "the original and foremost purpose of punishment in biblical law was the appeasement of God. . . . By taking 'impassioned action' to punish violators of His laws, expiation is made to God and God's 'fierce anger' turned away from Israel."[25] Impassioned action was taken not only against murderers, who destroyed creatures made in God's image, but also against anyone displaying sacrilegious or immoral or even uncivil behavior, all of which offended God and thus were grounds for execution because they put the community at risk of supernatural sanction. Executions were originally authorized by a religious leader (for example, Moses or Aaron) and later by a religious court (the Sanhedrin), though sometimes offenders were executed on the spot, reflecting the righteous anger of the community.[26] In each case, the aim was the same: "So you shall purge the evil from the midst of you."[27]

Most commonly, executions during the biblical era took the form of stoning. In the early biblical period (roughly 2000–1200 B.C.), before the settling of Palestine, the Hebrews were essentially a nomadic desert people. Stonings were rather unceremonious and probably quite brutal. A stoning might begin with a simple ritual gesture—for example, the harmed party or a witness to the crime might place a hand on the head of the offender to mark him for execution. "In an orderly proceeding the witness was to cast the first stone. [I]f others were necessary to produce death, the bystanders hurled them."[28] When the occasion permitted, the offender might also make a final statement, presumably asking forgiveness from God and perhaps also from the community. Later Jewish law described a more elaborate execution ritual involving two witnesses, though the essentials remained unchanged. The offender, standing on an elevated scaffold, would formally confess, then one of the witnesses would push him from the scaffold, and the other would drop the first stone on him. "If he still lived, all present stoned him."[29]

Given the considerable number of capital crimes, executions were probably quite common, especially during the early biblical era, when adjudicatory procedures were informal. (The word of credible witnesses, without other evidence, was enough to convict someone of a capital crime.[30]) The impression to be gained from the Bible and other historical sources is that those executed in this manner somehow came to terms with this terrifying punishment, bearing their fate with some semblance of dignity. It is more likely that the typical offender was mute with fear.[31] Those executions must have been terrifying. Following the lead of the witnesses, the citizens would arm themselves with stones and surround the offender, perhaps also taunting and ridiculing him before launching their onslaught of bruising rocks; they would stop only when the offender's bloody and lifeless form lay buried under the stones. In this manner, the community would act as one, cleansing itself of the guilt of the criminal and putting things right with God.[32]

Capital punishment in ancient Greece, particularly during the Bronze Age (3000–1000 B.C.), was essentially the same as that practiced by the Hebrews during the biblical period. "Stoning was the earliest form of community punishment among the ancients, for stones were the most natural and the most readily obtainable means of defense or attack."[33] Like the Hebrews, the Greeks restricted stoning for the most part to crimes that affected the community as a whole.[34] And among the Greeks, as among the Hebrews, the earliest stonings were unplanned outbursts of "violent indignation" that were "gradually sanctioned by custom and became a regular mode of punishment."[35] Likewise, the legally sanctioned, more refined stonings of later Greece closely resembled those practiced among the Hebrews of the corresponding biblical period.

When the offender came within four cubits of the place of execution, he was stripped naked, only leaving a covering before, and his hands being bound, he was led up to the fatal place, which was an eminence twice a man's height. The first executioners of the sentence were the witnesses, who generally pulled off their clothes for the purpose: one of them threw him down with great violence upon his loins: if he rolled upon his breast, he was turned upon his loins again, and if he died by the fall there was an end; but if not, the other witnesses took a great stone, and dashed it upon his breast as he lay upon his back; and then, if he was not dispatched, all the people that stood by threw stones at him till he died.[36]

Even after stonings were planned—that is, after they had become an authorized form of punishment following a primitive script—they could still degenerate into mob scenes. In one variant of stoning as planned punishment,
known as the "rebel's beating," a mob would use hands, staves, and stones to
beat the offender to death.[37]

Medieval Executions: Ceremonial Violence

Near the end of the ancient period, executions became for a time less common and less violent. The heights of civilization reached in classical Greece
and republican Rome (500 B.C.–A.D. 44) presumably made executions seem
barbaric. (The link between civilization and the death penalty will be examined in the next chapter.) The Imperial Age of Rome (A.D. 14–337), however,
saw a resurgence in executions. This time was famous for the arenas in which
Christians, criminals, and errant slaves were thrown to the lions before hordes
of cheering spectators. And after the Fall of Rome, in the early medieval period, sometimes called the Dark Ages (500–1000), executions became a fact
of daily village life. Executions in imperial Rome had had an element of
pageantry to them, however coarse and brutal those executions may have been.
By contrast, early medieval executions in many ways hearkened back to the
more primitive executions of antiquity.

Life in medieval Europe was a parochial and impoverished existence, particularly during the earlier years (the Dark Ages). Invasions from without and
disorder from within were constant threats. Disease ran rampant; mortality
rates were high.[38] The precariousness of the times may have bred an angry,
fearful, punitive psychology. In any case, punishment was distinctively arbitrary and harsh, a state of affairs "regarded with apathy by the public." Punishment was seen "as one of the chances of fortune, or one of the many crosses
laid on mankind by Heaven; a misfortune that might befall anyone, and which
must, therefore, be borne patiently."[39]

And publicly. Adjudication during the early medieval period was a bare-
bones, almost spontaneous public procedure often involving the entire community. In Nuremberg around the year 1000, for example, it was the
prosecutor's job to observe the crime and capture the criminal. His proofs
were physical—stolen goods retrieved from the criminal or parts of the bodies
of murder victims (for example, a finger, which the prosecutor himself had to
forcibly remove). Having chased down the criminal, secured the evidence,
and "fastened [it] to the culprit's back," the prosecutor, loudly announcing the
crime, would drag the offender (often literally) to the authorities and call for a
trial. The trial would be "held publicly in the market place, and anyone who
chose could follow the proceedings." Throughout, there was minimal formality and precious little decorum. If condemned, the accused would be executed by the aggrieved party, "who strung up the criminal on any suitable tree
or post."[40] A slow and ignominious death by strangulation would ensue before
the eyes of the townsfolk.

By the later Middle Ages, adjudication had become more formal and dignified. In the Nuremberg of 1400, for example, torture administered discreetly

in prison cells produced confessions, obviating the need to place stolen goods or expropriated body parts in evidence before the public. "Trials no longer took place in the market square, but in a special hall within the Rathaus [city hall], after the accused had been privately examined." Rules of evidence and procedure were increasingly elaborate. As in the early medieval period, punishment followed swiftly. The practice of allowing citizens to carry out executions, however, was abandoned.[41] Such was now "considered to be incompatible with the dignity of the court that had pronounced judgment; it also brought undesirable odium on the accuser." Executions were therefore assigned to an official of the court, usually the Zuchtiger, the man in charge of torturing suspects. By the close of the Middle Ages (1500), the Nuremberg court and its executioner behaved with considerable decorum and even civility:

> Orders were given to produce the prisoner in court. The executioner knocked at the door of the condemned cell, entered, apologising for the intrusion, bound the prisoner's arms, cast a white cloak about the victim, and led him between two chaplains to the Judgment Hall. Here the Bannrichter [judge] inquired of the Schöffen [jury] whether the judgment passed were in conformity with the law. Having received assurance of this, he ordered the court clerk to read out the sentence, after which the condemned man was at once led out to execution.[42]

From beginning to end, the Middle Ages were a time of periodic famine and almost constant scarcity, particularly of the bread and ale that were the staples of the peasant diet.[43] Still, this period was given to occasional excesses in the form of grand banquets and elaborate pageantries in honor of special events—including executions. As Barbara Tuchman reminds us, "outward magnificence" in entertainment was much valued during the Middle Ages. The contrast between the mundane tragedies of daily life and the occasional flamboyant celebration was striking. "Amid depopulation and disaster," observed Tuchman, "extravagance and splendor were never more extreme."[44] People made hay, as the saying goes, during those few moments in which the sun shone upon them; eating, drinking, and being merry virtually in front of their suffering fellows. Thus, in Nuremberg as the medieval period drew to a close, "guests at the sumptuous banquets and entertainments given in the splendid Hall of the Rathaus were not troubled by compassion for the poor wretches lingering, often enough under sentence of death, in the dark cells only a few yards below."[45]

Some of those poor wretches were destined for executions that were entertainments in their own right, gaudy pageantries of violence and prolonged, agonizing death. In such instances, a formal parade, replete with dignitaries in full dress, would convey the condemned to the place of execution, often the town square. Feelings would run strong and find immediate, if generally restrained, expression. Amid the unfolding violence, the condemned prisoner had a script to follow. He was, for example, required by custom to forgive the executioner, who was considered God's agent. The condemned would then be allowed to speak (sometimes shout) his piece to the crowd; it was expected that the prisoner's last words would be a more or less coherent declaration to the assembled citizenry that he had repented and was ready to meet his Maker. Some no doubt rose to the occasion, but most prisoners, we must suppose, were simply unable to summon the strength to play out their assigned roles, which required an almost superhuman composure in the face of adversity. (Executions were a popular, if perverse, form of entertainment; the condemned had almost certainly attended executions and therefore knew, from direct observation of the executions of others, the awful violence that awaited.) Trembling in terror, prisoners would be supported or otherwise propped up by some member of the scaffold party. Spectators, though not directly or formally involved in the execution, would be anything but passive observers of the drama before them—perhaps crying out in anger. On rare occasions, an unruly mob would storm the scaffold only to be repelled, sometimes at the cost of individual lives, by the gallows guards. The final act would be a sort of offering up—and also, pathetically, a holding up—of the offender, guilt acknowledged or at least not successfully contested, for execution. The crowd would respond, depending on the particulars of the case and the demeanor of the condemned, with piety or ridicule. With God and Man appeased, the criminal would be killed.[46]

And killed with a vengeance, in a spectacle of suffering arranged for the edification and admonishment of the assembled masses. One procedure was to hang the person, cut him down before he died, and then disembowel him or draw and quarter him—that is, carve out his intestines and cut him in four— while he was still alive. Another method was known as breaking on the wheel. "The prisoner's arms and legs were propped up on a wheel-like platform and were broken in several places by the use of a heavy iron bar. The mangled remains were then turned rapidly, scattering gore about until the unfortunate victim was dead." Breaking on the wheel was a variant of sawing the victim in pieces, "a popular medieval execution." With this type of execution, "the victim was usually hung up by his feet and sawed in two vertically by the executioner."[47]

Such might be the fate of a common criminal. A more grievous offender— a traitor or assassin—would be drawn and quartered in a most protracted and painful way, then beheaded for good measure. The grisly details of execution, including what was to be done to which parts of the miscreant's body, were sometimes specified in law. One such statute, of old if not venerable lineage, read as follows when applied to a group of traitors:

> Ye do respectively go to the place from whence ye came; from thence to be drawn upon a sledge to the place of execution, to be there hanged up by the neck, to be cut down while ye are yet alive, to have your hearts and bowels taken out before your faces, and your members cut off and burnt. Your heads severed from your bodies, your bodies divided into quarters, your heads and bodies respectively to be disposed of according to the king's will and pleasure; and the Lord have mercy upon your souls.[48]

In other scenarios for the execution of grievous offenders, molten wax would be poured in the offender's open wounds, and the flesh of his arms and legs torn with hot iron pincers. All the while, onlookers might exhort the executioner to greater violence. At the proper moment, just before death, the good confessor would commend the criminal's soul to God. Indeed, all the condemned might hope for at this juncture was escape into the hereafter.[49]

Executions of the Inquisition   Nowhere is medieval pomp and circumstance, and the complaisance with which violent executions were viewed, better illustrated than in the autos-da-fé—literally, "acts of faith"—of the Inquisition. At these public events, criminals, and especially heretics, were executed en masse. Autos-da-fé were more religious pageantries than mere civil ceremonies, providing an occasion "by which men gave a public and splendid proof of their warm zeal for religion." An auto-da-fé would be publicly announced thirty days in advance and would be scheduled to coincide with such momentous events as the coronation or marriage of a king or the birth of a royal child, "in order that they might be the more solemn and more authentic."[50] The pageantry would but thinly disguise the raw violence of the executions with which it culminated.

The pageant would begin with a grand procession. One such procession in Madrid, a pageant unto itself but typical of these affairs, has been described as follows:

A hundred coal-merchants, armed with pikes and muskets, marched front, because they furnished the wood which was employed in the punishment of those who were condemned to the flames. Next followed the dominicans, preceded by a white cross. The Duke of Medina Celi appeared next in order, bearing the standard of the Inquisition according to the hereditary privilege of his family. This standard was of scarlet damask; upon one side was embroidered a naked sword in a crown of laurel, upon the other the arms of Spain. Next was borne a green cross bound with black crepe. Several grandees and other persons, familiars of the Inquisition, marched after it, dressed in cloaks adorned with black-and-white crosses, and edged with gold lace. The procession was closed by fifty halberdiers or guards of the Inquisition, clothed in black-and-white robes, commanded by the Marquis of Povar, hereditary protector of the Inquisition in the Kingdom of Toledo.[51]

The procession, having passed the royal palace, would end at a grand stage, on which the auto-da-fé proper would take place. Replete with amphitheaters, balconies, platforms, and altars, the stage, stationed in the town square, was built expressly for the occasion. Dignitaries of the Inquisition, of the town, of the church, and of the kingdom would be arranged on the stage according to their prestige. Victims would be displayed on a platform in the lower center of the stage, closest to the crowds.

At the appropriate moment, the victims would be marched onto the higher levels of the stage and paraded before the king, then placed on the left side of the stage on a plain platform. This sad procession, in Madrid and else-where, was led by "twelve persons, male and female. . . with ropes around their necks, and torches in their hands, and carrochas or caps of pasteboard, three feet in height, upon their heads, on which their pretended crimes were represented in various manners." Others followed, some fifty or more in num-ber, wearing special cloaks of varying colors, often with representations of flames and the devil painted on them.

An elaborate ritual would then unfold on the stage, featuring many masses and special events—a marriage or coronation ceremony, for example—and lasting an entire day or more. Finally, the sentences of the condemned would be read, which alone would take hours. Those sentenced would proceed, one by one, into prominently displayed cages, "in order that they might be seen distinctly by everybody." A final mass would be said; the grand inquisitor would grant absolution, not pardon, to those who repented. The king would retire. At this juncture,

> the criminals. . . . were delivered over to the secular arm, and were carried upon asses to the distance of three hundred paces without the gate [of the town]. They were executed after midnight. The obstinate were burned alive, the repentant were strangled before they were cast into the fire.[52]

The crowd, at once terrified and edified, would disperse. The spectacle of vi-olence, devoid of compassion for the poor frightened souls caught up in it, would thus come to an end.

Early Modern Executions:
Refined Ritual, Subdued Ceremony

After the Middle Ages, executions gradually became more tame, though per-haps no less grisly. In the early modern period, roughly the sixteenth through the eighteenth century, public punishments became, in the main, less grossly violent than their biblical or medieval predecessors. Routine executions were marked by elaborate ritual; sensibilities appeared to have evolved considerably. Research on executions in England, Holland, and Germany indicate that in each of these countries, less violent methods came into favor in the early mod-ern period relative to the methods of execution used in those countries in earlier periods.

The English Experience Disemboweling and beheading were common and unremarkable in England during the Middle Ages. It was the custom to display the head of the condemned to show the crowd in no uncertain terms that the order of the court had been carried out. By the close of the eigh-teenth century, however, executions of this sort were rare; when beheadings did occur, they were apt to be seen as revolting spectacles. Even traitors were typically spared disemboweling, though disemboweling followed by behead-ing was the punishment specified in law, and long observed in custom, for such offenders. When traitors were merely beheaded in early modern Lon-don, the crowd would be visibly repulsed:

When the first stroke of the ax was heard, there was a burst of horror from the crowd, and the instant the head was exhibited there was a terrifying shriek sent up, and the multitude ran violently in all directions, as if under the influence of a sudden frenzy.[53]

An even more telling example of the change in sensibilities during this period was the introduction of a cap to "conceal the obscenely contorted features" of the hanged man, as well as to give "a certain privacy and decency in public death."[54] Garden-variety hangings of ordinary criminals during the early modern period, though both public and violent, were a far cry from the stonings of antiquity or the public tortures of the Middle Ages.

Early modern executions in England were carefully staged, if comparatively modest. Executions in England during this period generally were proper and dignified undertakings, marked by the ringing of church bells, special prayers for the condemned, and the final dropping of a handkerchief by the prisoner—if he was not overcome by fear—to signal his readiness to die. The condemned of rank and privilege would normally go to the gallows in their best clothes; those who could muster last words would give a sort of a speech marked by contrition.[55] Afterwards, the prison warden might schedule an official repast to mark the close of the execution ceremony. The governor of Newgate, for example, sent out invitations to a private party following each execution: "We hang at eight, breakfast at nine."[56] All very proper.

One explicit aim of these ceremonial executions, no doubt true to some degree of all public executions in all cultures, was education of the citizenry. English citizens, including schoolchildren, were encouraged to observe the condemned in their cells (the prisoners were exhibited for this purpose) and to attend their executions to see firsthand the fate of those who had gone bad and therefore "come to a bad end"—the end of a rope.[57] Executions in rural areas of England during the early modern period appear to have been undertaken with appropriate decorum, meeting with the approval of schoolmasters, parents, and other authorities. Crowds were generally small and well-behaved. The executions were of course awful, but that is what is meant by coming to a bad end—the kind of death others would do anything to avoid. The deeper lesson offered to the crowd was that of power—the authorities had it, they didn't. Break the sovereign's law and they, too, might one day be plucked from the safety of the crowd and hanged by the neck for all to see.

In London, things were often less decorous than in the countryside. The crowd could be quite raucous, with drunken revelry the normal state of affairs. Violence among the spectators was disturbingly common at these executions. (This violence might on occasion include a grim battle for the corpse, waged by the deceased's loved ones against the minions of anatomists seeking bodies for medical research.) For their part, condemned prisoners were often as drunk as the spectators, having imbibed freely at the traditional pub stops along the route to the execution site. Some of these prisoners were also nursing hangovers from parties held in their honor on the eve of their executions. A perhaps extreme yet instructive case is that of Renwick Williams, known as the Monster of London, who was executed during the late eighteenth century. His last evening on death row was anything but a solemn testimony to the wages of sin.

> The Monster sent cards of invitation to about twenty couples among whom were some of his alibi friends, his brothers, sisters, several of the prisoners, and others. . . . At four o'clock, the party set to tea; this being over, two violins struck up, accompanied by a flute, and the company proceeded to exercise their limbs. In the merry dance, the cuts and entrechats of the Monster were much admired. . . . About eight o'clock, the company partook of a cold supper, and a variety of wines, such as would not discredit the most sumptuous gala, and about nine o'clock departed, that being the usual hour for locking the doors of the prison.[58]

For the London crowds that came to Williams's hanging and those of others, executions were indeed gala affairs. On occasion, the executioners, themselves inebriated, joined the party. One drunken executioner made a concerted effort to hang the prisoner's confessor, who made the mistake of positioning himself too near the condemned man on the scaffold! Others pandered to the baser desires of the crowd, performing their jobs like actors in a music hall, even bowing deeply before the cheering masses.[59] The condemned were expected to do their part as well, which amounted to dying with panache and upholding their family name. Some did, and those are the ones that were written and sung about at the time, generating a kind of mythology of the brave condemned.[60] One mother is reported to have called out to her son as the noose was being tightened around his neck, "Son, I hope you will die courageously like your father."[61] Some public education! To be sure, as in times past, most prisoners died in abject terror, no doubt soiling themselves in the process, even as the crowd looked on, taking it all in. This, too, offers an education—that subjects of the crown should be properly awed by the might and majesty of law, as administered by the executioner.[62]

Graeme Newman explains these patently irreverent executions as the result of social dislocations, manifested in an extreme form in London, accompanying the demise of the medieval period and the emergence of the modern.[63] Unseemly gallows behavior proved quite persistent and, indeed, may have become an English tradition in its own right. The spectacle of an hysterical English crowd watching a man hang did not really change until executions were moved indoors during the latter half of the nineteenth century. Be that as it may, in early modern London, it is fair to say that in regard to executions, a pearl of ceremony was cast before an often unruly crowd of swine.[64]

The Continental Experience On the whole, executions were considerably more restrained and dignified in the continental Europe of the early modern period than in England.[65] On the Continent, ritual came more successfully to channel feelings and suppress spontaneity. Executions were held on a stage, with spectators cast in a more circumscribed (and more sober) role than their English brethren. The condemned, as well, were given less room for personal expression, both in their final hours and in their dress and deportment on the scaffold. (Ritual aside, it is probably true that most of these prisoners were numb with terror, like their English counterparts.) Executions were meant to have a certain purity, and even beauty, as ceremonies unto themselves. They might have evoked feelings, especially sadness, in observers, but these sentiments generally did not spill over and affect the conduct of the executions in any direct way.

Petrus Spierenburg, whose observations on early modern executions in Amsterdam are most illuminating, recounts the execution of one Hendrina Wouters, described as "the darling of eighteenth-century stagers of beautiful executions." (Again, these "beautiful executions" would be atypical, providing more tales of the brave condemned.) Having been tortured on the rack, Hendrina confessed to the crime of murder and was sentenced to death. She proved to be a most cooperative subject of the court.

> She thanked the judges for their merciful sentence, saying she deserved a more severe penalty. On Friday, when her death sentence was announced, she bade farewell to her husband and two children. Bystanders burst into tears. The preacher was very content. Although, while professing to be a Catholic, she proved unable to say the Lord's Prayer, he declared that she would pass away as a child of God. On the justice day he concluded his prayer by expressing the wish that it might have impressed the sinner and the spectators. He asked the Lord's blessing to descend upon her and the judges. Then Hendrina begged forgiveness once more. She remained humble and kept her eyes down. Approaching the cross, she expressed no fear but became even more cheerful. The executioner broke her arms and legs, but she kept on praying until she received a cut in her throat.[66]

The "beauty" of this execution is in the staging rather than in the method, though of course this execution is much less brutal in terms of its method than a disemboweling or dismemberment.

Executions in early modern Germany followed a script much like those in Holland. This script also created a certain number of "beautiful" executions that would be memorialized in their own right. "Elaborate and highly ritualized," these executions began with a "sentencing ceremony" in the town square, moved next to a formal procession in which the condemned were escorted "by troops and public officials of various kinds." The procession was carefully arranged: "representatives of the local guilds," crucial economic figures in the community, would be given positions of prominence; religious figures would lead the procession and preside on the scaffold. More ceremonies would unfold on the scaffold, before and after the execution proper, which would normally entail the decapitation of the condemned criminal—though even at this late date, "particularly serious offenders" were "broken on the wheel" in the medieval manner. Before the execution, there would be prayers, religious readings, and the singing of hymns and dirges by choirboys. If the offender were Catholic, a crucifix would be provided for him to hold during the execution, presumably as a source of comfort for one on the threshold of a terrifying death. No such palliatives were provided Protestant offenders.

Instead, local epileptics from the Protestant community would be summoned to the scaffold, coming forward with "glasses and mugs to catch the offender's blood as it spurted from the severed neck," which they would drink "as a cure for their affliction." (One can hardly imagine that the arrival of this ghoulish crew, outstretched cups in front of them, would offer comfort to the condemned!) After the execution, the ritual would end "with a sermon from the officiating priest or pastor, admonishing the crowd to heed the moral lesson of what they had just witnessed" and to share in the "collective expiation" offered by the execution.[67]

The assembled crowd generally behaved with decorum at early modern executions in Germany and Holland. This was considered altogether fitting for an execution ritual which was "an affirmation of official hierarchies and values" in the civil and religious realms. As the nineteenth century unfolded, however, executions in continental Europe became more secular (more "enlightened") and less religious; the social hierarchy of civil society became less stable and controlling, and an independent middle class gradually emerged. Executions became less an expression of shared community values and more an act of violence played out before a self-selected and increasingly working-class audience that might take umbrage at the proceedings, particularly if the offender were a sympathetic figure or if the execution were botched. Though less pronounced than in England, unseemly crowd behavior eventually became a problem in continental Europe, and hastened the abolition of public executions.[68]

Though flagrantly violent, executions in early modern Holland and Germany were more formal and restrained than those of their biblical or medieval counterparts.[69] Executioners of this period thought of themselves as craftsmen or even artists rather than mere purveyors of violence. Many doubled as torturers, on and off the scaffold, but this too was thought of as an art and not a primitive act of violence. For the executioners of early modern Europe, "branding becomes 'making an adorning design'"; the right way of torturing is "a clever reallocation of limbs."[70] All of justice is a stage; it is the appearance—the ritual—that is the meaningful thing. At the executions of this time, a penitent or at least unresisting subject—artfully mutilated, then cleanly killed—was displayed as a lesson in suffering for all to behold.

THE THRESHOLD OF ACCEPTED VIOLENCE

As a general rule, eyewitness accounts of executions in times past bespeak a familiarity with violence that is "largely unhampered by feelings of repugnance."[71] The threshold of accepted violence is lower in later times, reflecting more refined sensibilities that were sometimes violated or at least strained (as with early modern beheadings in England and, one supposes, breaking on the wheel in Germany during this period). But more important, at each juncture of history up to the early modern period, people show a considerable capacity for observing crude acts of violence without being repulsed by them. One sees sadness at Wouters's impending plight, which suggests an element of compassion typically absent in earlier executions, but the general civility of the proceedings implies that her execution does not trouble the executioner or the crowd. There is certainly no apparent repugnance at her bloody fate or at that of her contemporaries in Germany who faced decapitation. There are no reports of public revulsion at the sight of stonings (or crucifixions, another common mode of execution) during the biblical era or in other periods in antiquity. Nor is there evidence of revulsion at the sight of the gross bodily tortures that accompanied medieval executions.

Paintings of execution scenes on the Continent during the early modern period depict executions and their aftermath as entirely normal and unremarkable.

A few pictures from the seventeenth and eighteenth centuries show the Volewijk in winter. Men and women are skating on the frozen Y. Along the shore of the Volewijk there are *koek-en-zopie-tenten* (stalls with cakes and drinks). The customers do not even seem to notice the gallows behind them. A few others walk at the foot of the gallows and point at the corpses. No one looks embarrassed by the sight.[72]

These decent, eminently civilized people "saw the corpses" of the condemned and quite clearly "did not care." It was as if the bodies of the condemned were so many carcasses of beef hung out to dry.

Their London counterparts during this period lived in what was colloquially known as the City of Gallows, with bodies gibbeted—hung up in chains and left to rot in the open air—at every major crossroads. This was considered standard fare by the English, if not by visitors from the Continent. "No matter by what approach the stranger then entered London, he had the fact of the stringent severity of English criminal law most painfully impressed upon him by a sight of the gallows."[73]

Actual executions, however, both on the Continent and in England, were a different matter entirely. "Then the crowd came specially to watch the spectacle and did not want to miss a minute."[74] A public killing was exciting and worthy of interest, a communal and political event of some moment; residual bodies were empty of larger meaning. Executions occurred; public attention rose and fell, not in response to the tragedy of life lost but in response to the drama of life taken. The bodies of the dead may have lingered, but life in the community went on.

NOTES

1. Comment, "A Fondness for the Gallows," *The New Yorker* 68 (11): 4 (1992).
2. I borrow this term from Spierenburg. See P. Spierenburg, *The Spectacle of Suffering: Executions and the Evolution of Repression: From a Preindustrial Metropolis to the European Experience* (Cambridge: Cambridge University Press, 1984) for an insightful discussion of executions in Europe during the medieval and early modern periods.

3. We learn from Gatrell that "most felons went to their deaths in quaking terror." See V. A. C. Gatrell, *The Hanging Tree: Execution and the English People 1770–1865* (Oxford: Oxford University Press, 1994), 37.

4. Amnesty International's worldwide research confirms that, even today, those who are on the racial, economic, or political margins of their societies are selected out for execution at excessive and discriminatory rates. See *When The State Kills…The Death Penalty, A Human Rights Issue* (New York: Amnesty International U.S.A., 1989), 5.

5. This information is provided by the Death Penalty Information Center via the Internet. For updated information, consult: http://www.essential.org/dpic

6. Personal communication, Marie Deans, who has counseled many condemned offenders during their final hours in the death house. See more generally, N. Hentoff, "Executing the Retarded in Our Name," *Village Voice* 40 (8): 30–31 (1995), and *The Machinery of Death: A Shocking Indictment of Capital Punishment in the United States* (New York: Amnesty International, 1995).

7. See, for example, P. C. Ellsworth and S. R. Gross, "Hardening of the Attitudes: Americans' Views on the Death Penalty," *Journal of Social Issues* 50 (2): 19–52 (1994).

8. See *Fact Sheet #3*, National Coalition to Abolish the Death Penalty, 918 F Street NW, Suite 601, Washington, D.C. 20004.

9. This troubling subject is discussed insightfully in H. Prejean, *Dead Man Walking: An Eyewitness Account of the Death Penalty in the United States* (New York: Random House, 1993).

10. The seminal work on this subject has been done by M. L. Radelet, H. Bedau, and C. E. Putnam, *In Spite of Innocence: Erroneous Convictions in Capital Cases* (Boston: Northeastern University Press, 1992).

11. See U.S. Congress, Senate Committee on the Judiciary, Subcommittee on Civil and Constitutional Rights, "Innocence and the Death Penalty: Assessing the Danger of Mistaken Executions," staff report by the 103rd Cong., 1st sess., October 21, 1993, 11.

12. Comment, *Progressive* 59 (2): 10 (1995).

13. T. Sellin, *Slavery and the Penal System* (New York: Elsevier, 1976).

14. See T. Sellin, "Race Prejudice in the Administration of Justice," *American Journal of Sociology* 41 (1935): 312–317; A. Raper, *The Tragedy of Lynching* (Chapel Hill: University of North Carolina Press, 1933); and S. E. Tolnay and E. M. Beck, *A Festival of Violence: An Analysis of Southern Lynchings, 1882–1930* (Urbana: University of Illinois Press, 1995). During this same period, blacks were swept off the streets and into captivity, often for little more than loitering. Their fate was to be sent off to hard labor as contract prisoners and, later, plantation prison inmates, in many cases working the same farms and fields as had their ancestors in slavery. These penal regimes were, in fact, "worse than slavery," in the words of noted historian David Oshinsky, because inmates, unlike slaves, were cheap and hence expendable sources of labor; they would be worked to death and then simply replaced with new convicts who could be acquired at low or even no cost. See D. Oshinsky, *Worse Than Slavery: Parchman Farm and the Ordeal of Jim Crow Justice* (New York: Free Press, 1996). One version or another of these brutal penal regimes survived into the 1970s and even early 1980s. See A. R. Sample, *Racehoss: Big Emma's Boy* (Austin, Tex.: Eakin Press, 1984).

15. See, for example, M. L. Radelet, ed., *Facing the Death Penalty: Essays on a Cruel and Unusual Punishment* (Philadelphia: Temple University Press, 1989). See also M. Wolfgang and M. Riedel, "Race, Judicial Discretion, and the Death Penalty," *The Annals* 407 (May 1973): 119–133 and M. Wolfgang and B. Cohen, *Crime and Race; Conceptions and Misconceptions* (New York: Institute of Human Relations Press, 1970).

16. See S. E. Barkan and S. F. Cohn, "Racial Prejudice and Support for the Death Penalty by Whites," *Journal of Research in Crime and Delinquency* 31 (2): 202–209 (1994).

17. Since 1977, the period of the reemergence of the death penalty in America, roughly 350 people have been put to death; some 40% were African-Americans, though African-Americans make up only 12% of the larger population. (The overrepresentation of blacks among the executed was much higher in times past, especially in the South.) One may observe that blacks commit a disproportionate amount of violent street crime—roughly 40% today—and in a sense put themselves at higher risk for execution. (One might also attempt to make this claim in historical terms.) However, before drawing any conclusions, an important question to ask is, why do black Americans have a high rate of violent street crime? The answer: enduring social injustice.

More specifically, the evidence suggests that high rates of violent crime among African-Americans can be traced to the uniquely enduring and pernicious interaction of race, poverty, and injustice in American history, starting with the institution of slavery, giving way to decades of indiscriminate mob lynching, judicial execution, and incarceration in prisons modeled on slave plantations, and continuing today in urban ghettos and prisons that virtually hold captive our poor black population. Variously characterized as "truly disadvantaged" and comprising a hard-core "underclass," many African-Americans in times past and even today see "little reason to respect the law or to look down upon those who were punished and sent to jail" and much reason to view and treat authorities of the justice system with contempt. See Oshinsky (n. 14), 131–132. It is fair to say that no other minority group has faced such conditions of continuing deprivation and injustice, often under color of law. No other group has been forced to live for so long under what can only be called criminogenic conditions. In these various ways, our past haunts us, clothing the death penalty even today in a mantle of racism.

In addition to Oshinsky, quoted above, suggested readings on this troubling topic include the following: Tolnay and Beck (n. 14); J. R. Mandle, *Not Slave, Not Free: The African American Economic Experience Since the Civil War* (Durham: Duke University Press, 1992); W. J. Wilson, *The Truly Disadvantaged: The Inner City, the Underclass, and Public Policy* (Chicago: University of Chicago Press, 1987); J. Hagan and R. D. Peterson, "Criminal Inequality in America: Patterns and Consequences," in *Crime and Inequality*, ed. J. Hagan and R. D. Peterson (Stanford, Calif.: Stanford University Press, 1995), 14–36; C. R. Mann, "The Contribution of Institutionalized Racism to Minority Crime," in *Ethnicity, Race, and Crime: Perspectives Across Time and Place*, ed. D. F. Hawkins (Albany, N.Y.: State University of New York Press, 1995), 259–280; and R. J. Sampson and W. J. Wilson, "Toward a Theory of Race, Crime, and Urban Inequality," in *Crime and Inequality*, ed. J. Hagan and R. D. Peterson (Stanford, Calif.: Stanford University Press, 1995), 37–54.

18. See M. L. Radelet, "Race and Death," *Index on Censorship* 2 (1995): 124.

19. See D. C. Baldus, G. Woodworth, and C. A. Pulaski, *Equal Justice and the Death Penalty: A Legal and Empirical Analysis* (Boston: Northeastern University Press, 1990). To be sure, the crimes in which blacks kill whites may be technically more serious in legal terms—many are armed robberies gone bad and thus qualify as felony murders—but this crime pattern reflects once again the role of poverty and race in American society. To modify the famous statement by Willie Sutton, who robbed banks because "that's where the money was," blacks disproportionately rob whites because they are the ones with the money. The harsh penalties that attach to these crimes may reveal vestiges of a racial caste system in America, a caste system which was only formally dismantled a few decades ago but which still reveals itself in patterns of segregation in housing and other aspects of American life. Crossing the color line in the commission of a violent crime is indeed seen as legally more serious than violence among our black citizens, in part because social arrangements are such that the very act of crossing the color line is itself a threat to the larger social order, as it has been throughout our history.

20. See Radelet, *Facing the Death Penalty* (n. 15), 532 and Radelet, "Race and Death" (n. 18), 124–125.

21. Radelet, Bedau, and Putnam (n. 10).

22. Quoted in G. E. Goldhammer, *Dead End* (Brunswick, Me.: Biddle Publishing Company, 1996).

23. J. Reiman, *The Rich Get Richer and the Poor Get Prison: Ideology, Class, and Criminal Justice*, 4th ed. (Boston: Allyn & Bacon, 1995).

24. J. Jackson and J. Jackson, Jr., *Legal Lynching: Racism, Injustice, and the Death Penalty* (New York: Marlowe & Co., 1996).

25. "Punishment," *Encyclopedia Judaica*, 16 vols. (Jerusalem: Keter, 1971), 13:1386.

26. T. Sellin, *The Penalty of Death* (Beverly Hills, Calif.: Sage, 1982), esp. Chap. 1.

27. Deut. 17:7.

28. J. Hastings, ed., *Dictionary of the Bible*, 5 vols. (New York: Charles Scribner's Sons, 1898–1905), 1:527.

29. *The Interpreter's Dictionary of the Bible*, 4 vols. (New York: Abingdon Press, 1962), 4:447.

30. Later, evidentiary requirements became so strict as to preclude the use of the death penalty. See Sellin (n. 26), 15.

31. Execution myths are built around those who "die well," but in reality they are few in number. See Gatrell (n. 3), Chap. 1.

32. The connection between crime and impurity, with punishment serving as a means of cleansing for the community, survived in modified form virtually up to the modern period. During the Middle Ages, for example, offenders would be dragged on a leather slide to the place of execution so that their feet would not touch and hence pollute the ground. In the late Middle Ages, and even during the early modern period, condemned criminals would be driven in a cart, their coffins beside them, so that at no time would they touch the earth. This practice, Newman tells us, was part of the "officially worded death sentences. . . . [R]equiring the criminal to be kept from the earth until hanged thrusts him into the gulf between heaven and earth. The earth is saved from the criminal's demonical powers." G. Newman, *The Punishment Response* (Philadelphia: Lippincott, 1978), 37.

33. I. Barkan, "Capital Punishment in Ancient Greece" (Chicago, 1936), 41. In the ancient world, stoning was a natural, simple, and public method of execution. Other methods sharing these attributes to lesser degrees, generally reserved for more specialized offenses, included drowning, burying alive, beating to death with sticks, and immolation, or burning to death. For an account of the nature and import of executions by these various means, see G. R. Scott, *History of Capital Punishment* (London: Torchstream Books, 1950).

34. Barkan (n. 33), 53.

35. Ibid., 41.

36. Scott (n. 33), 19.

37. Ibid., 20.

38. D. Kagan, S. Ozment, and F. M. Turner, *The Western Heritage* (New York: Macmillan, 1979), 251.

39. A. Keller and C. V. Calvert, *A Hangman's Diary: Being the Journal of Master Franz Schmidt, Public Executioner of Nuremberg, 1573–1617* (Montclair, N.J.: Patterson Smith, 1973), 2.

40. Ibid., 29.

41. The process of excluding the public from a direct role in executions was probably a gradual one. We know, for example, that in sixteenth-century Halifax the citizens played a role—actual and symbolic—in the use of the Halifax Gibbet, a kind of guillotine that required the pulling of a long rope before the blade was dropped upon the neck of the offender, severing his head. "[E]very man there present doth either take hold of the rope (or pulleth forth his arm so near to the same as he can get, in token that he is willing to

see justice executed) and pulling out the pin in this manner, the head block wherein the axe is fastened doth fall down with such a violence, that if the neck of the transgressor were so big as that of a bull, it should be cut asunder at a stroke." See "Holinshed's Chronicle of 1587," quoted in Newman (n. 32), 293.

42. Keller and Calvert (n. 39), 34, 38, 37.

43. Kagan, Ozment, and Turner (n. 38), 290.

44. B. W. Tuchman, *A Distant Mirror: The Calamitous Fourteenth Century* (New York: Knopf, 1978), 12, xvii.

45. Keller and Calvert (n. 39), 2.

46. See Scott (n. 33) and A. Mencken, *By the Neck: A Book of Hangings* (New York: Hastings House, 1942).

47. H. E. Barnes, *The Story of Punishment: A Record of Man's Inhumanity to Man* (Montclair, N.J.: Patterson Smith, 1972), 242.

48. W. O. Douglas, *An Almanac of Liberty* (New York: Random House, 1954), 17.

49. This type of execution for grievous offenders was comparatively common in the Middle Ages. Isolated examples of this punishment can also be found in the early modern period. Notable among these is the case of Damiens the regicide, executed in Paris in 1757. See M. Foucault, *Discipline and Punish: The Birth of the Prison* (New York: Pantheon, 1977), 3–5.

50. Scott (n. 33), 26.

51. Spierenburg (n. 2), 28.

52. Ibid., 30.

53. L. Radzinowicz, *A History of English Criminal Law*, 5 vols. (New York: Macmillan, 1948), 1:26–27.

54. J. Atholl, *Shadow of the Gallows* (London: John Long, 1954), 108.

55. Radzinowicz (n. 53).

56. See Newman (n. 32), 144.

57. Atholl (n. 54), 73.

58. Radzinowicz (n. 53), 1:167.

59. Spierenburg (n. 2), 1:188–189.

60. Gatrell (n. 3), 29–30.

61. Atholl (n. 54), 75.

62. See, generally, Gatrell (n. 3).

63. Newman tells us that it was during this period, one of "the most sanguine in all English history," that

the feudal, medieval rhythm of life—the unhurried, detailed work of the master craftsman, the leisurely raising of sheep and spinning of cloth, the quiet tilling of the earth—was deeply disturbed. The merchants, traders, and industrialists were beginning to take over. The people were thrust headlong into the business of production. To make matters worse, the ordinary people were constantly embattled by wars, civil and international. The civil war, though fought with dignity, nevertheless was a war. And wars cannot circumvent the horrors of death. As if this were not enough, the people of England were visited frequently by terrible plagues—the worst one being the black death of 1666, followed soon by the Great Fire of London. Death was all around them at the time when the social and economic life of the country began to throb. All the basic fibers of English life had been subverted. . . . And in the crowded city of London the specter of death and killing loomed larger than ever. It is little wonder that by the time the eighteenth century was under way, the ordinary Londoner, soon to become known as one of the "working class," found himself gazing dumbfounded or yelling hysterically with the crowd at the foot on the gallows.

See Newman (n. 32), 130, 135.

64. See Radzinowicz (n. 53).

65. The orgies of execution that came in the wake of the French Revolution were a notable exception to this observation. These mass guillotinings were bloody spectacles, and the crowd, reeling from the infamous Reign of Terror of Robespierre and incensed at the political scapegoats paraded before them, might even cry out to see the heads of more infamous victims. The crowd's appetite for gore was not insatiable, however, and after the first few beheadings, their ranks would thin out. Be that as it may, this episode of raw public violence was quite unusual, both for France and for the continental Europe of the early modern period. See O. Blanc, *Last Letters: Prisons and Prisoners of the French Revolution, 1793–1794* (New York: Farrar, Straus & Giroux, 1987).

66. Spierenburg (n. 2), 65, 66.

67. Because this expiation included the offender, the blood of the condemned was considered spiritually pure and hence held the power to heal epilepsy, which was seen as a form of possession by the devil. See R. J. Evans, "Justice Seen, Justice Done?: Abolishing Public Executions in 19th-Century Germany," *History Today* 46 (4): 20–25 (1996). See also R. J. Evans, *Rituals of Retribution: Capital Punishment in Germany 1600–1987* (Oxford: Oxford University Press, 1996). Rituals involving the cleansing and healing power of the condemned on the scaffold were found in other cultures in the Middle Ages. For example, the touch of the condemned was thought to cure disease in medieval England. See Gatrell (n. 3). Healing scaffold rituals appear to have been common and more graphic in Germany.

68. Evans, "Justice Seen, Justice Done?" (n. 67), 20–25.

69. Wouters's execution was a sanitized version of breaking on the wheel as it was practiced in the Middle Ages.

70. Spierenburg (n. 2), 94. Visitors who approached London by sea might also be greeted by the sight of hanging corpses, in this instance those of pirates. "For more than four centuries, pirates were hanged at Execution Dock on the north bank of the Thames." Bodies of the "more notorious pirates" were displayed "at places along the river where they would be seen by the crews of all ships entering and leaving the port." See D. Cordingly, *Under the Black Flag: The Romance and Reality of Life Among the Pirates* (New York: Random House, 1995), 223, 225.

71. Ibid., 94.

72. Ibid., 91.

73. Radzinowicz (n. 53), 1:200.

74. Spierenburg (n. 2), 91.

2

Executions in America

The history of execution procedures in America—the execution rituals associated with the death penalty—roughly parallels that of executions in England and continental Europe. Executions in the colonial period and even on through the mid–nineteenth century, for example, were comparable to the early modern executions examined in Chapter 1. Later executions in the United States forged a modern script that, with its focus on technical method and bureaucratic procedure, may be uniquely American.

THE END OF PUBLIC RITUAL

Colonial executions, like their counterparts in Europe, were public. They were carried out on scaffolds that were centrally located and discretely elevated to accommodate the viewing public. Procedures were restrained and dignified, merging civil and religious authority:

> Magistrates and ministers designed public executions in the early American Republic as displays of civil and religious authority and order, as a "spectacle for Men and Angels." . . . As a civil ceremony, the execution exhibited the authority of the state. It sought to bolster order and encourage conformity. . . . As a religious ceremony, ministers used hanging day to remind the crowd of its own mortality and to demonstrate that God alone could redeem the sinful. Ministers instructed spectators that the

truly penitent could earn salvation. Execution day served as both a warning and a celebration. At the gallows the crowd received a lesson on the
consequences of crime and sin; on hanging day civil and clerical figures
offered proof that society worked properly and that God saved souls. Anyone who dissented from the proceedings did so subtly and infrequently.[1]

Colonial executions were well-attended, featuring high officials and common
citizens. The behavior of the crowd was generally restrained, though an air of
celebration—of confirmation of one's righteousness—would be apparent. The
execution process, not at all unlike that experienced by Hendrina Wouters
(see Chapter 1), was seen to have a beauty all its own.

Colonial executions were a communal undertaking of the first order. Research on these and subsequent public executions in America explicitly indicates what perhaps was only implied about the communal nature of executions
in Europe; namely, that the larger community typically saw themselves as "insiders" and the condemned as "outsiders"—that is, "foreigners, minorities,
and those literally not from the immediate community."[2] Execution lore, especially in Europe, makes much of the noble or wealthy who meet their fate
on the scaffold, but these are but a tiny minority of the condemned.[3] As a
general rule, those publicly condemned and executed were common folk of
no distinction. In the colonial context, Masur's analysis confirms that the condemned "were people for whom spectators might feel the least sympathy, and,
as a result, authorities hoped, the assembled would unite against the condemned to defend social stability."[4] This characterization of the condemned—
as outsiders, marginal to the community—applies to virtually all public
executions in America and Europe.

Those condemned to public execution often served as scapegoats. Their
executions, in turn, can be seen as a form or variant of human sacrifice. As
Davies has observed, "throughout the history of mankind, sacrifice,
vengeance, and penal justice were not separate notions but different facets of
the same process, needed alike to protect the state against the wrath of the
gods."[5] Like all scapegoats, the condemned typically are *in* but not *of* the community; unlike complete strangers, marginal members of a group are "suitable
substitutes for the whole group and so [can] be proper vessels for the whole
group's impurities."[6] (Complete strangers can work as scapegoats *if* they are
drawn from racial or ethnic groups that make up the marginal members of a
community; the dominant group is apt to see members of marginal racial or
ethnic groups as interchangeable, so even a stranger to a given marginal group
will be seen by the dominant group as a member of that group.) Likewise,
scapegoats can serve as stand-ins for the larger group's fears, since indeed the
dominant group *does* typically fear and loathe its marginal members (and others who resemble them), on whom they often project their worst fears.

The scapegoat, thus invested with group guilt and symbolizing all that the
larger group fears, can be banished on the scaffold in a ceremony of righteous
power, the object of which is to appease God, to unite the "insiders" of the
community in their shared status as special in God's eyes and in their own,

and, finally, to render the dominant group safe and secure from the sort of earthy dangers represented by the criminal they have offered up for punishment. Small wonder that crowds at public executions would be large and that, typically, there would be a spirit of festivity, of outright celebration, or at least smug self-congratulation. The group in attendance at the execution would be drawn together and rendered a real and special collectivity, not just an ordinary assembly of people. "The execution gala offers the exclusive sight of the dominant group asserting raw power, glorying in that power, celebrating their clarified identity," pure and alive and special, made whole by the killing off of deviant pretenders to their esteemed ranks.[7]

Public execution procedures had great staying power in America as they had in Europe. Masur's historical research revealed that, in America, "Many aspects of the [execution] ritual changed little throughout the seventeenth and eighteenth centuries."[8] Magistrates and other civil officials presiding over executions during this period saw in the crowds assembled at the gallows the assertion of a common social order drawn together against the threat posed by the offender. Sermons were a critical feature of executions; the themes, meant to apply to offender and citizen alike, were remarkably enduring. Masur determined that ministers used the language of "true and sincere penitence and salvation" as readily in 1650 as in 1790! These sermons—in effect featuring "recycled and refashioned phrases and arguments"—held "enormous currency" on execution day.[9]

By the turn of the nineteenth century, however, sensibilities began to change. Most notable was "the emergence of a middle class that valued internal restraints and private punishments."[10] For this social elite—and for their counterparts in Europe during the early modern period—"the death and suffering" of the condemned were "increasingly experienced as painful . . . because other people were increasingly perceived as fellow human beings."[11] The widening group of people considered human was the result of a growing "mutual dependence between social groups," well-exemplified in the middle class—the merchant and trading and service class—as societies became more civilized.[12] In effect, this privileged group "identified to a certain degree with convicts on the scaffold"; that is, they could see in the offender glimpses of their own humanity. These increasingly civilized people "disliked the sight of physical suffering: even that of the guilty," presumably because the guilty, no matter how serious the crime, were still fellow human beings to them.[13] The public spectacle of suffering offered by executions, variously entertaining and edifying in times past when applied to marginal and indeed often demonized groups, had become for them a source of distress, a cruel event to be avoided at all costs.

Changing sensibilities altered not only the perception of capital punishment in the abstract, but the nature of the crowds in attendance at executions. The enlightened elite, of increasingly civilized and refined sensibilities, studiously avoided executions.[14] Those who rallied around the scaffold were of a more coarse and vulgar nature; ironically, many were outsiders to the community who would travel to executions for the entertainment value. Their behavior often closely resembled the unruly English mobs discussed in Chapter 1 and was quite unlike the quiet and penitent—even if smugly self-righteous—community members much-praised for their decorum and restraint by Puritan ministers over the preceding two centuries. The condemned, as well, could prove unruly—failing to confess, claiming innocence—and would have to be visibly forced to play their assigned roles in the execution ritual. "Social authorities could no longer depict hanging day as a spectacle of civil and religious order" that had shared meaning to all citizens, God-fearing and criminal alike. "No longer could it be claimed," as had been done for centuries by magistrates and ministers, "that on execution day the entire community assembled for an effective lesson in morality and piety."[15]

Public executions came to "resemble 'county fairs' that attracted huge crowds of spectators to small towns."[16] Matters became even worse in the cities. Whereas a small town execution might draw a crowd of mostly outsiders numbering between eight and sixteen thousand, certainly a considerable gathering, urban executions could bring out crowds thirty- and forty-thousand strong, which is to say, assemblies the size of small cities. Public executions, wherever they were held, became commercial events, complete with admission tickets, preferred seating areas, and stands selling food and supplies.[17] These were "disgusting spectacles" to the social elite, in no small measure because the crowds drawn to them came for the crass carnival atmosphere rather than any serious moral or civic purpose. The elite also likely saw these crowds as a potential threat to social order and to state power, both of which were called into question by the rowdy behavior of spectators, though never really compromised. After all, the executioner always had his way and the crowds would always disperse and go home.[18] The deeper threat may have been to the image of civility so central to the elite vision of modern society.[19] If public executions can properly be thought of as a form of human sacrifice, these sacrifices would increasingly have appeared to have been offered in vain—or worse, offered up to satisfy the vanity of people who reveled in the kind of primitive violence that gave the lie to the notion that the death penalty was a decent, civilized sanction.

Public executions were outlawed state by state in New England and the Middle Atlantic region, indeed abolished entirely in these regions by 1845, and replaced by private hangings that were to be held discreetly behind prison walls.[20] Prison hangings, in turn, formed the new execution day ritual. These were modest secular procedures carried out before a small group of elite citizens who were required by class etiquette to behave with decorum and restraint. Private executions were not meant to be spectacles; nor were they ceremonies, with sacrificial overtones, as was the case with many public executions. Some advocates of private executions claimed that condemned prisoners would repent genuinely if removed from the gaze of the crowd. There had been a growing fear that public hangings had produced confessions cooked up for the masses rather than sincere professions of guilt, and certainly the stylized broadsheets handed out at executions, featuring a more or less standard formula of repentance, suggest that this was so.[21]

But repentance, true or otherwise, was not central to private executions. The central issue was to preserve a simple, quiet, uncontroversial, almost collaborative execution, in stark contrast to the occasionally unpredictable spectacles that could unfold on the public scaffold. Accordingly, there was serious talk of using drugs to anesthetize the condemned before they were privately hanged, so that "decorum, propriety, and civility were preserved, the control of vicious passions effectuated."[22] The result would be a tame execution marked by the apparent cooperation of the condemned; standing alone, with no scaffold platform from which to vent one's feelings, protest one's innocence, or secure forgiveness from the community, and shorn of any emotional support that might be wrested, however misguidedly, from the tumult and emotion of scaffold crowds—held secure in the firm and uncontested grip of the duly constituted authorities assembled around him, who now maintained complete and utter control of the proceedings.[23] Thus isolated from human passions, vicious or otherwise, executions would unfold "coldly, clinically, and in heart-stopping silence behind high prison walls," with the paradoxical result, reminiscent of executions today, that "a polite nation's brutality [would] be camouflaged" as an act of humaneness.[24]

The abolition of public executions, then, may have "only hid the cruelty" of execution "and so intensified it."[25] From this crucial transition—moving from passionate public executions to cold, clinical, private ones—we can trace the beginnings of the bureaucratic regimen of modern private executions. Today, psychological dehumanization born of social isolation—on death row or in the death chamber—serves as the anesthetic that facilitates efficient, impersonal executions that are virtually devoid of human sentiment. With lethal injection, a number of jurisdictions offer tranquilizers to the condemned, the better to further numb the human spirit and expedite the smooth unfolding of a process that so fully camouflages executions as to put them beyond recognition for what they are: premeditated acts of lethal violence carried out in the name of an ostensibly civilized society.

Public Executions—Legal and Illegal—in the American South

The retreat from public executions in America was much delayed in the South. There, the condemned were almost all blacks, who were considered by Southern whites to be less than fully human, comprising in their eyes a marginal, demonized group almost fully excluded from the protections afforded to members of the human community.[26] It is telling that one salient rationale for American slavery was that blacks possessed "racial traits" that made them, like primitive beasts of burden, "uniquely fitted for bondage."[27] Following the end of slavery, whites widely expected the demise of African-Americans on the assumption that blacks, being naturally dependent on superior whites, could not survive on their own. "Many believed that blacks would perish in freedom, like fish on the land. The Negro's 'incompetence,' after all, had been essential to the understanding—and defense—of slavery itself."[28]

A corollary belief held by many Southern whites was that blacks were natural criminals. In the harsh, smugly self-righteous words of a nineteenth-century Southern planter, "You can't find a white streak in 'em. . . . All the men are thieves, and all the women are prostitutes. It's their natur' to be that way, and they'll never be no other way."[29] Slavery, it was believed, had contained that criminality. With freedom, so the belief ran, came persistent, predatory, brutal crime, calling for severe punishment.[30]

The punishment of choice was often public execution by means legal or illegal. None of the social elite of this time identified with blacks as fellow human beings who should be treated with a modicum of compassion; no one sought to protect these black ex-slaves from humiliation and suffering on the public scaffold. Indeed, the outright elimination of blacks—there was much talk of black extermination after Emancipation—framed discussions of punishment. For one political party, the Radicals, "the 'Negro Problem' was how to control the blacks as they passed through bestiality and into extinction."[31] A 1905 editorial in a Texas newspaper stated, in a matter-of-fact tone, "Almost every day some negro brute assaults a white woman in this state, and often one to a half-dozen murders are committed in an effort to hide the crime. . . . If rape and murder by brutish negroes are to become common, the negro must expect extermination."[32] Confronted with an atavistic "criminal race" in their midst, Southerners resorted to legal and illegal executions—not to mention brutal penal servitude—on a regular basis.[33]

As a regular practice, or perhaps even a social institution of some standing in the community, lynchings were a Southern phenomenon that came to full flower with the passing of slavery, when blacks became subject to harsh legal and extralegal punishments.[34] This belies the popular image of slavery in America, which features the indiscriminate lynching of slaves, as in fact slaves were rarely executed by legal or illegal means. In a sense, the social control offered by executions was superfluous in their case. Slaves were already imprisoned—and subject to corporal punishment, often of a quite severe nature—on Southern plantations.[35] It is telling that the language of those who sought the abolition of slavery described the entire South as a prison for blacks, as when William Lloyd Garrison writes of "the Southern prison-house of bondage" in his preface to Frederick Douglass's now-classic narrative about his experiences as a slave.[36] Slaves also had great value as labor commodities. To kill a slave was to squander a considerable financial investment.

The emancipation of slaves ended the mass incarceration of African-Americans and set in motion forces that tore at the heart of the Southern world, threatening "to topple the class structure of Southern society and the racial caste system on which it was fabricated."[37] In all, some four million slaves were set free, "suddenly transformed from personal property to potential competitors."[38] Southern whites—beleaguered, afraid, and increasingly vengeful in the face of economic and social competition from free blacks—sought alternatives to slavery that would allow them to control and ultimately exploit the black population. The underlying theme was the preservation of white supremacy—maintaining the status of whites as the dominant, favored group, which was essentially undisputed during slavery. In essence, white supremacy meant racial purity. One strategy to preserve white supremacy featured sheer and often brutal violence. The aim: to reduce newly liberated African-Americans to slaves of fear, who would submit passively to the demands of the dominant white caste, quietly living out a segregated, inferior life. This strategy is perhaps best exemplified by the actions of terrorist gangs like the Ku Klux Klan and other marauding vigilante mobs that would frighten, maim, torture, and lynch black citizens well into the twentieth century.

No one defends lynchings these days, but lynchings were praised as noble acts of "popular justice" throughout the South after the Civil War and indeed well into the twentieth century.[39] "Lynch law is a good sign," observed the Georgia populist Tom Watson, "it shows that a sense of justice yet lives among the people."[40] And most popular these illegal executions were, especially in the South and, later, the West, after the migration of Southerners to Texas and beyond.[41] Hard as it may be to imagine today, lynchings were all the rage with the public and even with officials in the South, including a few governors, who not only deferred to the public will but often reflected its demand for vengeance. The comments of former Mississippi governor James K. Bardaman are indicative of the time: "If it is necessary every Negro in the state will be lynched; it will be done to maintain white supremacy."[42]

The killing ritual associated with lynchings recapitulated the mob violence of biblical stonings and the flamboyant violence of medieval executions.[43] The victim of lynch mobs would often be set upon by outraged citizens who would assault him mercilessly; the beaten and bloodied victim would then be mutilated, even castrated, while still alive. Many lynchings involved immolation—colloquially know as "Negro barbeques"—an excruciating procedure long-abandoned in legal executions and distinctly reminiscent of medieval witch hunts. (Historically, immolation has been reserved for those considered the very worst offenders, who "had to be instantly obliterated . . . not merely killed, but reduced to ash."[44]) Efforts would be made to prolong the killing, the better to inflict agony on the victim and entertain the crowd. It would seem that Southerners, seeing themselves surrounded and potentially overwhelmed by a brutal subhuman enemy, responded in turn with primitive violence, undeterred by any sense of empathy for the targets of their anger and fear.

The lynching of Sam Holt in Newnan, Georgia in 1899 provides a case in point. As with most lynching victims in the South, Holt, a black man, was accused of a violent crime against a white person, in this instance his employer. As was typical, passions ran high and raw vengeance was sought. Here is an excerpt from a news account of the event:

> Sam Hose [Holt] . . . was burned at the stake in a public road, one and a half miles from here. Before the torch was applied to the pyre, the Negro was deprived of his ears, fingers and other portions of his body with surprising fortitude. Before the body was cool, it was cut into pieces, the bones were crushed in to small bits and even the tree upon which the

wretch met his fate was torn up and disposed of as souvenirs. The Negro's heart was cut into several pieces, as was also his liver. Those unable to obtain ghastly relics directly, paid more fortunate possessors extravagant sums for them. Small pieces of bone went for 25 cents and a bit of liver, crisply cooked, for 10 cents.[45]

As extreme as this case may appear to our contemporary sensibilities, lynchings marked by ferocious violence were the norm rather than the exception.[46] Lynchings can be said to have followed a kind of script, but that script often called for exercises in frenzied mob violence, where blood lust ruled.

Certainly there were elements of human sacrifice in many lynchings. The targets were a marginal group reduced to demonized stereotypes, invested with blame for all that had gone wrong with Southern society after the Civil War and indeed on through to the Great Depression. As is typical in cases of human sacrifice, the target group undergoes "double transfiguration" so that "the victims are transfigured into aggressors, then violence against the group sacralizes the event as the dominant community is reaffirmed in its own purity."[47] As natural aggressors in the eyes of whites—and, moreover, thought to harbor an even more natural resentment against the white Southerners who had enslaved them—newly freed blacks were objects of great fear, in many cases bordering on hysteria. That fear, in turn, led to lynchings for behavior as variable as violations of racial etiquette (including "acting like a white man") and such violent crime as murder and rape. That fear also led on occasion to lynchings of obviously innocent persons—relatives or friends who were explicitly chosen by mobs as stand-ins when the alleged offenders could not be found.[48] As members of a scapegoat class, it would appear that, once the mob was on the move, *any* black person could serve as a suitable candidate for a lynching.

Of course, some crimes and some lynchings were worse than others. The murder of one's employer, as in Holt's case, perhaps had a special resonance. This crime could be symbolically linked with a deep-seated and much-feared scenario dating back to the period of slavery, in which the seemingly docile and trustworthy slaves rise up in revolt, kill their masters, and turn white supremacy on its head. Such fears, symbolized in the rebellion of Nat Turner and other renegade slaves, ran especially deep as the institution of slavery came into question with the approaching Civil War. And these fears ran rampant after Emancipation, when fears of "Negro retribution" for the abuses of slavery were quite common.[49] Rape was considered a particularly heinous crime, perhaps even worse than murder, and led to many of the most awful lynchings. Rape threatened white supremacy at its supposed genetic core by forcibly "polluting" the white gene pool. "It is a small exaggeration to describe white preoccupation with miscegenation and racial amalgamation as a regional paranoia" during this time, and, of course, the paranoid nightmare in this context was rape.[50]

Lynchings, like public executions, often drew crowds featuring a wide cross section of the community—rich and poor, men, women, and children. This was possible because, like public executions of the time, lynchings would often be announced in advance, the better to frighten blacks with the threat of impending violence and to facilitate attendance by whites from neighboring areas.[51] "Indeed, railroads ran special trains and frequently assigned extra cars to regular trains to accommodate the demands of lynch-minded white crowds numbering as many as 15,000."[52] A 1902 lynching in Mississippi, attended by five thousand people, featured not only special trains but "reserved seats" placed strategically near the lynching site "for the women who might desire them."[53] Many did. No empathy for the victims—blacks being seen as subhuman—deterred the social elite from their place at the lynching. No worries about humaneness deterred anyone, either. Humaneness was reserved for humans. With a demonized scapegoat, a member of the crowd or local community could see the lynching as itself a humane gesture in service of the larger human community on whose behalf the lynching victim was put to death.

Pictures of lynching scenes regularly show the festive, gloating mood characteristic of public executions. Members of the dominant group—including women and children—smile broadly, picnic baskets in hand. Others, arms raised, point with pride at the ravaged corpse, as if to say: "The wicked black is dead; long live the white race!" Some of the perverse enthusiasm generated by lynchings may have been captured by Langston Hughes in his poem, "Lynching Song."

> Pull at the rope!
> O, pull it high!
> Let the white folks live
> And the black boy die.[54]

In another poem, "Ku Klux," Hughes ends on a related theme:

> A klansman said, "Nigger,
> Look me in the face—
> And tell me you believe in
> The great white race."[55]

All too often, no amount of subservience would be enough to spare a man's life. The lynching victim, frequently hanged from the nearest tree, would become the latest manifestation of the "strange fruit" that adorned Southern trees. In lyrics made famous by blues singer Billie Holliday, the song "Strange Fruit" captures this grim scene:

> Southern trees
> Bear a strange fruit
> Blood on the leaves
> And blood at the root
>
> Black bodies swingin'
> In the Southern breeze
> Strange fruit hanging
> From the poplar trees.[56]

Pictures of mobs taken after a lynching have a curiously self-satisfied quality to them, as if the mob is sated, ready to savor their victory over evil. Pictures that caught the mob in action yielded a different image. By all accounts, members of the mobs were suffused with rage, straining to get at the victim, spitting and kicking and throwing rocks, sometimes hurting each other in the process. One account, that of James Cameron, who survived a Marion, Indiana lynch mob in 1930, is particularly compelling. Cameron tells us that the crowd chanted in unison, "Nigger, Nigger, Nigger," surging at him relentlessly as he was led to a tree just outside the jail, a tree that held aloft the bodies of two young black men who only minutes before had been beaten, mutilated, and then hanged by the very crowd that now sought Cameron's life. Hungry for its last victim, the crowd set on Cameron with what he called "demonic" ferocity. "Only the strongest and biggest were able to get in close enough to inflict inhuman pain," he reports. "The weaker ones had to be content with spitting on me and throwing things at me." Many threw rocks; others wielded bats and clubs. One can't help but see the scene as reminiscent of a Biblical stoning gone out of control. Even children got in their licks. "Little boys and girls, not yet in their teens . . . somehow managed to work their way in close enough to bite and scratch me on the legs." It would seem that all of the members of the crowd wanted a piece of Cameron—to inflict pain, to remember, to prove they were there.[57] Inexplicably, Cameron was spared and even allowed to drag himself, unmolested, back to his cell. (Cameron himself believes that God spoke directly to the crowd, ordering them to stop. No one from the crowd confirms this divine intervention, but then no one on the scene has ever offered *any* explication for the sudden cessation of Cameron's worst nightmare.)

Renewed in life and power, participants in a lynching would remember the event, dwell on it, and tell and retell it to others not fortunate enough to be in attendance. A desire for relics—for example, body parts or clothes wrested from the dead or dying and portions of the rope or of burnt wood; all seeming testimony to the sacrificial nature of lynchings—was a near universal feature of lynchings, bespeaking not only their memorable quality but bringing to mind once again executions of the Middle Ages. Souvenirs included "picture postcards of the proceedings . . . sold by enterprising photographers."[58] Accounts in newspapers offered detailed descriptions of lynchings, sometimes including feature stories about citizens prominently involved in the violence. Like legal executions of the time, then, lynchings were typically a source of civic and racial pride.

The statistics on lynchings of African-Americans in the South, though incomplete, tell a story of remarkable violence. We know lynchings were common during the Reconstruction period, from 1865–1877, a time marked by "a staggering increase in the amount of violence directed at blacks" in response to "the hysterical concern among many [whites] that the region was threatened by the prospect of 'Negro domination.'"[59] Reliable figures are unavailable, however, so the extent of the carnage cannot be assessed.[60] From 1882 through 1930, a period known as "the lynching era," statistics are better.

Local records and news accounts reveal that "on the average, a black man, woman, or child was murdered nearly once a week, every week . . . by a hate-driven white mob."[61] Capital punishment during this period, little more than "legal lynching"—an oxymoron peculiar to the South during this period[62]—claimed roughly as many black lives and served to reinforce the reign of terror sought by Southern whites.[63] The death toll during this period from all executions—mob lynchings and legal lynchings—totaled an incredible 4,291 black lives. Over the forty-nine years of the infamous lynching era, then, "an African American was put to death"—by legal or illegal execution—"somewhere in the South on the average of every four days."[64] If lynchings from the Reconstruction period are included, the gruesome lynching era—marked by one or more executions a week—then extends for over sixty years, covering a full three generations of free African-Americans!

Racism is, of course, at the heart of slavery and the orgy of lynching that followed Emancipation.[65] Racism also explains why the vast majority of people sentenced to death in the South during this period were black, why their alleged victims were reported to be white, and why many of these black men were publically hanged well into the twentieth century—a comparatively primitive and degrading procedure for a legal system to maintain at this late date. Public hanging as a legal sanction was created as a "conspicuous symbol of indignity" meant to shame and deter; hanging often produced "a slow and agonizing death," the ignoble manifestations of which—kicking, choking, and loss of bladder and bowel control—were easily visible to large crowds.[66]

One can only suppose that in such a climate it must have seemed right and natural that a group of law-abiding whites should assemble to view and celebrate, quietly or otherwise, the public degradation and demise of a black criminal. The victim might well be resigned to his fate; after all, he—again, almost all those legally executed were men—lived in a world in which lynch mobs could wreak carnage on his race with impunity, and in which law meant white law, pure and simple. A lawful public hanging might well be, for prisoner and audience alike, a comparatively normal and even decent undertaking, a kind of tame lynching with antecedents in times past, notably the early modern period with its staged executions calculated to hide any human sentiments that might blemish the proceedings.

The historical record appears to bear out these speculations. We learn that the ritual of twentieth-century public executions in the South had been streamlined relative to early modern executions but still offered resonances from that distant period; there was clearly a kind of ceremony, this time characterized by a certain bucolic simplicity. Conducted in woods and pastures, these executions were unobtrusive, almost natural events. In general, the condemned betrayed no profound emotions. The crowds, still quite large at that point in history, were sometimes loud and coarse but more often subdued in their reactions. Occasionally, some of the observers displayed sadness for the condemned, or perhaps resignation that a young black life had yet again come to an end on the scaffold.

Philippe Aries recounted the hanging of a young black man in Georgia in 1890. Though comparatively recent, the execution is striking for several reasons. First, the man was killed almost immediately after conviction. Second, he was executed in public, before a crowd of spectators. Third, the crowd displayed an easy familiarity with violence and death, though a simple, unadorned hanging was, historically speaking, fairly tame. Fourth, the condemned man, formerly a servant, was attended by his master, who "prepare[d] him for death and . . . play[ed] the role of confessor" even as the condemned man stood on the scaffold. Finally, the man went to his death with simple resignation, eating his last meal with relish, just moments before his execution, then mounting the scaffold with a deliberate step. "His bare feet did not tremble." His manner was "calm," "natural," and "completely dignified." His farewell was simple and direct: "'I'm all right now,' and very firmly, 'Good-bye, captain . . . good-bye everybody.'"[67] The account implies that the condemned man is a simple creature, savoring a last meal because it is an animal pleasure of the moment, unafraid of death because his attachment to life is so primitive.

Yet another execution was that of one Asbury Dixon, a black man hanged in 1902 in the town of Snow Hill, Maryland. On the eve of his execution, Dixon, his family, and his fellow prisoners congregated freely in the jail, singing religious hymns. Dixon sang "with a fervor and solemnity unsurpassed by any of them." He was resigned, prepared to die. Dixon's young son, Tema, "much interested in the singing of hymns and the farewells of the other prisoners to his father," tired, then fell asleep in his father's cell. The jailor let the boy stay, leaving him to sleep the night "in his father's arms." The parting of father and son the next morning was a wrenching experience for the man and his boy as well as the jailor. This was the private reality, where dehumanizing stereotypes could be shed. The public reality, of white justice begetting black death, awaited Dixon on the scaffold. The jailor, whatever his private personal sentiments, went about his duty without visible emotion. Dixon, too, displayed little feeling for the enormity of the fate that awaited him; he ate a hearty last meal, then smoked a cigar. On the scaffold, Dixon acknowledged the error of his ways, spoke of receiving forgiveness from the Lord, and said a gentle goodbye to the onlookers. Resignation to a force of nature beyond Dixon's or anyone else's control pervaded the execution, an event that was not an occasion for sadness or regret, but rather one of "the quiet little hangings [that] made a pleasant break in the monotony of farm life."[68]

Public executions would be held in some southern states well into the twentieth century. There were public executions in Mississippi and Louisiana, for example, in the 1940s and perhaps even as recently as the 1950s. (Executions were held in or around local jails in these states until 1955 and 1957, respectively, after which the execution process was centralized and moved to state prisons.[69]) Mississippi is the home of the first portable electric chair, which was in use in that state from 1940 through 1955; some seventy-three prisoners, fifty-six of them black (77 percent), were put to death in this chair, usually in local jails but sometimes in public. Newspaper accounts during this period sometimes carried pictures of these electrocutions. The 1940 execution of Willie Mae Bragg was reported in the *Jackson Clarion-Ledger* in this way:

> At the left, Bragg sits in the chair and looks on as guards strap his arms. . . . The picture at right was made as the first flash of electricity surged through his body. . . . Note Bragg's hands gripping the chair and his bulging in death's throes.[70]

It would seem that Bragg was a specimen and nothing more, a mere vehicle for an examination of the workings of the curious new machine that was the electric chair, an entity whose death could be dissected dispassionately, as if it were of no great consequence that his black life should end in this way.

Most executions using the portable electric chair were conducted within local jails but even these events had a semipublic character to them. When the executioner arrived with the electric chair in the back of his truck, it would cause a considerable stir. Pictures can be found featuring the executioner of this period, Jim Thompson, posing with the chair in front of a school. Surrounding the chair are Mississippi schoolchildren, all white, holding their books and looking on as if in the presence of a prized trophy.[71] Actual executions would, of course, draw much local attention. "[P]eople often surrounded the [jail] building to listen for telltale signs" of electrocution. In one typical instance, "A crowd gathered late at night on the courthouse square with chairs, crackers, and children, waiting for the current to be turned on and the street lights to dim."[72]

The execution of Willie Francis provides another example of a semipublic execution of a black man.[73] (This case is famous because the first attempt to execute Francis failed, but that is not important here.) Conducted in a rural Louisiana jail in the mid-1940s, this execution was marked by an air of casual informality, as if Francis's life, much like that of Willie Mae Bragg, were of little consequence. The room in the jail holding the electric chair was full to overflowing with local citizens, all white; the streets outside the jail were crowded as well, primarily with white citizens. The instrument of execution was a portable electric chair, installed in the jail on the morning of the execution by a prison captain and an inmate on assignment from the state penitentiary at Angola. Both the officer and the inmate were reportedly drunk, which almost certainly explains why the chair failed to kill Willie Francis.

Willie's demeanor on the day of his execution was calm and collected, even relaxed. Earlier that day, his head had been shaved by a fellow prisoner. Though at first uneasy during this procedure, Willie came to trade jokes with the prisoner as well as with the sheriff and deputy in attendance. "Everybody was being so nice to me," Willie was reported to have thought, "that for a while dying didn't seem like such a bad thing." (One can only imagine the hard life Willie led, to be so moved by simple gestures of kindness in the death house.) Though he later stated he was fearful, Willie indeed acted as if dying weren't such a bad thing. At one point, he was led near the electric chair and docilely started to seat himself of his own accord. He was stopped by the sheriff, who ushered Willie into a cell in an adjoining corridor for his last words with a priest. It was apparent to everyone on the scene that Willie was "fully resigned to his fate." Moments later, Willie was summoned by the sheriff.

> Willie looked at the sheriff, who said nothing but instead gave him a slight nod. Not fully understanding what to do, Willie left the cell, walked across the hallway, back into the execution room, and sat down in the chair. This time no one stopped him.[74]

The execution failed for technical reasons (the chair was not properly grounded), and the botched effort gave rise to a spate of litigation about whether or not a person could be lawfully "executed" twice. But the execution itself was only remarkable in its curious informality, the apparent result of a blending of pastoral sentiment with modern technology. Willie's second bout with the chair, roughly one year later, was orchestrated with more formality and, by modern standards, more professionalism. The chair worked, and Willie died.

Prison Executions: Private, Bureaucratic Procedure

The easy informality of executions like those of Willie Francis and Willie Mae Bragg unfolded as if it were right and natural that these alien creatures, so utterly unlike their executioners and the viewing public, be put to death. Executions of this sort are, of course, a thing of the past. Gradually over this century, executions came to take on a new meaning and a new, impersonal form in response to the growing perception of the humanity of the prisoners condemned to death. (This reciprocal process—recognition of the humanity of the condemned and a corresponding need to distance oneself from that humanity in order to kill the prisoner—appears to have occurred first in the North, the most modern part of America at this time, and only much later in the South, the region that was the least modern, as a general matter, and little short of primitive in relation to blacks, the main group subject to execution.[75])

Increasingly, executions were seen as acts of violence that were likely to reflect badly on the larger community, harden the public, and demean the condemned. Accordingly, executions became both less frequent and less public. They were moved into penal institutions, sometimes initially to jails (as seen most notably in rural areas in the South and elsewhere but also in some cities), where they would remain until state prison systems were sufficiently developed to take over the task. Eventually, all executions occurred within prisons. At first, these executions typically were performed in the center of the prison yard, which accommodated sizeable crowds; later, they were conducted in remote corners of the yard, thus restricting the viewing audience. Finally, executions were moved inside prison buildings, generally to the basements of death rows, which in turn were housed deep within the prison compound.[76]

Efforts were made to make executions as tame as humanly possible—and, thereby, it was hoped by the people on the scene, decent and humane. (Historical analysis suggests that while bringing executions indoors added greatly to the control of the event by officials, it may well have also added to—intensified—the suffering of the condemned, despite the conscious intent of those associated with private executions to make the process humane.) In practical terms, this concern with humanity meant that officials sought executions that were to be quick, painless, minimally disfiguring, and private. In particular, one scrupulously avoided anything that would draw a condemned prisoner's attention to an impending execution, such as a preview of the execution apparatus. Such an experience, by "unnecessarily sharpen[ing] the poignancy of the prisoner's apprehension," would in turn cause "those last torturous minutes to be even more unbearable."[77] In the process of trying to spare prisoners such suffering (and no doubt to lessen the discomfort of prison staff as well), executions became strained, hidden, and hurried undertakings. To paraphrase a mid-twentieth-century executioner, one stayed out of sight and worked as quickly and quietly as one could.[78]

Present-day executions could hardly be more different from executions in the past. Executions today are always conducted in secluded areas within prisons. Only a limited number of spectators attend and most do so for professional reasons; these witnesses maintain a discreet silence, though many are reportedly shaken by what they see. (It would appear that witnesses of modern executions, tame though these events may be in historical terms, routinely show symptoms of dissociation related to short-term trauma; we might suppose that witnesses to public executions in times past were often profoundly traumatized, though the term or even the phenomenon were unknown to them.[79]) Neither death nor killing is any longer a familiar part of daily life for the population at large; killings by officials are especially rare events, and are drained of their emotional import by secrecy (hardly anyone sees them) and euphemism (hardly anyone calls an execution a killing).

Speed and efficiency, too, almost certainly dampen the emotional resonance of the proceedings relative to earlier executions. Executions today are over within a matter of minutes. (By contrast, in early modern London it took upwards of two hours to get from the prison to the scaffold.) In extreme cases today, executions take as little as nine seconds from when the prisoner leaves his cell.[80] Often, observers hardly know that a killing has occurred. Nor, claimed one famous hangman, does the prisoner! "The execution was over so quickly," states Syd Dernley, who carried out executions in England as recently as the 1950s, "that the condemned man could scarcely have registered what was happening to him."[81] It is perhaps not surprising, then, that now and again prisoners would escape from lynch mobs and run straight into the arms of the official executioner. Relating one such story, a correctional official in Georgia observed,

The point is that a good executioner's better than a mob. The guy knew he was gonna die. He chose between a professional and a bunch of bloodthirsty crazies. I would have done the same thing: at least a professional's gonna get it over with fast.[82]

Today's executions are highly bureaucratic jobs with clearly delineated roles, responsibilities, and procedures articulated in execution protocols. All behavior is spelled out by the prison authorities and occurs in the context of rigidly enforced bureaucratic routines. Of course, most prison work, indeed most work in general, is bureaucratized these days. But the execution of prisoners is an extreme case, and for good reason. Killing and dying are elemental activities, and so we thoroughly "encase" them, as it were, within sterile but comforting bureaucratic procedures.[83] The process is ritualistic, by virtue of its mechanical precision, but bureaucratic executions are not true rituals. Rituals, like bureaucratic procedures, allow people to disengage from their normal roles. But with true rituals, this disengagement occurs in the service of a larger undertaking—some form of cleansing or celebration—that has larger communal meaning. The bureaucratic execution is an end in itself, recognizing only its own internal logic.

Citizens not officially connected with an execution play a restricted, impoverished role in these proceedings. As in times past, crowds may assemble during executions, though today's crowds are small by historical standards; with the exception of executions of well-known offenders, these crowds grow smaller by the day. (Executions have become so routine to the public that some executions barely merit media coverage.) People may mill about outside the prison gates, sometimes protesting or applauding the executions taking place within, but they have no real awareness of what is going on. The prison staff, in turn, are barely aware of these groups, considering them little more than a nuisance. Certainly these groups have no meaningful involvement in the execution process. Even the execution of notorious offender Ted Bundy, seen by many as the personification of evil, drew a crowd of no more than two thousand, enormous by today's standards but small in historical terms. The Bundy crowd was isolated in a cow pasture far from the execution site, where their tasteless antics were played out in a seeming parody of public executions from days gone by. The best they could muster was an effigy execution, and even that did not engage the attention of the entire crowd.[84]

Loved ones—of the condemned and of the victim—are also on the periphery of modern executions. The family and friends of the condemned have limited opportunities to visit in the death house. Though in some states relatives or friends of the offender or victim (or both) can attend executions, their numbers are limited. So, too, is their behavior sharply circumscribed, in line with the bureaucratic rule of impersonality. The admonitions to witnesses given at Louisiana's Angola Prison, paraphrased by Sister Helen Prejean, are typical. There, the warden "emphasizes to all witnesses—victims' families included—that during an execution there must be 'no emotional outbursts, no obscenities uttered, no undignified behavior of any kind.' They have designed a process, he says, that 'protects everyone's rights,' including those of the one being executed. 'They have a family too. A circus atmosphere is not in anyone's interest.'"[85]

Surely no one would want witnesses from the victim's family celebrating the execution of their loved one's killer in the death house, but the warden's premise would seem to be that any strong emotions are inherently inappropriate at an execution, despite its being an event that brings together people deeply affected by violence and is itself a deeply affecting act of violence. At least one other warden expressed irritation to a reporter over a family that couldn't seem to stop crying as their loved one's execution approached. Their behavior upset *him*, not the condemned prisoner, during the man's last meal, which the warden himself had arranged over the initial objections of the prisoner—as if the condemned prisoner's unwillingness to eat on schedule bespoke a sadness that was somehow out of bounds, a kind of resistance to the execution routine. "You aren't making things any easier," the warden was reported to have planned to say to the weeping family after the last meal was over. It is not clear whether he did or not. By all indications, the ease and efficiency with which the execution was to be carried out were the paramount issues at stake to the warden.[86]

Even the condemned are curiously removed from today's executions, present more in body than in spirit. The condemned spend years on death row awaiting their fate; not, as in the past, a mere few days or weeks. (A corollary of our modern concern for humanely administered executions is our desire to allow inmates to explore every avenue of appeal before we execute them. This greatly lengthens the prisoner's stay on death row.) During their lonely and barren confinement, the condemned die a slow psychic death; numb submission to the executioner has become the norm in the death house.

MODERN EXECUTIONS AND
THE ILLUSION OF HUMANENESS

America, perhaps more than any other country, has tinkered with the mechanics of legal executions in a search for the "perfect" method. In operational terms, perfect means the most tame and reliable method of killing made possible by existing technology. Our preferred methods have evolved over the centuries. Beginning with the rather simple and unambiguous violence of hangings and shootings (by firing squads)—which involved direct and unembellished applications of techniques used elsewhere in the world and, in the case of hangings, in practice for centuries—we moved on to the relatively complicated but more tame killings made possible by twentieth-century technology: the gas chamber, the electric chair, and most recently, lethal injection. In a sense, our history lives on in today's execution methods, since each is still in use since the advent of the contemporary death penalty in 1976. In descending order of frequency, at year's end 1996, there have been a total of 223 executions by lethal injection, 128 by electrocution, 10 by gas, 4 by hanging, and 2 by firing squad. If we look back over the twentieth century as a whole, the predominant method has been the electric chair, which has taken well over four thousand lives. The method of the future would appear to be lethal injection. Presently authorized in thirty-two states—in contrast to electrocution, authorized today in only eleven—lethal injection is far and away the most frequently used method these days and for the foreseeable future. Executions by either of the two most common methods today, lethal injection or electrocution, share an important feature: each lends itself to impersonal bureaucratic procedures and the appearance of quick, bloodless, and even painless deaths.

Today we have an elaborate and largely clandestine bureaucracy to carry out death sentences, and we use technologically sophisticated modes of execution. The changes are telling. Slowly but inexorably we have distanced ourselves from the reality of the death penalty. We now kill efficiently and, above all, impersonally—"without anger or passion," to use Max Weber's fine phrase—like so many functionaries in the business of justice.[87] The contemporary execution procedure is unlike any of the premodern procedures—even those followed in executions at the turn of this century. Though modern executions are obviously violent in that they entail the forcible taking of life, the technical process is typically quick, clean, and precise, and ostensibly free of physical pain. Such, then, is the nature of progress. We have come a long way from the public slaughters of the past.

Or have we? We normally think of modern execution methods as humane because they are physically painless. Certainly these methods appear painless, but appearances can be misleading. Barnes, for example, has cited anecdotal evidence from earlier in this century that casts doubt on the presumed painlessness of electrocution, which has been the most common method of execution in use in America in the twentieth century.[88] More recently, Denno has marshalled an impressive array of scientific evidence on this subject that, once again, raises the unsettling prospect that, despite disclaimers by some experts and executioners, and despite the comparatively tame execution scene associated with the electric chair, "death by electrocution may inflict 'unnecessary pain,' physical violence, and 'mutilation'" in violation of the Eighth Amendment.[89]

Electrocutions are probably painful, and may be excruciatingly so. We now know that the considerable electricity generated by the chair largely circumvents the brain, which is insulated by the skull, and instead passes through the body and out the leg. Thus, while massive surges of electricity are coursing through his body, the prisoner is almost certainly conscious; nerve activity—which carries the sensation of pain—remains intact. We have convinced ourselves that prisoners don't experience pain in large part because they do not move or speak, which of course would be natural reactions to pain. But prisoners in the throes of electrocution do not move or speak because they are physically paralyzed; they can only sit, frozen and mute, in an enduring painful spasm. In the words of Harold Hillman, a neurobiologist,

> It is usually thought that the failure of the convict to move is a sign that he cannot feel pain. He cannot move because all of his muscles are contracted maximally. A physiological effect that in itself is enormously painful and further prevents the prisoner from crying out or providing other outward signs of other massively painful effects of electrocution such

as third degree burns and an enormous heating up of the bodily fluids throughout the body. . . . While the subject remains conscious, strapped into the chair, paralyzed yet aware of the gruesome burning of his body, it is scientifically and medically certain that death is not instantaneous.[90]

Things are almost certainly worse when electrocutions are botched. Then, electricity must be applied more frequently; sometimes electrocutions take up to fifteen minutes to finally kill the prisoner. Over this century, about one out of every nine or ten electrocutions has been botched. (Public executions were probably botched at a much higher rate, at least judging by anecdotal accounts.) We may expect more botchings in the coming years. Most electric chairs are old. Poor electrode connections, the most common cause of botched electrocutions, will if anything grow more common as electric chairs deteriorate.[91]

It is chilling to think that the very measures we have used to assure ourselves that modern executions are tame and hence painless may in fact be profoundly misleading. As it happens, even modern, proficient hangings—the kind seemingly over in seconds, producing a hangman's fracture and a quietly dangling body—are likely to be painful. We tend to think otherwise, once again, because most of these hanging victims are paralyzed, not unconscious, and strangle to death unable to move or otherwise express pain.[92] Earlier hangings, for example in the Middle Ages or in the American South, produced visibly painful strangulations replete with people struggling for life. In such instances, the pain and indignity were seen as proper features of an execution. A modern hanging, in contrast, *looks* like a good, clean kill by a master craftsman. Syd Dernley, the modern English hangman quoted earlier, maintained that not only were his hangings quick—over in seconds—but painless. "Certainly he suffered no pain," contended Dernley, referring to the typical prisoner hanged in a twentieth-century English prison.[93] Dernley may have been wrong on both counts. The hanged man may have lingered for minutes, not seconds, and suffered considerable pain. Prisoners are not cut down, in the case of hanging, or otherwise removed from the execution apparatus until a "decent interval" has passed. Whatever may be the motivation for this decorous pause in an otherwise brutal execution ritual, one effect is to maintain the appearance that death is quick and painless. By the time we remove the body of the condemned from the execution apparatus, any evidence of life or pain in death has passed from the scene.

Former Supreme Court Justice Brennan, in his eloquent dissent from denial of certiorari in *Glass* v. *Louisiana*,[94] made a compelling case for the violence of electrocution, which he maintained was a clear violation of the Eighth Amendment. In that same dissent, Brennan cited evidence that criminals executed in the gas chamber—by asphyxiation—suffered great pain over a number of minutes; that method, too, Brennan concluded, was a violation of the Eighth Amendment. The gas chamber was meant to be a successor to the electric chair. There was no mutilation of the body; no powerful surge of raw electrical power. Gas was thought to kill quickly and quietly. Few states adopted this method, however. It was expensive—a gas chamber is a fairly elaborate technical undertaking, requiring considerable upkeep. The mechanics of execution by lethal gas are comparatively complex. There is also an element of danger; lethal gas can leak from the chamber, endangering witnesses, or can kill anyone who enters the chamber before it has been properly cleared. The gas chamber may have fallen into disfavor because of the association of lethal gas with the genocidal campaigns of the Nazis in World War II, which occurred shortly after the first American gas chambers were put in place. Perhaps most important, prisoners in the gas chamber appeared to suffocate in a slow and painful way, though again, some experts wrote off these reactions—including head-banging, drooling, gasping for air, and even moaning—as post-mortem responses rather than death agonies. In a 1994 case, *Fierro* v. *Gomez*, the United States District Court for the Northern District of California reviewed evidence on the effects of the gas chamber and supported Justice Brennan's Eighth Amendment claim. The court "concluded that the time it takes for the lethal gas to kill an inmate combined with the degree of pain inflicted on the inmate warrants the use of another method of execution."[95]

Most executions today are carried out by lethal injection, clearly the tamest and most apparently painless method of execution yet devised. Here, too, however, controversy reigns. Some anesthesiologists question whether lethal injection is as painless as it appears, contending that it may, like hangings, produce a paralysis that masks a slow and painful death by suffocation. In *Chaney* v. *Heckler*,[96] the court referred to "known evidence concerning lethal injection which strongly indicates that such drugs pose a substantial threat of torturous pain to persons being executed."[97] The court noted that, when using the mixture of barbiturates and paralytics required by law, "even a small error in dosage or administration can leave a prisoner conscious but paralyzed while dying, a sentient witness of his or her own slow, lingering asphyxiation."[98] Such dosage errors would, therefore, produce botched executions. Other problems emerge as well, falling under the heading of botches or glitches. For example, it is often hard to locate veins in which to insert the needle on offenders with long histories of drug use, a category that includes many, if not most, condemned prisoners today. At other times, there have been malfunctions of medical equipment. Even in a properly administered execution by lethal injection, the prisoner has a long and emotionally painful wait while strapped to the gurney—sometimes upwards of an hour.[99]

Lethal injection, then, offers a paradoxical execution scene. A supine inmate, seemingly at rest, appears to drift off into a sleep that merges imperceptibly with death. This is, in its essentials, the ideal modern death—a death that occurs in one's sleep, painlessly.[100] The reality may well be completely different. The interval on the gurney, reminiscent of rest but actually a case of forced restraint, can certainly be considered a kind of torture of its own; and once the drugs are introduced, what follows may well be a death by slow suffocation—likewise, a kind of torture. All of this unfolds before us as we congratulate ourselves on our humaneness and, more macabre still, as the immobilized offender comes to realize the deception of execution by lethal injection and, unable to struggle, recognizes his inability to communicate his distress to the world. He may endure a final insult to his dignity in the form of an experience of complete and utter helplessness while others smile benignly, as if all is well with a world that kills heinous murderers with such kindness.

Pain is subjective, and it is impossible to know with certainty the experience—or range of experiences—of those who undergo execution. No one can come back from the dead to tell us about executions. Botched executions, where the offender lingers on before death, do not offer opportunities for us to assess the experience. The Francis case, where the chair failed and he lived to be executed another day, is of no help because the chair did not administer electricity of any magnitude, and hence his experience sheds no light on actual executions. Since we cannot know for sure, we must acknowledge that it is *possible* that modern executions are painless or at least comparatively pain-free, as maintained by many advocates of modern execution methods from the electric chair to lethal injection. Certainly, one can envision a lethal injection process in which the anesthetic used, in nature and amount, is such that no consciousness of physical pain is possible—much like an overdose of an anesthetic. This still leaves unexamined the *psychology* of modern executions. Here the crucial point is that, though restrained by historical standards, today's executions, even if largely or even entirely free of physical pain, are *purely destructive* undertakings that can and should be rejected on that ground alone.

MODERN EXECUTIONS AND
THE ORDEAL OF DEHUMANIZATION

Modern executions neither appease God nor involve or affirm the community. Instead, these execution procedures smack of a mechanized, mindless "nihilism." Byron Eschelman, a former chaplain at San Quentin and a participant in many executions, makes this point in a strident yet compelling way:

> Society is expert at cold-blooded, unemotional, businesslike, professional killing. The death penalty is routine, ritualistic, even-tempered, assembly-line annihilation. The state becomes a legal "Murder, Inc.," serving respectable citizens who pay taxes to get the job done.[101]

There is even a kind of "countdown for death" detailing the condemned prisoner's last hours, as though his execution were a mere technical drill.

The official countdown of the final hours of inmate Cain (an unfortunate pseudonym), part of San Quentin's official execution schedule during Eschelman's tenure there, embodies the modern execution procedure. Comparable execution protocols exist for each and every modern execution method, including lethal injection.[102]

No community, not even the impoverished community of the prison, can draw emotional sustenance or larger meaning from the pseudoritual detailed in modern execution protocols, which are as lifeless as the corpses they are

	S	M	T	W	T	F	S
							89
						X	X
	X	X	X	X	X	X	9
	10	11	12	13	14	15	16
	17	18	19	20	21	22	23
	24	25	26	27	28	29	30
	31						

When	Where	Who	What
A.M.			
1:00	Holding Cell Area	Death Watch Officers	Maintain regular entries on the log sheet.
3:00	Holding Cell Area	Watch Lieutenant	Makes routine checks with the death watch officers during their shifts.
4:00	Holding Cell Area	Watch Lieutenant	Telephones count to control center.
6:15	Holding Cell Area	Death Watch Officers	Ask Cain what he wishes for breakfast.
7:00	Employees' Dining Room	Supervising Cook and Correctional Sergeant	Prepare and deliver breakfast for Cain and the death watch officers.
7:15	Holding Cell	Chaplain	Offers religious services and counseling. May remain until after the execution if Cain asks him to, or may return after 9:00.
8:00	Death Cell	Watch Lieutenant	Checks and dispatches log sheet to warden.
8:10	Gas Chamber	Chamber Operator and Chemical Operator	Arrange necessary chemicals and test the chamber.
9:00	Employees' Lounge	Citizen Legal Witnesses	Sign official register.
9:30	Holding Cell Area	Chamber Operator	Unrolls strip of green rug leading from the cell to doorway of gas chamber.
9:40	Administrative Area	Associate Warden Custody	Drives sedan with warden and associate warden administration about 150 yards from Administration Building to entrance of witness area.
9:45	Holding Cell Area	Warden and Associate Wardens	Accept last wishes and messages from Cain.
9:52	Holding Cell	Lieutenant	Unlocks Cain's cell; asks him to remove all of his clothing, including slippers. Cain dresses only in new blue jeans and a white shirt.

When	Where	Who	What
9:55	Holding Cell	Chief Medical Officer and a second doctor	Affix stethoscope on Cain's chest with sterile tape, rubber tube extending through shirt front.
9:55	Employees' Lounge	Correctional Lieutenant	Escorts official witnesses and institutional staff to entrance of gas chamber witness area.
9:58	Witness Area	Associate Warden Administration	Signals for entrance of witnesses. Correctional officer no. 1 stationed to left of chamber; correctional officer no. 2 on right inside iron railing. Medical technical assistant on raised steps available for first aid to witnesses.
10:00:30	Holding Cell	Lt.-in-Charge of Execution, Death Watch officers, and Chamber Operator	Escort Cain from cell to chamber. Strap Cain to Chair B, which is the nearest to the connection for the stethoscope hose.
10:01:30	Observation Area	Correctional Officer	Closes steel door and spins tight the locking wheel.
10:02:30	Observation Area	Warden	Orders executioner to proceed.
		Chamber Operator	Removes safety pin from lever. Depresses mechanical action. Cyanide gas generates in chamber.
10:03	Gas Chamber	Cain	Unconscious.
10:13	Observation Area	Medical Officer	Confirms death of Cain.
10:15	Observation Area	Warden	Passes report of time of death to associate warden administration through porthole in door.
10:17	Observation Area	Chamber Operator	Starts exhaust pumps to clear chamber of gas.
10:21	Observation Area	Associate Warden Administration	Informs official witnesses of time cyanide pellets dropped and time of death.
10:25	Administrative Area	Warden	Returns by car and telephones office of governor.
10:30	Observation Area	Official Witnesses	Sign affidavit as they leave observation area.
10:35	Warden's Office	Warden	Meets press.
P.M.			
1:00	Gas Chamber	Hospital Crew	Remove body from chamber to prison morgue. Fingerprint.
2:00	Hospital	Medical Officer	Completes death certificate.
3:00	Administrative Office	Secretary	Prepares notice to court, transmitting affidavit of death.
4:00	Control Center	Control Sergeant	Subtracts one from institutional count.
4:15	Administrative Office	Records Officer	Assembles case folder for deposit in archives.
4:30	Warden's Office	Warden	By request, sends letter confirming execution of Cain.

meant to produce. Nor can the condemned find support or purpose in these proceedings. Execution procedures in earlier times, however brutal, at least allowed the offender "abundant opportunities to establish for himself a public character" and to die with a "display of courage and dignity."[104] (Even in the case of lynchings, the fortitude of some offenders, such as Sam Holt, noted previously, met with reluctant approval.) One's behavior on the scaffold offered the hope of redemption—of one's (public) character, at least in a limited degree, and of one's (private) soul. This is no longer the case. Brave or cowardly, penitent or unrepentant, the offender's death is immaterial because almost no one sees it and few people these days attach existential or religious meaning to the way in which one approaches one's death. Indeed, the *point* of the modern bureaucratic execution procedure is to *suppress* any real-life human reactions on the part of the prisoners or their executioners. Human reactions—displays of character or faith—would interfere with the efficient administration of the death penalty and indeed draw unwanted attention to the violence of the proceedings.

The impersonality of the modern death penalty makes it distinctively brutal. Admittedly, this is a curious proposition. We explicitly seek humane executions. Whereas in times past we physically assaulted the condemned as a community or selected executioners brutal enough to kill them before our eyes, today we select personnel for execution teams who are, among other things, civil and accommodating to the needs of the prisoners during their last hours. To be sure, we do not pick such men, nowadays referred to as deathwatch or execution team officers, entirely out of the goodness of our hearts. Their interpersonal skills promote a decent sort of social control and facilitate the smooth execution drill that is the hallmark of the modern death penalty.[105] Perhaps the prisoners sense that there is an element of duplicity in this, however well-meaning it may be. Though most of the condemned appreciate the attention of the deathwatch officers, both they and the officers remain emotionally aloof from one another. The result is a civil but impersonal proceeding that gives company but not comfort to the condemned (see Chapters 6 and 7).

Executions today are disturbingly, even chillingly, dispassionate. If you doubt this, listen to Caryl Chessman's fictional rendering of a modern execution. Himself a death row inmate, Chessman vividly depicted the pain of a lonely, anonymous death, a death predicated on one's personal insignificance. Though fictional, even melodramatic, his account is authentic. Chessman knew, as we all know, that death is a profoundly personal experience. He knew as well that today's condemned prisoner suffers the ignominy of an impersonal death inflicted by faceless bureaucrats. This prisoner is reduced to the status of an object and disposed of according to a schedule.

Your waiting is over.
Three of the executioner's assistants come for you. The cell door is unlocked, opened. You're told quietly, impersonally, "It's time."
It's time to die, to be executed.

You stand there for an instant, unmoving. Perhaps you take a last drag on your cigarette, drop the butt, step on it. Three pairs of eyes watch you.

"Go to hell!" you scream defiantly. "I'm not going! Do you bastards hear me? I'm not going!"

They hear you. But you're going nevertheless. They'll take you by force if necessary. They have a job to do.

You can whimper. You can cry out to God to help you, to save your life. But don't expect a miracle. He won't intervene. So ask only for the strength to die like a man.

You can shrug. You didn't think it would come to this, but it did. And here you are, at the end of life's road, about to take that last short walk.

Automatically your legs move. You're walking, mechanically—out through the death watch cell entrance, around the bend in the short hallway, through a doorway. And there it is. The gas chamber. No stopping now. No turning back. You're hustled into this squat, octagonal, glass and metal-sided cell within a room. Its elaborate gadgets don't interest you. Quickly you find yourself seated in the chair. The guards strip you down. Their movements are swift and sure, smoothly rehearsed. The stethoscope is connected.

There! The job is done.

"Good luck," says the guard captain in charge.

Then you're alone. The guards have left. The metal door has closed. The spoked wheel on the outside of that door is being given a final turn.

Everything is in readiness! This is the dreadful, final moment. While the physical preparations were underway, while you moved, it wasn't so real. Activity blocked full realization. It was like watching a gripping scene in a movie, where the camera had been speeded up and the action had carried you along with it, irresistibly. You had only a blurred awareness that it was leading to this. But now that you're physically immobilized, there's a jarring change. The camera slows. You see; you absorb; the scene unfolds with a terrible clarity. For an instant, time is frozen. Your thoughts and sensory impressions are fragmented, each one stabbing at you like a needle.

The warden is at his post. So is the executioner and the attending physician. On the opposite side of the chamber, behind a guard rail less than four feet from where you sit, stand the official witnesses, their eyes riveted on you through the thick glass. In a matter of minutes, you'll be dead. They're here to watch you die.

The executioner is signaled by the warden. With scientific precision, valves are opened. Closed. Sodium cyanide eggs are dropped into the immersion pan—filled with sulphuric acid—beneath your metal chair. Up rise the deadly fumes. The cell is filled with the odor of bitter almond and peach blossoms. It's a sickening-sweet smell.

Only seconds of consciousness remain.

You inhale the deadly fumes. You become giddy. You strain against the straps as the blackness closes in. You exhale, inhale again. Your head aches.

There's a pain in your chest. But the ache, the pain is nothing. You're hardly aware of it. You're slipping into unconsciousness. You're dying. Your head jerks back. Only for an awful instant do you float free. Your brain has been denied oxygen. Your body fights a losing ten-minute battle against death.

You've stopped breathing. Your heart has quit beating.

You're dead.

The minutes pass. The blowers whirr. The ammonia valves are open. The gas is being driven from the cell. The clerical work is being done.

That's your body they're removing; it's your body they take to the prison morgue. No, don't worry about that cyanide rash on your leg.

If you have no one to claim your body and you're not of the Jewish or Catholic faith, you'll be shipped off to be cremated. You'll come back to the prison in a 'jar.' You'll go to Boot Hill.

If your body is claimed, a mortician will come for it. He'll take you away to a funeral parlor, prepare you for burial, impersonally. Services? Well, that's up to your people. Then burial. The end. But not really the end.

An aged mother may be weeping silently. She carried you in her womb. She gave you birth. And your life came to this.

"Mommy," a little girl may ask, "where's Daddy?"

Cruelly, a playmate may tell a small son, "Your old man died in the gas chamber!"

A young wife is dazed, numb.

This is your legacy to them.[106]

Chessman had seen the execution process at work when many of his fellow condemned were taken to their deaths. He coped with the threat of his own execution, according to a psychiatrist who interviewed him on a number of occasions, "by thinking of himself as the attorney in the case rather than as the condemned man." When this stratagem failed, as it did periodically, Chessman would talk with his psychiatrist "about the feelings of torture that he experienced waiting for death. At times, he felt that he could no longer tolerate the pain, the anxiety, and the fear. At such times, he expressed a wish to get the suffering over with."[107] Chessman never dropped his appeals, but his appeals did finally run out. After twelve years on death row, Chessman took his last walk.

As Chessman's fictional account implies, and as I will attempt to prove in Part II and especially Part III of this book, executioner and condemned alike are dehumanized in today's executions. They are morally dead—dead as persons—even as their bodies move to the cadence of this modern dance macabre. Each participates in a peculiarly subtle and insidious form of torture that prepares them for their respective roles in the execution process. This is not justice but rather, in Camus's wise reckoning, administrative murder.[108] To be sure, these arrangements make executions easier and more palatable. Indeed, given our modern sensibilities, there may well be no other way we can execute a person. But at bottom these dehumanizing procedures hide a reality that we must face head on—namely, that the death penalty is utterly out of step with our current standards of decency and has no place in our justice system.

CIVILIZATION AND THE DEATH PENALTY

The reasons for the change in the administration and ultimately in the meaning of the death penalty are rooted in the civilization of punishment.[109] Civilization proceeds unevenly, sometimes undergoing dramatic setbacks (witness the primitive quality of life after the fall of the Roman Empire), but, in general, civilization advances over time. In each subsequent age, people's awareness of and empathy for the humanity of others increases, expanding to include even deviant others. There is, then, a growing distaste and even revulsion for punishments that feature the public infliction of pain and finally a rejection of punishments that involve the infliction of any visible bodily pain at all.[110] Thus our modern, highly civilized sensibilities reject violence, especially public violence, as a means of punishment.

It is reasonable to suppose that when a culture or civilization is at its height, its members' emotional bonds to one another and their awareness of their shared humanity are strong. One salient result is that criminal sanctions are both less harsh and less readily used. This is true relative to the standards of the times, in that people reject as cruel the punishments they have inherited from their ancestors. This is also true objectively. Violence per se becomes, to varying degrees, objectionable, and is reduced as much as possible given the available means of execution. No clearer example can be found than that of classical Greece. Solon reigned during a period of great civilization. Though he inherited Draco's incredibly arbitrary and brutal system of law, in which virtually all crimes were capital offenses, he rejected this "draconian" code and replaced it with one of the more progressive criminal codes of any historical period. The death penalty was rarely administered at all, and incarceration was rarer still.[111] Moreover, when executions did occur in classical Greece, the method used was ingestion of hemlock, a comparatively painless poison that was self-administered by the condemned in a private and supportive milieu. The prototypical execution of the time was that of Socrates, who chose the hour of his death, conversed freely with his disciples until the end, and died in their comforting presence.[112]

Of a piece with the retreat from inflicting physical pain in punishment is the move away from spontaneous, face-to-face forms of bodily punishment. Typically, the violence of executions is muted by ritual, which functions as a sort of psychic buffer, separating the community from the condemned. (Executions in classical Greece are an extreme and perhaps unique case. The execution ritual is self-administered in private, obviating the need for an executioner and obscuring the underlying violence of the process.) Finally, as is true today, capital punishment becomes an isolated, ritualistic, mechanical event unto itself. In this context of remote and rigidly orchestrated bodily punishment, the community is profoundly removed from the proceedings, and even the participants in the process have virtually no human contact at all. It is a paradox of the modern death penalty that, having come to more fully appreciate the humanity of those we punish, we must suppress our awareness of that humanity, indeed suppress the humanity itself, if we are to carry out executions. Hence, we first kill the person, the moral entity, by a process of dehumanization. Then we kill and dispose of the body. This can be a smooth and efficient procedure, but never a just one.

With the civilization of punishment has come a gradual recognition of the finality of death. The death penalty is now seen as a final and irrevocable sanction.[113] The finality of death heightens the awesome and awful reality of the death penalty and, in turn, heightens our need to distance ourselves from the punishment process. However painless and impersonal the penalty of death may one day become, execution is increasingly perceived as an annihilation of the person. This is a uniquely modern perception. In earlier times, people shared the comforting belief that the death penalty, though surely violent, left the truly final matters in God's hands. We did His work, observing recognized ritual forms. He, and often the condemned as well, understood and approved (and, when necessary, forgave). Today we can take but cold comfort in the death penalty, if we take any comfort in it at all. The extreme nature of such a sanction gives us added impetus to distance ourselves from executions, even to the point, as we see today, of using bureaucratic procedures that psychically and morally numb us to the reality of the death penalty.

The evolution of the death penalty might be summarized as follows. Killing criminals, particularly in public, came to be seen as a revolting spectacle as people began to appreciate the humanity of those being killed, and hence to empathize with the humiliation and degradation wrought by their punishment. In response, executions became more tame, with savage communal stonings giving way to increasingly restrained and impersonal execution ceremonies and rituals. Thus, the killing of Hendrina Wouters in early modern Europe, though flagrantly violent by modern standards, was quite civilized compared with earlier executions; and the hanging of Asbury Dixon in twentieth-century America was so civil as to hide the violence of the death penalty. Subsequently, executions were physically hidden from the public by moving them behind the walls of penal institutions until finally, today, executions take place only in remote prison cell blocks, beyond the ken of all but a handful of official observers. Eventually, the violence of execution came to be hidden even from the participants themselves. This was done by bureaucratizing executions, thereby dehumanizing the various participants and muting their moral sensibilities. Of course, executioners know that they kill people, though some of them do not like to be called executioners. They are so caught up in the procedural concerns that mark the modern execution drill, however, that the violence of executions is effectively hidden from their awareness.

In the past, we were in the main less aware of our shared humanity and mortality, and so the enormity of executions escaped us. Violence against others, especially outcasts, was unremarkable. We could execute criminals spontaneously and without remorse. Even planned executions could still be casual or cordial or even festive, in part because the participants did not recognize the awful finality of the proceedings. As we came to sense our shared humanity and mortality, and thus to recognize the violence of the death penalty, executions became morally and psychologically problematic events. Public execution rituals became less accepted and were gradually replaced by private procedures. Executions today carry this evolution to its logical conclusion: We have replaced meaningful ritual with mechanical ritualism. The result is a bureaucratic execution procedure that abrogates our humanity under the guise of justice.

NOTES

1. L. P. Masur, *Rites of Execution: Capital Punishment and the Transformation of American Culture, 1776–1865* (New York: Oxford University Press, 1989), 26.

2. Ibid., 39.

3. Some members of the nobility were executed in England and France in the medieval and early modern periods, but not many. A few rich men and women were put to death, but again this was rare and unusual. "[A]part from the execution of a few wealthy forgers or murderers, most of the hanged were poor and marginalized people—'the very lowest and worst of the people . . . the scum both of the city and the country,' as Elizabeth Fry amiably described her Newgate charges in 1818." V. A. C. Gatrell, *The Hanging Tree: Execution and the English People 1770–1868* (Oxford: Oxford University Press, 1994), 8.

4. Masur (n. 1), 39.

5. N. Davies, *Human Sacrifice: In History and Today* (New York: Morrow, 1981), 52.

6. M. Fearnow, "Theatre for an Angry God: Public Burnings and Hangings in Colonial New York, 1741," *The Drama Review* 40 (2): 25 (1996). See, generally, R. Girard, *The Scapegoat* (Baltimore: John Hopkins University Press, 1986) and M. Douglas, *Purity and Danger: An Analysis of Concepts of Pollution and Taboo* (Harmondworth, Penguin, 1970).

7. Fearnow (n. 6), 27–28.

8. Masur (n. 1), 39.

9. Ibid., 40, 45.

10. Ibid., 5.

11. P. Spierenburg, *The Spectacle of Suffering: Executions and the Evolution of Repression: From a Preindustrial Metropolis to the European Experience* (Cambridge: Cambridge University Press, 1984), 185.

12. Ibid., 204.

13. Ibid., 204.

14. Gatrell argues that the crowds at public executions, right up to the end, had a fair representation of social elites. See Gatrell (n. 3), Part I. I view the evidence for this assertion as scanty. No such claims have been made about the crowds at public executions in America. It is of course possible that elites became both less willing to attend and less willing to admit attendance at executions.

15. Masur (n. 1), 96.

16. D. W. Denno, "Is Electrocution an Unconstitutional Method of Execution? The Engineering of Death over the Century," *William and Mary Law Review* 35 (2): 564 (1994).

17. Ibid., 564.

18. This point is made by Gatrell (n. 3).

19. The seminal work on the significance of crowds at public executions has been done by Gatrell, who observes that "the deepest anxiety of the modernizing state was that the unleashed passions of the scaffold crowd mirrored the state's violence too candidly. The crowd had come to seem like a repudiated *alter ego* or shadow-self which spoke too truthfully for a progressive nation to tolerate. The crowd gave the lie to the great world's representation of itself as civil, benign, and humane." Gatrell (n. 3), 23–24.

20. Masur (n. 1), 94.

21. Masur (n. 1) discusses this subject insightfully under the heading, "Gallows Literature."

22. Ibid., 22.

23. Gatrell (n. 3), 24.

24. Ibid., 24.

25. Ibid., 24.

26. An insightful discussion of executions legal and illegal in the South as a product of "a cultural tradition of exclusion" of blacks from the human community can be found in J. W. Marquart, S. Ekland-Olson, and J. R. Sorensen, *The Rope, the Chair, and the Needle: Capital Punishment in Texas, 1923–1990* (Austin: University of Texas Press, 1993).

27. K. M. Stampp, *The Peculiar Institution: Slavery in the Ante-Bellum South* (New York: Vintage Books, 1956), 8.

28. D. M. Oshinsky, *Worse Than Slavery: Parchman Farm and the Ordeal of Jim Crow Justice* (New York: Free Press, 1996), 19.

29. Ibid., 32.

30. See, generally, Oshinsky (n. 28).

31. S. E. Tolnay and E. M. Beck, *A Festival of Violence: An Analysis of Southern Lynchings, 1882–1930* (Urbana: University of Illinois Press, 1995), 90.

32. Quoted in Marquart, Ekland-Olson, and Sorensen (n. 26), 7.

33. See Oshinsky (n. 28).

34. There were lynchings in the South prior to the freeing of the slaves, but they were relatively few in number; the targets were mostly poor whites who were in some sense marginal to the community. See F. Butterfield, *All God's Children: The Bosket Family and the American Tradition of Violence* (New York: Knopf, 1995).

35. T. Sellin, *Slavery and the Penal System* (New York: Elsevier, 1976).

36. W. L. Garrison, preface to *Narrative of the Life of Frederick Douglass: An American Slave, Written by Himself* by F. Douglass (New York: Penguin, 1968), 2.

37. Tolnay and Beck (n. 31), 5.

38. Ibid., 57.

39. Fox Butterfield observes that "The word 'lynching' probably took its name from Captain William Lynch, a backcountry settler of Scotch-Irish descent who lived first in Virginia and later in South Carolina. In the 1760s, he and his neighbors developed the custom of handing out swift and violent justice to 'lawless men' by flogging or killing them. Due process and evidence were not always necessary." Butterfield (n. 34), 55–56.

40. Tolnay and Beck (n. 31), 18.

41. This migration pattern and its consequences for many types of violence is discussed in Butterfield (n. 34).

42. Tolnay and Beck (n. 31), 25.

43. Legal punishments in the South sometimes took on a medieval character as well. As recently as 1856, a Maryland law was enacted that "provided that a Negro convicted of murder should have his right arm cut off, his head severed, his body divided into four parts and . . . the head and quarters . . . set up in the most public place near where the crime was committed." R. Ginzburg, *100 Years of Lynching* (Baltimore: Black Classic Press, 1988), 224.

44. See Fearnow (n. 6), 30.

45. Tolnay and Beck (n. 31), 23.

46. See, for example, Oshinsky (n. 28), 101–102.

47. Fearnow (n. 6), 31.

48. See, for example, Ginzburg (n. 43), 166, who reports a 1922 Texas lynching as follows: "A posse was unable today to track down a negro who allegedly attacked the wife of the local Sheriff. The posse tracked down the uncle of a negro who is suspected of the crime and lynched him instead." Oshinsky makes this point as well. "'You don't understand how we feel down here,' a white Mississippian told a visitor in 1908. 'When there is a row, we feel like killing a nigger whether he has done anything or not.' Whites liked to believe that their mobs were punishing real crimes by dangerous Negroes. If they happened to lynch the wrong person—well, that too served a purpose by reminding other 'niggers' of their place." See Oshinsky (n. 28), 100.

49. See, generally, Oshinsky (n. 28).

50. Tolnay and Beck (n. 31), 76. Racial discrimination in the use of the death penalty has been most pronounced and most enduring in the case of rape. See Marquart, Ekland-Olson, and Sorensen (n. 26), 56–58, who note that "When males from an African-American background raped an Anglo female, the case was approximately thirty-five times more likely to result in capital punishment than a prison sentence" whereas few white men were executed for rape in the South. More striking, "In only one case did the rape of a black female result in a death sentence and actual execution."

51. R. M. Brown, *Strain of Violence: Historical Studies of American Violence and Vigilantism* (New York: Oxford University Press, 1975).

52. J. G. Miller, *Search and Destroy: African-American Males in the Criminal Justice System* (Cambridge: Cambridge University Press, 1996), 53.

53. Oshinsky (n. 28), 101.

54. A. Rampersad and D. Roessel, eds., *The Collected Poems of Langston Hughes* (New York: Knopf, 1994), 214.

55. Ibid., 252.

56. See Campbell v. Wood 18 F. 3d 662, 695 (9th Cir. 1994), 701.

57. See J. Cameron, *A Time of Terror: A Survivor's Story* (Baltimore: Black Classic Press, 1982), 72.

58. Miller (n. 52), 52.

59. Tolnay and Beck (n. 31), 171–172.

60. Ibid., 172.

61. Ibid., ix.

62. A. Raper, *The Tragedy of Lynching* (Chapel Hill: University of North Carolina Press, 1933). See also H. Shapiro, *White Violence and Black Response: From Reconstruction to Montgomery* (Amherst: University of Massachusetts Press, 1988). The research of Marquart et al. in Texas reveals that "the line between legal and illegal hangings was often razor-thin."

Marquart, Ekland-Olson, and Sorensen (n. 26), 2.

63. Tolnay and Beck (n. 31), 100.

64. Ibid., 100.

65. There was also a racist orgy of imprisonment of freemen following the Civil War—the Southern prison system, initially based on contract labor, later on plantation prisons, was virtually created to replace slaves with prisoners whose punishment, marked by an incredibly high death rate, was in many respects "worse than slavery." See Oshinsky (n. 28).

66. See Denno (n. 16), 679. All execution methods produce macabre death scenes, but the spectacle of the dangling corpse is considered among the most degrading of all. For a general discussion of execution methods and the indignities they inflict, see F. Drimmer, *Until You Are Dead: The Book of Executions in America* (Secaucus, N.J.: Carol Pub. Group, 1990).

67. P. Aries, *The Hour of Our Death* (New York: Vintage, 1982), 28.

68. A. Mencken, *By the Neck: A Book of Hangings* (New York: Hastings House, 1942), 34.

69. Marquart, Ekland-Olson, and Sorensen (n. 26), 13.

70. Oshinsky (n. 28), 206.

71. Ibid., pictures positioned on unnumbered pages between numbered text pages 146 and 147.

72. Ibid., 207.

73. A. S. Miller and J. H. Bowman, *Death by Installments: The Ordeal of Willie Francis* (New York: Greenwood Press, 1988).

74. Ibid., 10, 8, 8.

75. The spread of electricity to different parts of the country provides a measure of modernization. By 1930, and certainly by no later than 1940, the entire country was "electrified." See T. P. Hughes, *Networks of Power: Electrification in Western Society, 1880–1930* (Baltimore: Johns Hopkins University Press, 1983). Note that the lynching era ended around 1930, after the nation was more or less fully wired for electric power and when electrocution was the execution method of choice in most states.

76. R. G. Murdy, "Brief History of Capital Punishment in Maryland," *Report of the Committee on Capital Punishment to the Legislative Council of Maryland* (1962), Sec. 1, 1–4.

77. Royal Commission on Capital Punishment, 1949–1953. Report presented to Parliament by Command of Her Majesty (September 1953), 253.

78. R. G. Elliot, *Agent of Death: The Memoirs of an Executioner* (New York: Dutton, 1940).

79. Much of the evidence on this score is anecdotal. I know I was warned by the warden of the prison I studied that I might experience some shock when I served as an official witness at an execution in his prison. (I did.) A recent study of media observers of executions would appear to bear out the folklore on this subject. See A. Freinkel, C. Koopman, and D. Spiegel, "Dissociative Symptoms in Media Eyewitnesses of an Execution," *American Journal of Psychiatry* 151 (9): 1335–1339 (1994). The authors of this study report that "journalists who witnessed an execution experienced a high prevalence of dissociative symptoms . . . similar to that of people who endured a natural disaster." (1338). The professional role of media observers and even of researchers like myself should serve to buffer stress. Witnesses in attendance for purely personal reasons may therefore experience more stress, or stress of longer duration, than that described in the research.

80. Royal Commission on Capital Punishment (n. 77).

81. M. Trevelyan, "Dead Men Tell No Tales, but the Hangman Does," *Dallas Morning News*, 25 November 1989.

82. M. Lesey, *The Forbidden Zone* (New York: Farrar, Straus & Giroux, 1987), 135–136.

83. I am indebted to my colleague, James Lynch, for the interesting image of encasement offered by bureaucratic procedures.

84. See J. A. Paredes, and E. D. Purdum, " 'Bye-bye Ted . . . ' Community Response in Florida to the Execution of Theodore Bundy," *Anthropology Today* 8 (2): 8–11 (1990). These authors see parallels between today's execution and human sacrifice. My view is that those parallels only applied when executions were public.

85. H. Prejean, *Dead Man Walking: An Eyewitness Account of the Death Penalty in the United States* (New York: Random House, 1993), 105.

86. I. Solotaroff, "The Last Face You'll Ever See," *Esquire* 124 (2): 92 (1995).

87. M. Weber, *The Theory of Social and Economic Organization* (New York: Oxford University Press, 1947), 340.

88. See H. E. Barnes, *The Story of Punishment: A Record of Man's Inhumanity to Man* (Montclair, N.J.: Patterson Smith, 1972), 243.

89. Denno (n. 16), 557.

90. Ibid., 640.

91. Ibid.

92. Ibid., 686.

93. Trevelyan (n. 81), 4C.

94. Glass v. Louisiana 471 U.S. 1080 (1985).

95. See "Selected Recent Court Decisions," *American Journal of Law and Medicine*, Vol. XX (3): 334 (1994).

96. Chaney v. Heckler, 718 F. 2d 1174 (1983).

97. Ibid., 1177.

98. Ibid., 1191.

99. S. Trombley, *The Execution Protocol: Inside America's Capital Punishment Industry* (New York: Anchor Books, 1992), 14.

100. See Aries (n. 67). The meaning of death in the modern era and its significance for the justice of the death penalty are discussed at some length in Chapter 9.

101. Quoted in S. Levine, ed., *Death Row: An Affirmation of Life* (New York: Ballantine, 1972), 167.

102. See, for example, Trombley (n. 99), 104–116. Other protocols are on file with the National Institute of Corrections.

103. A. L. Smith and R. M. Carter, "Count Down for Death," *Crime and Delinquency* 15 (1): 77–92 (1969).

104. These observations were made by Lofland following a comparison of contemporary American execution procedures with those used in England in the eighteenth and nineteenth centuries. See H. Bleackley and J. Lofland, *State Executions Viewed Historically and Sociologically* (Montclair, N.J.: Patterson Smith, 1977), 308, 321.

105. G. R. Scott, *History of Capital Punishment* (London: Torchstream Books, 1950).

106. C. Chessman, "Trial by Ordeal," in *Death Row: An Affirmation of Life*, ed. S. Levine (New York: Ballantine, 1972), 15–17.

107. I. Ziferstein, "Crime and Punishment," *Center Magazine* 1 (2): 84 (1968).

108. A. Camus, "Reflections on the Guillotine," in *Resistance, Rebellion, and Death* (New York: Knopf, 1969).

109. Elsewhere I have discussed the civilization of punishment at some length. See R. Johnson, *Hard Time: Understanding and Reforming the Prison* (Belmont: Wadsworth, 1996), 78–90. For an unusually thoughtful discussion of this subject from a philosophical

perspective, see J. H. Reiman, "Justice, Civilization, and the Death Penalty," *Philosophy and Public Affairs* 14 (2): 115–148 (1985).

110. Psychological pain, too, becomes less tolerable as a form of punishment. Where once we aimed to inspire terror among those sentenced to confinement, now incarceration most powerfully evokes shame. Often, we will accept mere contrition or simple submissiveness from a prisoner as evidence that he is being adequately punished. See Johnson (n. 109).

111. Note that in late republican and Augustan Rome—that is, Rome at the height of its civilization, corresponding to classical Greece—"voluntary self-banishment," or exsilium, "became a legal institution, when magistrates were strictly ordered to allow the condemned person time to escape before executing the capital sentence." See *The Oxford Classical Dictionary*, 2nd ed. (Oxford: Clarendon Press, 1970), 426.

112. By the standards of the time, and perhaps even by contemporary standards, execution by hemlock was humane. See I. Barkan, "Capital Punishment in Ancient Greece" (Chicago, 1936), and J. Gorecki, *Capital Punishment: Criminal Law and Social Evolution* (New York: Columbia University Press, 1983). Hemlock kills by a process of refrigeration that proceeds

from the lower extremities upward. . . . The head is taken with dizziness, the mind becomes obscured, the sight is warped, the eyes roll haggardly, the knees weaken, the throat is pinched, and the extremities become numb. Death comes as a swoon when the circulation and respiration are abated. (Barkan, 75–76).

Executions were private. "Only the prosecutor . . . had the right to witness close at hand the punishment of the victim," to spare him the "insults of enmity" (81). Like Socrates, persons condemned to die would have the supportive companionship of others, whether colleagues, friends or family, during their last moments (75–76).

113. See, for example, Camus (n. 108).

PART II

Waiting to Die

A Study of Modern Death Rows

Death Row is a unique environment. Its monotony and repetitious predictability create to varying degrees a ritualistic sensory deprivation environment: the constant beige flat hard steel, the endless rows of rivet heads protruding like the tiny helmets of buried soldiers in a battlefield cemetery, the constancy of iron bars, the grey concrete. Rather than being bombarded as in any other contemporary twentieth century American environment, the eye wanders seeking stimuli, escape. Death Row creates a withdrawal of the senses, an inward turning, a necessity to self-stimulate, to remain centered, to keep from slipping off into bizarre fantasies of persecution and dull-eyed madness, to keep the mind intact.

STEPHEN LEVINE
DEATH ROW

The reality of this waiting place for death is difficult to grasp. It's not a ward in a hospital where sick people wait to die. People here wait to be taken out of their cells and killed. This is the United States of America and these are government officials in charge and there's a law sanctioning and upholding what is going on here, so it all must be legitimate and just, or so one compartment of my brain tells me, the part that studied civics in high school, the part that wants to trust that my country would never violate the human rights of its citizens.

The red block letters say "Death Row."

My stomach can read the letters better than my brain.

SISTER HELEN PREJEAN
DEAD MAN WALKING

The place was a dungeon, full of men who were as good as dead.

MICHAEL LESY
THE FORBIDDEN ZONE

I fear that death row means a gradual killing of my humanity,
which is more painful than any execution can ever be.

DEATH ROW PRISONER

3

Death Row

Conditions of Confinement

oday's condemned prisoners spend years, often a decade or more, on death row. They live in a segregated area of the prison, often in close proximity to the instrument of their death. During the deathwatch, when a prisoner is only hours from execution, he is guarded by men who are also his executioners. Allowed only the barest existence, particularly during those final hours, condemned prisoners are warehoused for death. It is, after all, only the body of the condemned that must be delivered to the executioner, and though prisoners who have been certified insane cannot be executed, their state of mind short of that extreme condition is irrelevant. The essence of death row confinement was captured by a condemned prisoner who observed, "A maggot eats and defecates. That's all we do: eat and defecate. Nothing else. They don't allow us to do nothing else." Such an existence, he maintained, amounts to a "living death."[1]

Condemned prisoners are permitted to do more than simply eat and defecate in solitary confinement, but the powerful perception persists among the condemned that they cannot do much more than that. The psychological impact of death row confinement is such that most condemned prisoners gradually waste away as human beings. By the time they reach the deathwatch, the condemned lead lives not much richer than that of a maggot. In short, though a bit exaggerated, our prisoner's description is basically correct. Death row is indeed a living death, a place where the body is preserved while the person languishes and ultimately dies awaiting execution.

This is no new discovery. Albert Camus knew it some thirty years ago and concluded from it that capital punishment amounted to death with torture.

> As a general rule, a man is undone by waiting for capital punishment well before he dies. Two deaths are inflicted on him, the first being worse than the second, whereas he killed but once. Compared to such torture, the penalty of retaliation seems like a civilized law. It never claimed that a man who gouged out one of his brother's eyes should be totally blinded.[2]

Once we have examined more fully the psychology of capital punishment— the waiting, killing, and dying, as seen by both prisoner and staff—I shall attempt to confirm and extend Camus's assertion about the torturous nature of life under sentence of death, then examine the implications of this position for the justice of the death penalty.

To address these issues more fully than was possible through existing research, I interviewed, for the first edition of this book, death row inmates, death row officers, execution team officers, and others (for example, the prison warden) involved in executions. I also observed two executions; one as an official witness, the other as a behind-the-scenes observer of the execution team. Over the intervening years since the first edition of the book was published, I reinterviewed a number of participants in the original study as well as some additional staff associated with the execution process. I served yet again as a firsthand observer at an execution, studying the execution team in action. The setting for my research was a southern state (which remains unnamed to protect the identities of the staff, especially those serving on the execution team). The state provides a reasonably representative view of the death penalty in the United States today. It has a sizeable population of condemned prisoners (about fifty) exposed to a normal contingent of officers who maintain a level of security that is typical of contemporary death rows. In addition, the state conducts executions regularly. As is the case in most other states with an active death penalty, executions are carried out by a trained team of correctional officers.

What I found in my research confirms that the cumulative confinement experience of condemned prisoners—from death row to the deathwatch and, finally, to the death chamber—is profoundly dehumanizing, resulting in nothing less than the literal moral death of the person, who is reduced to a compliant object of execution. Accordingly, we begin our examination of the psychology of capital punishment where the killing and dying begin: on death row.

DEATH ROW CONFINEMENT IN
HISTORICAL PERSPECTIVE

Separate confinement for the condemned, away from the masses of criminals awaiting lesser punishments, is a relatively recent practice, probably beginning with the early modern period, when prisons, then known as "bridewells" (after a London jail), became more common. During that period, some condemned prisoners appear to have been treated fairly decently for the short interval between sentencing and execution. In early modern Nuremberg, for example, prisoners were held in a condemned cell for three days, during which they were "allowed a liberal table, provided by charitable people, and visitors had free access to [them]."[3] Wealthy or notorious English offenders of this period might throw themselves a farewell party on death row. The Monster's Ball, detailed in Chapter 1, is a case in point. Though I know of no account of the state of mind of Nuremberg prisoners or even of Renwick Williams (the Monster), it would not be at all surprising to learn they tried to drink themselves into an enduring stupor. We know that for many condemned Englishmen, the final procession—with its notorious pub stops, noted in Chapter 1—was undertaken in a state of inebriation, with the typical offender "actually drunk out of his mind" by the time he reached the scaffold.[4] Perhaps it is to be expected that "Those with money could spend their last days in Newgate in dissipation" as well.[5] We see that Williams was not alone, though he was in the minority in Newgate, which catered primarily to the poor. For him and others in his situation, dissipation often would be the greater part of valor, in the condemned cells and later on the scaffold.

For most offenders in early modern England, at least, confinement would be a brutal and degrading experience. The prisons of this day were squalid human warehouses. Condemned prisoners would be held in confinement for weeks and even months, left to await—and contemplate—a terrifying public death. Many were veritably consumed with fear. "In the long weeks or months between arrest, incarceration, trial, and execution, most of these people had no chance of sustaining the equilibrium which would equip them for the brave death of legend. Every circumstance from the conditions of their imprisonment to the blood-curdling exhortations of the clergyman was calculated to break their spirit."[6] As a result, "Most wretches had already betrayed their terror in the dark silence of the condemned cell," long before they reached the scaffold.[7]

For much of the eighteenth century, prisoners sentenced to death in London were confined in the "Condemned Hold" located in the gloomy cellars of Newgate Prison, a setting with the ambiance, if not indeed the institutional lineage, of a medieval dungeon. The penal regime at this time allowed regular prisoners easy congress with outsiders, including wives and lovers, children and pets, prostitutes and drink merchants. There was even "a gymnasium of sorts" and a "Free and Easy Club" to organize social life.[8] All this required money. The poor could—and sometimes did—rot in their own juices. The worst conditions were reserved for the condemned, who were kept in strict isolation. The relevant statute instructed that the

> jailor or keeper to whom such criminal shall be delivered for safe custody shall confine such prisoner to some cell separate and apart from the other prisoners, and that no person or persons whatsoever, except the jailor or keeper, or his servants, shall have access to any such prisoners, without license being first obtained.[9]

One is left with the impression that, in this area of Newgate as throughout the prison, the rich could obtain special privileges. For them, "licensed" visitors and perhaps amenities as well would almost certainly be available, even though they were technically held in solitary confinement. A regime of solitary confinement for impoverished condemned prisoners, at least, appears to have been authorized in English law for roughly a century, then repealed because of its severity.

By the nineteenth century, solitary confinement of the condemned was no longer permitted, but the general confinement regime appears to have become much more restrictive. Conditions remained nothing less than awful for the typical prisoner. Gatrell uses as a case in point the conditions of confinement and general confinement experience of Joseph Harwood in Newgate in 1824, which his research reveals are typical of the time period. Harwood "was crammed with two or three others into a Newgate cell measuring eight feet by six." The condemned cell was barely furnished and dimly lit (by candle). Ventilation was provided by "a hole in the prison's three-feet-thick front wall, crossed by two frames of close iron bars." One can only imagine the smells in these cells, as men had to relieve themselves in chamber pots—and indeed did so in English prisons well into this century. An observer on the scene described the Newgate cells that held Harwood as "beastly." In these cramped, close quarters, Harwood and his fellow condemned were "half-devoured by vermin of the most loathsome description." For the typical condemned prisoner like Harwood, there was no "liberal table" and certainly no ball or banquet. "The food was bread, water, and gruel." The prisons of this day, unlike the closed and isolated penitentiaries that followed them, allowed some movement outside the cell and even some contact with the outside world, though much less than had been available a century earlier. "By day Harwood had access to two communal rooms and the prison's press-yard, a gloomy space flanked by bland stone walls topped with spikes. . . . A gate of iron bars permitted prisoners to communicate with friends across a short passage terminated by another barred gate, watched by turnkeys." It was not clear whether Harwood had friends with whom to communicate, or how common such communication was among the condemned.[10]

What is clear is that signs of stress and breakdown were evident in the condemned cells. Suicide attempts were common; condemned prisoners deteriorated rapidly and visibly. Firsthand accounts tell us that the "demeanors" of the condemned "change as the weeks dragged on, as they crept into the condemned pew in the prison chapel, 'stupefied' and 'looking around them vacantly as if unconscious of their state.'"[11] Hair would turn gray, skin would wrinkle, weight would fall off. The focus on daily chapel as a context in which to assess deterioration is no accident. Visits to the chapel were a source of enormous stress. "The pew for the condemned was a black-painted box below the pulpit. A coffin rested meaningfully on the table in its centre."[12] Prisoners were arrayed by category; a place was set aside for teachers and children, who might learn valuable moral lessons about life and death even before the arrival of execution day. "With women prisoners screened by curtains in one gallery, those due for transportation in another, the non-capital convicts beneath them, and the schoolmaster and children in pews by themselves, this artfully arranged assemblage would be required daily to pray 'for those now awaiting the awful execution of the law.' "[13] The chapel was a setting of palpable fear— "the fear of God and damnation," giving vent in groans, fainting, faces of "ashy paleness" and "short, sharp, screams" of barely contained hysterics.[14] The effect, if not indeed the aim of daily chapel and indeed the entire condemned regime, was "to break the spirits of capital convicts so that they may make no physical resistance to the hangman."[15] And break they would. Duly terrified and morbidly repentant, they would play their roles in the public execution script or at least fail to resist the authorities, who would if necessary carry them—literally—through the proceedings.

All the while prisoners suffered under sentence of death, officials would openly go about the business of preparing for the execution. "Gallows were noisily tested, graves openly dug, the condemned assessed face-to-face for the drop appropriate to his weight, build, and neck defects, and his coffin brought casually into view."[16] Executions were public and well-attended (see Part I). No effort was made to hide their grisly violence. Everybody—no one more than the condemned—knew full well that the scaffold was a "site of physical pain" and that no ceremony could change the fact that "hanging was never meant to be a dignified or peaceful quietus."[17]

The regime of psychological and spiritual terror so evident in the daily chapel routine at early modern Newgate is a thing of the past, but vestiges of other death row practices from this time were in evidence at the turn of the twentieth century in American prisons. Conditions of confinement on death row remained spartan, for example, though uniformly so, with no exceptions for the rich. The occasional ball or party of the early modern era had been transformed into a somber and certainly sober last meal available to one and all. Though last meals in American prisons could be fairly elaborate repasts (most were not), the means or status of the prisoner did not determine what he ate or did on his last night. Within the sharp limits of death row confinement, American prison officials leave "nothing undone to make the short lives of their condemned as comfortable as possible"[18]—much like those who, centuries earlier in Nuremberg, offered a "liberal table" to the condemned on their final days. (There appears to have been no special care for the condemned in early modern England's Newgate, other than services which the rich could acquire for themselves.) Music was permitted in many American death houses well into the twentieth century; however, no festivities—music with dancing, for instance—were allowed, as they occasionally were in early modern Newgate. But the *feelings* music would evoke were not yet taboo in American prisons as they are today, in large measure because the process of bureaucratization was not yet complete.

One corollary of the relative informality of the death penalty at the turn of the twentieth century in America was a preoccupation in prisons, as well as in the newspapers and movies of the day, with what amount to "brave deaths of legend" played out in the death house and perhaps drawing historical inspiration from notable public deaths in times past. At the heart of these legends were people who remained visibly unique individuals even as they faced execution. As late as the 1930s at Sing Sing, we see pockets of prebureaucratic informality in the execution process that allowed for notable expressions of individuality on last walks and even while the condemned were seated in the electric chair.[19] "Condemned men have been known to make peculiar requests," notes Sing Sing's Warden Lawes, who granted more than a few in his time. "There was the fellow who insisted on wearing a white shirt; another wanted a tie."[20] Surely this is reminiscent of earlier executions, where one's outfit was the subject of considerable care and pride.[21] Another prisoner, sporting a nonchalance not at all unlike some of his flamboyant counterparts in the medieval and early modern periods, "tried to walk to the Chair on his hands with his feet in the air."[22] A certain "flair for showmanship" apparent in the hand-walking convict was seen in others among Sing Sing's condemned as well. One such character in this modern catalogue of the brave condemned was a "hymn-signing negro who almost ran to the Chair, kissed it reverently and sang a sermon on how, to him, it was a chariot swinging low to life everlasting and a harp among the angel choirs."[23] One prisoner, following a despised fellow gang member to the chair, "asked for a rag, carefully wiped off the Chair and said: 'I've got to rub it off after that rat sat in it.'"[24] This sort of death was memorialized in gangster movies.

Perhaps the most revealing case, itself seemingly drawn from a Jimmy Cagney gangster movie, was the young man who "paid little or no attention to the priest, strode rapidly to the Chair, with a swaggering gait, and seated himself, all the while puffing furiously at a large cigar between his lips." Puffing on a cigar, mind you, even as he is being strapped into the electric chair! Ever defiant, "he gazed sneeringly at the witnesses while the attendants fumbled with the straps." Note that he is calm and collected, almost in control of the proceedings, much like a nobleman who behaves with panache on the scaffold. No priest for him; no contrition or remorse. It is the lowly, common, custodial attendants who are nervous and weak; the meek, passive, cowardly witnesses who earn his wrath. "Suddenly his eyes blazed. With a quick movement he threw the lighted cigar toward the nervous group. It struck one of them between the eyes. 'You're a bunch of ———,' he yelled, and died with a curse on his lips."[25] One can only imagine what he called the hapless witnesses or how they reacted. That this prisoner had the presence of self to behave as he did, as well as the opportunity to do so afforded him in the execution routine, speaks volumes about the lingering capacity for individuality on the threshold of execution, even at this late date. The condemned man was somehow above it all; everyone else was a captive of an emergent but not fully mature bureaucratic process. It was Warden Lawes's explicit goal at this time "to let routine rule" in the execution process.[26] He admitted failure in this regard. It would be some time before routine came to fully dominate the execution process, and when it did, brave deaths of legend became a thing of the past.[27]

Executions in America at the turn of the twentieth century were generally private. Though these death were effectively hidden from the public, who could only read about them or view recreations of these events in movies, there was still an openness among the participants about the killing and dying at the heart of the death penalty. On Sing Sing's death row at the turn of the century, for example, the condemned were quite directly exposed to executions and their aftermath.

> The execution chamber was immediately adjoining [the condemned prisoners' cells], and the little green door which led to it and death was in plain view of the condemned prisoners awaiting execution. The last short walk took the prisoner past the cells of some of these awaiting execution, and all could hear the hum of the deadly motor and even the noise made by the drills and saws used in the autopsy immediately after the execution.[28]

Tame by historical standards—Hendrina Wouters withstood much worse, as we saw in Chapter 1—these executions were nevertheless out of step with modern sensibilities. Indeed, they "tended to drive even the strongest mind insane and resulted in desperate efforts being made to effect an escape."[29]

In 1922 a new death row was built in Sing Sing, known formally as the Condemned Cells. A distinctive feature of this death row was that it afforded the prisoners some insulation from the sights and sounds of death. Still, the Sing Sing prisoners called their new home "the slaughterhouse." (They called the death house area "the dance hall," which is either an oblique reference to execution-eve festivities of centuries past or, more likely, a reference to "dancing" on the end of a rope when hanging was the method of execution in use in New York. The adjoining morgue was the "ice box," which requires no explanation.)[30] They lived on death row in solitary confinement under oppressive custody. There were to be no farewell parties in the slaughterhouse.

Sing Sing's death row was a remarkably secure custodial environment. The prisoners spent all but fifteen minutes of each day locked in their cells. "While locked in the cell, no condemned prisoner [could] see another," though conversation was possible. Prisoners were "dressed in," meaning that, on arrival, they were assigned "clothing . . . of such quality that it [could not] easily be used to make a rope to be used in an attempt at suicide by hanging."[31] Only one prisoner succeeded in taking his life in Sing Sing's Condemned Cells.[32]

A concerted effort was made to prevent makeshift weapons from falling into the prisoners' hands. In their cells, prisoners wore felt slippers instead of shoes; during their brief periods of recreation, they wore special shoes with soft insteps, which made them less formidable weapons. Eating without knives and forks, instead using comparatively harmless spoons, prisoners were also denied the use of pepper, which could be used to temporarily blind an officer. The prisoners were shaved and even manicured by the officers. Cells contained "no movable object" but the prisoner, who moved only rarely and not far. "In fact," stated Warden Lawes, "the condemned prisoner [was] in the same position as a rat caught in a wire-caged trap."[33]

Sing Sing was not in any way unusual. (Life on San Quentin's death row, for example, followed a virtually identical pattern.[34]) The psychology of life in this and other wire-caged traps reflected the desperate situation of the prisoners. The condemned were chronically tense and deeply despondent. Facing reasonably swift and certain execution—the wait then was at most a matter of months—these prisoners were evidently a dangerous and unstable lot, requiring close confinement to hold them safely. In the words of one prisoner,

> The men in death row have nothing to lose except the hope of a commutation. In the mood of despair that gripped us all, tempers were short, nerves frayed. It was enough to put one prisoner within striking distance of another for murder to be done. It was enough to leave a prisoner alone for seconds, if he meant to take his own life. Neither of these possible occurrences was acceptable to the authorities, if only because they implied that a prisoner still held within himself certain liberties they couldn't touch. If you could kill yourself, or the man in the next cell, it meant that you didn't belong to them entirely. And from the moment the gates shut behind you, everything was calculated to give you the opposite impression: that you were their property.[35]

That such a regime actively reduces the person to so much state property, to be dispatched in the execution chamber, is a central theme of this book. This outcome—the compliant condemned—has been sought in different eras in different ways, presumably with varying degrees of success. In early modern Newgate, we see something approaching psychological terrorism, with many offenders consumed by raw fear bordering on horror in the condemned cells. In modern Sing Sing and later American death rows, we see a regime of isolation and regimentation as the context and source of a demoralization that is, it would seem, increasingly widespread as the century unfolds and the bureaucratic process takes hold. Variants on a theme of dehumanization would seem to characterize confinement under sentence of death, whatever may be the particulars of the penal regime or the execution process.

CURRENT CONDITIONS ON DEATH ROW

Conditions on most death rows have changed little since the officials of Sing Sing built their new and improved wire-caged trap. Perhaps this is to be expected. Death rows are located in prisons; prisons have been and remain today painful, depriving environments. Indeed, "one of the striking things about prisons is that we make no bones about the fact that we intend them to be uncomfortable."[36] Death row is not managed like the rest of the prison, however, and condemned prisoners are not treated like regular inmates. Always, "the condemned live with the barest services, the minimum contact, the slightest concern."[37] As I have observed elsewhere,

> Death row is the most total of total institutions, the penitentiary most demanding of penitence, the prison most debilitating and disabling in its

confinement. On death row the allegorical pound of flesh is just the beginning. Here the whole person is consumed. The spirit is captured and gradually worn down, then the body is disposed of. A century ago prisoners were subjected to the discipline of silence. Today on death row, this silence may prove endless.[38]

Death row is the extreme case of the pain and deprivation of imprisonment, the prison's prison.

The peculiar silence of death row stems from the empty and ultimately lifeless regimen imposed on the condemned. These offenders, seen as unfit for life in even the prison community, are relegated to this prison within a prison and held—sometimes even today in virtual solitary confinement—for periods measured in years rather than days or months. Typical maximum security prisoners spend about eight to twelve hours a day in their cells; typical death row prisoners spend twenty to twenty-two or twenty-three hours a day alone in theirs. Death row prisoners leave their cells to shower (often handcuffed) and to exercise (in a restricted area, sometimes fittingly called a "recreation cage"). If one has visitors, he leaves his cell to receive them. But visits occur under heavy guard, are restricted in frequency and duration, and become increasingly rare as a prisoner's stay on death row continues. There may be an occasional trip from the cell to the law library for the self-proclaimed "writ writer"—an inmate lawyer of sorts. Otherwise, condemned prisoners remain in their cells. They are, with few exceptions, ineligible for prison jobs or correctional programs, or even the usual forms of prison recreation, such as sports and movies. Deemed beyond correction, they typically are denied access to even the meager privileges, amenities, and services available to regular prisoners.

In general, the custodial routine of death row varies little from state to state. A nationwide survey of death row living conditions conducted in 1979 revealed that

> most DSIs [death sentence inmates] cannot work at prison jobs, cannot attend education classes, clubs or religious services, have much less opportunity for exercise and recreation and much less adequate facilities and equipment [than regular prison inmates]. DSIs have little human contact. . . . Many are shackled for trips within the prison. Most eat in their cells and are separated from visitors by barriers. . . . [T]he lives of DSIs are grim. . . . Perhaps more important than any single deprivation is the fact that the impact and effect of each restriction is exaggerated because of the more general deprivation of being kept in cells most of every day and isolated from almost all contact with other human beings.[39]

Aside from a smattering of essentially cosmetic reforms in a number of prisons—access to educational classes in some systems; the availability, on paper at least, of mental health counseling; modest increases in out-of-cell time and access to visitors; and, in a few states, the availability of part-time work—death rows today are essentially indistinguishable from their counterparts in earlier years.[40]

Detailed descriptions of individual death rows, whether civilian or military, holding hundreds of prisoners or only a handful, bear out these observations. The death rows of Florida's Starke Prison, a civilian death row with a population surpassing three hundred, and Fort Leavenworth Penitentiary, a military death row with a population of fewer than ten, are virtually indistinguishable. Each is located in the prison's segregation unit, and each conveys the impression that one is "deeply embedded in the prison—lodged, figuratively, in its bowels—shut off from light and liberty."[41] The tomblike ambiance of the physical setting complements the empty existence of its inhabitants.

- In Florida, each condemned man is housed in a separate 6×9 foot cell, from which [three] departures are scheduled each week. Two of these are for showers, when the man is handcuffed and permitted to walk a short distance down the tier to a special shower cell. The third exit is [for] exercise . . . in an enclosed blacktopped area. No visits to the prison library, chapel, or gymnasium are permitted. . . . No education or work opportunities are available to the prisoner, and opportunities for counseling are extremely limited. . . . Most of the day is spent reading, watching television, and talking with one another.[42]

- On death row at Fort Leavenworth the cells were typical segregation cells and in fact were alongside and connected to the maximum security cells. The difference was that in front of these six cells was a steel caged area. This steel cage encompassed all six cells and provided the exercise room for the inmates. Death row inmates never left the confines of the caged-in cells except to shower, and they were placed in leg-irons when so engaged. Once a day for one hour each prisoner was permitted to exit the cell into the caged area to exercise. The rest of the death row inmate's time was spent in his cell.[43]

These descriptions, drawn from materials available in 1983, remain accurate today—as a general rule, little of consequence changes on these or any other death rows.

Florida's death row has been moved to a new facility, but the regimen remains unchanged. The stated purpose of Florida's new death row is to provide "the maximum level of security and total segregation of these 'worst-of-the-worst' inmates."[44] If such is possible, Florida's death row prisoners today are even more isolated than they were a decade ago. Maximum security in Florida's contemporary death row means virtually no contact with other prisoners and only the most limited contact with the custodial staff. "While in their cells, inmates will have no visual contact with one another and they will not be able to communicate" with one another, at least not directly.[45] (On other death rows in which such isolation of prisoners is sought, the inmates have been able to make some contact with one another through the use of "peepers"—mirror fragments appended to makeshift handles—that afford a limited if distorted form of visual communication.[46]) "The only people with whom inmates will have contact will be the correctional officers walking the floor" as the officers go about their hourly rounds to maintain a regular count of their captives.[47] It is telling that fleeting contact with an officer conducting a count—an impersonal, thoughtless activity, in the main—is seen as providing "death row inmates a greater opportunity to communicate with staff."[48] Such is the degree of social isolation on death row that the prospect of a nod or wave from a passing officer is taken for a species of human relations.

In one federal case, the court described in detail the conditions of death row confinement in the state of Tennessee in the mid-1980s. The plaintiff, one Mr. Harries, had lived on death row for a number of years.

Mr. Harries lives in a six by eight foot cell, which contains a toilet with a wash basin in the toilet well. A bunk bed is provided for his use, which takes up about one-third of the cell. Lighting in the cell consists of one sixty-watt light bulb; additional lighting is available by use of an electrical hook-up, but this must be done at the inmate's expense. There is no window in Mr. Harries' cell and ventilation within his cell consists of blowers drawing out stale air. According to Mr. Harries, the ventilation is so poor that cigarette smoke stains his cell walls and toilet odors frequently make it difficult for him to sleep. Also, fumes from the respondents' [prison officials'] use of oil-based paints [for the walls and such] result in difficulty in normal breathing. . . . The ventilation problem is exacerbated when the humidity increases due to steam created from the showers of inmates. . . .

Mr. Harries is confined in his cell for twenty-three hours per day. Respondents permit him to exercise during the day for forty to forty-five minutes and to shower daily for ten to fifteen minutes. . . . The exercise area is too small for running and the number of inmates in the yard restricts them from walking. Moreover, even when the inmates are outside to exercise, the grate that covers the exercise area restricts the sunlight from shining through. While the respondents have provided a set of weights for inmates, many are unable to use them. When the weather does not permit inmates to go into the small exercise area, during the winter or when it rains, no exercise is afforded to inmates. Thus, according to Mr. Harries and other death-row inmates, it is not unusual for inmates not to exercise for a week or more during such times. . . . At all other times, including the taking of his meals, Mr. Harries remains within his cell. The temperature in Mr. Harries' cell averages, according to the respondents, between eighty and eighty-five degrees Fahrenheit. . . . A stipulation jointly submitted by counsel for the respondents and Mr. Harries indicates that the temperature within his cell on July 11, 1984 was ninety degrees. . . . [T]he stipulation indicates that the temperature within Mr. Harries' cell may reach uncomfortable and potentially life threatening limits. . . .

Turning to the area of food service to [death row] inmates, it is undisputed that prior to the commencement of this lawsuit, food served to inmates was cold. . . . The court . . . is concerned about the credible assertions of Mr. Harries that he discovered part of a mouse in his food. . . .

> [Finally,] inmates receive no religious services or counseling from respondents and the respondents prohibit any such services from outside sources.[49]

Mr. Harries, though a prisoner of death row in the 1980s, might just as well have been held in Warden Lawes's Condemned Cells at Sing Sing during the 1920s.

The court in the *Harries* case concurred in this assessment, finding the conditions of Mr. Harries's confinement to be offensive to contemporary standards of humanness. As result of this and subsequent holdings with respect to Mr. Harries's contentions,[50] reforms were put in place on death row. The centerpiece of the reform effort was a three-tiered death row confinement system in which prisoners who avoid disciplinary infractions for specified periods of time are allowed progressively more freedoms within the death row environment. This includes more association with other condemned prisoners and more access to out-of-cell activities such as educational programs, religious services, counseling, and even jobs—first on the tier, later in the regular prison. Tennessee's death row is now housed in a modern facility, so physical conditions have improved considerably.[51] No information is available in the research literature or from official documents of the Tennessee correctional system on the quality of life on this reformed death row. It is therefore impossible to determine if these changes, valuable in themselves, have measurably improved the quality of life and adjustment on Tennessee's death row or in any way helped prisoners come to grips with their impending executions.

DEATH ROW REFORMS:
THE ILLUSION OF CHANGE

Some contemporary death rows are more accommodating than the essentially solitary-confinement based regimes we've reviewed, having been liberalized as a result of legal consent decrees developed by reformers and correctional administrators.[52] A few of these settlements have been quite successful, though they have typically been piecemeal rather than comprehensive efforts. Some reforms have reduced cell time, sometimes also increasing the amount of recreation time prisoners have while out of their cells. Other reforms have expanded prisoners' opportunities for contact visits. The most comprehensive death row reforms were achieved in Texas and appear to have served as the model for reforms of the Tennessee system.

On January 3, 1986, Texas initiated a "death row activity plan" that groups death row prisoners into two categories: "work-capable," which at last accounting covered roughly 40 percent of the prisoners; and "death-row segregation," covering roughly 60 percent of the prisoners. (These figures appear to have remained fairly constant over the last ten years; I am aware of no comparable figures for the Tennessee system.) Those deemed capable of working are assigned a "meaningful job" as prison jobs go, primarily as laborers pulling four-hour shifts in a garment factory located near death row. Moreover, officials are "to provide a reasonably balanced range of recreation, work, programming and other out-of-cell activity" to work-capable inmates. Regular death row inmates, though still essentially segregated, also benefit. They are allowed "three hours of out-of-cell time five days a week" and are given access (in their cells) to "religious and educational programs" as well as psychological counseling. (However, segregated prisoners who are found to pose a danger upon release from the cell may be placed in a "Death Row Segregation—Non Recreation" category.) The frequency and length of visits remain restricted for all of Texas's condemned prisoners, however, and physical contact with visitors is prohibited altogether. When a work-capable inmate receives an execution date, he is immediately segregated until either he is executed or his execution date is vacated. If his date is vacated, he can return to work.

The reactions of the prisoners are mixed but generally favorable. Though some of Texas's work-capable prisoners compare themselves to slaves in death camps—their labor is unpaid and they may one day be put to death—others stress that the reforms break up the monotony of the day and offer small but important freedoms.[53] And friendships. "Unlike other death-row prisoners, who are isolated in their cells for most of the day, the factory workers form deep friendships. Here, unlike the rest of death row, whites, blacks and Latinos all mix easily together." This makes for a more congenial daily regime, but heightens the impact of executions; the "sudden disappearance" of a fellow worker who was known as an individual is made "all the more painful."[54] A few prisoners hope that, should their death sentences be commuted, their work experience and solid adjustment will help them make parole.[55]

Reforms of death row confinement conditions are laudable on purely humanitarian grounds. Such reforms—in Texas, Tennessee, and elsewhere—are also practical, given that today's condemned prisoners face years of confinement. Solitary confinement may have been defensible as an across-the-board policy when prisoners faced a few weeks or months or even a year or two on death row. But when the stay on death row stretches, as it does today, to five, ten, or even fifteen years or more, such confinement becomes at best an oppressive, last-ditch option for unmanageable prisoners.

After careful study of the pertinent consent decrees, John Carroll and I concluded that these reforms, though likely to please some prisoners and satisfy the courts, "will only nominally improve the quality of daily life on death row." It is our view that

> a few hours of exercise and of the company of one's fellow prisoners are no doubt to be preferred to solitary confinement, but years of the circumscribed existence that is death row will certainly remain a numbingly boring and ultimately debilitating experience. After all, only so much can be said and done by prisoners who share the essentially eventless limbo world of death row, no matter how much time they spend out of their

cells and no matter how diverse the hobbycraft programs or work experiences that are available to them. Contact visits [where available] will help to relieve the isolation and boredom of life on death row, yet they are, in the final analysis, but brief interludes in this lonely regime of confinement.[56]

Death row, Carroll and I concluded, by its very nature remains a prison within a prison, delimited by the violent sanction it serves.

Case Study of a Failed Reform

The original study on which this book is based, conducted over a three-year period from 1987 to 1989, involved, in part, a reformed death row. (The focus of my study was the execution process, examined in Part III.) What I found in this study, conducted after my collaboration with Carroll, confirmed our earlier conclusion that the quality of life under sentence of death is subject to only slight improvements. While some of the details of the death row regime I studied have changed in the years since the first edition of this book, the essential conditions remain unchanged.

The site for the study was a death row housed in a southern prison. I interviewed at length twelve officers, eight men and four women, each of whom was designated a trained and experienced security technician. The interviews were focused,[57] covering the nature and quality of work on this death row, but there was no predetermined set of questions. Each officer was asked to describe his or her assignment on death row, and the interview proceeded from there. The aim of the interview was to learn how the officers perceived their work, and this was aided by allowing them to determine what aspects of the job they viewed as salient. I then met for about an hour with sixteen condemned prisoners housed in one area of death row (my access to the prisoners was limited by the prison authorities). My discussion with the prisoners did not constitute a genuine interview. It was more like a gripe session, but a useful one in that their concerns dovetailed with those of other prisoners interviewed more systematically. I reviewed all pertinent documents pertaining to the organization and management of the death row environment. Though this part of my research is at best tentative and exploratory, I came away with lasting impressions of the environment.

The prisoners on this death row are afforded considerable liberties by death row standards. They are allowed out of their cells in groups of up to eight men to spend time in a common dayroom, sometimes for as long as five hours a day; they are served meals outside their cells, in the dayroom; they have opportunities for as much as ten hours a week of outdoor exercise; they are offered group religious services; and visits are regularly permitted, with prisoners sometimes allowed physical contact with their guests. Some inmates are allowed, within limits, to work; all have access to an educational counselor. A psychological counselor is on call three days a week. The courts would surely approve these arrangements. Yet for all these reforms, this death row is still oppressive, with a social climate not much different from that of Warden Lawes's Condemned Cells.

This death row, like all death rows, is formally defined—and aptly described—in the prison's institutional operating procedures (IOPs) as "a special housing unit set aside for the strict control and maximum security management" of condemned prisoners. There is a tight chain of supervision and command; all activities on death row must be approved in advance in writing, and staff are monitored regularly. Only certified officers, specially trained as security technicians, can work there. Vigilance is stressed; security is demanded. Cell searches, for example, are done three times a day, once on each shift. The IOPs read as follows: "During cell searches, inmates are required to be removed from the cell in restraints, searched, and held on the tier under the supervision of a certified officer." I observed a number of these searches and can attest that the procedures are thorough and intimidating. By any measure, the level of control on this death row is high.

Prisoners are housed in semicircular configurations of cells, called pods, each containing two tiers of eight cells. Each pod has a dayroom that abuts the cells and offers indoor recreation, mostly cards and television. The dayroom is enclosed within bars. These bars are interrupted by a cement-and-glass control booth, located half within and half without the dayroom. Each booth holds one officer, known as a pod control officer, who opens and closes all cell doors as well as all doors leading to and from the housing pod. All prisoners in the dayroom are within easy view of the pod control officer at all times. This officer can also speak with the inmates by means of an intercom system. Another officer sits in a hall just outside the pod, alongside the bars, and is able to observe and interact more directly with the prisoners.

The prisoners, then, spend a number of hours each day out of their cells in a dayroom, under the gaze of the pod control officer and interacting, if they so choose, with the hall officer. It is fair to say that these dayrooms are, in essence, large communal cells that function as extensions of the prisoners' individual cells. Each group of condemned prisoners, while in their cells or in the dayroom, is securely segregated from the general prison inmate population. In one prisoner's words, "We have absolutely no contact with general population prisoners." The same can be said for condemned prisoners in other areas of death row. Each pod functions as a death row within the larger death row, set apart from the rest of the world.

Prisoners periodically leave death row and go to other locations within the prison. When they do so, they move under heavy security. It is as if they drag the death row regime behind them, shackled to it by the chains that bind their hands and feet during these excursions. As dictated in the prison's IOPs,

> Inmates shall be placed in restraints prior to leaving the cells. The restraints shall consist of handcuffs and safety chain. The inmates shall be thoroughly searched by frisk upon exiting and entering the cell. Strip searches can be conducted if the officer in charge has reason to believe an inmate has a weapon or personal contraband.

Typical destinations within the prison include the medical section and visiting area. In each instance, security procedures are stringent: "Upon arrival at the back door of the Medical Department," for example, "leg restraints shall be placed on the inmate. The inmate shall remain in leg restraints at all times while being treated, unless otherwise requested by the attending medical employee." For visits, which are preceded and followed by strip-searches, "hand restraints may be removed at the discretion of the Chief of Security, but at no time will hand restraints be removed without the use of leg restraints."

Inmates also leave death row proper for outdoor exercise, in this case in small groups. The recreation area is a large outdoor cage topped with barbed wire and housing a basketball court. Since, here, the prisoners are only a few fences away from freedom, security procedures are elaborate. As specified in the IOPs, a ranking officer and four correctional officers go to the

> pod area to begin pulling inmates for recreation. The lieutenant or sergeant will position himself by the pod control room. The correctional officers working in teams of two will go to the cell door of the inmate coming out for recreation. The lieutenant or sergeant will communicate to the pod control room officer which cell door to open and when. The correctional officers will restrict their activities to one tier at a time. The pod control room officer will not be allowed to open more than one cell at a time.
>
> Each inmate will pass the clothes that he will be wearing to the recreation yard through the food slot to the officer for inspection. Each inmate will be handcuffed through the food slot. . . . [T]he inmate will come out of his cell in his shorts. Under the supervision of two correctional officers, the handcuffs will be removed, and the inmate will be allowed to dress. The inmate will be recuffed with his hands behind him and ordered to the dayroom area where he will be supervised by the lieutenant or sergeant.

The prisoners are then escorted to the recreation area. An officer "shall remain outside the recreation yard and shall maintain radio contact with the tower and the building."

It is nowhere recorded in the official IOPs, but this death row is haunted by an escape that occurred several years back. At that time, security procedures were poorly articulated, and little attention was paid to the implementation of those procedures that were in force. As a result, six inmates returning from outdoor recreation (then unrestrained) were able to take a hostage, gain access to the control area, leave the death row building, and commandeer a truck that was allowed off the prison grounds because the inmates were able to convince the gate officer that they had a bomb in their possession (it was a TV wrapped in a blanket). That was a correctional nightmare, though fortunately no one, officer or civilian, was hurt during or after the escape. To some degree, the security concerns at this prison are a legacy of that escape. But security is a salient concern on all death rows. If this death row differs from its fellow death rows on the matter of security, the difference is one of degree, not kind.[58]

As on all death rows, the officers who work here rank security as their main concern, with prevention of escapes as their top security problem. Security is a virtual obsession with the death row commander. Working on death row is, in his words, a "battle of minds," and the lines of conflict, in his eyes, are clear: "They want out; we must keep them in." In this continuing battle of wits and wills, no one can afford to be casual or relaxed. Or friendly. As specified in the IOPs,

> All staff assigned to work in the Death Row Unit(s) . . . shall avoid any personal discussions. Employees *must not* be too familiar or discuss personal items of interest with the inmates. Employees must conduct business and activities on a professional basis and be observant at all times and be knowledgeable of all duties.

There is no such thing as small talk here. The death row commander warns his staff to "speak cautiously, and always ask yourself 'why' when someone is talking to you—what is he *really* after?"

This death row, like its unreformed counterparts, is seen by both the keepers and the kept as cold, lonely, and often frightening. For their part, the inmates bemoan the constant pressure, the feeling of being hemmed in and harassed by their keepers, their vulnerability to the guards, and the threat of personal debilitation. In their far-ranging grievances, they echo concerns uncovered in more systematic research on prisoners of solitary-confinement death rows. One prisoner, who has spent some nine years on this death row, may have captured the tempo of life in this environment when he observed,

> Not a day passes that I do not fight just to get out of bed. And in the late hours of the night, it takes much strength just to keep a grip on my sanity. I have spent many hours at my window, standing on my toilet at the air vent, pleading with men who were considering suicide. . . . I have been on that very edge myself.

In this man's view, our reformed death row emerges as "a psychological nightmare that very few survive." I heard nothing in my session with the prisoners to belie this claim.

As executions have become more common since the publication of the first edition of this book, the social climate on this death row has become, if anything, even more taxing and traumatic for the prisoners. Prisoners on this death row today report that the psychological nightmare not only continues but has gotten worse. The escalating pace of executions has taken a toll in human suffering. A prison reformer and informal counselor to the condemned on death row and in the death house, with close and continuing contacts with many of the prisoners, was reinterviewed for this edition of the book. She told me that "the mood on death row today is one of hopelessness." It is, at bottom, a regime palpably constrained by loss. No one, not even the innocent, get out alive. As one man told her, "the innocent get life in prison; everybody else is gonna get killed here." In this grim world, the IOPs may change—some more restrictive, others less—but the social reality is one of growing isolation. Prisoners keep to themselves more, talk to others less, trust no one. They are driven inward, away from each other, into their cells, which

serve as cold, concrete havens of last resort. Increasingly, the condemned feel
cut adrift in a silent world that is circumscribed by gray walls and violent death.

BACK TO THE FUTURE:
HIGH-TECH SOLITARY CONFINEMENT
ON MODERN DEATH ROWS

Oklahoma's death row offers a revealing case study of a modern, high-tech
human warehouse for the containment and execution of condemned prisoners. Known by the bland name H–Unit, it offers a human existence so lifeless
that its nondescript name—a letter in the alphabet, devoid of any intrinsic
meaning—somehow seems fitting. H–Unit was expressly built as a thoroughly
modern penal establishment, a kind of futuristic rendering of solitary confinement. A planning document for H–Unit notes, "The state-of-the-art design
of this unit maximizes security and control, while providing inmates and staff
with a safe, modern environment in which to live and work."[59] For the words
security and *control*, substitute *isolation*; for the word *modern*, substitute *sterile*.
H–Unit is nothing if not solitary and sterile; a cold, oppressive human waste-
land in which prisoners are interred—confined underground—in utterly self-
contained cell blocks replete with dimly lit and sparely furnished concrete
cages. It is telling that in a recent anthology of death row poetry, covering
death rows from around the nation, the editor remarks that "The most common image in these poems is of cold—cold steel, cold cell, cold death." Death
row, we learn from the poetry of the condemned, "is like being trapped under
ice."[60] By this reckoning, H–Unit is the quintessential death row.

Located on the grounds of the Oklahoma State Penitentiary, H–Unit serves
as a "super-maximum security" adjunct to the larger prison.

> Constructed of entirely concrete with living accommodation sited effec-
> tively underground, H–Unit is an electronically controlled facility
> designed to minimize contact between inmates and prison staff. Prisoners
> are confined for 23 or 24 hours a day in windowless cells allowing virtu-
> ally no natural light and no natural air. No work, recreational or voca-
> tional programs are provided.[61]

All male death row prisoners in Oklahoma are held in H–Unit. Other prisoners are confined there as well, but only for short periods of time. Death row
prisoners are the only long-term residents of this facility.

It is both ironic and telling that H–Unit was conceived as a reform institution, meant to be an improvement over an old-fashioned and physically primitive solitary-confinement regime. As made clear by an assessment team
working under the auspices of Amnesty International (AI), H–Unit represents
a giant step back from the death row conditions it was meant to improve upon.
As the AI report notes, "in some important respects conditions are worse in

H-Unit than they were on the former death row, particularly as regards access to natural light and air, the exercise facilities and contact with staff and others."[62] Indeed, H-Unit is worse than many, perhaps most death rows. As the AI report notes, "most prisoners under sentence of death in the USA are held in segregated death rows. However, few appear to impose restrictions as severe as those in H-Unit and many death row prisoners have more out-of-cell time and association with fellow inmates; some engage in prison work or other programs."[63]

It is a painful irony for the condemned that the cells on this quintessentially modern death row are today's answer to the medieval dungeon— cramped, barren, dark, and devoid of human character.

> The cells in the housing area are 7'7" by 15'5" and have two poured concrete bunks on either side of an uncovered toilet and sink. There is no other furniture in the cells apart from two concrete shelves on the back wall which serve as "tables" and two similar shelves above these for TV sets if prisoners can afford to purchase them from prison stock. Prisoners are not allowed to pin anything on the walls, which are unpainted concrete. The cell doors are solid metal, except for the upper part which has a plexiglass window with thick bars on the outside. . . . The only light inside the cells is provided by two bare light bulbs positioned at eye-level at the back of the cell where the bunks and shelves are situated.[64]

Almost no outside light makes its way into the cell blocks. When the lights in the cells are turned off, even on a sunny day, the cells are enveloped in near total darkness.

As in dungeons of old, life on H-Unit is essentially limited to these impoverished, barren cells.

> Prisoners are confined to [their] cells for 23 hours a day during weekdays and 24 hours a day at weekends. The only out-of-cell time is a 15 minute shower three times a week; an hour's exercise five times a week in an enclosed concrete yard if weather permits; visits (for those who have them); and limited access to the prison's law library. Up to ten inmates at a time may also attend a religious service once a week under makeshift arrangements in a corner of the quad. All meals are eaten in the cells. No work, educational or vocational programs are provided.[65]

As if to add insult to injury, inmates complain that the food is poor and the servings small. Often, meals are served cold. Inmates claim they have poor access to medical, dental, and psychiatric services—some feel they are treated as if they are terminal pariahs, beyond the reach of medical care or indeed human compassion.[66]

A limited exercise regimen is offered in sharply constricted facilities, settings more like dog kennels than recreation yards. "Prisoners exercise in a 23 by 22 foot yard surrounded by 18 foot high solid concrete walls. The roof is constructed of girders covered with wire mesh. There is no view to the outside."[67] Little is provided in the way of equipment. There is merely empty, exposed space, lacking even the simple amenity of a drinking fountain or a chair to sit on.

> The H–Unit yards have no facilities apart from a bench press with weights welded to it which all the prisoners interviewed said was difficult or impossible to use. There was no shelter from the rain or heat of the sun in summer and no drinking fountain. . . . [No] more than five prisoners may exercise on the yard at a time. The only facility available for recreation is a handball court and the yard is so small that, even with only five inmates it is not possible to do anything else if handball is being played. There is nowhere to sit . . . [which] made the yard almost impossible to use for inmates who were elderly or suffered from joint diseases and/or were on crutches.[68]

Solitary death rows breed claustrophobic reactions—the feeling that the walls of the cells are closing in, that the very air in cramped cells is in danger of running out. Prisoners on solitary-confinement death rows routinely see themselves as "the living dead," their death row worlds as settings that impose "a living death."[69] Modern high-security facilities—sterile, empty, marked by a suffocating routine—do nothing to dispel these sentiments.

> The solid walls of the exercise yard, together with the lack of windows in cells, means that prisoners are virtually confined to a concrete world in which they never see a blade of grass, earth, trees or any part of the natural world. Most prisoners interviewed said this was the most stressful aspect of their confinement. . . . Several prisoners likened confinement in H–Unit to being locked in a tomb.[70]

Some prisoners became visibly depressed and withdrawn in this unnatural environment. Deeper, long-term reactions of this sort—suggested by prior research[71]—were beyond the ken of the AI team, which was limited to a short visit at the facility.

Physical containment, social isolation, and impersonal control are central objectives of all death row regimes. On Oklahoma's H–Unit, these functions reach absurd and even tragic extremes. The setting, in a nightmare version of a futuristic world, features remote control of convicts caged nearly—and in some cases, totally—around the clock, under the dominion of officers who issue commands that emanate from distant control centers by way of intercoms. The very regime itself bespeaks dehumanization in all its essentials.

> H–Unit was designed to be a "non-contact" facility, minimizing direct physical contact between prisoners and prison staff, and each quad is managed from a central control room through which guards can operate the unit electronically. Correctional staff do not routinely patrol the cell area, apart from the "key-men" who open the beanholes [food slots] three times a day to pass food to the prisoners. Most communication between

guards and prisoners takes place through the intercom in each cell, which is operated from the control room. When prisoners are let out to shower or go to the yard, the cell doors are operated electronically and they are supervised by staff from the other side of the bars.[72]

When contact occurs, it is buffered by the constraining hardware of custody. "On the few occasions when prisoners do have direct contact with guards—for example when being taken to attorney visits, the law library or the medical room—prisoners are placed in handcuffs and leg-irons and are escorted by at least two correctional officers."[73] The absence of human contact is the norm, extending from the daily cell-block regime to visits with loved ones, attorneys, and even to religious services.[74] Given the strain of social isolation on the normal psyche, it is troubling that there was no full-time psychiatrist at H-Unit as recently as 1994, when Amnesty International released its report. One former psychiatrist "told Amnesty International that he had little contact with mentally ill prisoners on H-Unit and indicated that they did not receive adequate treatment or monitoring."[75]

In the original plan, and for a time, H-Unit prisoners were confined one to a cell. With crowding, most cells are now doubled up. Confining two men to a cell "was widely reported to be a source of great stress in the conditions of close confinement on H-Unit. Prisoners described the experience as being permanently locked in a box with someone from whom there was no escape."[76] And since there are no alarm buttons in the cells, the prisoners are left to their own devices when trouble develops, as has occurred with some regularity according to the prisoners. Privacy concerns are also salient. "The fact that prisoners both showered and exercised with their cell partner increased tensions and some prisoners said they refused exercise—or arranged to exercise on alternate days only—in order to have some brief time and space to themselves."[77]

Here, as in other death rows, condemned prisoners are treated like desperately dangerous men requiring extreme conditions of confinement. Ironically, death row prisoners, as a general rule, may be less of a security threat than regular maximum security prisoners. In a lawsuit dealing with attorney visits on H-Unit, a U.S. District Judge stated that "Death row inmates pose no greater security risk than any other high-maximum security inmate. . . . Institutional behavior is generally better for death row inmates because such behavior may be used as evidence in mitigation or commutation proceedings."[78] (Experiences in states like Maryland, which confine condemned prisoners in the general maximum security population, bear out this observation.) This holding did nothing to change conditions on H-Unit, which are driven more by deep-seated fears than by rational policy. The AI report maintains that Oklahoma's death row violates a host of international standards, most notably Article 5 of the *United Nations Universal Declaration of Human Rights*, as well as a number of prison standards set by the American Correctional Association.[79] Shortly after Amnesty International's report was released, Oklahoma officials defended their regime on the grounds that it provided the kind of custodial control necessary for the protection of the staff and the containment of desperate convicts. On top of that, *added* restrictions—strip searches before and after *any* exit from a death row cell—were put in place.[80]

Oklahoma's death row gives us a glimpse of solitary confinement in the modern penal dungeon that may well be the death row of the future. One cannot help but note that the chilling human environment this death row offers brings to mind the regimen of solitary confinement ruled unconstitutional in the *Medley* case a century ago. Medley was subjected to solitary confinement in a Colorado prison prior to execution. The Supreme Court, drawing on English history, ruled that solitary confinement was unconstitutional because of its severity and because it comprised a second sanction, in addition to that of execution. The court held that in historical terms, solitary confinement had been used as "a further terror and peculiar mark of infamy" that could be added to the death penalty and, hence, that such confinement was not merely incidental to the penalty of death but must be considered "an additional punishment of the most important and painful character."[81] That character, I will argue, is one of torture. Though today's courts may not be receptive to this argument, there can be little doubt that, from the prisoners' point of view, confinement under sentence of death is a separate and painful punishment that, more even than the method of execution, captures the essence of that which is truly degrading about the modern death penalty.

A DEATH ROW BY ANY OTHER NAME . . .

There are two basic death row regimes: reformed and unreformed. The unreformed regime offers unadorned long-term solitary or near-solitary confinement. The condemned prisoner spends the bulk of each day alone in his cell. When out of the cell, he is alone or in small groups and is heavily restrained and closely guarded. (Most condemned prisoners in America spend time on solitary-confinement death rows; this is also the most common death row regime in foreign countries with the death penalty.)[82] The reformed model of death row offers the condemned prisoner greater time out of the cell. This time is generally spent in dayrooms appended to the cell block. There, the prisoner engages in such diversions as ping-pong, chess, and cards. (In some instances, the prisoner of a reformed death row is allowed to work for a portion of the day.) The dayrooms that capture much of the prisoner's out-of-cell time are, in essence, congregate or group cells that are removed from the larger prison community.

In the solitary death row, then, the prisoner is in isolation, an outcast who feels himself buried alive. In the congregate death row, the prisoner is a kind of leper confined with his disease-mates to a steel and concrete colony. To be sure, the differences between these regimes are real and are the hard-won product of many legal battles. Prisoners recognize and appreciate the differences. (As we have seen, Texas's and Tennessee's reformed death rows allow inmates who adjust well to work at regular prison jobs during the day. A few states allow better behaved prisoners to mingle in the general population, with other maximum-security prisoners, at least while they are years away from execution. These privileges are deeply appreciated by most condemned prisoners.) But in neither the solitary nor congregate death row regime is there a meaningful effort to help prisoners come to terms with the awful fate that awaits them.

Willie Turner was a prisoner of Virginia's death row, a reformed regime. As his experience makes clear, death row is not so much an environment as it is a way of life—and death. In his words,

> It's the unending, uninterrupted immersion in death that wears on you so much. It's the parade of friends and acquaintances who leave for the death house and never come back, while your own desperate and lonely time drains away. It's the boring routine of claustrophobic confinement, punctuated by eye-opening dates with death that you helplessly hope will be averted. It's watching yourself die over the years in the eyes of family and friends, who, with every lost appeal, add to the emotional scar tissue that protects them . . . from your death, long before you're gone. . . . I've spent over 5000 days on death row. Not a single waking hour of any of those days has gone by without me thinking about my date with the executioner. If I don't think of it myself, then something brings it to my mind, like some other prisoner talking about his future, or somebody being executed, or somebody not being executed because of a stay. Dozens of times a day for 5000 days. All that thinking about it [execution] is like a little dying, even if you're on the best death row on earth.[83]

Nobody fully adapts to the pressures of death row confinement. As Willie Turner has said, reflecting on his many years on death row, "nothing could have prepared me for the despair and the frustration, for the loneliness and the abuse, for the shame and the sorrow, for the hopes raised and dashed, for the dreams and nightmares of my death that my seventeen years facing my own advancing demise have served up to me."[84] After seventeen years, Turner was known as the Dean of Virginia's death row, in recognition of his long tenure and thoughtful commentary on life under sentence of death. He was executed a few months after giving his affidavit about his experiences on death row.

From the prisoners' point of view, even the most experienced prisoners, all death row regimes offer much stress and little hope. All reforms put in place to date are ultimately futile, because they do nothing to prepare the prisoners for their fate or to change the basic fact that death rows exist to facilitate impersonal, bureaucratic executions. This grim job they do well and with increasing frequency by dehumanizing those—inmate and staff alike—who are a part of the killing routine. A comprehensive assessment of the psychological devastation that is played out on our nation's death rows, affecting both the male prisoners and, to a lesser degree, the staff, is the aim of the next chapter.

WOMEN ON DEATH ROW

There are roughly fifty women on death row in America today. Women represent about 2% of condemned prisoners in America and about 2% of prisoners sentenced to death in any given year. Since 1608, roughly 520 women have been put to death in America; this represents about 3% of the 19,000-plus legal executions that have taken place in America. Only one woman—Velma Barfield—has been put to death since the return of the modern death penalty in 1976.[85]

Oklahoma's death row for women, not unlike the men's unit, is a modern facility featuring high security. Condemned women—five at last count—"are housed inside a locked and isolated unit." There they are confined in "single locked cells for 23 out of 24 hours each day" in a setting that, like a typical men's death row, is aptly described as "a prison within a prison." Condemned women are isolated from the regular prison population and from each other. Recreation is allowed for an hour a day, in "a small locked outdoor exercise cage . . . when weather permits and if correctional officers have the time to escort and observe them." When out of their cells, the women are "handcuffed and shackled." They are not permitted contact visits. When surveyed about their adjustment, the women voiced concerns about "loneliness and isolation" as well as "emptiness and loss." At least one woman used the imagery of "existential death," a variant on the notion of living death so commonly voiced in death rows for men. On Oklahoma's death rows, then, both men and women would appear to be classed among the dangerous and undeserving, requiring close custody.[86]

I am aware of no national survey comparing death rows for men and women. Such literature as exists suggests that Oklahoma's death row for women is in the minority. (Though not alone. California's death row for women is comparable.)[87] Nevertheless, it would appear that, in most states, the contrast between men's and women's death rows is quite sharp. More often than not, condemned women are held in settings that are cozy and congenial, more like group homes or even private homes than like prisons or death rows. In these settings, condemned women are not seen as a danger, so a relaxed regime is maintained. "When I visited male death-row inmates in other states," noted a female journalist, "they were separated from me by a glass wall, and sometimes handcuffed to a belt." By contrast, on Alabama's death row for women, she continued, "I am locked in the inmates' cells, with the guard coming by only every half hour." The setting was inviting. "On the sunny, plant-rimmed patio, the atmosphere is completely relaxed." Almost. "Except for the screams of a disturbed prisoner from inside the building, we might be spending the afternoon on someone's screen porch."[88]

In this journalist's experience, "The loose structure of the death row at [Alabama's] Julia Tutwiler Prison is typical of those housing women around the country." So, too, are the pleasant, highly individualized surroundings. "The Florida death row is painted peach. In Texas, for example, in the bungalow containing the state's female death-row population of six, the cells border a day room with area rugs and a small library." Even work takes on the form of a cozy cottage undertaking. "In one cell the women have set up a workshop for making Cabbage Patch–like dolls that sell for $25." The condemned women entertain the writer as though she were a guest in their home. "Neelley offers me a choice of Diet Coke, Coke, or Sprite. I can see the purple sheets on Harris' bed, needlework on the walls, and Neelley's collection of angels above her bed. I am in someone's house."[89]

All of this may change when and if women are executed with any regularity. Women facing a realistic threat of execution may pose—or be seen to pose—a danger. There may also be a premium placed on distancing oneself from women on the threshold of execution, so that they may be more efficiently and impersonally put to death. Custody provides distance; cells and bars and deadening routines separate keeper from kept, making an execution less personal, less compelling. A home, put under heavy guard, becomes a prison. Something like a men's death row regime, already in evidence in some states, may become the norm if and when executions for women occur with any regularity.

NOTES

1. R. Johnson, *Condemned to Die: Life under Sentence of Death* (Prospect Heights, Ill.: Waveland Press, 1989), 116.

2. A. Camus, "Reflections on the Guillotine," in *Resistance, Rebellion, and Death* (New York: Knopf, 1969), 205.

3. A. Keller and C. V. Calvert, *A Hangman's Diary: Being the Journal of Master Franz Schmidt, Public Executioner of Nuremberg, 1573–1617* (Montclair, N.J.: Patterson Smith, 1973), 36.

4. V. A. C. Gatrell, *The Hanging Tree: Execution and the English People 1770–1868* (Oxford: Oxford University Press, 1994), 37.

5. Ibid., 36.

6. Ibid., 40.

7. Ibid., 38.

8. P. Linebaugh, *The London Hanged: Crime and Civil Society in the Eighteenth Century* (Cambridge: Cambridge University Press, 1992), 29–30.

9. The authority for this confinement was Act 25 George II, c. 37, "An act for the better preventing the horrid crime of murder," quoted in *In re* Medley, 134 U.S. 160 (1889), 170. It is not clear if condemned prisoners convicted of crimes other than murder were so confined or were given the freedoms allowed for regular prisoners in Newgate. See Linebaugh (n. 8), 29–30.

10. Gatrell (n. 4), 42.

11. Ibid., 43.

12. Ibid., 44.

13. Ibid., 44.

14. Ibid., 44.

15. Ibid., 44.

16. H. Bleackley and J. Lofland, *State Executions Viewed Historically and Sociologically* (Montclair, N.J.: Patterson Smith, 1977), 288.

17. Gatrell (n. 4), 45, 51.

18. L. E. Lawes, *Twenty Thousand Years in Sing Sing* (New York: R. Long & R. R. Smith, 1932), 335.

19. In earlier executions, in the medieval and early modern periods, execution ritual allowed for expressions of individuality. The goal of modern executions, only achieved after some time, was to exclude individuality from the execution process.

20. Lawes (n. 18), 296.

21. For a considerable period of time, men and women in early modern England dressed for their executions with what Gatrell called "sartorial gaiety." The tradition lasted longer for women than men. Gatrell tells us that the prison reformer Elizabeth Fry learned through her work with condemned women that the "'chief thought' of nearly every condemned woman in Newgate 'relates to her appearance on the scaffold, the dress in which she shall be hanged.'" Gatrell (n. 4), 36–37.

22. Lawes (n. 18), 296.

23. Ibid., 329.

24. Ibid., 329.

25. Ibid., 291.

26. Ibid., 330.

27. It is my impression that "brave deaths of legend" persisted in the form of humorous or defiant last words, which appear as late as the 1960s but occur with decreasing frequency since the 1930s, the period about which Warden Lawes wrote. Over the past decade, last words appear particularly banal, perhaps showing the more or less complete bureaucratization of the execution process. For some colorful last words of condemned prisoners in the 1950s and 1960s, see A. Wallace, ed., *The Book of Lists #3* (New York: Morrow, 1983). The somewhat irreverent "Au Revoir Les Inmates," available on the Internet at http://www.one.net/~tdaniels/cooking.html, offers the seemingly uninspiring last words of contemporary condemned prisoners.

28. L. E. Lawes, *Life and Death in Sing Sing* (New York: Sun Dial Press, 1937), 161.

29. Ibid., 162.

30. Lawes (n. 18), 6.

31. Lawes (n. 28), 162, 163.

32. In absolute terms, suicides are more numerous on today's death rows, but since the number of condemned prisoners and their length of stay on death row have increased greatly, it is unclear whether the rate of suicides is higher or lower than in times past.

33. Lawes (n. 28), 164.

34. C. T. Duffy with A. Hirshberg, *Eighty-Eight Men and Two Women* (New York: Doubleday, 1962).

35. I. Zimmerman with F. Bond, *Punishment without Crime* (New York: Clarkson N. Potter, 1964), 119–120.

36. R. Johnson and H. Toch, eds., *The Pains of Imprisonment* (Prospect Heights, Ill.: Waveland Press, 1988), 13.

37. B. Jackson and D. Christian, *Death Row* (Boston: Beacon Press, 1980), 28.

38. Johnson (n. 1), 121.

39. J. F. Else, E. Kudsk, and J. Meyer, "Living Conditions of Death Sentence Inmates in the U.S." (unpublished paper, 1981; available from J. F. Else, School of Social Work, University of Iowa, Iowa City, Iowa 52242). John Conrad and I conducted an informal

survey of death row living conditions during 1983 and 1984. Our impression was that little had changed on our nation's death rows since the Else et al. report.

40. C. A. Nesbitt, R. L. Howard, and S. M. Wallace, *Managing Death-Sentenced Inmates: A Survey of Practices* (American Correctional Association) (St. Mary's Press: Washington, D. C., 1989) and A. Wunder, "Survey Summary: Living on Death Row," *Corrections Compendium* XIX (12) (December 1994): 9–21.

41. Johnson (n. 1), 43.

42. M. L. Radelet, M. Vandiver, and F. Berardo, "Families, Prisons, and Men with Death Sentences: The Human Impact of Structured Uncertainty," *Journal of Family Issues* 4 (4): 595–596 (1983).

43. P. Dumm, personal communication following a visit to Fort Leavenworth's death row, spring 1983. I have it on the authority of current military personnel that procedures have remained unchanged since then (Maj. J. Tyler, personal communication, summer 1989).

44. See W. A. Stimpson, "A Better Design for Safer Detention on Death Row," *Corrections Today* 53 (4): 159 (1991).

45. Ibid., 159.

46. Prisoners on Louisiana's death row in Angola Prison routinely used peepers to get "a view of the hallway and anyone visiting the area. The peepers are used in cell-to-cell conversations as well. Men in isolated cells often grow weary of talking to walls, windows and bars. A human face, even if viewed through a makeshift mirror, adds meaning to a destitute existence." See W. Rideau and R. Wikberg, *Life Sentences: Rage and Survival Behind Bars* (New York: Times Books, 1992), 265.

47. Stimpson (n. 44), Note 2 at 159.

48. K. Flack, "In Florida: A Look at Day-to-Day Death Row Operations," *Corrections Today* 55 (4): 76 (1993).

49. Groseclose *ex rel.* Harries v. Dutton, 594 F. Supp. 949 (1984), 959, 960, 961.

50. Stressing the bleak physical milieu, the long periods of cell time and attendant idleness, and the absence of any type of attention to the unique psychological stresses faced by the condemned, the court in the *Harries* case held Tennessee's death row to be in violation of the Eighth Amendment prohibition of cruel and unusual punishment. However, on appeal the circuit court subsumed the *Harries* case under Grubbs v. Bradley, 552 F. Supp. 1052 (1982), a prior prison-conditions suit covering the entire Tennessee prison system. In *Grubbs*, the court had taken a narrow view of the Eighth Amendment, holding that "the mere fact that inmates may tend to degenerate as a result of incarceration is not actionable." Only "serious physical or psychological deterioration [that] is inevitable" violates the cruel and unusual punishment clause (1124). The presumption is that "core" protections afforded by the Eighth Amendment pertaining to "food, clothing, shelter, sanitation, medical care, and personal safety" would have to be violated to produce serious and inevitable deterioration (1122). In this circuit court's rendering, the Eighth Amendment would seem to require us to preserve the body of the prisoner—which is to be fed, clothed, maintained in clean and hygienic conditions, and held safe from harm—while allowing us to ignore the person. As a result of *Grubbs*, a special master was appointed to oversee reforms on death row and indeed throughout the prison system.

51. See *Death Row Programming and Management: Policy and Procedures Manual*, Tennessee Department of Corrections, Effective September 1, 1992 (unpublished document). This and other death-row and execution-related correctional documents are available from the National Institute of Corrections Information Center, 1860 Industrial Circle, Suite A, Longmont, Colo 80501 (800 877 1461).

52. A summary of these reforms can be found in R. Johnson and J. L. Carroll, "Litigating Death Row Conditions: The Case for Reform," in *Prisoners' Rights Sourcebook: Theory, Litigation, Practice*, ed. I. Robbins (New York: Clark-Boardman, 1985), 8.3–8.33.

53. Ibid., Note 6 at 8.11–8.12. For a more detailed discussion of this reform effort, focusing on the work experience of the prisoners, see J. R. Sorensen and J. W. Marquart, "Working the Dead," in *Facing the Death Penalty: Essays on a Cruel and Unusual Punishment*, ed. M. L. Radelet (Philadelphia: Temple University Press, 1989), 169–177.

54. Muir, "Worked to Death in Texas," *The Observer Magazine*, 27 February 1994.

55. Johnson and Carroll (n. 52), 8.11–8.12. For a more detailed discussion of this reform effort, focusing on the work experience of prisoners, see Sorensen and Marquart (n. 53), 169–177.

56. Johnson and Carroll (n. 52).

57. I have used focused interviews in prior research. See, for example, Johnson (n. 1), 11–15 and R. Johnson, *Culture and Crisis in Confinement* (Lexington: Lexington Books, 1976), esp. 31–34. For a general discussion of focused interviews, see R. Merton and P. Kendall, "The Focused Interview," in *The Language of Social Research*, ed. P. Lazarsfeld and M. Rosenbert (New York: Free Press, 1955).

58. Security levels on death rows in Texas and Alabama, neither of which has experienced an escape, are essentially the same as those reviewed above. See Sorensen and Marquart (n. 53) and Johnson (n. 1).

59. Amnesty International, *Conditions for Death Row Prisoners in H-Unit, Oklahoma State Penitentiary* (New York: Amnesty International U.S.A., May 1994), 1.

60. J. Zimmerman, *Trapped Under Ice: A Death Row Anthology* (Brunswick, Me.: Biddle Publishing Company, 1995), 9.

61. Amnesty International (n. 59), Summary.

62. Ibid., 2.

63. Ibid., 3.

64. Ibid., 5.

65. Ibid., 7.

66. Ibid., 20. This complaint has been noted on several death rows in the United States and abroad. See Johnson (n. 1) and L. Vogelman, "The Living Dead: Living on Death Row," *South African Journal on Human Rights* 5 (1989): 183–195.

67. Amnesty International (n. 59), 11.

68. Ibid., 11–12.

69. Perceptions of death row as a living death and of condemned prisoners as the living dead are widespread and of enduring lineage in America and around the world. See, for example, Johnson (n. 1) for American prisoners; Vogelman (n. 66) for South African prisoners; and M. Hector, *Death Row* (London: Zed Books, 1984), 44 for Jamaican prisoners.

70. Amnesty International (n. 59), 13.

71. Much of this research is reviewed in Johnson (n. 1) and R. Johnson, "Life Under Sentence of Death," in *The Pains of Imprisonment*, ed. R. Johnson and H. Toch (Prospect Heights, Ill.: Waveland, 1989), 129–145.

72. Amnesty International (n. 59), 15.

73. Ibid., 15.

74. Ibid., 17.

75. Ibid., 21.

76. Ibid., 19.

77. Ibid., 19.

78. Ibid., 24.

79. Ibid., 28.

80. A. Hamilton, "Oklahoma Inmates Allege Reprisals after Critical Report," *Dallas Morning News*, 1 August 1994, 1A, 9A.

81. *In re* Medley (n. 9), 170, 171.

82. See, for example, P. Hodgkinson and A. Rutherford, *Capital Punishment: Global Issues and Prospects* (Winchester: Waterside Press, 1996), 174 and accompanying notes. For the particular case of Jamaica, see Hector (n. 69), 44.

83. Turner v. Jabe, para. 22, declaration of Willie Lloyd Turner, pursuant to petition for writ of habeas corpus, April 27, 1995.

84. Ibid., para. 22.

85. V. L. Streib, "Capital Punishment of Female Offenders," (unpublished manuscript, Cleveland State University, Cleveland-Marshall College of Law, 1995). For a thoughtful examination of the execution of females in American history, see V. L. Streib, "Death Penalty for Female Offenders," *University of Cincinnati Law Review* 58 (3): 845–880 (1990).

86. All observations about Oklahoma's death row for women are drawn from K. A. O'Shea, "Woman on Death Row," in *Women Prisoners: A Forgotten Population*, ed. B. R. Fletcher, L. D. Shaver, and D. G. Moon (Westport, Conn.: Praeger, 1993), 85–86.

87. See, for example, M. Marlette, "Confining the Condemned," *Corrections Compendium* 17 (1): 1, 6 (1992).

88. T. Rosenberg, "Dead Woman Walking," *Harper's Bazaar* 411 (February 1996): 110–122.

89. Ibid., 110–112.

4

Living and Working
on Death Row

D eath row assaults the senses with the sights and sounds—and sometimes the smells—of death. "Don't tell me about the Valley of the Shadow of Death," says Mumia Abu-Jamal, a prisoner on Pennsylvania's death row. "I live there."[1] He lives there alone, with the image of death giving substance to his world. All condemned prisoners do. Death row reeks with the threat of death. For the condemned, death gives meaning and purpose to every facet of his world, defining:

- *place*—the prisoners live on death row; typically spend their final hours in the death house, confined to a death cell; they meet their fate in the death chamber;

- *process*—time on death row is called dead time; life on death row is known as a living death; the final hours of confinement are called a deathwatch, which usually unfolds in the death house, while the prisoner is confined in the death cell, awaiting the reading of the death warrant, which occurs on the threshold of the death chamber;

- *people*—the team that carries out the execution is the death team or deathwatch team or simply the execution team; those on whom the team labors are of course condemned to death; and, finally,

- *outcome*—death by execution, by whatever means necessary as defined by the jurisdiction in question.

Death constrains death row; death row constrains those condemned to die. Condemned captives-cum-corpses suffer an existence rather than a way of life—they are the living dead until the execution team can "get them dead," to paraphrase one prison warden. That such an existence brings psychological devastation in its wake hardly requires elaboration.

Donald Cabana, a former warden with considerable experience working with the condemned, tells us that death row "is a place that exacts a toll in human destruction."[2] Any death row. All death rows. Always. And a heavy toll, at that. Charlie Jones, warden at Alabama's Atmore Prison, concurs. Jones, like Cabana, has run a solitary-confinement type death row and has overseen a number of executions. He states bluntly that death row reforms, ultimately, are cosmetic, even though he takes a legitimate pride in reforms he has personally instituted in Alabama. "I don't give a damn what you give him," he states uncompromisingly, "you've done some damage" by the sheer fact of confining the prisoner under sentence of death.[3] That damage affects the keeper and the kept, Cabana and Jones agree, although each acknowledges that the heavier burden by far falls upon the condemned. In this chapter we examine this damage by turning our attention first to the prisoners, later to the staff. In the chapters comprising the next section, we will examine the human dimensions of the killing and dying, the taking and the yielding of life that is at the heart of the death penalty.

With only rare exceptions, condemned prisoners are demoralized by their bleak confinement and defeated by the awesome prospect of death by execution. Worn down in small and almost imperceptible ways, they gradually but inexorably become less than fully human. At the end, the prisoners are helpless pawns of the modern execution drill. They give in, give up, and submit; yielding themselves to the execution team and the machinery of death.

The reforms examined in the preceding chapter do nothing to reduce the dehumanization experienced by condemned prisoners. In no instance in even the most extensively reformed death row are condemned prisoners prepared in any way for the ordeal they must face. And as executions occur with increasing frequency, a trend that has gathered considerable momentum in recent years, there is every reason to believe that conditions of confinement on death rows will continue to become more restrictive. I noted in the first edition of this book that a return to a standard regime of solitary confinement was a real possibility. Oklahoma's H-Unit, reviewed in the preceding chapter, stands as a monument to this troubling trend.

Deathwatch regimes remain as they have been throughout this century, retaining vestiges of confinement practices from centuries gone by. No death row reforms undertaken to date affect the deathwatch, the period that culminates death row confinement and ends in the execution of the prisoner (see Part III). This period continues to be one of virtually unmitigated solitary confinement under conditions of total security. As we shall see, the stress of life under sentence of death reaches its zenith during the deathwatch.

LIVING ON DEATH ROW: THE
PSYCHOLOGY OF HUMAN WAREHOUSING

The bleak quality of life on all death rows, reformed and unreformed, reflects their common goal: human storage. This goal dictates that condemned prisoners be treated essentially as bodies kept alive to be killed. This concern for preserving the body without regard for the quality of life reaches an extreme in suicide prevention efforts that amount to treating the person like a piece of meat.

Philip Brasfield, for example, reported that a suicidal prisoner on death row in Texas, where Brasfield himself was also confined while under sentence of death, was

> placed in a straightjacket that was left open at the back to secure him to a bare mattress on the bunk. In addition, handcuffs were placed on his wrists. A crash helmet much like a motorcyclist would wear, was placed on his head and there he lay for weeks, helpless, alone, and drugged. The care and feeding he received was from the inmate porters. At times, he'd call for assistance for over an hour before a guard would open the door and untie him so he could urinate.[4]

Similar procedures apply to inmates whose mental health problems present trouble. On the reformed death row I studied (see Chapter 3), an inmate testified to these procedures.

> Should any individual with psychiatric problems present a problem [to staff], his cell will be stripped of all belongings (including clothing and hygiene items), and he is subject to be chained to the cell's bare steel bunk. This has happened to me, personally, and I have seen the same happen to other men.

Yet another example of preserving the body but ignoring the person was related to me by Alvin Bronstein of the American Civil Liberties Union's (ACLU's) National Prison Project. One of his condemned clients required triple-bypass heart surgery but refused treatment. Officials allegedly urged the prisoner to undergo surgery so he could be alive for his execution, at one point asking Bronstein to argue their case with his reluctant client. Bronstein declined. The prisoner subsequently died of a heart attack.[5]

Daily procedures on death row embody the storage premise quite explicitly. "Neat and efficient," in the words of social scientists Jackson and Christian, these procedures are tellingly described in terms that objectify the prisoners. For instance, Jackson and Christian tell us that

> death row inmates get showers one at a time. The noun takes a verb form: "I'm going to shower the row now," the guard says. "I'm opening one-row cell 13 to shower Jones." One is "being showered" rather than "taking a shower." The option is the guards', always. The same thing happens with recreation; it becomes a verb: "I'm going to recreate group three

now," the guard says, meaning he will let one-quarter of the men on the row out of their cells and into the small dayroom.[6]

The immediate result of such efficient storage arrangements is a radical reduction in the prisoner's privacy. Indeed, prisoners typically claim that on death row one has no privacy at all. In the words of Caryl Chessman, who spent twelve years on San Quentin's death row before his execution in 1962,

> You have no privacy. Day and night, you're watched closely. Having claimed it, the state is jealous of your life. Every possible safeguard is taken to prevent you from cheating the executioner—by digging, cutting, or assaulting your way to stolen freedom; by self-destruction; by fleeing to the world of the insane. You've come to the wrong place if curious eyes and the probing beams of flashlights make you uneasy.[7]

A present-day death row prisoner seconded Chessman's observations, reminding us that nothing essential has changed on the row:

> They read your mail. Take a visit, they're standing over your shoulder. They know everything you're saying. You shower and they're watching you. At night they're shining flashlights in your cell. You never have a free moment.[8]

Regular prisoners are permitted to develop an informal society and, to some extent at least, police themselves.[9] But the margin for failures of control on death row is exceedingly narrow. The prisoners are watched closely—though not continuously, as in the death house—and without apology.[10]

Held powerless on death row, condemned prisoners also come to feel powerless—that is, alone and vulnerable. Many—as many as seven out of every ten[11]—deteriorate in measurable ways. All are to some degree weakened and demoralized. Those condemned prisoners who reach the deathwatch, examined in Chapters 6 and 7, are subjected to constant surveillance and experience complete loss of privacy. Made susceptible by their death row confinement, they collapse under the substantial pressure of the deathwatch. In the final analysis, they are reduced to dehumanized objects that are mere pawns in the modern execution process.

Powerlessness

Close confinement combined with almost constant surveillance renders death row inmates powerless to alter or influence their daily existence in any meaningful way. Their lives are monotonous and lonely, and they are predictably bored, tense, and depressed. Chronic irritability and periodic lapses in personal control can leave prisoners feeling alienated from themselves. The prisoner comes to see himself as essentially a stranger in a strange land.[12] Powerlessness and its emotional sequelae, established in the *Harries* case as key factors in the cruelty of Tennessee's death row (see Chapter 3), affect prisoners on all death rows. The reason is straightforward: All death rows are, at bottom, sterile, eventless, oppressive environments that demoralize their inhabitants as a direct function of the setting's emphasis on custodial repression.

Death rows offer deadening, unchanging routines as a central feature of existence. On Louisiana's death row, at Angola Prison, "The occasional call-outs, and mealtimes, are the only contact a condemned prisoner has with other inmates. The dominant activity of death row is shower time."[13] Most of the prisoner's time is spent in the cell, vegetating before a TV set or leaning against the cell bars wielding a peeper in a strained effort to glimpse another human face. "Men in isolated cells often grow weary of talking to walls, windows and bars. A human face, even if viewed through a makeshift mirror, adds meaning to a destitute existence."[14]

The isolated life on death row produces, in many inmates, a kind of self-imposed retreat from others. Many prisoners even refrain from outdoor exercise, the only chance they get to shake off the isolation of their cells and speak directly with other inmates. A death row security officer at Angola tells us that "Death row inmates don't go out on the yard too regular. They have the privilege but they don't take advantage of it. I talk to them and try to get them to go out, to get a little fresh air and sunshine, but they seldom do."[15] These prisoners add self-imposed isolation to the state-imposed isolation of the death row regime, consigning themselves to a life that is, in the view of one death row inmate on San Quentin's death row, a kind of nightmare version of the movie *Groundhog Day*, a comedy in which Bill Murray's character, Phil, lives the same day over and over again. The movie is funny and even insightful; Phil uses his redundant existence to perfect his coping skills, land the woman of his choice, and go on to become a better person. The story line as applied to death row is quite different. There, each day is a redundant experience of failure and rejection—of being powerless to effect change, cut off from supportive human contact, vulnerable to others in a world where people want you dead. Each day the condemned are a little more dead—more like passive objects and less like autonomous beings—than the day before. The inmate who compared life on death row to the Murray movie had, for a time, a column that others would put on the Internet for him. His Internet pseudonym: Dead Man Talking.

The experience of powerlessness—of being an object imbedded in a routine—is magnified on solitary-confinement death rows, in which warehousing for death takes its most blatant, unvarnished form. The barren dimensions of the condemned prisoners' lives on such death rows are evident in the empty diversions they employ to occupy their time. In the prisoners' words,

■ I've got so bored at times, I used to hook cockroaches together, sort of like they was a team of mules, to drag a matchbox around on the floor to pass time. I mean that may sound weird to you or somebody else, and it might be. Matter of fact I just flushed a little frog down the shit jack the other day that I had back there [in my cell]. It came up through the shit jack. I kept him back there a couple of weeks and I kicked roaches and things to feed him. Just any little old thing. . . . To more or less keep your mind off the damned chair and the things that you're seeing around you. Anything to occupy your mind.

- I got a big dictionary. I look in there and I read—just look at words, I can't even pronounce the words I be looking at, you know, but I read the meaning to them. I like doing stuff like that. It's hard to stay at that thing, you get sleepy—without moving—you can't stay up but an hour at a time, you have to lay back down. I can't seem to settle down in my cell. Like, I spend 23 1/2 hours in there and I can't ever come to peace with myself. It irritates me all the time.[16]

Long hours in the cell are a source of psychological pressure and emotional turmoil. All prisoners experience some pressure; for some, the experience is almost disabling. For example,

I sit in that cell, you know, and it seems like I'm just ready to scream or go crazy or something. And you know, the pressure, it builds up, and it feels like everything is—you're sitting there and things start, you know, not hearing things, things start to coming in your mind. You start to remember certain events that happened, bad things. It just gets to a person. I sit up at night, you know. You just sit there, and it seems like you're going to go crazy. You've got three walls around you and bars in front of you, and you start looking around, you know, and it seems like things are closing in on you. Like last night, when I sit in there and everything's real quiet, things, just a buzzing noise gets to going in my ears. And I sit there, and I consciously think, "Am I going to go crazy?" And the buzzing gets louder; and you sit there and you want to scream and tell somebody to stop it. And most of the time you get up—if I start making some noise in my cell, it will slack off. And it sounds stupid, I know, but it happens. . . . [S]ometimes I wonder if I don't get it stopped, I'm going crazy or something. And you know, maybe tonight when I lay down it's not going to break when I get up and try to make some noise.[17]

Against the suffocating vacuum of the cell, a chance to place a simple order at the commissary can be an exhilarating, liberating experience—a small freedom so sweet it accentuates the bitter constraints that envelop one's life on death row.

They have one day which is a store day. That one day actually is to these people on death row like Christmas and all they actually get is cigarettes and candy or cookies, and that's actually become to be a thing like Christmas. I've surveyed it from watching the guys and everybody gets excited and they are actually more happy on Tuesday when they get that little package. But you see this is actually what we have been reduced to as far as being men, trying to be a man, finally enjoying a little thing like a cookie. To me it's actually absurd, this actually affects me to that point and there is no way out of it, there is no way to rebel against it.[18]

Prisoners on reformed death rows generally have more autonomy than those on solitary-confinement death rows. (I say generally because reformed death rows go through periodic lockdowns, during which the prisoners are kept in solitary confinement as punishment. On the reformed death row I studied, one such lockdown lasted a full five months.) These prisoners normally have the company of their dayroom companions to fall back on, and this can, no doubt, be a source of comfort, giving them a sense of a more normal and at least minimally autonomous daily life. Contact with other prisoners, however, can be a double-edged sword. One's fellows can be a source of pressure, harassment, and sometimes violent victimization, all of which add to feelings of helplessness. As a case in point, on our reformed death row a man was brutally attacked by a fellow prisoner in the dayroom. The victim was paralyzed for life.

Even congenial conversations in dayrooms (for those on reformed death rows) or with men in neighboring cells (for those in solitary confinement) offer only limited opportunities for autonomous action or emotional support. Eventually, one says and does all that one can say and do in the compressed world that is death row. One's social life, as it were, becomes numbingly redundant and oppressive in its own right. It is worth recalling that Sartre's notion of hell was of being confined for eternity with people one despises. For many prisoners, perhaps especially on reformed death rows, the fact that they have "no exit" from other condemned prisoners may make their confinement a kind of hell. It is, in my view, entirely fitting that a wide-ranging anthology of writings from death row goes by the title, *Welcome to Hell*.[19]

The enduring difficulty is that on death row—any death row—everything remains the same. "It's continuously having the same walls, the same bars, the same papers, the same books," said one condemned prisoner. "Nothing changes. Only the outside, the light. We have day and we have night, we have day and then we have night." People become fixtures, as unchanging as the schedule. A paradoxical dependence is bred; routines come to hold in check the very resentments they produce. "If something changes, it's like a shock to you," observed one inmate. "You'll hear them yelling and screaming and everything else."[20] With the inevitable return of routine, the inmates retreat once more into the familiar, however impoverished it may be.

Loneliness

Though familiar, the routine on death row offers little real comfort—to the prisoners, that is. For the staff, routine can become an end in itself, a means of distancing themselves from the prisoners. Too often, the staff become insensitive to the human tragedies unfolding among the condemned; they seem unwilling or unable to offer meaningful support. "Caring," observed one group of researchers studying death row officers, "is simply not part of the job."[21] "Nobody is going to help you," confirmed an inmate. "Nobody is going to give you a kind word. Nobody is going to ask you, 'How's it going, how's your day? Is everything coming out okay?' You're totally ignored." Nor do other prison officials fill the emotional void. Like the occasional citizen's groups that tour death rows, "they just look in the cage and they go away."[22] Though these are almost surely overstatements on the part of the inmates—

some officers and officials say they care, and try to show it—they indicate widely and firmly held perceptions of the social reality on death row. Almost to a man, condemned prisoners feel abandoned by the prison staff, denied simple human compassion, treated "as if already dead."[23]

Feeling abandoned by the prison staff often goes hand in hand with feeling abandoned by the world. The custodial regime not only insulates guards from prisoners, it also isolates prisoners from the moral and social community of the outside world. Inmates suffer "a symbolic isolation that comes from living with the fact that 12 members of your community have determined that you are a worthless person who should no longer be permitted to exist." Prisoners may feel "so isolated that it is nearly impossible to share a religion with those on the outside." As time passes and they gradually exhaust their appeals, prisoners may feel further removed from the world of the living. One reason is that fewer people are apt to write or visit in support of a lost (or losing) cause.[24] Another is that failed appeals mark progressive stages in the killing and dying process, "pull[ing] layers of legal legitimacy over a corpse that hasn't quit moving and complaining yet."[25]

Their isolation on death row contributes to the weakening and often the dissolution of the prisoners' relationships with their loved ones. In one condemned man's words, "While most people rely on their families for their major source of support, it is not at all uncommon for this resource to be unavailable to death row prisoners."[26] One reflection of this sad fact is an empty visiting room. "On the death row visiting day," Jackson and Christian tell us, "the room is usually empty. It is rare for even two death row inmates to get a visit at the same time."[27]

Visits are a precious but rare—and precarious—commodity in the eyes of the condemned. Visits are not matters of right but rather privileges that can be—and, in fact, regularly are—suspended at the discretion of prison officials.[28] Officials discourage visits through a variety of restrictive rules and regulations. For example, visits can take place only on certain days and for limited periods of time. This creates logistical problems for the prisoners' loved ones. And though no physical contact is allowed during typical visits, the staff nevertheless carefully monitor all visits. What is worse, after all visits, inmates are shackled and subjected to thorough body searches, even when the visits involved no physical contact. For some prisoners, the pain and humiliation engendered by such treatment outweigh the pleasure of the visit. One prisoner could barely suppress his rage when describing his experience with visits.

Your people come to this place. You go down and you sit down for an hour or whatever you stayed and you get your mind away from this place. And just as soon as you come in after having enjoyed yourself for a little bit, just as soon as you get up from out there and walk in here, they strip you, look up your asshole and in your mouth and strip search you and handcuff you behind your back and drag you back up that hall. Well, you see, they just broke your whole fucking visit. You would have been better off, in a way, if you'd just stayed in your cell and if you could have slept

through that hour. . . . I mean that's the kind of attitude that leaves you
with after they fuck with you. Knowing your people drove and went
through all this trouble to come see you, to give you an hour or something. Then they have taken the fucking time to figure out a way to fuck
it up for you.[29]

Condemned prisoners tend to see the death row regime as a calculated
and gratuitous assault on their humanity. For them, the physical setting is puni-
tively spartan; rules and regulations are means to inflict pain.[30] The intrusive
procedures associated with visits do much to fuel the prisoners' angry perception that their keepers mean them harm.

Aside from humiliating searches, the rules regulating visits with condemned
prisoners make these encounters strained and potentially divisive. Visiting
arrangements for Florida's condemned, under which visitors are continuously
observed, have been found to impede the flow of information and emotional
support between families and condemned prisoners, "thereby sustaining rather
than alleviating feelings of isolation and uncertainty."[31] The visiting routine on
Alabama's death row frustrates any attempt at congenial conversation. The visiting situation in Alabama, as I stated after observing visits there firsthand, is
more akin to a wake than to a supportive family gathering.

The priorities on [Alabama's] death row seem almost unforgivable in regard to visits. The routine surrounding visits might be compared with the
preparations for a funeral. Noncontact visits, in particular, seem peculiarly
reminiscent of the viewing at a wake. The inmate sits alone in an enclosed
chamber, neatly dressed and carefully groomed, almost as if on display for
his loved ones. The need to shout across the barrier separating the inmate
and his visitors precludes intimate conversation and results in awkward
interludes of silence. Visitors speak as much among themselves as with
their prisoner; they appear nervous and out of place. The prisoners, too,
seem ill at ease.[32]

It is hard to be natural when yelling to loved ones or when officers are looking over your shoulder, perhaps eavesdropping as well. In turn, truncated conversations and awkward interludes of silence can leave people feeling confused
and lonely: What did she *really* mean by this pause or that phrase? The prisoner, on returning to his cell, is left to wonder. And worry.

As a general rule, states Abu-Jamal, the condemned prisoner in Pennsylvania, visits on death row "are an exercise in humiliation." These demoralizing
visits are, moreover, experienced by many inmates as an *intentional* effort to
destroy the human relationships that sustain condemned prisoners. "In Pennsylvania, as in many other death states, noncontact visits are the rule. It is not
just a security rule; it is a policy and structure that attempts to sever emotional
connection by denying physical connection between the visitor and the inmate."[33] The empty existence on death row may, in any case, render prisoners
mute during visits. They and their loved ones live in utterly different worlds,
with little or no common ground to draw on to sustain communication

(though more accommodating visiting conditions would certainly improve matters). After years of noncontact visits and, for many inmates, ultimately, no visits at all, the result is that "Prisoners are as isolated psychologically as they are temporally and spatially. By state action, they become 'dead' to those who know and love them, and therefore dead to themselves. For who are people, but for their relations and relationships?"[34] Unrewarding visits thus reflect and reinforce the prisoners' basic sense of alienation from the world of the living. As a result, most condemned prisoners describe themselves as abandoned by the free world and left to their own devices to endure their confinement.[35]

Vulnerability

Held powerless under conditions of indifference and neglect, prisoners tend to resent their guards, who are the nearest at hand to blame for their helpless and lonely state. Prisoners also come to feel vulnerable to harm by their keepers. Alone and defenseless when in their cells, living at all times in harsh and deprived conditions, convenient objects of contempt, condemned prisoners feel vulnerable to abuse from their keepers. Condemned prisoners are usually held in the most secluded quarters of the prison—a condition that, absent effective supervision of the guard force, invites, indeed almost authorizes, abuse. Their stark vulnerability may be apparent from the moment prisoners set foot on death row. One prisoner put the matter like this:

> The biggest fear is when you walk onto this place. I've seen one man walk out there and he stood right there and he broke down and cried. I've seen more come in here and live three days and start praying. I've seen them come in here and cuss the day they was born because of fear. I've seen grown men come in here and get down and pray like kids. And cry.[36]

Condemned prisoners see death row as a law unto itself, one based on the premise "Might makes right." As one prisoner observed, "They can do anything they want to you. Who's going to stop them?" Power, many say, emanates from the butt end of the baton or billy club that is often standard equipment for death row officers. This weapon, sometimes tellingly called an axe handle by the prisoners, functions as both a symbol of violence and an instrument of social control. As one prisoner observed,

> You have to more or less watch what you say to these guys because if they want to get you back, they could easily do that. You're on your way out to the yard, the guy could say as soon as you get out of the center—around that little bend—where the rest of the guys couldn't see you, they could easily claim "well, he turned around and hit me," "he turned around and I thought he was attacking me," or "he pushed me." And one whack with one of those axe handles up against your head, if you're not going to be dead, you're going to be insane for the rest of your life. And then you're not going to be able to help no one. . . . I am really afraid of that. I'm trying to hold on to my own common sense, you know, because I feel that is one of the main factors that I do have that is still mine. My

knowledge that I can think and my ability to learn and do my own research on my own case. I feel that if I got hit with one of those sticks, I wouldn't have that much sense. So, I live in constant fear of that actually all the time."[37]

In a curious throwback to an earlier—and more primitive—era in penology, San Quentin's death row features guards armed with machine guns patrolling the catwalks and the outdoor recreation area. To my knowledge, San Quentin is unique in this regard; no other prison in the United States features armed officers within the prison's perimeter. San Quentin's death row, intimidating even to hardened convicts, is housed in Eastblock, a cell block that has been described by one condemned prisoner as "cavernous, dark, loud and smelly." Keepers and kept, we learn, move about in hazy, "subdued light" that is "filtered by dirt and grime on the windows" of the exterior walls, adding an element of almost surreal gloom. Cells are small and cramped, bare and uninviting. Life outside these tiny habitats always brings with it a tangible presumption of risk. "All the Guards that are not on the gunrails are required to wear bullet proof vests; in case there is an incident where shots are fired, they will have protection."[38]

Condemned prisoners at San Quentin have access to outside recreation, but they must undergo strip-searches to get there and then must contend with the danger posed by their fellow inmates as well as that posed by armed officers, who shoot into the enclosed recreation area with some regularity in efforts to control prisoner behavior.

> The first time I went to the yard, a few days after I arrived in Eastblock, I was walking around the yard to get my bearings and to check out my environment a bit. As I made a few circuits around the compound, I noticed the concrete had a lot of holes in it. Later, I was leaning against the wall talking with one of the guys and I commented on the poor workmanship of the concrete. The guy looked at me as if I was drooling on myself. He snickered and said, "That's not poor workmanship, it's because of poor marksmanship." It turns out that all the chips I had noticed were from the bullets fired into the yard during altercations. It was at that point that I began to wonder if I really wanted to hang out in a place where part of the exercise program was dodging bullets.[39]

The yard on San Quentin's death row also provides an unimpeded view of the death house, which for some inmates is frightening and depressing, and reason enough to stay in one's cell.

> I think that what finally made up my mind for me is the "Chimney." Everyday that I went to the yard, I would end up leaning against the wall. As I leaned there, I could watch what was going on around me. At the end of the row of yard compounds is where the Gas Chamber is located. Sticking out of the roof of the Chamber is a huge green pipe, used to vent the poison gas after an execution is carried out. I would catch myself staring at this pipe everyday and wondering if that pipe would someday

be venting the poison gas used to execute me. It was soon after this that I decided that I didn't really want to hang out in the yard any longer.[40]

The self-isolation of prisoners on death row, then, may plausibly feature elements of retreat into the comfort of routine as well as retreat from the threat of danger that lurks outside the cell door. Yet the cell can provide but a limited sanctuary, since it is policed by officers, who can enter at will, bringing the threat of violence with them. At San Quentin, at least, the vulnerability of prisoners in cells is highlighted when officers on catwalks shoot onto the tiers to maintain order, with some bullets and debris making their way into the cells. This may not happen often, but from my own visits to San Quentin's death row I know that it does happen, and that it is a source of fear among the prisoners.

Abuse, including violence, may be implicitly if unintentionally authorized in the training of many death row officers. Colin Turnbull's research revealed that death row officers' training emphasized "combat duty" and made "no attempt to help the guard approach the extremely difficult task of maintaining appropriate human relations [with condemned prisoners]."[41] This surely applies to the armed officers at San Quentin, if not indeed to their colleagues in bulletproof vests patrolling the tiers. The profound suspiciousness of the officers on the reformed death row I studied, a suspiciousness demanded by their superior officer, promoted a combat mentality among many of these officers. Cabana, when he was warden at Parchman Prison in Mississippi, praised the custodial skills of officers, particularly those on death row, who looked for threat in even such innocent-sounding activities as Bible study.[42] Informal socialization on the job, moreover, is apt to alert the guards of any death row to the potential dangers of their work, reinforcing the apparent value of a cold and even pugnacious stance with the inmates. One prisoner put this matter plainly:

> They got us one sorry motherfucker right here and that's the only way I know how to put it. One of the most sorriest motherfuckers right here that could be working in a penitentiary. Now he comes to work and sits his ass down right up there, and sits there and tries to figure out a way to fuck somebody back there on death row. And he's the one that shows the others how to do us. . . . It's just like father teach son—that's their routine. When a guard comes here, instead of giving him [formal] training and everything and teach him how he should cope with these things in prison and stuff, they bring him right up here, put him under one of the worst sons-of-bitches there is here. Then father teach son. Then it's just a very short period of time until they have built up this attitude and they look at you the same way he does. . . . Now I been in down here since way back. So a whole lot about the outside, I don't know nothing about it. But about these sons-of-bitches, I do. And that's why I say, when a guy come into here and he say, "Well, there goes a good guard." Shit. It won't be three days before he's just as sorry as the next motherfucker.[43]

One can readily imagine the threat posed by a "sorry motherfucker" with a gun, as in the unique and troubling case offered by San Quentin.

Many condemned prisoners believe that their keepers, with or without provocation, would resort to violence.[44] Indeed, some prisoners' fear of violence from their keepers merges with their fear of execution. One prisoner, visibly afraid, had this to say:

> When you're on death row and you're laying down in your cell and you hear a door cracking, you'll think of where it comes from. When you hear it crack. And when you hear the keys and everything, when something like this happens, the keys come through here: I'm up. I'm up because you don't know when it's going to take place. The courts give you an execution date, that's true. But you don't know what's going to take place between then and your execution date. You don't know when you're going to be moved around to the silent cell over here. That's right down the hall, what they call a waiting cell. You don't know when you're going to be moved down there. And this keeps you jumpy, and it keeps you nervous, and it keeps you scared.[45]

Such fear, which borders at times on raw panic, may be more prevalent among condemned prisoners than one would imagine. It bespeaks the profound vulnerability these prisoners feel, and the deep distrust they have for their keepers.

Coping and the Crucible of Deterioration

Many condemned prisoners describe death row as a human pressure cooker. Tension is pervasive, pernicious, and, in varying degrees, disabling. Symptoms of depression and lifelessness are common. Deterioration in some form affects many, if not most, death row prisoners at various points in their confinement. "The main thing," said one condemned prisoner, "is the mental pressure: you're always depressed. But I think another main thing is the physical deterioration of the body. You sit up there and you just feel yourself getting weaker, you know? Your back hurts, ya know? You're sick a lot—cold and low blood. You lose your energy."[46] The threat of deterioration can be a source of considerable anxiety, leading prisoners to question their capacity to maintain their psychological equilibrium. "I'm already walking on a hairline of being sane and insane," observed one prisoner, "I could fall either way at any time."[47]

Some prisoners do in fact become psychiatric casualties of death row. I was able to study one such man who had, in the brutally frank words of a fellow prisoner, "done cold left himself." Our exchange on this man's history of deterioration went as follows:

> When I first come down here, he talked good, he could carry on a good conversation, he could talk real good. We used to talk to each other, you know. But it's got to where now sometimes at night he would be sitting down there in his cell and he'd tear up pieces of cloth all night long, tear his mattress all night long, get at the bar and yell out "Mama, Mama," continuously at the top of his lungs. And you can't sleep with

that there going on. Yell out other people's names and so forth. I think, I think he needs help, a lot more than what he's getting up there.

Do you think it's a psychiatric condition now?

I think it's worked into that, yeah. Because every time somebody mentions the chair—every time someone mentions this thing in here, walking around it or anything, he flies off the handle.[48]

Few inmates were supportive of this man, who had become an irritant. Others resented him because they thought he was faking mental illness. A few taunted him, at least until his symptoms made it apparent that he was profoundly disturbed.

Anytime someone mentions the electric chair, he gets real uptight?

Yeah, he gets uptight. One of the inmates will joke with him about it, or say something to him in a way, I call it smart cracking, just to see if he's going to do it again. Which isn't right, but they do it. They yell at him; they say something like, "Hey, he's the first to go" and a bunch of other stuff that they make up and say to him. This'll trigger him off. I mean, it would trigger me off.

Do you think they want to trigger him off?

They do sometimes. But they got to where, I don't know, that's been about a year or something ago, and he hasn't got out of it yet. They've quit joking as far as, you know, revving him up. But he hasn't got better. It's just with him, it's just a thing that's with him and he does, he needs, he needs help, I mean, you know, a doctor's help.[49]

By the time I interviewed this man (for an earlier book), he impressed me as being "only a shell of a person." I caught him in a lucid period, one of few. He'd been transferred to the local jail in his hometown to pursue legal matters, and the respite from death row gave him a second wind, one long enough at least to report on his psychological demise. Here is our exchange.

This place here just caves in on you. The same thing every day, that just stacks up on top of you, ya know what I mean? So I got out from under it, ya know what I mean? Like a brand new life, man. Like I just came in yesterday. I feel relaxed a lot more now, and I can hold a better conversation with you because of the time I spent in court. . . .

But before I started going to court and things, my mind just flips out on me. . . . I done flipped out three or four times in different tiers, you know? My mind just right up and leave me. I didn't expect the thing to happen. And everything just, you know, how you just go. I can't explain it and everything that has taken place, but I just flipped out.

This happens from out of nowhere?

Just out of nowhere. Just flipped out . . . I stayed up for weeks at a time. I don't know why, I just couldn't go to sleep. . . . I'd be depressed and lost. Like the officers would come by and they'd talk to me, some of them, and say I was lost, man, say "it was like you was in another world, man" ya know? I say, "yeah, that's the way I felt, like I was in another world." I felt sometimes for weeks at a time that I wasn't even here."[50]

During his weeks of mental absence, this prisoner would hear voices that would tell him to set fire to his cell. He would stop eating. He would hold loud conversations with himself and with his neighbors, some of whom would tease and taunt him out of frustration. The only thing missing from his life was help, from professionals or peers.

I do not know what has become of this clearly disturbed prisoner. The subjects of that book—and this one—were given anonymity, so I never connected the names of persons with the interviews I conducted. It is possible that this man has been executed. Mentally ill people like him have been put to death in the past and continue to be today.[51] We may expect more such executions over the coming years. Mentally ill prisoners are particularly vulnerable to environmental pressures, pressures that are growing worse on death rows across our nation as the pace of executions picks up. Marginally adjusted prisoners will see their coping deficits shade into psychoses; psychotics will see their mental disorders reach extreme states of distress.[52] All the while, the other death row prisoners will see in these tragic human breakdowns living reminders of what the future may well hold for them as their execution dates inexorably draw near.

A Living Death

The cumulative impact of death row, as noted by the court in the *Harries* case, is an "overall sense of defeat."[53] The sources of this defeat emanate from the various conditions of confinement we have reviewed. In the words of Rideau and Wikberg, both inmates at Angola Prison and authors of noted essays on that prison's death row, the typical condemned prisoner's experiences can be summed up as follows:

> Frustration gnaws at his gut. Loneliness embraces him daily, driving him deeper into a world of nothingness. Fear—a constant, never-changing fear—eats away at his sanity. Two years ago, three years ago, today, tomorrow—the same, all the same; there is no inkling that the torture will end. Hope has become merely a flickering candle whose light pales quickly before the all-engulfing feeling of devastation.[54]

Abu-Jamal, an African-American, draws attention to the role of racism on death row. He gives the stark example of differential conditions available for recreation, a key outlet for death row prisoners. "The cages were for the blacks on death row. The open yards were for the whites on the row." In his view, this could be no accident. "The blacks, due to racist insensitivity and sheer hatred, were condemned to awaiting death in indignity. The event provided an excellent view, in microcosm, of the mentality of the criminal system of injustice, suffused by the toxin of racism."[55] Evidence from other sources indicates that racism may be a factor in some of the uglier encounters between staff and inmates on death row. As one inmate observed just after his arrival on death row, "I was looking at the chair and they said. "Bring him on in here." They showed me the chair and they said, "Yeah, we are going to sit your ass in there." You know, they were calling me nigger and shit. They were asking why I did what I done and did I want to die . . ."[56]

The cumulative destructiveness of death row for minority prisoners Abu-Jamal expressed this way:

> Mix in solitary confinement, around-the-clock lock-in, no-contact visits, no prison jobs, no educational programs by which to grow, psychiatric "treatment" facilities designed only to drug you into a coma; ladle in hostile, overtly racist prison guards and staff; add the weight of the falling away of family ties, and you have all the fixings for a stressful psychic stew designed to deteriorate, to erode one's humanity—designed, that is, by the state, with full knowledge of its effects.[57]

Research on life under sentence of death has not systematically explored the role of racism in shaping the experiences of African-American inmates on death row, though the problem of racism in our society and in our prisons, not to mention in the administration of the death penalty in times past and today, is well known.

Putting aside any unique problems that may be borne by black prisoners, the literature on the subject of reactions to death row confinement draws attention to a pervasive and profoundly human problem of hopelessness. In one prisoner's words,

> You can hear its empty sound in the clanging of the steel doors, in the rattle of chains, in the body searches, in the lack of privacy, in the night sounds of death row, and you can see it in the eyes of the guards who never really look at you, but are always watching to see that you do not commit suicide.[58]

The "normal" reaction in such an environment, observed the noted psychiatrist Seymour Halleck, who testified as an expert in the *Harries* case, features "depression and lethargy."[59] (Harries himself showed signs of psychological deterioration that a number of experts attributed to the conditions of his confinement on death row, an attribution supported by a body of empirical research and accepted by the court.[60]) Prisoners of other death rows bear out this observation, describing death row as a "living death" and themselves as the "living dead." As one prisoner poignantly observed, "You need love and it just ain't there. It leaves you empty inside, dead inside. Really, you just stop caring."[61]

Death row prisoners, to restate Halleck's point, give up on life as we normally know it. They exist rather than live. That existence, however, can be deceptive to outside observers, even to correctional officers and officials on the scene. For on a social level, death row prisoners, and, to a lesser extent, their keepers, create a make-believe world premised on denying the reality of the death penalty. Prisoners talk tough and act cool, posturing even within the cells that cage them, desperate to deceive themselves and those around them.

An intriguing example is provided by reactions to the passing of the old year and the coming of the new, which is accompanied by New Year's Eve celebrations on at least some death rows; celebrations that are not entirely unlike those taking place outside the prison. One inmate found humor in the situation.

> I am always amused on New Year's Eve. At the stroke of midnight, a lot of guys will start cheering and whistling. I could never figure out why. There is a cartoon that I am reminded of whenever the guys start cheering. It's called "Mr. Boffo." A regular theme of "Mr. Boffo" is something called, "People [Unc]lear On The Concept." Whenever I hear the cheering, I think to myself, here is the essence of people not clear on the concept. Since time is something that we all have very little of (on Death Row) I think that to cheer the passing of time is one of those bizarre ironies that are common in a situation like this.[62]

Cheering the *passing* of time on death row is one thing; still being alive is a kind of victory. It would be an equally bizarre irony if the death row inmates cheered the *coming* of a new year, as most New Year's revelers do. This, too, would be an example of people unclear on the concept, because the new year does not bring a fresh start for condemned prisoners so much as it brings them closer to death. In either case, any form of New Year's celebration gives a profoundly misleading image of death row to the outside world. People who conclude from such celebrations that life is carefree or easy on death row are, to echo the sentiments of our inmate, "unclear on the concept," not unlike those who once thought that the singing of field slaves was an expression of contentment with their lot in life.[63]

Humor is used by death row prisoners to bolster a facade of manliness, as well as to distract attention from inner doubts and turmoil. The prisoner who found humor in the curious cheerfulness of condemned men on New Year's Eve may thereby find some relief from his own anxieties about his impending mortality; the revelers almost certainly get some relief from inner turmoil through their celebration, especially if they are able to secure "home-brew"— homemade alcohol—to ring in the new year. In both instances we see denial, and denial is a psychological gambit that always comes home to roost. As one prisoner of a solitary-confinement death row put it,

> The row ain't serious; it's a lot of funny things happening on the row. Everybody seeing who can be the funniest, you know. So, I contribute in that there, too. I figure if I contribute in that, that will keep me going halfway. But I figure now when things really get hard and everybody stops joking, that's when you are going to see about ten people just bug out from the jump. All of us are going to bug out sooner or later.[64]

Things "get hard," to complete the prisoner's point, when someone is executed—as happens these days with increasing regularity. These executions would seem to be both the logical and the psychological culmination of death row confinement.

WORKING ON DEATH ROW

Tension and Fear

The condemned prisoner's life on death row is grim, a fact that is well known to their more thoughtful keepers. "For nearly five years," states Donald Cabana, a former warden of Mississippi's Parchman Prison, "I watched in amazement, wondering how men survived the rigors of being confined to a cell for twenty-three hours a day" in the "forlorn place" that was the death row under his charge. The lot of those who guard death row is singularly unrewarding as well. "Just working in the place was degrading," states Cabana, in reference to a time when Parchman's death row was an "environment . . . charged with anger and open hatred between convicts and guards." More recently, under Cabana's guidance, death row took on a more professional ambiance, staffed by officers who "did their jobs well" and "treated the condemned men with respect." Even so, "Little Alcatraz," the revealing nickname of Parchman's death row, remained a dehumanizing place for captive and captor alike. Even the best death row is "a different world" from the rest of the prison, to quote Cabana; a place that takes some of the humanity of "both the keepers and the kept."[65]

Work on death row is a stressful and often frightening assignment that too readily lends itself to indifferent and even abusive treatment of the condemned prisoners. Proactive wardens like Cabana can reduce the harms, but the problem lies in the structure of the job. Death row guards are enjoined solely to preserve the bodies of the condemned—to feed them in their cells or in common areas, to conduct them to out-of-cell activities, to watch them at all times. In large measure, the officers are reduced to intrusive waiters and unwanted escorts. Moreover, the death row guard's role is in some respects an impersonal and hence symbolically dehumanized one: The officer's character as a distinctive person, though not stripped from him, is rendered largely irrelevant to how he carries out his work as a death row officer. Not surprisingly, like the prisoners, the guards are bored and tense much of the time. Some even report being depressed by their circumscribed, thankless jobs.

Relations between guards and inmates have been described as either overtly hostile, with harassment and counterharassment a common form of exchange,[66] or impersonal, with little or no contact.[67] (Death rows can also vary between these extremes, sometimes hitting a decent middle ground, as appears to have happened in Parchman's "Little Alcatraz.") To be sure, the condemned and their keepers usually accommodate one another to some degree, and a few death row officers are even able to transcend the limitations of their role and develop normal, if generally superficial, human relationships with death row prisoners. Nonetheless, death row officers are, for the most part, professional custodians; they may be tactful and even courteous, but not "chummy."[68] "They don't make friends," said one prisoner of such guards, "they just do their job and go home."[69] Tension is high, affecting officers and inmates alike.

Neither is fear of violence restricted to inmates. Officers, too, feel vulnerable as they go about the work of guarding condemned prisoners. Officers regularly cite the dangers posed by the prisoners as justification for the custodial restrictions on death row. Guards are quick to point out that condemned prisoners are men of proven violence with little to lose in trying to escape. It is widely believed that because the prisoners face execution and often live in the most depriving environment the prison has to offer, they feel free to attack or even kill guards. What more can we do to them? worried officers ask. The guards thus come to fear the potential violence of their captives just as the prisoners fear the potential violence of their keepers. Too often, shared fears give way to mutual hate.[70] The peace on death row can seem precarious indeed.

Fears harbored by officers may be especially pronounced on reformed death rows, because the inmates are out of their cells in small groups and hence are a more potent threat. The security-related concerns of many of the officers on our reformed death row appeared to be rooted, at least in part, in fear.

For some of these officers, my interviews revealed, fear lurks in the background. Said one officer, "You know in the back of your mind who you're dealing with, what they are, but still you don't bring it to the surface." Other officers spoke of conscious fears. The prisoners, they believe, are violent men bent on escape. These officers work under constant pressure. As one said, "They will hurt you to get away. You've got to watch them all the time. You know if these guys get a chance, you're gone. They'll kill you. They've all killed before." In the words of another officer, "There was always that thought in my mind, 'If they ever get out of here, I'm as good as dead.' I feel they don't have anything to lose. If we get in their way, they just get rid of us quick." Security procedures are in place to restrain the prisoners and protect the officers, but they fail to reassure. Assessed against a backdrop of fear, regulations appear flawed. "If they want to escape, they can," said one officer with an air of futility. "Somebody's going to slip up somewhere along the line."

The officers' fears are not indiscriminate. There are periods of high risk and hence high anxiety, though different officers expressed different concerns. For one, it was "taking inmates to recreation" that required extreme caution. For another, "Counts are scary. I worry there'll be one hiding 'round the corner and I'll have to go and find him." According to a third, "Open areas bother me. I'm uncomfortable working in the open area [in the hall] near the control station." One officer, though calm on the surface, found almost *any* occasion a source of fear because he was intimidated by the prisoners' crimes. He readily admitted that some prisoners were less fierce than one would expect, given their crimes, but he took no comfort in this. "You can't judge a book by its cover. You've never seen him mad."

A troubling and pervasive sign of fear is that officers see themselves as potential hostages. "The inmates constantly threaten to take hostages," said one officer. Some of it is joking, he acknowledged, but the risk of one day becoming a hostage "is very real." That fearful eventuality preoccupies a number of officers, who envision scenarios that would result in their being taken hostage. A common fear is that a harried, and thus distracted, control officer will open the wrong door at the wrong time, unleashing a group of inmates on a defenseless hall officer. The officers respond to such intimidating contingencies with a grim fatalism, taking the attitude that they should do what they can to control their own lives and let other matters sort themselves out.

> Anybody can get attacked or taken hostage at any time. But I just have a job to do, and I just go ahead and do it and hope that nothing will happen. I just try to do my job, be alert and observant, and nothing should go wrong. If it does, I'll just have to deal with it.

As another officer put it, "You know who you're dealing with, *what* you're dealing with, but you have to deal with it as it comes. You do what you have to do in the line of your duties, your job. You focus on what you're doing."

Fear can directly affect the way officers do their jobs. A common but dangerous temptation, born of fear, is to appease prisoners to gain their cooperation. (Inmates do not note or mention officers' use of this approach, perhaps because they see such officers as friendly to their immediate interests.) One officer stated the premise underlying appeasement quite baldly: "Anybody facing death, they gotta be dangerous. If he calls and he needs something, you got to try to get it for him." Such officers are said by their colleagues to bend or even ignore the rules "to keep it calm in there and to make their day go by." Other officers are said to get "too personally involved." They "play" with inmates rather than controlling them, and are "slap happy" and "sloppy" in following procedures. These officers, according to their colleagues, say to inmates, "'You're my buddy.' Slap 'em on the back and say, 'You're my partner. I know you're not going to hurt me because we're stick buddies.' This is no place to play. If you get that far gone, I think you better get out." Obsequious guards make their fellow officers nervous. The problem for the staff, and for the weaker inmates they must protect, is that appeasement corrodes the officers' authority and undermines control, lowering the general level of security. "We're supposed to be a team," complained one officer, "and what happens to them happens to me." If a colleague trembles visibly, he is useless as an officer. What is worse, his presence emboldens the more predatory prisoners, which in the long run spells trouble for officers and inmates alike.

Some officers go to the other extreme and become overbearing and abusive. This response, as we have seen, is salient in the minds of the prisoners. As Radelet et al. observed, "Relations with the correctional officers are fragile, with one hostile guard easily able to overshadow relationships with those who are more humane."[71] A major reason for this fragility is fear. Ever on the defensive, abusive officers are quick to take personal offense and quick to intimidate and harass prisoners in retaliation. Under conditions of solitary confinement, officers of this type may have the upper hand because prisoners are locked in their cells. They may even set the example for other officers to follow.[72] On less restrictive death rows, however, abusive officers are more apt to be seen by their colleagues as a liability.

Contrary to appearances (and inmate perceptions), most abusive officers are not gratuitously hostile. Rather, condemned prisoners are a trial for them, taxing their limited self-control. Though the prisoners are, in the view of most officers I interviewed, reasonably well-behaved on a day-to-day basis, the officers pointed out that the prisoners are not easy to be around. They characterized the inmates as impatient, touchy, demanding, and given to wide mood swings that sometimes end in tirades. Such, said the officers, is the pressure of life on death row. To get into a "cursing match" with the prisoners is tempting, noted one officer, but he resists because to do so "would put me at their level." Unfortunately, this officer felt that some of his colleagues regularly lower themselves to the level of the prisoners, becoming defensive about their authority and abusive with prisoners. Wherever these officers go, this man maintained, they stir up trouble.

> We have some hard cases. I could have everything calm, but this one guy wouldn't be there but two seconds and he'd rile 'em up so. When he left, you could hear the inmates down the hall, he'd rile 'em up so. . . . Just some small remark or something he'd know would get 'em riled.

Since trouble is seen as contagious, given the pressure of life on death row, abusive officers are as much of a problem as their lax colleagues. In the one instance, abuse may provoke an incident. In the other, timidity may invite trouble. Either way, other officers—and the prisoners—suffer.

The fears of the prisoners and guards, though quite real, are not necessarily realistic. It is by no means clear that death row guards would be eager to harm their captives if the opportunity arose. Certainly the officers cannot simply enter prisoners' cells and carry them off to the execution chamber on a whim. (Fearful prisoners can acknowledge this last point intellectually, by the way, but not emotionally. They still feel starkly vulnerable.) Nor is it clear that condemned prisoners, most of whom face years of legal appeals and therefore have reason to hope for reprieve, are desperate enough to callously harm or kill a guard to escape the executioner or to exact revenge.

But the fear persists on this and other death rows, with harmful consequences. A prisoner of a solitary-confinement death row described the consequences as follows:

> There seems to be too much security. There seems to be an abnormal amount of fear in the guards simply because we have a death sentence and that makes it hard for us to have the same courtesies that we should—that other inmates have. For example, the guards are so afraid of us where they won't get close to us or they won't come up and talk to us when we need something done seriously. It could be a medical problem or something. And because of this fear in the guards, we don't get the assistance we need like other inmates do. . . . You can easily tell it's fear in the officers and other employees of the institution. Just because we have this death sentence, people are so afraid of us that they don't want to get close to us and because of this very thing we just don't get what I would say [is] the com-

passion that we need or the assistance that we need. Sometimes it's hard to find the right word, but I know that it is something that we don't get that every man, regardless of his condition, should have.[73]

The main casualty of fear, then, is simple human compassion, the absence of which contributes to the distinctively cold interpersonal climate on death row.

Human Services

Yet fear need not contaminate all encounters on death row. Implicit in the above-quoted prisoner's insightful observations about the corrosive effect of fear is the hope that individual officers and inmates can, through more open interaction, come to know one another and use that knowledge to suspend, or at least place in perspective, the stereotypes that divide them. That hope sometimes bears fruit. On the reformed death row I studied, three officers, admittedly a minority, suppressed their fears and went about their jobs as responsible correctional officers. Two of these officers were women. Like good officers of either gender in any correctional setting, they saw themselves as figures of authority whose job was to help the inmates cope with the pains of imprisonment.[74] In their view, condemned prisoners, like all other prisoners, are entitled to a range of basic human services, and these officers provided those services as a matter of course.

One officer listed by rote some examples of human services provided on death row: "You must provide phone calls, supplies, commissary, legal and personal calls [call the switchboard for them], toilet paper, soap, towels. The list goes on." Paradoxically, security is on that list of services, even on death row. For these officers, security means more than merely preventing escape. It also means protecting the inmates and the officers. In one guard's words,

This is a security job: to keep them protected while they're here and to keep them from getting out. Anytime they go anyplace within the building or outside it, they have to have waist chains, leg irons, and all this stuff. So you have to act as a buffer between them and the inmates who are "free." So it's a form of protective custody. You have to protect them from the other inmates because they can't protect themselves.

Condemned prisoners need protection from each other as well. Stress builds up on death row, and men under pressure sometimes act out. Violent men sometimes act out violently, so fights are one periodic consequence of stress on death row with which the officers must deal. Such fights are usually broken up on command. When they are not, the regular death row officers do not enter the dayroom, where they might be taken hostage, but instead call in a twelve-man tactical team, which restrains the prisoners. In this way, both the inmates and the officers are protected.

Sometimes officers go a step beyond efficient provision of services. In the words of one such officer, they "develop a friendly-type relationship" with the prisoners. Having come to empathize with the prisoners in their difficult situation, they are moved to respond to the prisoners' legitimate concerns. "It may be a simple thing to you and me, but if it's something that's pressing them, then they want it done today. They don't have a lot of business. The least thing that comes up is important."

These more responsive officers occasionally find themselves in a helping role. Interactions may start with a request for a basic commodity, such as toilet paper, and end in an informal counseling session.

> The man may start a conversation which eventually brings out a problem they're struggling with. For example, problems with girlfriends. They ask me because I'm a female. Or [problems with] kids or cooking, things they know I know about.

At other times, such officers may simply offer a friendly word to lift a prisoner's spirits. "Sometimes you just smile to cheer them up sometimes. Sometime they're looking sad, you say, 'What's wrong? It's not that bad. Cheer up.'" The fact that prisoners may not tell them what's wrong or visibly cheer up is a disappointment—none of the officers claimed success as informal counselors—but it does not discourage the officers from trying to be of help. Their job, they say, is a thankless one. These officers behave as they do to satisfy their own personal and professional standards, not to win praise or recognition from the prisoners.

Such officers are explicitly aware of the limits of a human service role on death row. Quite consciously, they try to be friendly without becoming friends, to be responsive without kowtowing. They don't appease; they simply care enough to serve and protect. In their view, the ideal officer "doesn't get too close but gets close enough to deal with them and accept them for who they are." If a guard gets too friendly, prisoners "can ask you for favors, and you can get caught up in things." The objective is to be a concerned professional—that is, "to deal with them on a one-to-one basis but not get emotionally involved with them." These officers see themselves as correctional professionals who must go about their work in a civil and responsive but fundamentally businesslike way.

US AND THEM: THE DIVISIVE ROLE OF EXECUTIONS

Executions cast a long shadow over death row and impose a stark limit on the degree of emotional involvement that is possible between officers and inmates. As one prisoner on a solitary-confinement death row observed, "We know within ourselves that no matter how courteous a guard tries to be to us, we know what he will do in the end. And so that right there makes us guard against them."[75] Contrary to the view of this and, indeed, most condemned prisoners, death row officers normally are not involved in executions; the execution team is assembled from officers who have had little or no contact with the prisoner prior to the deathwatch. Still, complicity is obvious in that the death row officers expressly hold the prisoners for the purpose of execution. Some of the guards of our reformed death row recognized this complicity; others did not. In any case, the prisoners hold each and every officer accountable. "You can feel the tension in the air after an execution," observed one officer. "I think they are angry at anybody with a [correctional] uniform."

Anger is not the only emotion to follow in the wake of executions. Prisoners may also feel a sense of loss. Some condemned prisoners, on this and other death rows, develop among themselves a primitive notion of community.[76] The execution of one of their fellows is therefore a loss. Their sense of loss accentuates feelings of powerlessness and vulnerability; it reaffirms in no uncertain terms the lonely fate that awaits the condemned prisoners. The complicated mix of sentiments evoked by the execution of their fellows can seem overwhelming and inexplicable; only rage at the death row officers, the culprits once removed from the execution team, offers relief. In the words of one prisoner,

> I wanted to understand why Mike was being taken from me, but it was impossible. Each day I have to interact with the same guards who came to the unit and took him from me. These guards were the same guards who were telling me, "Joe, Mike is a good man. *They* shouldn't kill him." Each time I heard a guard say that, I could feel the anger churning within me. What they were saying made no sense to me. I wanted to scream, "NO!" I wanted to tear down the prison walls and make *them* stop. I hated them. . . . Before that day four other friends had been executed: men whom I ate with, talked with, played with, argued with—men whom I came to know as friends and shared a life bond with. Men whom no matter what their crimes, I *could not* see as anything but human beings . . . men whose tears I saw, whose flesh I touched, whose pain I still feel. I still know the hopelessness, I am still with the guards who took them away to be executed, and I am still trying to understand.[77]

Some of the death row officers, too, develop a sense of community with at least some of the prisoners. The executions of these prisoners are a loss for the staff as well. Parting with prisoners one has come to know and like can be at once touching and depressing. An officer on our reformed death row, supervising a prisoner's last visit with his family, reacted in a revealing way.

> The reality of that last family visit really made me feel bad. His daughter didn't even know him. It was depressing to be there. It's supposed to be part of the job, like being a doctor or something. You lose a patient and that's just it, but it's not that easy. You never forget this type of thing, but you can put it behind you.

For this officer, one "loses" a prisoner to execution. Like any genuine loss, it doesn't come easily.

To be sure, officers on this and other death rows more typically remain aloof from condemned prisoners or even treat them abusively. They do not see executions as emotionally wrenching events, nor do they take pleasure in them. They behave as they do, in part, to avoid the emotional hurt that in-volvement with prisoners would bring. "You can't be buddy-buddy," said one officer, "you've got to keep it business." This business is a matter of life and death, killing and dying. Death row officers, however, are not simply waiting to kill the prisoners, whatever the prisoners may feel. In many ways, the offi-cers, too, are pawns in the death penalty drama. The officers know that con-demned prisoners either have their sentences changed by appeal or commutation, in which case they never see them again, or they are executed. In either case, but particularly when prisoners are executed, most officers feel it is better not to have known them well.

More concretely, one officer told me that he kept his emotional distance from the condemned because he might be the one to escort them to the death house. The death house, which in the state under study is located in another prison, is where the executions occur. There, another group of correctional officers takes over, conducting the deathwatch and carrying out the execu-tion. It is to the experience of these officers, our modern executioners, that we now turn.

NOTES

1. M. Abu-Jamal, *Live From Death Row* (Reading, Mass.: Addison-Wesley, 1995).

2. D. A. Cabana, *Death at Midnight: The Confession of an Executioner* (Boston: Northeastern University Press, 1996), 148.

3. Quoted in G. E. Goldhammer, *Dead End* (Brunswick, Me.: Biddle Publishing Com-pany, 1994), 108.

4. P. Brasfield with J. M. Elliot, *Deathman Pass Me By: Two Years on Death Row* (San Bernardino: Borgo Press, 1983), 91–92.

5. A. Bronstein, personal communication.

6. B. Jackson and D. Christian, *Death Row* (Boston: Beacon Press, 1980), 14.

7. C. Chessman, "Trial by Ordeal," in *Death Row: An Affirmation of Life*, ed. S. Levine (New York: Ballantine, 1972), 4.

8. Jackson and Christian (n. 6), 94.

9. See G. Sykes, *The Society of Captives* (New York: Atheneum, 1966); J. Irwin, *Prisons in Turmoil* (Boston: Little, Brown, 1980); and R. Johnson, *Hard Time: Understanding and Reforming the Prison*, 2nd ed. (Belmont: Wadsworth, 1996).

10. For an insightful discussion of privacy and incarceration, see B. Schwartz, "Depriva-tion of Privacy as a 'Functional Prerequisite': The Case of the Prison," *Journal of Criminal Law and Criminology* 63 (1972): 235–236.

11. I and Professor Stanley Brodsky of the University of Alabama independently found seventy percent of Alabama's condemned prisoners to be showing signs of deterioration. My finding, based on content analysis of interviews, was that "7 of every 10 prisoners diagnosed themselves as suffering physical, mental or emotional deterioration in what was typically portrayed as the interpersonal vacuum constituting the human environment of death row." See R. Johnson, "Life under Sentence of Death," in *The Pains of Imprisonment*, ed. R. Johnson and H. Toch (Prospect Heights, Ill.: Waveland Press, 1988), 132. Brodsky found a seventy percent deterioration rate for this same population using

objective personality tests. Brodsky's results are reported in depositions pertaining to Jacobs v. Britton, No. 78–309H et al. (S.D. Ala., 1979).

Other studies have described the problem of deterioration as common among condemned prisoners but have not provided statistics on the prevalence of symptoms. See R. Johnson, *Condemned to Die: Life Under Sentence of Death* (Prospect Heights, Ill.: Waveland Press, 1989) (Chapter 6 contains a fuller ethnographic description of deterioration among Alabama's condemned than that found in the article cited above); Jackson and Christian (n. 6), 174–189 (examining Texas's death row); L. West, "Psychiatric Reflections on the Death Penalty," *American Journal of Orthopsychiatry* 45 (1975): 689–700 (covering death row prisoners generally); H. Bluestone and C. L. McGahee, "Reaction to Extreme Stress: Impending Death by Execution," *American Journal of Psychiatry* 119 (1962): 393–396 (covering death row prisoners at Sing Sing); and J. Gallemore and J. Panton, "Inmate Responses to Lengthy Death Row Confinement," *American Journal of Psychiatry* 129 (1972): 167–172 (covering death row prisoners in North Carolina). In 1968, Congress heard testimony on the problem of deterioration among the condemned. See U.S. Congress, Senate Committee on the Judiciary, *To Abolish the Death Penalty: Hearings before the Subcommittee on Criminal Laws and Procedures*, 90th Cong., 2nd sess., March 20 and 21 and July 2, 1968, S. 1760.

12. C. M. Lambrix, "The Isolation of Death Row," in *Facing the Death Penalty: Essays on a Cruel and Unusual Punishment*, ed. M. L. Radelet (Philadelphia: Temple University Press, 1989), 199.

13. W. Rideau and R. Wikberg, *Life Sentences: Rage and Survival Behind Bars* (New York: Times Books, 1992), 264.

14. Ibid., 265.

15. Ibid., 270.

16. Johnson, *Condemned to Die* (n. 11), 48.

17. Ibid., 49.

18. Ibid., 51.

19. J. Arriens, ed., *Welcome to Hell: Letters and Writings from Death Row* (Boston: Northeastern University Press, 1997).

20. Jackson and Christian (n. 6), 232, 226.

21. M. L. Radelet, M. Vandiver, and F. Berardo, "Families, Prisons, and Men with Death Sentences: The Human Impact of Structured Uncertainty," *Journal of Family Issues* 4 (4): 596 (December 1983). For many regular prison guards, caring, expressed as a concern for delivering human services and thereby ameliorating the stresses of confinement, is a central feature of their work. See H. Toch, "Is a Correctional Officer, by Any Other Name, a 'Screw'?" *Criminal Justice Review* 3 (1978): 19–35; R. Johnson and J. Price, "The Complete Correctional Officer: Human Service and the Human Environment of Prison," *Criminal Justice and Behavior* 8 (3): 343–373 (1981); L. Lombardo, *Guards Imprisoned: Correctional Officers at Work*, 2nd ed. (Cincinnati: Anderson, 1989); and Johnson, *Hard Time* (n. 9), Chap. 8.

22. Jackson and Christian (n. 6), 90, 19.

23. Brasfield with Elliot (n. 4), 80.

24. Lambrix (n. 12), 198, 200, 200.

25. Jackson and Christian (n. 6), 31. See also Lambrix (n. 12).

26. Lambrix (n. 12), 199.

27. Jackson and Christian (n. 6), 15. See also Johnson, *Condemned to Die* (n. 11); Radelet, Vandiver, and Berardo (n. 21); and B. Eshelman, *Death Row Chaplain* (New York: Signet Books, 1972).

28. M. Vandiver, "Coping with Death: Families of the Terminally Ill, Homicide Victims, and Condemned Prisoners," in *Facing the Death Penalty: Essays on a Cruel and Unusual Punishment*, ed. M. L. Radelet (Philadelphia: Temple University Press, 1989), 133.

29. Johnson, *Condemned to Die* (n. 11), 54.

30. Ibid., 50.

31. Radelet, Vandiver, and Berardo (n. 21), 605.

32. Johnson, *Condemned to Die* (n. 11), 115.

33. Abu-Jamal (n. 1), 9, 11.

34. Ibid., 9, 11.

35. Johnson, *Condemned to Die* (n. 11), Chap. 1; Radelet, Vandiver, and Berardo (n. 21); and Jackson and Christian (n. 6), 100–109.

36. Jackson and Christian (n. 6), 78.

37. Johnson, *Condemned to Die* (n. 11), 70–71, 71.

38. "Dead Man Talking," the Internet, http://www.monkey.hooked.net/monkey/M/Hut/deadman/deadman.html, col. 4.

39. Ibid., col. 5.

40. Ibid., col. 5.

41. C. Turnball, "Death by Decree: An Anthropological Approach to Capital Punishment," *Natural History* 87 (1978): 54.

42. Cabana notes that Connie Evans asked to meet with another condemned prisoner for an informal Bible study session as Evans's execution drew near. Cabana was "reminded by an ever diligent security supervisor that it could be part of a plan to escape or create a disturbance of some kind . . ." Cabana viewed the admonition as "appropriate and appreciated," though he "chose to grant Evans his request." Cabana (n. 2), 178.

43. Johnson, *Condemned to Die* (n. 11), 65.

44. Ibid., Chap. 4.

45. Ibid., 74.

46. Ibid., 103.

47. Ibid., 106.

48. Ibid., 106–107.

49. Ibid., 107.

50. Ibid., 106–109.

51. K. S. Miller and M. L. Radelet, *Executing the Mentally Ill* (Newbury Park, Calif.: Sage, 1993), 73 and generally. This is a thoughtful and moving work on the plight of the mentally ill condemned prisoner. For a heartbreaking account of the travails of daily life for mentally ill prisoners, as seen by the prisoners themselves, see H. Toch, *Mosaic of Despair: Human Breakdowns in Prison* (Washington, D.C.: American Psychological Association Press, 1992), esp. Chap. 4.

52. If the psychotic prisoners are properly diagnosed, they will be determined to be incompetent to be executed because they do not understand the punishment they face; they will then be transferred to a hospital for the criminally insane and subjected to treatment, the object of which will be to render them competent to be executed. See Miller and Radelet (n. 51).

53. Groseclose v. Dutton, 609 F. Supp. 1432 (D.C. Tenn. 1985), 1436.

54. Rideau and Wikberg (n. 13), 263.

55. Abu-Jamal (n. 1), 34.

56. Johnson, *Condemned to Die* (n. 11), 83; see also page 136 for a discussion of racism and larger societal and criminal issues as seen by black death row prisoners.

57. Abu-Jamal (n. 55), 29–30.

58. J. M. Giarratano, "The Pains of Life," in *Facing the Death Penalty: Essays on a Cruel and Unusual Punishment*, ed. M. L. Radelet (Philadelphia: Temple University Press, 1989), 195.

59. *Groseclose* (n. 53), 1436.

60. See n. 11.

61. Johnson, *Condemned to Die* (n. 11), and Jackson and Christian (n. 6).

62. "Dead Man Talking," (n. 38), col. 9.

63. "I have often been utterly astonished . . . to find persons who could speak of the singing, among slaves, as evidence of their contentment and happiness. It is impossible to conceive of a greater mistake. Slaves sing most when they are most unhappy." F. Douglass, *Narrative of the Life of Frederick Douglass: An American Slave, Written by Himself* (New York: Penguin, 1968). It may well be that condemned prisoners joke most when they are most unhappy on death row.

64. Johnson, *Condemned to Die* (n. 11), 112, 96.

65. Cabana (n. 2), 80–81, 148.

66. Johnson, *Condemned to Die* (n. 11), Chap. 3.

67. Radelet, Vandiver, and Berardo (n. 21), 596, and Jackson and Christian (n. 6).

68. Toch (n. 21), 19–35.

69. Personal communication from a death row inmate, as part of an unpublished survey of death row living conditions conducted by John Conrad and myself (1984).

70. Johnson, *Condemned to Die* (n. 11), 69.

71. Radelet, Vandiver, and Berardo (n. 21), 596.

72. Johnson, *Condemned to Die* (n. 11), 69.

73. Ibid., 60.

74. Lombardo (n. 21), and Johnson (n. 9).

75. Johnson, *Condemned to Die* (n. 11), 64.

76. Ibid., Chap. 7.

77. Giarratano (n. 57), 194–195.

PART III

In Cold Blood

A Study of Modern Executions

Now it is a terrible business to mark out a man for the vengeance of men. But it is a thing to which a man can grow accustomed. . . . And the horrible thing about public officials, even the best . . . is not that they are wicked . . . not that they are stupid . . . it is simply that they have got used to it.

G. K. CHESTERTON

I can take or leave executions. It's not a job I like or dislike. It's a job I've been asked to do. I try to go about every job in the most professional manner I can. If they would stop the death penalty, it wouldn't bother me. If we had ten executions tomorrow, it wouldn't bother me. I would condition my mind to get me through it.

EXECUTION TEAM OFFICER

There's nothin' to it. It's no different to me executing somebody and goin' to the refrigerator and getting a beer out of it. . . . They all look the same. It's just a procedure, and they happen to be part of it. . . . I go there to do a job, and I do it and leave.

SAM JONES, STATE EXECUTIONER, LOUISIANA, 1983–1991

5

Death Work

A Modern Execution Team

The execution of Gary Gilmore, carried out in 1977, marked the resurrection of the modern death penalty. The event was big news and was commemorated in a book by Norman Mailer, *The Executioner's Song*,[1] later made into a movie. The title is deceptive. Like others who have explored the death penalty, Mailer tells much about the condemned but very little about the executioners. Indeed, if we examine Mailer's account more closely, the executioner's story is not only unsung, it is also distorted.

Gilmore's execution was quite atypical, even if his crime was not. He was sentenced to death for killing two men in cold blood, for no apparent reason. Viewed from the outside, his own death had a similar ring of nihilism. Gilmore, unrepentant and unafraid, refused to appeal his conviction—under a then-untested capital statute. There is no doubt that he could have contested his case for years, as many condemned prisoners have done since his death. But Gilmore, who had already served some twenty-two years of his young life behind bars, would have none of that. To him, prison was death; life in prison was a kind of living death in its own right. Death by firing squad gave him a chance to offer blood atonement for his awful crimes (a notion that resonated with his dark Mormon obsessions[2]), as well as a kind of immortality as the man who put the executioner back to work.

Relishing his notoriety and his perverse power, Gilmore dared the state of Utah to take his life, and the media repeated the challenge until it became a taunt that may well have goaded officials to action. (There was even a *Saturday*

Night Live skit depicting him fixing his make-up in preparation for his execution.) His brother Mikal, who spoke with Gary near the end, states that "Gary remained fierce and unswerving in his determination to die." And to use lawyers for the state of Utah, primarily, but death penalty advocates as well, to bring about his death. Gilmore

> transformed them into his servants: men who would kill at his bidding, to suit his own ideas of ruin and redemption. By insisting on his own execution—and in effect directing the legal machinery that would bring that execution about—Gary seemed to be saying: *There's really nothing you can do to punish me, because this is precisely what I want, this is my will. You will help me with my final murder.*[3]

A failed suicide pact with his lover staged only days before the execution, using drugs she delivered to him by a kiss in an intimate visit, added a hint of sex and melodrama to the already compelling human drama. Gilmore's final words, "Let's do it," seemed to invite—even, perhaps, command—the lethal hail of bullets from the firing squad. That nonchalant phrase, at once fatalistic and brazen, became Gilmore's epitaph. It clinched his outlaw–hero image and found its way onto tee shirts that confirmed his celebrity status.

As befits a celebrity, Gilmore was treated with unusual leniency by prison officials during his confinement on death row. He was, for example, allowed to hold a party on the eve of his execution, during which he was free to eat, drink, and make merry with his guests until the early morning hours. As we have seen, this was not unprecedented: Notorious English convicts of centuries past would throw farewell balls in the prison on the eve of their executions (see Chapter 1). For the record, Gilmore served Tang, Kool-Aid, cookies, and coffee, later supplemented by contraband pizza and an unidentified liquor. Periodically, he gobbled drugs obligingly supplied by the prison pharmacy. He played a modest arrangement of rock music albums but refrained from dancing.

Gilmore's execution, like his parting fete, was decidedly out of step with the tenor of modern executions. Most condemned prisoners fight to save their lives, not to have them taken. They do not see their fate in romantic terms, and they do not host farewell parties of any sort. Nor are condemned prisoners, with the exception of some slated for lethal injection, given medication to ease their anxiety or gain their compliance. The subjects of typical executions remain anonymous to the public and even to their keepers. They are very much alone at the end.

The focus of my research, in contrast with Mailer's account, is on the executioners themselves as they carry out typical executions. In my experience, executioners—not unlike Mailer himself—can be quite voluble, and sometimes quite moving, in expressing themselves. I draw on their words to describe the death work they perform in our name.

DEATH WORK AND DEATH WORKERS:
DEFINING PARAMETERS

Executioners are not a popular topic of social research, or even of conversation at the dinner table or cocktail party. We simply don't give the subject much thought. When we think of executioners at all, we imagine men of questionable character who work stealthily behind the scenes to carry out their grim labors. We picture hooded forms hiding in the shadow of the gallows, or anonymous figures lurking just out of sight behind an electric chair or a firing blind or outside a gas chamber, or, most recently, beyond a curtained partition, syringe in hand, in an execution chamber made to look like a hospital room. We wonder who would do such grisly work and how they sleep at night.

This image of the executioner as a sinister and often solitary person is, of course, a holdover from earlier times, when executions were public and executioners were scorned as evil, contaminated by the death work that was their livelihood. Their lives might be placed in jeopardy by an angry crowd, by relatives of the condemned, or by superstitious neighbors. They were often afforded a hood or cloak while at work to protect their identities, which would offer them a token shield against harm. Some of these execution traditions, or at least remnants of them, linger on even today. Thus it is that a few states hire free-lance executioners and engage in macabre theatrics. Executioners may be picked up under cover of darkness at lonely country crossroads; some still wear black hoods to hide their identity. They slip into the prison unnoticed, do their work, then return to their civilian lives.

In Florida, this scenario is played to the hilt. A hooded executioner is picked up before daybreak at a designated spot and driven to the prison by a corrections official. He wears the hood at all times—before, during, and after the execution. He is escorted to the execution chamber at the prescribed time (which in Florida is at sunrise), and, on cue, he pushes a button that activates the electric chair. When the man is dead, the executioner, hood still in place, "is driven back and paid"—in cash, to further protect his anonymity. (In some states, the doctors who administer lethal injection are afforded an "executioner's cloak"—official anonymity, not a garment—to protect their identities; they, too, can be paid in cash to further shield them from scrutiny.[4]) Florida's executioner meets with no man face-to-face. "You won't be seeing him," a Florida Department of Corrections official told a journalist. "Not on this side of life."[5]

Some executioners forgo secrecy. For example, the executioner's name is a matter of public record in Alabama and Mississippi. In these states, "'the dirty little secret' of capital punishment is neither fetishized nor veiled."[6] Here we find no hooded figures, no blood money collected in cash. These executioners—in Alabama, the warden; in Mississippi, a ranking correctional officer—are popular figures in the community, told by passersby on the street to "Keep up the good work."[7] Sam Jones, Louisiana's civilian executioner responsible for nineteen deaths, was initially reluctant to be photographed; however, he eventually went public, allowing interviews with local newspapers and *Playboy* magazine, even appearing on television. These men see themselves as doing a job, as professionals who approach their work without passion or prejudice. Matter-of-fact, Jones describes himself as "a normal John Doe that walks the streets every day. I work and live a normal social life."[8] How ironic that an executioner would characterize himself in such a way—as a John Doe, a nameless corpse—as if in subconscious recognition that it takes a dead (dehumanized) man to kill other men in cold blood for a living.

The very presence of an official executioner, particularly when drawn from outside the ranks of the prison system, may give comfort to skittish prison administrators. In one warden's words, "We can honestly say that we didn't do it."[9] The warden's point almost seems to be, "Nobody did it—no one is responsible—if we don't know who did it or if he is not one of us." That warden, of course, is spouting sheer nonsense. Correctional officials are *always* involved in executions, even if they themselves do not directly carry out the killing. The plain fact is that formal executioners, whether shrouded in secrecy or working more or less as public figures, do not orchestrate the execution process. The warden or his designate does. As former warden Cabana notes, "my hand was on the lever as well. The executioner could not, would not, proceed until I gave the order."[10] Neither the warden nor the executioner can go to work until after the prisoner has been escorted to the death chamber and fastened to the execution apparatus. At that key juncture, the executioner merely flips a switch, pulls a lever, or pushes a button, "something a child, an animal, or even a machine could do."[11]

Formal executioners are almost peripheral to the modern execution process. This process starts on death row, the bleak and oppressive "prison within a prison" where the condemned are housed for years awaiting execution (see Part II), and culminates in the deathwatch, a brief period, usually twenty-four to forty-eight hours long, that ends when the prisoner has been executed. This final period, the deathwatch, is supervised by a team of correctional officers—variously known as the tactical squad, the strap-down team, the deathwatch team, or simply the execution team—who typically report directly to the prison warden. It is generally the warden who reads the death warrant; as noted above, he signals the executioner to start the machinery of death. The warden, depending on his personal proclivities, may be more or less involved with the condemned prisoner over the period of his confinement and execution.[12]

The warden or his representative presides over the execution. In many states, it is a member of the execution team, acting under the warden's authority, who plays the role of executioner. Though this officer may technically work alone, his teammates are apt to view the execution as a shared responsibility. As one member of a deathwatch team told me in no uncertain terms,

> We're all as a team, together. We all take a part of the killing, the execution. So, this guy that pulled the switch shouldn't have more responsibility

than the guy that cut his hair or the guy that fed him or the guy that watched him. We all take a part in it; we all play 100 percent in it, too. That take[s] the load off this one individual [who pulls the switch].

The formal executioner—in this case, the head of the deathwatch team—concurred. "Everyone on the team can do it," he said, "and nobody will tell you I do it. I know my team." My research confirmed these claims.

The correctional officers who serve on deathwatch teams are expressly selected and trained to carry out executions. They are executioners, in my view, even when they are assisted by an outsider who is hired to complete the formalities of the execution—to flip a switch or push a button, thus taking the life of a prisoner he may have never even seen. By contrast, the deathwatch team officers must serve, observe, and control the prisoner, then escort him to the death chamber and secure him for execution—if they do not also perform the execution themselves. It is they who are the most active in the conduct of executions; it is they who carry the heaviest psychological burden.

The officers of these deathwatch teams are, for all intents and purposes, our modern executioners. I studied one such team, composed of eight seasoned male officers of varying ranks. (A ninth officer, a woman, seated the witnesses but was not otherwise involved in the execution. The team is very much a man's world.) The team had carried out five electrocutions when I began my research. I interviewed each officer on the team after the fifth execution, following the same general format that I had used with the death row officers.[13] Again, my aim was to elicit and explore the officers' perceptions of their work by allowing them to delineate the execution process as they saw and participated in it. At the start of each interview, I posed open-ended questions about each officer's role in the execution process. These questions, in turn, led to others about how the officer was trained to do his job, about how he felt about and perceived the executions he had helped to carry out, about his observations of the prisoners as their executions drew near, and about the effects on him personally of his involvement with executions. I then served as an official witness at the team's sixth execution and as a behind-the-scenes observer during their seventh, at which point I informally reinterviewed each of the officers.

I also interviewed the warden, the prison's operations officer, and a member of the prison's treatment unit who had advised a condemned prisoner who was later executed. In these interviews, again focused but using open-ended questions, I probed the dimensions of each person's role in the execution process, their perceptions of the individual condemned inmates they had observed, and the effects, if any, their involvement in the execution process may have had on them as individuals. In addition, I interviewed a counselor affiliated with a prison reform organization. The counselor had assisted both of the men whose executions I'd observed, in each case staying with them through all but the final minutes of the deathwatch. I also interviewed a journalist who had spoken with one of the condemned prisoners both before and, by telephone, during his deathwatch. These latter interviews were almost exclusively aimed at reconstructing the experiences of condemned prisoners during their final hours. After the publication of the first edition of this book, I observed yet another execution—as a behind-the-scenes observer—and interviewed the officers and warden again. (By this time, two officers had left the team; I interviewed their replacements.[14]) The results of this research form the substance of this and the following two chapters on the psychology of capital punishment.

THE DEATHWATCH TEAM

Members of the deathwatch team referred to themselves, with evident pride, as simply "the team." This pride was shared by correctional officials. The warden praised them as solid citizens—in his words, "country boys." (Some of the officers were in fact from urban areas and about half were African-Americans, but they all qualified as country boys in the warden's eyes because of their reliable characters.) These men, the warden assured me, could be counted on to do the job of execution and do it well, however unpleasant they might find the experience to be. As a fellow administrator put it, "it takes a certain amount of grit" to serve on the execution team. Continuing, he mused,

> What's the expression? "When the going gets tough, the tough get going." A certain amount of professionalism [is required] there. . . . An execution is something [that] needs to be done, and good people, dedicated people who believe in the American system, should do it. And there's a certain amount of feeling, probably one to another, that they're part of that—that when they have to hang tough, they can do it, and they can do it right. And that it's just the right thing to do.

In the eyes of the warden and other prison officials, an execution is a good man's burden, shouldered stoically for us all.

The official view of an execution is that it is a job that has to be done, and done right. The death penalty is, after all, the law of the land. In this context, "done right" means that an execution should be proper, professional, and dignified. In the words of a prison administrator,

> It was something, of course, that had to be done. We had to be sure that we did it properly, professionally, and [that] we gave as much dignity to the person as we possibly could in the process. . . . You gotta do it, and if you've gotta do it, it might just as well be done the way it's supposed to be done—without any sensation.

In the language of the respondents, "proper" refers to procedures that go off smoothly, and "professional" means without personal feelings that intrude on the procedures in any way. The phrase "without any sensation" no doubt expresses a desire to avoid media sensationalism, particularly if there should be an embarrassing and undignified hitch in the procedures—for example, a prisoner who breaks down or becomes violent and must be forcibly placed in the electric chair as witnesses, some from the media, look on in horror. Or, perhaps worse, a botched execution.[15] Still, the phrase may also be a revealing slip of the tongue. For executions are indeed meant to occur without any human feeling, without any sensation. A profound absence of feeling would seem to embody the bureaucratic ideal for the modern execution.[16]

There is, to be sure, no room for passion or even for emotion in the professional execution sought by prison administrators. Condemned prisoners are not supposed to be dragged kicking, screaming, or weeping to their deaths. They are meant to go to their deaths with dignified dispatch, if not decorum ("graciously," to quote one of the execution team officers). The point is, I suppose, that an execution should be, or should at least appear to be, a punishment to which one submits voluntarily, if reluctantly, rather than a calculated act of violence one resists at all costs. It boils down to a matter of appearances, and appearances matter to everybody on the scene, particularly the officials. There is, then, an execution etiquette. Part of death work is making sure that this etiquette is observed.

The view of executions held by the officers of the team parallels that of correctional administrators but is somewhat more restrained. The officers are closer to the killing and dying and are less apt to wax abstract or eloquent in describing the process. Listen to one man's observations:

> I look at it like it's a job. I don't take it personally. You know, I don't take it like I'm having a grudge against this person and this person has done something to me. I'm just carrying out a job, doing what I was asked to do. . . . This man has been sentenced to death in the courts. This is the law, and he broke this law, and he has to suffer the consequences. And one of the consequences is to put him to death.

From where the deathwatch officers sit, the important yet "dirty" job of execution must be done in a workmanlike manner. No one is proud of the blood or the mess, the sights and smells of violent death. As one officer observed, "It's nothin' to be proud of; it's just a job to do, one way or another."

The job of execution offers many opportunities for abuse. The prisoner could, for example, be strapped in the chair in an intentionally demeaning or painful way. But no one on the execution team seeks to inflict suffering on the condemned prisoner. Their reasons are rooted in a practical notion of humaneness: Abuse is not only unprofessional but impractical, because it is likely to trigger resistance. Accordingly, the officers have modified equipment such as the face mask to reduce both the prisoner's discomfort and the likelihood of shifting or squirming; the team members try to cinch down the body straps gently to avoid causing pain as well as to avoid provoking any struggle from the prisoner. All the officers, like the prison administrators, want a smoothly orchestrated, professional execution. In their view, however, such executions are neither acts of patriotism (as some of their administrative supporters would have it) nor acts of murder (as some of their free-world critics would have it). Rather, executions are, in the team's eyes, lawful and arguably humane penal sanctions. For the men of the deathwatch team, that is enough.

Which is just as well, since only a few members of the execution team support the death penalty outright and without reservation. Having seen executions close up, some of the team officers have lingering doubts about the justice or wisdom of this sanction. What puts these officers off is not so much the violence of execution—violence comes with the territory in the penitentiary. Besides, many of the officers have encountered violence in the military or in the free world. But violence in prison and elsewhere is usually situational and reactive, occurring when there seems to be no alternative. Such violence need not be justified, in the eyes of the officers. Executions are different because they are arranged. When asked, "Does being part of a planned life-taking process trouble you?" two men responded as follows:

- (Sigh) That's a good question. That's a real good question. (Sigh and long pause) It do, in a sense, and it don't. It probably—if it do, it's 'cause every person that's put on this earth, I feel, is created equal, you know, and they [are] put on this earth to do, to handle some type of problems and whatever. They got to live to do that. But my old grandfather had a saying, you know, "Do unto others what you want them to do unto you." So when you kill somebody, you should be killed. . . . [But] the execution, the killing itself, don't bother me. I was in the service eighteen months in Nam. I was on body patrol, far as when they dropped napalm and you went in and picked up dead bodies and stuff, put 'em in body bags. I guess another part of it, I live in a ghetto. I see a lot of life and death over there, you know. It really don't bother me, you know. Even inmates here get killed, you know. I've saved a couple of inmates here who have been cut up real bad as well as taken the dead bodies out from here that been killed. So the killing, it really don't bother me.

- There is turmoil, even for someone that I didn't like per se and might not care if he lives or dies, okay? But the violence doesn't bother me. Out in population, you may have to subdue someone or whatever. Certainly, if you subdue someone improperly, you could give them a lethal blow or whatever. So, then, you know, working on the tower, we have firepower. Okay, push may come to shove and we may have to use it. . . . [But with an execution] I ask myself, "Am I doing the right thing? Is this just or unjust? Do we have the right to take a man's life?"

A number of their colleagues entertain similar concerns. Nevertheless, the members of the deathwatch team can be counted on to do the difficult job of execution, because all of them accept without question the authority of the law and hence conclude that the matter is essentially out of their hands. Somebody's got to do it, say these men in unison and with conviction, because it's the system. And if we're the ones to do it, they continue, at least we'll do it right. One officer put the matter this way:

I've seen it. I know what it is. I've smelled it. I've tasted it. I've felt it. . . . I'm not sure the death penalty is the right way. I don't know if there is a right answer. So I look at it like this: If it's gotta be done, at least it can be done in a humane way, if there is such a word for it. 'Cause I know it can be a nasty situation. Executions have been here for a long time. And for a long time it's been done, you know, unprofessionally and for primitive reasons. The only way it should be done, I feel, is the way we do it. It's done professionally; it's not no horseplaying. Everything is done by documentation. On time. By the book.

EXECUTIONS BY THE BOOK

Arranging executions that occur "without any sensation" and proceed "by the book" is no mean task, but it is a task the execution team undertakes in earnest. The tone of this enterprise is set by the team leader, a man who takes a hard-boiled, no-nonsense approach to correctional work in general and death work in particular. "My style," he says, "is this: If it's a job to do, get it done. Do it and that's it." He seeks out kindred spirits, men who see killing as a job—a dirty job one does reluctantly, perhaps, but above all a job one carries out dispassionately. In his words,

> I wouldn't want to put a man on the team that would like it. I don't want nobody who would like to do it. I'd rather have the person not want to do it than have a person who wants to do it. And if I suspected or thought anybody on the team really's gettin' a kick out of it, I would take him off the team. . . . I would like to think that every one of them on the team is doin' it, is doing it in the line of duty, you know, carryin' out their duties.

Not all officers are candidates for death work. Only volunteers are sought, and though a fair number step forward, only a few are chosen.[17] The team leader screens the volunteers carefully. He knows the officers at the prison from his long years of service there, and his friendly, down-home country style invites them to admit any difficulties they may experience. Reluctant or squeamish candidates are encouraged to move on to different assignments without fear of sanction or prejudice.

> I would know what type of officer you have been, because I've been working with you and seen the way you conducted yourself. I'd sit down and talk to you and tell you what, what we gonna do and what's expected of you, and ask you, "Do you think you could handle it?" And if you told me you thought you could, why, I'd start training you. And then if I saw a weakness or something, that you're falling back, why then I'd ask you, you know, "Do you have a problem with it?" And then I would take you back and sit you down and tell you, if you did have a problem with it, had anything against it or you thought you had anything against it, you ought to just drop out. And nothing would ever be said. We'd just carry it on through.

Those volunteers who are selected to serve on the team are, by all accounts, the cream of the correctional officer corps. They are seasoned, mature, and dependable officers; level-headed types who have proven time and again that they know how to cope with the daily tribulations of work in the prison. Physically and emotionally strong, they take orders well but can also be counted on to use discretion. Common sense and cell-block finesse enable them to relate to and understand convicts. In the warden's words, these officers "can look condemned prisoners in the eye and tell them 'no' when they have to and not get them upset." Some of the officers credit military combat experience as their baptism of fire. All have proven that they can keep cool and handle the pressure that is endemic to the prison community. The observations of one officer, confirmed by the team leader, substantiate this last point:

> I volunteered because of my [military] service background and my job background here. They were looking at experience, more or less, number one. And they were also looking for (pause) the people who had been through a lot of stress—stress from inside the institution—that could handle stress more. The overall thing was to deal with the stress and pressure. . . . As long as I've been here, I have been used, more or less, as the person to handle the big problems and straighten them out.

Executions always have the potential to become big problems, so this officer feels he has found his niche on the deathwatch team.

In part to avoid any problems, big or little, the deathwatch team has been carefully drilled in the mechanics of execution. The execution process has been broken down into simple, discrete tasks and practiced repeatedly. The team leader described the division of labor in the following exchange with me:

> The execution team is a nine-officer team and each one has certain things to do. When I would train you, maybe you'd buckle a belt; that might be all you'd have to do. . . . And you'd be expected to do one thing, and that's all you'd be expected to do. And if everybody do what they were taught, or what they were trained to do, at the end the man would be put in the chair and everything would be complete. It's all come together now.
>
> *So it's broken down into very small steps?*
>
> Very small, yes. Each person has one thing to do.
>
> *I see. What's the purpose of breaking it down into such small steps?*
>
> So people won't get confused. I've learned it's kind of a tense time. When you're executin' a person, killing a person—you call it killin', executin', whatever you want, the man dies anyway—I find the less you got on your mind, why, the better you'll carry it out. So it's just very simple things. And so far, you know, it's all come together; we haven't had any problems.

This division of labor allows each member of the execution team to become a specialist in one specific task, an expert technician who takes pride in his work. Here's how two officers saw their specialized roles:

- My assignment is the leg piece. Right leg. I roll his pants' leg up, place a piece [an electrode] on his leg, strap his leg in. . . . I've got all the moves

down pat. We train from different posts; I can do any of them. But that's
my main post.

- I strap the left side. I strap his arms and another man straps his legs and
another one puts his head in the cap. But my job is strapping his left arm
in. . . . I was trained with those straps. The way those straps is on the
chair, see, I have to know, you know, exactly where each thing is.

The implication is not that the officers are incapable of performing multiple
or complex tasks but simply that it is more efficient to focus each officer's efforts on one easy task. "Every man I got down there can carry the job," the
team leader maintained. "We may cross-train . . . but when it comes down to,
to the time a man goes into the chair, everybody does only one thing and
that's it."

On-the-Job Training

An integral part of the training is realistic rehearsals, with team members cast
as recalcitrant surrogate prisoners, or "dummies," so that the team can anticipate problems and practice the restrained use of force.

We might set up a training, and I might be the dummy, you know, the
dummy. And I sit in the chair, they put on the arm straps and stuff, and I
might buck, you know, whatever, resist them putting me in the chair. So
we can practice this. We go through stuff like this. And we have had one
officer that nearly got his arm broke in the practice. . . . We have different
people we use for dummy. We might carry a small person through, or a
big person, or somebody, you know, trying to basically size the person
[the prisoner] up. If you've got a man that's scheduled to go and he's
gonna be big, I'd use myself or somebody else big.

Each inmate presents a different set of physical characteristics that must be not
only "sized up," to quote the officer, but also accommodated. Straps must be
adjusted so they will be tight enough; exact placement across an inmate's body
will vary as well, so a rehearsal with a similar-sized "dummy" allows the team
to determine, in one officer's words, "where *exactly* the straps have to go, and
to make adjustments."

Serving as the dummy during execution rehearsals at once demands and
promotes trust in one's peers. Imagine the role: Officers march you into the
death chamber, strap you in an electric chair, and fasten your arms, chest, and
legs. With you pinioned, they affix a cap to your head and cover your face
with a leather mask. Electrodes are then connected to the cap and your right
leg. All this occurs in an electric chair that, though obviously not activated at
the moment, is the real McCoy, capable of shooting twenty-five hundred volts
of electricity through your body.

The team leader, who routinely plays the role of surrogate prisoner, described the experience as "peculiar." Explaining, he observed, "Well, when I
first started, it was peculiar, you know, because when they put the mask on me,
you know, you can't really tell what the person is doing. You feel helpless."

Another officer on the team, more voluble than his leader, chose the word "weird." He, too, stressed the helplessness he felt when strapped in the chair.

> It's kind of weird. You feel totally helpless, you can't move, you can't see, you can't speak. It's total darkness. All you can hear are sounds around you. It's definitely weird. It's kinda like puttin' you in another world. . . . You get a little queasy, I guess from being helpless. You can't fight it. This is total helplessness.

According to the team leader, the officers submit to this stressful procedure[18] out of trust and commitment. "You have to trust your peers. You have to trust people. And like I said, it's a team, and you trust and love one another, so you go on and do it for the team." Each of the deathwatch officers shares the leader's devotion to the team: At some point, each has volunteered to play this trying role, doing so quite consciously out of dedication to the team.

Practice is meant to produce a confident group that is capable of fast and accurate performance under pressure. Time is crucial in the execution trade: The less time spent securing a prisoner for execution, the less opportunity there is for things to go wrong. A smooth execution drill unfolds rapidly and conforms to institutional operating procedures (IOPs). Practically speaking, doing an execution right means, perhaps above all else, doing it fast.

> We've got a time schedule for everything that we do. The head man has got to see that everything is going according to the clock. The clock— we're timed on everything. There's a certain time—you gotta go by the IOPs on the thing, and each thing has gotta be done at a certain time. . . . You know everything you've got to do. You just got to, you just got to do it in a certain time, a certain time you got to do this. The schedule is boss. You've got to break it down to the schedule, every last minute.

The rewards of practice are reaped in improved performance. Executions take place with increasing efficiency and, eventually, with precision. "The first one was grisly," a team member confided to me. He explained that a certain amount of fumbling made the execution seem interminable. There were technical problems as well: The generator was set so high that the body was mutilated. The execution chamber stank of burnt flesh, described as having a greasy odor reminiscent of fatty pork. (Air fresheners were subsequently installed throughout the death house.) But that is the past, the officer assured me. "The ones now, we know what we're doing. It's just like clockwork."[19]

TEAM COHESION

"We're a Family"

In the execution training, individual tasks are emphasized and the team members are called upon to function as automatons. The team itself, however, is a warm and even intimate primary group, a close-knit group its members can trust at all costs. The team's work environment—the death house—is a home

away from home. The officers of the team work together to handle the problems and pressures posed by death work. In their words,

- The team is very close. I guess we're probably . . . closer than any of the
  officers in here. . . . Comes from working close together. It's real, real
  close, you know. We really don't have nobody [else] to talk to. And we'll
  share ideas and things, we'll go off and sit down and just talk and share
  ideas. How we feel or how it's affecting us. We, I guess, have confidence
  in one another, trust. Just a good group of people.

- There's more closeness than in any other group I've seen in the system, as
  far as working together. And one thing we do—we got this thing with
  the team—we talk to each other. If we got a problem, we go and talk to
  each other *first* about it before we go off [and get upset]. . . . Everything
  that we do stays there [and gets worked out], you know what I'm sayin'?
  That's the way we operate.

- We are very, very close-knit. When we got a problem from an execution,
  we all go down in the basement, the execution chamber—we call that our
  home—draw the curtains, and go in the back, and we'll talk. One guy
  may say, "I don't think I can make it tonight." And we'll sit down and say,
  "C'mon, what's the problem? Let's talk it out. . . . " Then we have to
  remind him, "the law says that this is what has to be done, and we have to
  do it."

As one officer succinctly put it, "We're not a team, we're a family. In the
prison, we fuss, cuss, and threaten each other constantly. But down there [in
the death house], we're a family."

At first blush, such sentimentality may seem strained or fabricated, but it is
neither. Individual people may function as cogs and, in groups, may be deployed in mechanical fashion as the sum total of those cogs. But this is almost
never the whole story. Such arrangements violate essential human needs for
purposiveness in action and relationships with others, needs the team members meet through the primary-group relations that exist among them. Each
and every officer comes to see himself as a man among men he likes and ad-
mires, working together to complete a critical task in service of the larger social good. The team thus functions as a psychological safe harbor and a moral
reference point—which is to say, a source of support and direction as the officers go about the business of death work. In the niche provided by the team,
officers feel more confident and assured; the demands of death work become
a manageable routine. In one officer's words,

> When I first started, I was nervous. I told them I was nervous. I think
> they could sense it anyway, but I told them I was nervous. I was scared to
> death of my reactions, of how I was gonna react to seeing a man
> executed. Would I get so excited I might pass out, maybe embarrassing
> everyone? That would be unprofessional. I didn't know how I'd react. I
> didn't know once the switch threw whether I'd lose everything in my
> stomach or not. . . . I didn't [lose control], because I had the family. They
> were there. They gave me all the support I needed through the first one.

Then after that it just became a job. It just became a normal job. You build up your self-confidence so that when the time comes, you just do what you got to do.

"Now," the officer concluded with evident satisfaction, executions "seem like something we do every day."

The Private World of the Execution Team

The team that binds these men as a primary group operates in a world of its own, a world that is tailored to promote and reward the efficient conduct of executions. In a number of ways, the team is actually, and not just symbolically, set apart from the rest of the world during practice sessions and particularly during the deathwatch. For one thing, the death house in which the team carries out its duties is located in the basement of a building on the periphery of the prison compound. Though the death house is within the prison's massive walls, it is removed from the daily ebb and flow of life in the penitentiary.

You just get down there and you're pretty much left alone. . . . It's physically located in the basement. And even the windows—they have windows, but there's an earth mound outside and you can look up and you only see the bottom of people's feet as they're walking by. (laughing) And you're isolated, you know. People sometimes tend to forget about you, too.

Team members work in pairs during the deathwatch. These pairings (four in all) have evolved into stable partnerships. The formal reason for pairing the officers is to promote security, but the resulting partnerships strengthen each officer's bonds to the whole team as well as to his individual partner. When any given pair of officers is on duty during the twenty-four hours of the deathwatch, the remainder of the team sets up camp in the officers' lounge. This, once again, removes the execution team officers from interaction with the regular prison community.

We set up a place to sleep, almost a camp here. Because we got to rotate, you know, at night, through the night. When some of us are sleeping in [one area], we can walk and come up here [to another area] and drink coffee and eat, whatever.

These arrangements allow for continuing interaction between partners, reinforcing a sense of teamwork and shared purpose. Particularly as the time of execution draws near, the team uses its camp as a place to build esprit de corps and to get ready—"psyched up"—for the execution.

The team's camp also shelters the officers from potentially harsh scrutiny by outsiders, whether in the prison or from the larger community. Paradoxically, most prison inmates most of the time are indifferent to the workings of the execution team.

[Inmates] think that the people that is going to be electrocuted have deserved it. They went through all the process of the courts, and some of them been on death row for five or six years, and they figured they've, they've been fair to them.

Fellow officers, however, can be another matter. They may show jealousy and resentment, approval or disapproval. In any case, the team considers these reactions distracting, and best ignored.

Your fellow workers back here is more harder on you than maybe the inmates. You know, they give you the ol' silent treatment. Funny vibes you get from them, I don't know. . . . Some of 'em disapprove, and some of 'em pat you on the back. I really learnt don't pay no attention to it. Pay no attention one way or another.

The team also sees the media as a critical audience that must be kept at bay. Reporters are said to lurk outside the prison waiting to interview people involved with the execution, so the officers are content to stay where they are until the execution is over. Then, they know, they will be free to go about their business. "News people are funny," said the team leader. "They'll run over the top of you to get a story. But after the story is over with, they'll, they'll leave just as quick as they come in, you know." Meanwhile, according to another officer, "Being up there together and isolated from everybody gives us a little better feeling."

Physical isolation is complemented by the social isolation of self-imposed secrecy. Team members do not want others to know the details of their in-volvement in executions. Said one officer, "We look for a person who is very secretive, you know, and can keep things to himself. 'Cause this is very sec-retive, you know, what my part is and what his part is." Officers do not speak of their activities to outsiders. Their presumption is that outsiders simply wouldn't understand because, in one officer's blunt reckoning, "They hadn't been there." (I became an insider, it would seem, because I offered the officers a chance to speak openly and anonymously about their concerns. From the start, the officers encouraged me to attend an execution to form my own assessment of their operations.) Officers are even hesitant to let members of their families know any details of the execution process or their roles in it: "Well, we, we were sworn to secrecy. When I first got on the team, I wouldn't even tell my wife what I was doing. The deal was, keep it among ourselves. Whatever we say or do down here has got to stay down here, you know." Team members particularly fear that if the person who plays the for-mal role of executioner were to be identified as an individual, he would be stigmatized by others for what is really a team activity, and perhaps singled out and abused by vengeful convicts.

An Elite Unit

The deathwatch team, set apart physically and by its self-imposed social isola-tion, quite explicitly sees itself as an elite. As one officer observed, "It's an honor among ourselves to be on the team. I wouldn't go out on the street and broadcast that I'm on the execution team, but I'm proud of it." And rightly so. As befits an elite unit, the team receives privileges and perks. The officers are not paid a separate fee for carrying out executions, but the long hours mean overtime pay. Isolation from the regular prison routine allows small but special freedoms: the extra smoke or cup of coffee when they want it, the chance to mingle with their colleagues and to be their own boss much of the time. (Being isolated in the death house means being on their own a lot.) The camp mentality mentioned earlier lends itself to a suspension of normal work routines. There is a sense that on the deathwatch the officers are liberated from the mundane constraints of daily prison work.

Clearly, the team is an important group engaged in an important enterprise. After all, those who work at matters of life and death are protected from the hassles of everyday prison work. Furthermore, a direct line of command connects the team with the warden, which attests to the gravity of the team's task and gives the officers the heady sense that finally they can stand or fall on their collective merits.

> One thing that relieved us of a lot of stress was [that] we worked for the warden. When he activated us, we worked for him; that's who our orders came from. Came, you know, through the team leader and then to us. Anybody else, they couldn't come and, you know, disrupt you. So everybody knew what they had to do, and they just did what they had to do. You know, if you did it wrong, *you* did it wrong. You know what I'm sayin'?

In the prison work environment, one is subject to the conflicting directives and evaluations of various sector and shift commanders, and the rules of the game are often a hodgepodge one negotiates at one's peril.[20] Being on "the warden's team," entrusted with a special and clearly defined mission, is a privilege. "That team works on their own," confirmed the warden. "I never interfere. They know what they're doing. If they can't solve a problem, they'll bring it to me." In correctional circles, this is more than a job. It is almost, one suspects, an adventure.

These gratifying arrangements motivate the team members to do their work well. The officers think of themselves as skilled death-work technicians. Functioning as an autonomous team allows them to focus their technical skills to good result. Away from the madding crowds of the cell block and yard, following an explicit procedure and reporting to a single, supportive boss, the team is free to do well what it feels it does best:

> We think of ourselves as a special team. And I even heard one of [the officers] remark one time—tension got bad in the back and we were having a lot of problems [with the regular prisoners], and he walked up to me and he said, "When are we going to go back down in the basement and do what we do best?" Said, "Hell, I'd rather do the work down there than back here."

"We like to think we're the best in the nation," added another officer. "Nobody," he assured me, "does a better execution than we do."

A Modern Execution Team

This team was, to my knowledge, the first execution team to be studied and described. After the publication of the first edition of this book, a study of Missouri's execution team was undertaken by Steve Trombley and published in a book fittingly entitled *The Execution Protocol: Inside America's Capital Punishment Industry.*[21] The dynamics of Missouri's execution team, using lethal injection, offer an *exact* parallel to those of the execution team I studied using the electric chair. There is a detailed protocol in which every step in the execution process is laid out clearly, broken down into small steps, and rehearsed so that things go off like clockwork. Trombley reports that "During the execution, each event is timed with a stopwatch and logged by the operations officer, who is in the death chamber."[22] There is even a rehearsal with an officer from the team similar in size to the prisoner to be executed so that problems in the management of the offender can be simulated.[23] The focus is on teamwork and on the maintenance of morale; all members take responsibility for the execution and all members stress humaneness, defined as the "desire to ensure that the inmate's suffering is reduced to a minimum."[24] Close custody prevails during the deathwatch, with one or more officers observing the condemned prisoner in his solitary cell at all times.[25] Prisoners are told what to expect, "step by step," so there are "no surprises."[26] The prisoners cooperate, following the ritual, submitting to social control. "So far, we have not had to manhandle an inmate to get him in there to put him down."[27] The shared view is that "The constant practice, the breaking down of the process into specific roles, the clear understanding on the part of staff precisely what their role is," yields an execution procedure that is "competent, professional, and stress-free."[28]

My research and that of others reveals that bonds of solidarity are an essential feature of modern execution teams.[29] Established and nurtured in the private world of the deathwatch team, these ties are forged in commitment to a common purpose and tested in countless rehearsals. These human connections are the psychological cement that holds an execution team together under the pressures of death work. "It's really a team when you get down to the last hour, you know. You've got to be in, in conjunction. You've got to be ready to work together, to know this man's gonna be with me when I go down there to the death house." The men stress their professionalism as agents or instruments of the state and their respect for one another's skills, which have been tested in the ultimate context of the taking of life. When officers are called upon to take a prisoner to his death, they all draw strength from the knowledge that they are part of a modern execution team.

NOTES

1. N. Mailer, *The Executioner's Song* (Boston: Little, Brown, 1979).

2. Gilmore was much influenced by his mother, who early on saw her son as the criminal of the family. She also passed along a version of Mormonism that brought with it a preoccupation with violence. States Mikal, "They saw themselves not only as God's modern chosen people, but also as a people whose faith and identity had been forged by a long and

bloody history, and by outright banishment. They were a people apart—a people with its own myths and purposes, and with a history of astonishing violence." A central tenet of Mormonism, at least at the outset and as understood by the Gilmores, was blood atonement. "If you take a life, or commit any comparable ultimate sin, then your blood must be shed. Hanging or imprisonment would not suffice for punishment or restitution. The manner of death had to be one in which your blood spilled onto the ground, as an apology to God." M. Gilmore, *Shot in the Heart* (New York: Doubleday, 1994), 10, 17.

3. Ibid., xi.

4. See, for example, A. A. Skolnick, "Physicians in Missouri (but not Illinois) Win Battle to Block Physician Participation in Executions," *Journal of the American Medical Association* 274 (7): 524 (August 1995).

5. I. Solotaroff, "The Last Face You'll Ever See," *Esquire* 124 (2): 93 (August 1995).

6. Ibid., 95.

7. Ibid., 95.

8. W. Rideau and R. Wikberg, *Life Sentences: Rage and Survival Behind Bars* (New York: Times Books, 1992), 4–5, 316–317.

9. E. Johnson, "Some States Prepare for First Executions in Twenty Years or More," *Wall Street Journal*, 6 November 1984, 1. Lesy described the division of labor associated with executions, beginning at the top, with the warden, as a series of psychological "cutouts" that the individuals performing the labor use to minimize or even deny their involvement in executions. See M. Lesy, *The Forbidden Zone* (New York: Farrar, Straus & Giroux, 1987), 135–157. This warden exemplifies Lesy's point. Yet the warden and the officers of the execution team I studied did take responsibility, individually and collectively, for the executions they carried out. They asserted that executions are lawful sanctions, and as agents of the law they have nothing to hide from themselves or others. How they prepared themselves psychologically to carry out their perceived duty is a more complicated matter, often involving elements of psychological denial (especially of the humanity of the victim), but they did not deny or downplay their responsibility for executions.

10. D. A. Cabana, *Death at Midnight: The Confession of an Executioner* (Boston: Northeastern University Press, 1996), 17.

11. Rideau and Wikberg (n. 8), 317.

12. There are marked variations on this score. The warden of the prison I studied kept his distance from the process. He showed up to read the death warrant and signal the start of the execution but was otherwise uninvolved with the execution process. Donald Cabana reports that he was very much involved with the execution process, including being present for rehearsals; he was very much involved in the lives of the condemned prisoners, even during their final hours and minutes. See Cabana (n. 10).

13. For a discussion of focused interview procedures, see Chap. 3, Note 57.

14. One officer retired, the other died. To date, the team has had no dropouts, and morale remains high.

15. The team I studied was more concerned about losing control of the situation and having to use violence than they were with the prospect of a technically botched execution. Experience suggests, however, that when an execution is botched, the staff are deeply affected. "I remember the scene vividly," reports Commissioner Thigpen, present at a botched execution in Alabama's Atmore Prison. "I could not find adequate words then or later to express how much I regretted what had taken place. The members of the execution team who had failed to connect the chair correctly to its power source apologized time and again for their error. Steps were taken immediately following that event to eliminate the possibility of the same error occurring again. Still, that does not relieve you of the fact that you know a mistake had occurred that caused unnecessary suffering." See M. L. Thigpen, "A Tough Assignment—A Former Commissioner's Thoughts on Carry-

ing Out Executions," *Corrections Today* 55 (4): 58 (July 1993). At this execution, it was apparent to all involved that the execution had been botched. In other situations, outside observers may see an execution as flawed while the execution team does not, particularly if they conclude, rightly or wrongly, that no added distress was caused by any problems of implementation.

16. This view is widely shared by those associated with execution teams. As Warden Charlie Jones of Alabama's Atmore Prison put it, "You want to do it right. You've got to do it, and you want to do it in the most humane way possible. The least little annoyance in the routine can throw the whole thing out of kilter." See G. E. Goldhammer, *Dead End* (Brunswick, Me.: Biddle Publishing Company, 1994), 107. For other expressions of these and related sentiments, see the various articles under the heading, Special Focus—Managing Death Row, *Corrections Today* 55 (4): 56–99 (July 1993).

17. Great care in the selection of execution team members is the norm in the field, though it is not always the team leader who selects the officers on the team. See, for example, Cabana (n. 10), and Special Focus—Managing Death Row (n. 16).

18. The words of the officers are testimony to the stressful nature of the experience. As it happens, there is also objective evidence. Cabana reports that one of his officers, who served as a volunteer for a gas chamber rehearsal, showed a "heart rate [that] was wildly erratic." See Cabana (n. 10), 161. We can only imagine what condemned prisoners experience when they are secured to the execution machinery. The notion of "total helplessness" used by one of my respondents would seem appropriate, though perhaps "total terror" would be even more apt.

19. Terms like *clockwork* or *machine-like precision* are commonly used to describe executions carried out by well-trained teams of officers. See for example S. Trombley, *The Execution Protocol: Inside America's Capital Punishment Industry* (New York: Anchor Books, 1993), and Special Focus—Managing Death Row (n. 16).

20. L. X. Lombardo, *Guards Imprisoned: Correctional Officers at Work*, 2/e (Cincinnati: Anderson, 1989).

21. Trombley (n. 19), esp. 104–116. Donald Cabana's *Death at Midnight* (n. 10) examines executions in Mississippi's Parchman Prison. Cabana places more emphasis on his role as warden in charge of the execution process and less on the role played by the execution team. To the extent that the workings of the team are examined—the protocol, practice, rehearsals, etc—the parallels are once again exact.

22. Trombley (n. 19), 112.

23. Ibid., 116.

24. Ibid., 107.

25. Ibid., 108–109.

26. Ibid., 114.

27. Ibid., 114.

28. Ibid., 223.

29. The group dynamics of execution teams have not been explicitly discussed in the literature to any great extent, though the bonding of execution team officers is now well known to practitioners. The remarks of Warden Martin of Broad River Correctional Facility in South Carolina are instructive on this score: "As the execution date drew closer and the preparation grew more intense, our team became extremely close." See G. N. Martin, "A Warden's Reflections—Enforcing the Death Penalty with Competence, Compassion," *Corrections Today* 55 (4): 62 (July 1993). In my occasional work as a consultant on execution related matters, I have found that recognition of this bonding effect is quite common. See, generally, Trombley (n. 19).

6

Deathwatch

The Final Hours

The deathwatch team goes to work during the last hours before an execution. In the state under study, the deathwatch starts at eleven o'clock the night before the execution and ends at eleven o'clock the next night, when the execution takes place. At least two officers are with the prisoner at all times during that period. "If we thought maybe we had one [who] would commit suicide," stated the team leader, "we'd probably stay with him and sit there for forty-eight hours." The tasks of the deathwatch team are service, surveillance, and control. Their ultimate objective is to keep the prisoner alive and "on schedule"—that is, to move him through a series of critical and cumulatively demoralizing junctures beginning with his last meal and ending with his last walk. When the time comes, they must deliver the prisoner up for execution as quickly and unobtrusively as possible.

Critical junctures during the deathwatch include the prisoner's final visit with loved ones; a last meal; the boxing of the prisoner's personal possessions for distribution to relatives or friends; the shaving of the prisoner's head and right leg (to increase conductivity); a final shower, after which the prisoner changes into a fresh set of clothes for the execution; the transfer of the prisoner to the death cell, which is devoid of personal possessions of any kind; the reading of the death warrant; and finally the prisoner's last walk, to the death chamber and the electric chair. These junctures make up the schedule to which the officers refer as they move the prisoner toward his execution. After studying the general process by which the prisoner is controlled, we will examine how the schedule unfolds to accomplish an execution.

One would expect anybody, particularly a condemned prisoner with a history of violence, to resist execution by turning his rage on his keepers, or, failing that, himself. Officers are alert to these eventualities right up until the prisoner is in the chair. Like their colleagues on death row, the team officers appear to see the prisoner's situation in Hobbesian terms, with self-preservation the prisoner's most basic instinct or right. As Walter Berns has reminded us, it was Hobbes's view that "a man who is justly and legally condemned to death nevertheless retains the right to defend himself; indeed, he retains the right to kill his guards or anyone else who would prevent him from escaping."[1] But resistance is so rare as to be a nonissue. Even on death row, before execution is imminent, most prisoners see resistance as futile, even demeaning. "Either way it go," said one such inmate, "out the cell peaceful like, or you swing at them and hit them in the head and they bust you in the head—they gonna drag me around and strap me in the chair and go and turn on the juice."[2]

SOCIAL CONTROL

The typical prisoner is thoroughly defeated—in a word, dehumanized—by the time he commences his last walk. He is beyond resistance. To understand this phenomenon, one must think of the entire period the prisoner spends in confinement awaiting execution, on death row and during the deathwatch, as a continuous social control process. Waiting, worrying, plagued by nightmares that play out the grisly details of execution and by raw anxiety about how he will hold up under the pressure, the prisoner is worn down by the stress of confinement under sentence of death. This stress undermines his integrity as a human being and weakens, if not eliminates, his capacity to resist the will of his keepers.

On death row, the emphasis is on maintaining secure physical custody of the prisoner. Compliance is coerced when it is not forthcoming. By contrast, *social* control is the emphasis in the deathwatch. Shackles and cuffs are available here as they are on death row (see Part II), but modern execution etiquette does not permit a bound prisoner to be taken to his death.[3] The condemned prisoner must be under the social, not physical, control of his keepers; he must submit to the execution routine. The officials' goal, and in the end perhaps the prisoner's as well, is a smooth, orderly, and ostensibly voluntary execution, one that looks humane and dignified and is not sullied in any way by obvious violence.

Keeping the Prisoner Calm

Broadly speaking, the job of the deathwatch officers "is to sit and keep the inmate calm for the last twenty-four hours—and get the man ready to go." Keeping a condemned prisoner calm means, in part, serving his immediate needs. It is paradoxical to think of the deathwatch officers as serving the condemned, but the logistics of the job make service a central obligation of the officers. In the words of one officer,

> Well, you can't help but be involved with many of the things that he's involved with. Because if he wants to make a call to his family, well, you'll have to dial the number. . . . If he wants a cigarette, well, he's not allowed to keep matches, so you light it for him. You've got to pour his coffee, too. So you're aware what he's doing. It's not like you can just ignore him; you've gotta just be with him whether he wants it or not, and cater to his needs.

The officers cater to the condemned because contented prisoners are easier to keep calm and under control. Each and every officer on the team says this is so. But one can never trust even a seemingly contented prisoner facing execution. The deathwatch officers see condemned prisoners as potentially explosive, and literally stay an arm's length away from the prisoners when they hand things into their cells. Quite understandably, the officers are ever alert for trouble in their encounters with these prisoners. In their words,

- You always expect the unexpected. . . . You don't know what, what a man's gonna do. He's liable to snap, he's liable to pass out. We watch him all the time to prevent him from committing suicide. You've got to be ready—he's liable to do anything.

- We are very much concerned about security and him hurting himself. At the least little sign he's gonna attempt to hurt himself, we have to get on in there. . . . We look for mood swings, changes in attitude. Becoming argumentative. Anything out of the ordinary.

- Well, I'm thinking, always thinking. If this happen, what we gonna do? If that happen, what we gonna do? You never relax.

The prisoner is never out of at least one officer's sight, and a light is always burning in his cell. Records are maintained with a scrupulous attention to detail: "We record everything, missing nothing. If he turns over in his bed, we note it. How much he eats, how much coffee he drinks, how many cigarettes he smokes—we record it all." Surveillance is constant, and control, for all intents and purposes, is total.

One officer likened his security role to that of a football linebacker. Always on his toes, he must take in the big picture and be on the alert for any behavior that portends trouble. Another man consciously reads between the lines of his conversations with the condemned in an effort to get a handle on what the man is thinking.

- I'm very security-minded. You have to [be]; you can't be relaxed. It's just like playing football, you know. If you play linebacker, you can't be relaxed, you got to stay on your toes, you got to keep going at all times. . . . The guy might talk about he want to do this, he want to do that. He want this and he want that. He be pacing the floor. You know, you can tell the guy be getting ready to do something. The sound of his voice, you know, the way he talk to you, the way he walk. You watch everything. If you do relax, you get knocked down. You have to watch the whole thing.

- It's just hard. You never know what a man's gonna do when a man is doomed to die. I expect anything from him. I expect him to do anything to get out of this situation. Because he's already backed up to the wall. And the only thing between him and his freedom is me—when I'm down there. So I have to try to keep aware of where he is mentally. Even if it's to take him away from what he's thinking about. I don't want to have to wonder about nothin'. And I don't think he's gonna tell me the truth every time I ask him. I don't expect the truth, but from what he's telling me, he gonna answer my second question. My second question is, "What are you thinking?" Because I know he's thinking about something.

Both officers agree that if they don't anticipate and control any problems, the problems will control them. In particular, they, like the officers on death row (see Chapter 4), fear that a desperate inmate might try to injure or even kill an officer, either out of revenge or simply to delay the execution. The fact that the deathwatch prisoner is almost never out of his cell diminishes this fear, but it lingers as a background concern.

Maintaining Emotional Distance

Relations between the officers and their charges can be quite intense. Watching and being watched are always engaging activities, particularly when the stakes are life and death. These relations are, nevertheless, impersonal; there are no grudges, but neither is there much evidence of compassion or fellow feeling. The deathwatch officers are civil but cool, as are most death row officers (see Chapter 4). But most deathwatch team officers carry this deportment to the extreme, keeping a profound emotional distance from the men they are about to kill.

And no wonder. The utter and unremitting impersonality of their job symbolically dehumanizes the members of the execution team. This enables the officers, while on the job, to approach executions not as feeling persons but as bureaucrats of violence. The dehumanization these execution team officers experience is far more pervasive than that experienced by their colleagues on death row.

To keep their distance from the prisoner, the execution team officers erect "barriers," to quote the warden, between themselves and the prisoner. The officers concurred with this assessment. To do otherwise, they maintained, would make it harder to execute the condemned prisoner. A more personal relationship with the prisoner might even be a kind of hypocrisy, one officer noted, because one might like him and still have to kill him. The attitude of the officers is thus that the prisoners arrive as strangers and are easier to kill if they go out the same way.

- If they talk to me, I'll try to answer them. But I don't start no conversations. I try to avoid being with them as much as possible. I really don't want to get acquainted with someone, you know, when you're gonna kill him that night. I guess it could be a psychological thing there, you know. If you didn't know him that might make it a little easier. But you could be around a person so long that you might get to know him, you might like him or think pretty much of him, and I really don't want to think that I might like a person, then you got to go on to kill him that night. So, you know, to me it, it's kind of a hypocritical thing, you know, to get to know him.

- I don't like particularly to talk to the men. I just figure we wouldn't, we wouldn't have anything in common to talk about. I'm getting ready to electrocute him, and he's getting ready to die, and we just don't have anything in common. . . . It would be the best if you didn't, didn't know him. It's the best not to know him.

It is, the officers contend, literally "us against them." The officers are a team; the prisoner stands apart. The gulf that separates them, the officers might say, is as wide and deep as infinity.

Still, the officers learn that it is hard not to have at least intimations of empathy for a fellow human being in trouble, even if one goes out of one's way to remain aloof from him. The warden, certain that his officers throw up emotional barriers in self-defense, was equally convinced that "they get more personally involved than they will ever tell you or me." He may have a point. Remember, the officers must serve and observe the prisoner, so they are necessarily involved with him to some degree. Final visits, too, can be moving, tearful events, and these occur in the immediate presence of a group of officers. To be sure, the officers are there en masse for the purpose of security, but they cannot fail to note the human drama that is unfolding before their eyes. These encounters may not touch them deeply, but they almost certainly do touch them.

Officers may also find that they are called upon to execute prisoners they have come to know and even like over their years of work in the prison system. This happened to one of the officers on the team, at an execution carried out after the publication of the first edition of the book. "Well, it was pretty rough," he told me, "if you know the man a long time, it kind of gets to you a little bit." The officer found that it was impossible to stay aloof from this prisoner during the deathwatch.

We talked, we kidded a lot. He said, "If I need a phone call, I'll get the other guard to make it." Because I have a speech problem. So he said, "By the time you get the words out, I'll be gone." I said, "OK." He was just kidding. Anyway, we got along pretty good.

Later, when the chaplain and this prisoner prayed together minutes before his last walk, the officer joined them. "So, I stayed around and we prayed with him and the chaplain. We all prayed together. Then it was over with." The chaplain was moved. "I told him, 'That was really, really fine. You really were wonderful.' He said, 'He was my friend.'" When it came time for the prisoner's last walk, this officer volunteered. "I'll take him by the arm and walk him on in," he told the others, taking on a role that was new to him, for the sole purpose of helping the prisoner get through the ordeal.

By his account, the officer learned two lessons that night. The first is that "it is good to get close to a man because you can talk to him if he's got a problem. You can try to help him." There is, then, a possible human services role open even to executioners caught up in what is otherwise an impersonal bureaucratic proceeding. The second lesson modified the first. "I think that it is good to help, but you've got to try and keep your distance a little bit, too. Because after it is over, it will affect you. It affected me." Saddened but enriched, he considers himself a better officer as a result of the experience.[4]

This officer's experience makes it clear that to maintain emotional distance from condemned prisoners, officers must *actively* suppress their natural feelings of kinship with fellow human beings. This they are trained to do, both as prison officers and as members of the team. In the warden's words, "from the cradle to the grave, correctional officers are told, 'Don't get personally involved,' and that's what they try to do." This advice is part of the training officers receive and is reinforced in their daily prison work on and off death row.[5] (A similar process may operate with high-level correctional officials as well.[6]) They become expert at denial, which in the warden's view amounts to "tucking things in the recesses of their minds, where they don't have to deal with it." One effective technique the officers use is to remind themselves of the gruesomeness of the condemned prisoner's crime and the justice of his punishment. Note the following exchange between a team officer and myself:

> We don't see him all that much or talk to 'em, but, I mean, a human being is a human being. But you, the way you get around getting to like 'em, you read the papers and things, and you brush up on the case and just see what this man has done, you know. And when you find out that he drove nails through a woman's, an old woman's hand and nailed her to a chair and set the house on fire with her in it, then you kinda get to saying, "Well, this man here, he can't be no good."
>
> *Even if you have feelings for him, knowing what he did makes it easier?*
>
> I wouldn't have feelings for him; I wouldn't get that close to him. I wouldn't let myself get, get that way.
>
> *So you see it as a problem. You just don't let yourself get close?*
>
> Right, it's a problem. Like I say, you read the newspaper, and you try to find out all the dirty things that he done. (Laughing) So, so you say, "Well, okay, it's okay. It's all right, all right to put him to death."

Officers must psych themselves up during the last hours before an execution, a point I shall return to later. Dwelling on the details of the crime helps them get in the proper frame of mind for an execution.

Calculated Camaraderie

Two specific officers on the team are regularly assigned to guard the prisoner during his last five or six hours, the period during which the critical junctures mentioned earlier take place. They are given the delicate but essential job of keeping the prisoner calm and on schedule as the hour of execution approaches. (The officer who participated in the execution of a condemned prisoner he considered a friend, discussed above, was assigned this role for that execution only, due to staffing problems in the prison that impinged on team officers. It may be that his unfamiliarity with this manipulative role, or his unsuitability for it, accounts in part for the more personal approach he took.) As a general matter, these officers become more involved with the condemned prisoners than do their colleagues. Indeed, they *seek* relationships with the condemned. But these relationships are calculated and superficial, and are sought for the control they offer. In effect, the *job* of these officers is to establish relations, and they do so *solely* to achieve control over the prisoner. In the end—and until the end—they use this relationship to manipulate the prisoner's behavior so that he will comply with the etiquette of a dignified execution.

These officers work together to keep the prisoner occupied. They pour the man's coffee, light his cigarettes, listen to his stories, laugh at his jokes. They are unfailingly courteous, notes the chaplain, "even when there's been some guys, that at times because of fears or anxieties or whatever, have lashed out at them. I've never seen them respond with anything other than kindness." Unlike their more taciturn and aloof colleagues on earlier shifts, these officers make a conscious effort to talk with the prisoner, to engage and relate to him. In the words of one of these men,

> It's a critical time. The guys down there, they don't know whether they're going or not until the last minute. And during that period of time, they're constantly going through different mood swings, and I just stay there and try to keep them on an even keel. Whichever way they fluctuate, I go with them. There's me and another coworker of mine; we sit with them for the last hours. We're the only two that's there. And we're able to communicate. So far, we haven't had any problems, anybody getting disruptive right at the end or trying to commit suicide or anything. We just keep them right there and keep talking to them.

The point of these conversations is not merely to pass time; it is to keep tabs on the prisoner's state of mind, and to steer him away from subjects that might depress, anger, or otherwise upset him. Sociability, in other words, quite explicitly serves as a means of social control—keeping the man on an even keel and "on schedule" for a controlled execution. Relationships, such as they emerge for these officers, serve purely calculated ends. There may be an element of emotional involvement here, as the warden would have it, but clearly any fellow feeling is secondary to the task at hand as seen by these officers, sometimes vividly referred to as "getting the man dead." What dominates here is impersonality—indeed, impersonality at its worst: masquerading as concern for the stranger one hopes to execute with as little trouble as possible.

A more or less constant stream of conversation seems to be at the heart of this enterprise. The impression one gets is that ideally the staff would keep the man talking until the very end, which would come swiftly and without warning. As one officer said,

> Talking to him helps, you know. It moves the time faster, you know. If I see this person going—you know, getting really upset—I just try to talk with him, you know. Just bring up any type of subject not dealing with death, just anything. You don't want the inmate to be looking at his watch, or looking at the clock and saying "Wow, it's almost eleven, it's almost the twenty-sixth and I'm going to die the twenty-sixth." You know, you don't want that. You want it like this: As soon as he come up on that time [for the execution], boom! it's over.

Knowingly or unknowingly, chaplains, lawyers, and visitors may play a role in the denial process. They, too, wish to distract prisoners from the ugly reality that awaits them.

Unintentional Collusion

Relatives and others who call the prisoner, or who accept his calls, serve the useful end of buffering the emotional impact of the execution on the prisoner. Condemned prisoners have access to a telephone in their cells, and they can use it at length. The officers are well aware that conversations, whether with themselves, with visitors, or with callers, keep the prisoner's mind off the electric chair and make it easier for them to keep him calm and on schedule. "I just love it when outsiders stay with the man or talk [on the phone] with the man," the warden admitted. "They take the last-minute heat; it takes pressure off the team." It is almost as if these outsiders were an extension of the team. Indeed, the warden considered one chaplain, who was good at helping prisoners find some mental peace, as an honorary member of the execution team.

The prospect of collusion in relationships between the condemned and their supporters may be especially problematic for attorneys. Attorneys fight to keep their clients alive. Ironically, they do so with a commitment to professionalism that is shared by the warden and the members of the execution team. Once the prisoner's avenues of appeal have been exhausted, however, or when the prisoner has knowingly waived further appeals, professional obligations of attorneys impel them to help their clients die with some semblance of dignity. This means helping prisoners to conform to the official routine, and doing so themselves, so that the execution goes quickly and smoothly. The attorney for John Evans III, who had become demoralized on death row and had relinquished his appeals, described how he dealt with the prison warden.

> I thanked him for his professional attitude and his courtesy. I thanked him for making it easier for John and his family. We shook hands.
> I had to wonder at our roles. We were professionals. He was the executioner and I was the defense lawyer. Here we were thanking each other

for being so professional. One pro to another. For doing what? Making a hard job bearable? For helping reduce tensions all around? For making it go down easier?

Damn, I thought. This man is going to kill John in about three hours. He is going to pull the switch and shoot electricity through John's head and fry his brains out. That's exactly what he's going to do.

And here I am thanking him for being a pro. What was I doing in all this? Another pro. A respectable cog in this grotesque machinery of butchery. My job was to help provide a clean execution. I should be screaming and shouting. I should make them drag me out of there—create a scene. I should make it as hard and tough and as sick and inhumane as it was. I should be making my voice heard in this ritual of cruelty. I should make these bastards hear my voice and know what the hell they are doing.

And yet my rage gave way to thinking about John and his suffering. I had to serve him. And serving him meant taking my role as set out in the rites of execution. . . .

I had to be strong for John. If it was easier for him to accept his death and make peace within himself, then I would do all I could do to help him.[7]

Evans was executed in Alabama in 1983. In Alabama, the warden serves as the executioner.

The prisoner's supporters may collude in the execution process, as the warden would have it, but at least they are trying to help someone they care about in a time of great need. The role played by the final pair of deathwatch officers is, in contrast, a pseudosocial, strained affair. Yet the prisoner's hunger for human contact is such that even here there are moments of surface congeniality that he may find comforting. In one instance, even the last meal, voluntarily shared with an officer, was marked by apparently lighthearted banter.

These perverse arrangements are almost certainly mutually exploitative. People are friendly, but no friendships are born; there is laughter but no happiness or joy. "You treat him like an acquaintance, maybe, not a friend." Each party has a hidden agenda: The prisoner denies his fate and escapes momentarily into convivial fantasy; the guard moves his man through the execution schedule and closer to his fate, all the while keeping the prisoner's "mind at ease, his feelings under control." The officers, at least, are clear on their agenda. As one officer explained in the following exchange with me, the talk and the laughter were all in a day's work:

People that you think would have problems out of, being the last day, we don't have any problems out of 'em. Half the time me and the individual person be laughing. We just be laughing, you know. The guy's laughing and I'm laughing.

Do you develop a kind of friendship with the man, do you think, or is that too strong of a word?

Well, I don't look at it as a friendship thing. I look at it, myself, as an overall job. The man know what he done, and he know what he got to do, you know, and it's my job to get him through it. And I more or less put myself in condition for to get him through them last hours. No matter what it takes. I sit down and eat with him, the last meal, and all that. Anything he want to do, I sit down and do with him. . . . Shoot, one of 'em actually asked what to order and we didn't know what to order so we ordered McDonald's food for 'im. He ate Big Macs and I ate Big Macs, you know. And talk and laugh and whatever, you know.

So, you're kind of like a companion whose purpose is to get them through this last journey. And in the process (pause), well, in the process, do you develop any friendly feeling for these guys?

I don't look at it as being a friendly feeling. I just look at it as getting the job done. . . . It's a pleasant conversation, but you still have that sense [that] he's sitting there talking to you but he's thinkin' 'bout this whole matter, you know. He never forget what he's got to do later on, you know.

Neither, one can be sure, does the officer forget.

THE FINAL HOURS: CRITICAL JUNCTURES IN AN EXECUTION

As time grows short, prisoners may ask their guards what, in general terms, awaits them. The prisoners seem to want an overview of the process so that they can prepare themselves for what is to come. As a general rule, they don't want to know the gory details of execution, and the officers have no intention of allowing them to dwell on such troubling matters. To help put the prisoners at ease, though, the officers map out the execution process short of the execution itself. In one officer's words,

The last five or six hours, guys start asking what's going to happen to 'em and stuff like that—you know, what's going to happen to his property—and I more or less start running down to him what goes on up until the last fifteen minutes, you know. They appreciate that. I tell them nothing wrong; I'm telling them like it is. More of them worry, "Is my family going to get my personal property?" "Will I be able to talk to my people on the telephone or whatever?" You know, and you explain to them, this is what goes on up until a quarter to eleven. But I never get on a basis of saying, "Hey, you know, this is what's going to happen to you in the chair. . . . This is what goes down at the end." I never get on that basis. If a man start talking about the chair, I change the subject. 'Cause you try to keep them calm, and I don't want, you know, myself, to get them upset.

Exchanges of this sort demonstrate the persistence of denial, even on the threshold of execution. Condemned prisoners use denial as a psychological defense mechanism, first on death row, then during the deathwatch.[8] The prisoners don't want to hear about their executions, at least not in specific, personal terms, and the guards, who also benefit from this denial, don't want to tell them. So the prisoner talks to his executioners about procedures in the abstract and remains calm, even as his private sadness and fear grow apace.[9]

Generally speaking, the mood becomes more somber and subdued during this final period, as the execution draws near. Though, as noted earlier, one prisoner ate a hearty last meal in the ostensibly congenial company of a death-watch officer, most eat little or nothing at all. At this point the prisoners, in a last-ditch effort steeped in denial, may steadfastly maintain that their executions will be stayed. The pathos of this effort comes through, even in the retelling. One man proclaimed his execution to be "inconceivable." Such bravado is belied by the prisoners' loss of appetite, which reveals deeper doubts and fears and is taken by the officers to be a sign of weakening resistance. "You can see them going down," said one officer. "Food is the last thing they got on their minds."

Next the prisoners must box the meager worldly goods that they have brought with them to their death house cell. They have already given up many of the things that they possessed in their death row cells; items ruled to be either superfluous (no one needs jogging shoes or basketballs in the death house) or potential weapons (hobbycraft items may fall into this category, given the desperate situation of the prisoner) were confiscated and put aside when the prisoner arrived at the death house, in accordance with regulations. The staff, at this point, inventories all of the prisoner's possessions, including those already put aside, records them on a one-page checklist form, packs them in boxes, and marks them for disposition to family or friends.

Prisoners are visibly saddened and even moved to tears by this procedure, which at once summarizes their lives and underscores the imminence of their death. Up until this time, the prisoners have been gradually shedding unnecessary psychological baggage. One man, for example, simply forgot the names of his fellow condemned, though he had lived with them for years and felt himself to be a member of the death row community. The other prisoners no longer existed for him; their demise, so to speak, made it easier for him to face his own death. Relinquishing his property was a different matter. This amounted to abandoning *any* claim to a relationship with something outside himself. This radical step made oppressively real that which had been conveniently unconscious. The loss of his property hurt, since it clearly symbolized his coming loss of life. (To make a difficult situation worse for this man, some of his prized possessions, which had been stored away when he first entered the death house, turned up missing when his property was inventoried. The prisoner assumed that some prison official had stolen them because he saw the prisoner as a dead man who would have no need for material things.) At this point, with or without complications, strong feelings are apt to come to the surface, threatening unpredictable behavior. Sensing this, the officers step up security. Said one of the officers, "I really get into him; I watch him real close." The execution schedule, the officer pointed out, "is picking up momentum, and we don't want to lose control of the situation."

This momentum is not lost on the condemned prisoner. Critical milestones have passed. The prisoner now moves in a limbo devoid of food or possessions; he has seen the last of such things, unless he receives a stay of execution and rejoins the living. At the next critical juncture, his identity is expropriated as well: His head is shaved, along with his face and right leg. Shaving facilitates a palatable electrocution. It reduces the physical resistance to electricity and minimizes singeing and burning. But the process has obvious psychological significance as well, adding greatly to the perceived momentum of the execution.

The shaving procedure is quite public and intimidating. The condemned man is taken from his cell and seated in the middle of the tier. His hands and feet are cuffed, and he is dressed only in undershorts. The entire deathwatch team is assembled around him. They stay at a discreet distance, but it is obvious that they are there to maintain control should he resist in any way or make any untoward move. As a rule, the man is overwhelmed. As one officer told me bluntly, "Come eight o'clock, we've got a dead man. Eight o'clock is when we shave the man. We take his identity; it goes with the hair." This taking of identity is undeniably a collective process—the team makes a forceful "we," the prisoner their helpless object. The officers are confident that the prisoner's capacity to resist them is now depleted. What is left of the man erodes over the remaining three hours before the execution. In the words of another officer,

> When you get to the point of shaving the man's head, that usually will take just about all the strength a man has out of him. It's not long before he actually becomes a walking dead man. Because he knows that there is no more hope after that point. I've done six executions, and it's the same way for all of them. I have seen no change in it. Like when Delilah cut Samson's hair, that was it. It took all of his strength. There was nothing left.

After the prisoner has been shaved, he must then shower and don a fresh set of clothes for the execution. The clothes are unremarkable in themselves, though the prisoner must surely notice that buttons and zippers have been replaced by Velcro (to prevent his body from burning during the electrocution). Their real significance is symbolic, for this outfit marks the prisoner as a man ready for execution. As if to underscore this symbolism, the condemned prisoner is then weighed and photographed; his recorded image is then entered into a display case with the many others, dating back nearly to the beginning of the century, who have been executed at the prison. Physically "prepped" and with his picture and vital statistics saved for posterity, the prisoner is then stored, in effect, in an empty tomblike cell, the death cell. All that is left is the wait.

During this final period, the deathwatch area takes on a distinctively funereal ambiance. The officers are quiet, moving about gingerly so as not to disturb the prisoner. One might say they behave much like attendants at a wake or funeral. They are exceedingly courteous to visitors, offering chairs, including their own, and coffee—even, in one instance, the last cup in the pot. Visitors, in turn, treat the officers cordially. The officers, ever prompt and responsive though never obsequious, give the inmate anything he is allowed, such as coffee, juice, or a light for his cigarette. (The officers are solicitous, but they remain wary; the prisoner, ever wary himself, responds with subdued politeness.) The officers clean scrupulously to keep the area presentable to officials, who drop in and out periodically. These officials, too, are quiet and reserved, even reverent. They speak in hushed tones, as though they were visiting a grave.

Held in this increasingly lifeless milieu, the prisoner can normally count on his attorney, a chaplain, and a personal counselor for emotional support and advice. Like the team officers, these people see the prisoner's despair and deterioration. Unlike the officers, however, they try to help the prisoner cope on his own terms. A counselor who had been present at a number of executions told me that the aim of her advice, as well as that of the chaplain, depends on the status of the execution. If the prisoner has not yet exhausted his appeals, she tries to help him maintain a balance between "preparing for living and preparing for dying." Ideally, at this point, she continued, the prisoner "should be 'on hold,' ready to go either way." As execution becomes imminent, however, her objective shifts to helping the man "escape the horror" of execution.[10]

I know from my prior research that condemned prisoners do contemplate their executions, even years before their date with the electric chair. They shudder at the physical violence of electrocution and the indignity it visits on the body. "I already have an understanding about electricity," said one man, "it's not hard for me to imagine what an experience it would be."[11] They fear they will suffer great pain. Staff do not—or cannot—acknowledge this. Not only do wardens and execution team members, almost to a man, maintain that electrocution is painless—like a bolt of lightning, it is thought to instantly shatter the nervous system, rendering the prisoner unconscious—they contend that the prisoners themselves take comfort in the swift and painless death promised them by the chair. (It would thus be no consolation to prisoners or staff to know that most authorities maintain that electrocution is likely to be quite painful, and that at least one medical authority has compared electrocution to burning at the stake.[12]) Prisoners also agonize over their last walk, fearful that they will break down and leave behind a legacy of cowardice. As one man put it, "Don't nobody want to go out and the word you left behind is that you broke down." (A related concern—that prisoners will "mess" themselves on the last walk or in the death chamber—is sometimes voiced as a source of dreaded embarrassment.[13]) For years, prisoners have lived with a domino theory of executions; every execution, however distant, has seemed to move their own a bit closer.[14] This theory is entirely false—each case runs its own course of appeals—but no matter. Now they are next, and they are about to fall, perhaps painfully, perhaps ignominiously.

There is really no way to soften these hard realities—to deny the violence of forced death or the pressure of a last walk. Yet in the death house, as the hours wind down, the concerns of the prisoners shift from those that obsessed them over the preceding years. The *method* of execution and associated indignities recedes in significance and the *fact* of execution—of impending death—takes center stage. Interviews conducted since the execution team switched to lethal injection a few years back reveal that "the method is a detail," in the words of their counselor, "not a big deal to these men." While one man in the death house conceded that "it's probably better to get shot up than fried up"—better to face lethal injection than electrocution—"it's not all that much better." It is the counselor's considered opinion, rendered after assisting men facing both methods of death, that "all the men in the death house are stunned." Continuing, she stressed that "they don't dwell on the means"—on the chair or gurney and how one gets there—but focus instead on "the traumatic process" of which they are helpless captives.

The focus of discussion with the prisoner who stands on the threshold of execution reflects these concerns. In the words of the counselor, that focus is "not on what's going on around [him] in the death house, not on execution and being killed, but on dying and moving on to the next life." The prisoner is counseled to "let go, and go wherever it is you're going." Prisoners, many of whom devoutly wish for an afterlife, try to heed such counsel. Advice of this sort may be intellectually suspect (a theme developed in Chapter 9) but is as good as any in this situation. (After all, the condemned man has little hope of forgiveness from us, which is why we have sentenced him to a lonely, violent death.[15]) The execution team would no doubt concur in this advice, which encourages the prisoner to go to his death without resistance or struggle. This counsel, by promoting both denial and passive submission to the death work routine, furthers the prisoner's decline toward death.

DEFEATED MEN

The prisoner at the point of execution is more like an object without sensation than a flesh-and-blood person on the threshold of death. Officers had much to say about this phenomenon:

- We talked a lot among ourselves about this, and we think that when he realized that, that he's had it, is when we cut his hair off and put him in this other cell. We strip the cell [across from his old cell] and put him in this cell [the death cell]. He don't have any personal things over there or anything. Just a sheet and so forth, a mattress in it. And I think that's when he definitely thinks he's had it. . . . [He's] just calm, he just kinda accepts that this is it. I think it would be like, like almost being in a trance.

- We're cutting his hair and shaving their legs and all that stuff, and it's just more or less normal. It's just, just very quiet. . . . Most times, he's quiet.

We, you know, we tell him to move his head as we shave his head or whatnot. We tell him to shower and put his clothes on. He's, he's quiet. He responds to it, and he doesn't show no animosity towards you, towards any officer. . . . That's when it dawns on 'im it's gonna happen.

- When they come out of the shower, they go into a different cell; we put them in a different cell then, the death cell. Nothing but the bare essentials: the bed, the sheets, mattress, and clean clothes, that's it. Most of the time, they want a Bible, and pencil and paper to write a letter. . . . They don't say anything.

By the accounts of the deathwatch officers, these prisoners are beaten men, shells of their former selves, mentally dead or dying. Exhausted or, more properly, drained of spirit, the condemned surrender to the execution. According to the officers,

- His mind goes first. . . . All resistance disappears, they're exhausted. I think he make it up in his mind then, you know, that he's ready to go. He blocks everything out, you know, as far as where I'm gonna be tomorrow, what I'm gonna do, you know. I know what I've got to do. There's no more pain, no more sorrow. I'm going. And that's it, gonna get it over with. I don't have to fight the lawyers and the judges and the courts no more.
- They work it out in their minds and they accept it. . . . A lot of 'em die in their minds before they go to that chair. I've never known of one or heard of one putting up a fight. . . . By the time they walk to the chair, they've completely faced it. Such a reality most people can't understand. 'Cause they don't fight it. They don't seem to have anything to say. It's just something like "Get it over with." They may be, they may be numb, sort of.
- They go through stages. And at this stage, they're real humble. Humblest bunch of people I ever seen. Most all of 'em is real, real weak. Most of the time, you'd only need one or two people to carry out an execution, as weak and as humble as they are. They're really a humble bunch of people.

In these astute assessments, the officers of the execution team would seem to concur with the French existentialist Albert Camus, who saw the condemned prisoner on the threshold of execution as devoid of autonomy, "no longer a man but a thing waiting to be handled by the executioners."[16]

These humble, beaten "things" seem to their keepers to be barely human and alive. But they are not dead yet, and so the officers remain vigilant. For some of these prisoners, the officers assume, a thin and precarious line may separate quiet defeat from an hysterical and perhaps violent collapse of personality. Emotions are always muted during the deathwatch; near the end they are taboo. There is no music in the death house in the final hours because music moves people, sometimes awakening deep feelings.[17] Even consoling a man during the final wait might move him to tears, which in turn might precipitate an outright breakdown. An officer made this point in the following exchange with me:

> You don't want to console them, you know, 'cause then you be letting them slip back into a suicidal state. That's the most critical point.
>
> *Consoling them would make them suicidal?*
>
> I think so. I look at what they're facing—you're talking about being hit with electricity. Number one, it's much easier for them to take their own selves out than to face that. It's a real critical point. They might do anything.

In point of fact, many prisoners on death row do give serious thought to suicide as an alternative to execution (in one study, more than half).[18] Compared with execution, suicide seems to these prisoners a more dignified way to die, and one that leaves their families a more respectable legacy. Others, fewer in number, would like you to believe that they will stage a last stand, perhaps taking an officer or two with them. (One sometimes hears this brand of tough talk, a form of bravado, in group discussions with condemned prisoners.) Though few prisoners commit suicide at this juncture (none, to my knowledge, have ever hurt or killed an execution team officer), the team understandably treats them with caution. From the team's perspective, the prisoners are like dormant volcanoes—the surface calm reassures, but cataclysmic violence may not be far below.

Though by all accounts defeated and demoralized, the prisoners are not simply walking corpses the staff can direct toward the electric chair. In the warden's view, "They're numb, acting like 'I can't believe what's happening to me' or 'here I go, let's get it over with,' but I think they're very cognizant, all the way." "Very cognizant" may be an overstatement, if the officers on the team are to be believed. So, too, Camus's assessment of the condemned as "things" may be an overstatement. Still, the prisoners seem to retain a primitive sense of dignity, or at least a reflex sense of decorum, and in this respect they show some awareness of what is happening to them. From this residuum of real or feigned humanity, the condemned and his executioners forge an informal contract that goes something like this: The prisoner, obviously in distress, is admonished to walk to his death like a man, in conformity with the official script; the executioners, in control of themselves and the situation, imply that, in exchange, they will do the job cleanly and without a hitch. A fatal collusion ensues. Here's how one officer saw this delicate process:

> They get to a point where they don't know where they are. They don't really know what's happening. . . . I seen most of them right there at the end. They weaken to the point where they'll be almost crying, and I tell them, I say, "Well, you don't want to go out like that." I say, "People be here in a minute—pull yourself up." And they'll go ahead and get back on key where they were. That works every time for me. . . . They don't want to go out like that.

It is the unanimous view of the officers that the inmates want to "hold up for the row." In one officer's reckoning, "they want to go out like men." "We try to instill in them death with dignity," said another officer, "we don't want to see them falling apart."

Of the many inmates executed by the deathwatch team, only one man broke down at the end. (Pathetically, he had to be almost carried to the chair, with his eyes closed.) The others, though they did not break down, may well have been emotionally fragile. After all, "they don't really know what is happening," as the officer on the scene said, but they must sense the gathering violence of the execution. Fear and hate and impotent rage almost certainly stir within these men, threatening to overwhelm them, portending futile violence or demeaning tears. For this reason, all must be urged to pull themselves together and walk to the chair like men.[19]

Whatever may be the deeper psychic life of condemned prisoners on the brink of execution, they wait meekly to be escorted to their deaths. The people who come for them, joining the two officers who stayed with the prisoner during his final hours, are the warden and the remainder of the deathwatch team, flanked by high-ranking correctional officials. The warden reads the court order, known popularly as a death warrant. This is, as one officer said, the "real deal," and nobody misses its significance. As he explained,

> They know what the real deal is, you know. When it's time to go, I more or less have drawed out a picture for the man, saying, "Hey, this is it."
> This is the real deal right now. And when they see people come in there and start reading the court order to 'em, they know what the real deal is.

The condemned prisoners then go to their deaths compliantly, captives of the inexorable, irresistible momentum of the situation. As one officer put it, "There's no struggle. . . . They just walk right on in there."

In the end, condemned prisoners suppress whatever residual thoughts and feelings they may have, giving themselves over to the execution process. They go to their deaths one slow and controlled and methodical step at a time, numb to the awful violence that awaits them. In this, paradoxically, they may resemble their executioners, who also seek peace from troubling feelings in mindless, mechanical conformity to the modern execution drill.

BEHIND-THE-SCENES PREPARATION

While the officers in the death house prepare the prisoner for execution, the remainder of the team must get ready to carry out the act. Most of their preparations take place in the team's camp, away from the prisoner and the two officers assigned to guard him. Some of these activities are mechanical. The chair is tested and made ready. (The prisoner may hear the dull thud that accompanies the flood of electricity, and even imagine that he smells the burning of residual flesh from executions past. This upsets and embitters some prisoners, who feel that the staff are *assuming* that they are as good as dead, but this result is unintentional.[20]) The cap and leg piece must be soaked (first in brine, then in cold fresh water); the electrode connections must be buffed clean. Mostly, however, the officers of the team try to ready themselves emotionally.

Psyching Up

The officers say they must "psych up" for the challenge that awaits them. "Anything can happen," one man assured me, "and we have to be ready for anything." The officers are tense, and it shows. They relate their anxieties and share ways to deal with problems; they trade jokes and insults, and tell war stories about recalcitrant inmates they subdued in times past. Their behavior is not solely a form of release. It is purposive, serving at once to calm the nerves and get the adrenaline pumping. In the words of the officers,

- We do have to get psyched up, 'cause a lot of times you never know if we're gonna have to use force to put the man in the chair or not. We never have, but we always try to get ourselves in a position that we can do it if we have to do it. And we discuss who's going in the cell, who's gonna take him out, and how we're gonna do it without gettin' ourselves hurt.

- You have to get yourself psyched up for this thing, I tell you, you got to get psyched up. And the way we do it is we play jokes, you know, act the fool, whatever. . . . Most of the time, we get to talking about things that happened back in here, you know. "I whupped that old inmate," you know, things like that. "We, we got him out of that cell and whupped him," you know, things like that. Something that we all can relate to. "Do you remember about the time that this happened?" Or something like that.

Even gross racial slurs can be exchanged with impunity, as is revealed in this exchange:

> We're always laughing and joking. We say a lot of things that come out sometimes right crude that shouldn't be said. It stays on the team, and no one ever gets mad at the other one; even when they say something wrong, we don't take that much offense in it. For instance, like there's mostly blacks on the team. We can call one a nigger (pause), and he don't get mad.

> *So you guys are pretty close then?*

> Yeah. I don't believe you would ever hear a conversation anyplace and say the names and say the things we say, anyplace. I've never heard of it before. . . . Like, one guy, I joke with him, and he outranks me. And he's black but is lighter-skinned. He looks like a Chinese fellah. Now and I told him if he just comes to be disgusted and didn't want to do this, he could always come live with me and be my laundry boy. (Laughing) He done turns and says, "Go to hell, white man!" (Laughing) You know, we could say things and not neither one of us ever get mad.

Crude jokes may also be made about executions. "We make jokes about it. You know, we say, 'Well, what if the current goes out? Get a baseball bat.' Stuff like that." Some people may think "we are very sick individuals," this officer conceded, but the point is to let off tension.

It goes without saying that some of these activities would offend outsiders. The officers know that, but still, none of this behavior divides or weakens the team. Rather, these antics and insults reaffirm the team's primary-group bonds (see Chapter 5). One can say unspeakable things to one's "family," and doing so under stress may help affirm that reassuring bond. (By the same token, one keeps any differences of opinion to oneself. "We do not want to be divided. So our feelings, our personal feelings, what we think about a prisoner, say, we try to keep it to ourselves and we see that that makes for a more united team.") Psyching up in this way also promotes a collective state of mind marked by a confident and aggressive readiness for the task at hand. The "we" comes to feel very much ready to take on one of "them," in the unlikely event that force is required.

The team may also rehearse the execution during the waning hours of the evening to make certain that everything is in order. I observed one such rehearsal, which involved five separate enactments of the last walk and the strapping in of an officer serving as surrogate for the prisoner. There was considerable tension, which gave rise to nervous jokes of the gallows-humor variety and a bit of clowning around. (To the extent that these rehearsals are audible to the condemned prisoner, we can only suppose that they are a source of considerable anxiety.) But the rehearsal was no laughing matter. It involved real physical exertion as well as palpable emotional strain. Some officers were sweaty and short of breath when the practice session ended. Others were tense, and one was said to be "smoking" with nerves. Everyone was occupied with thoughts of the upcoming execution.

One man spoke for many of his colleagues when he observed, "I go over and over it in my mind. I play out problems and work out solutions. I want to be ready." Many such concerns are mundane but strategically critical. "What if he kicks?" this man wondered. "So I put my knee on his foot when I strap him in." But mostly the officers, like the condemned prisoner, simply wait. And again as with the condemned prisoner, a calm exterior may mask inner turmoil. In the words of one officer, "The surface is cool. Inside, we're balls of fire, we're jumping, the adrenaline is pumping." Primed for action, they must bide their time until they are signaled to proceed. "It's like the clock stops," observed one man. "But when the warden says 'It's time,' then time flies." The rest is action and reaction, following a well-rehearsed plan.

Administrative Concerns and Chronic Uncertainty

The administrative staff members who orchestrate the execution must also ready themselves. They, too, are preoccupied and tense. War stories about prior executions are trotted out. Discussion drifts to such fundamental matters as the fleeting nature of life ("here today, gone tonight" was one anxious joke), crime and punishment (especially the prisoner's past crime and impending punishment), and the so-called criminal personality (and how the criminal in question fits this reprehensible and immutable type, and is thus a living specimen of pure evil). As among the deathwatch officers, there is much talk among administrators about the condemned man's offense, talk that implicitly justifies the upcoming execution. At the execution for which I served as an official witness, it was noted with nervous humor that the prisoner in question had even raped his mother! As if that were not enough, his sister—and only personal visitor—was said to be afraid of him. The message was clear: The world would be a better place without him.

Let me hasten to add that this is not the stuff of standard prison shoptalk. Prison staff generally don't want to know a prisoner's offense. They believe that such knowledge may lead to prejudgments that, in turn, may interfere with their handling of the offender as an inmate. It is well known, for example, that lifers, some of whom have committed heinous offenses, are terrible citizens but model prisoners. "Take the prisoner as you find him" might be the prison guard's motto. For those under the death penalty, this motto doesn't hold. Prison personnel *want* to know the condemned prisoner's offenses in all their gross and revolting details, perhaps because they *don't* want to know the inmate—at least, not any more than is necessary to control and then execute him.

Just as the inmate doesn't know until the end whether or not he will be executed, so too the staff don't know whether or not they will be asked to do their jobs. Executions are scheduled for the end of the day, at 11 P.M., to give the prisoner a full day to prepare himself and initiate any last-minute appeals.

> They're [at] eleven o'clock at night. That gives the person a full day to make peace with God, and his lawyers and his family, and [to] use every opportunity through the legal system. If [the court is] gonna give him a stay, it has time to do that. By law, when they set the date, it has to be done that day. If you can't do it before twelve o'clock midnight, then, by law you have to start all over. It has to go back to court for a new date. So, eleven o'clock is probably about the closest time you can set that'll let all the process take place, and yet still have time to carry out the order on that particular day.

Last-minute appeals to the courts, the governor, and no doubt God as well are of course quite common. Correctional officials must make sure all legal avenues of appeal have been exhausted before they proceed with an execution. A phone line is kept open, and the status of the execution is checked one last time before the execution commences at the appointed hour.

> We want to be absolutely sure that nobody makes a mistake. I mean, it's the kinda thing you can't have mistakes. No such thing as a mistake. And so it's a fail-proof system, so that when it comes time to do it . . . we know that it's proper to do it. 'Cause I don't wanna walk out there in front of the media and tell them, "Gosh, we're sorry, ya know, the governor called at 10:59 and said 'no' but we'd already done it."

The prospect of delays at the eleventh hour, as it were, keeps administrators on edge and raises the chilling specter of a premature execution. These delays also complicate the job of the deathwatch team. Uncertainty about whether an execution will take place or not makes it hard for the team to remain mentally and emotionally ready.

> If everything go when it's supposed to, then it's not too bad. But you get an on-and-off thing, like the court gettin' involved, that's rough. Like with one fella, we's executin' him and, uh, that thing drug on. It be on one hour and off the next hour. And your adrenaline builds up. You have to build up, and then you get building up and then all at once they say, "Hey, it's not goin' to be tonight; it's off." Then you got to come all the way back down. And fifteen or twenty minutes later, they say, "It's back on again." And here you got to go up, pump back up, and it's really hard on ya. Courts, lawyers, and the governor—when they get into it, it's an unsure thing, and it's, it's pretty hard on ya.

One officer even likened the experience to torture. "You crash. Your metabolism just drops. And then when it's back on, you got about a minute and thirty seconds to get up again. And you got to be professional about it and make no screwups. It's emotionally painful."[21]

HOLDING UP UNDER PRESSURE

The team always works under great pressure, and the prospect of making a mistake looms large as the time of execution approaches. The team operates under the gaze of correctional administrators as well as of official witnesses, the latter group including representatives of the media. Any mistake, especially one that might add to the suffering of the condemned, will be noted, embarrassing the team.

> You're tense because you don't want to make a mistake, because you've got twelve witnesses watching you do that thing. All right, say you drop the headgear. You're getting ready to put the headgear on—which is not my job, but I'm just using this as an example—and you dropped it. It would be a very embarrassing thing with people watching you and this man sitting here waiting to die. (Laughs nervously) And you drop the thing and—it's just, it's a lot of tension.

The prospect of having to use force is ever on the minds of the officers, but actually doing so is almost unthinkable. That would not be a mistake so much as a disaster. The officers' collective nightmare is a botched execution, especially one involving force. "You don't want to get in a situation where you have to fight a man to the chair," stated one officer. "I think that would leave a mental scar on you worse than anything."

From the perspective of the deathwatch team, the execution is quite public. The whole world watches through the reporting of media representatives, who find newsworthy any snags that occur in the execution drill. (A flawed execution is national news. A more typical execution is usually only noted by the local media.) The team leader likened the situation to that of being in combat and having to scrupulously check one's machinery to make sure that it will work under fire.

> It's a whole lot like you're going in combat, you know. You don't know whether your equipment's gonna work—you got a good idea your equipment's gonna work—99 percent—but that 1 percent it might not work, you know. And you know executions are big news; people hear all over the world—England, overseas—you know, everywhere—and naturally you want everything to go as smooth as it can. So far we haven't had any problems and everything's carried out real well, normal, but I guess you always have that fear that it won't go off right.

The troops who make up the execution team have to be attended to as well, if I may pursue the team leader's combat metaphor. As is revealed in this exchange with me, the team leader finds himself measuring, and often modulating, the mood and temper of his execution team as they prepare for battle:

> They go up, and they come down. They get to talkin'—some of 'em will get to talkin' real fast, you know. Maybe you got a better word, but I call it climbing the ladder, you know, and I have to kinda talk 'em down, you know, get 'em settled down. And then I see 'em go down the ladder—they're way down here—and then I have to bring them up, you know, to a level. Yeah, they go through, they go through changes.
>
> *So you have to keep them at a place where they can do their jobs? And they're trying to keep the inmate at the same place, right?*
>
> Yes, uh-huh. They're trying to keep the inmate cool, right. (Laughing) So it's, it's challenging. . . . You don't know how your people gonna act during or after [the execution], so I'm not only watchin' the inmate, I'm havin' to watch my team, too. And so far we haven't had nobody [on the team] crack up, but you know it could happen, and I realize that it could happen.

The execution team has held up admirably under pressure. That is an achievement, the team leader contended, that he and the warden have come to expect but cannot take for granted. It is, they know, a product of discipline and commitment that must be renewed, singly and collectively, at each execution the team is called upon to perform.

NOTES

1. W. Berns, *For Capital Punishment: Crime and the Morality of the Death Penalty* (New York: Basic Books, 1979), 21.

2. R. Johnson, *Condemned to Die: Life under Sentence of Death* (Prospect Heights, Ill.: Waveland Press, 1989), 90.

3. Executions at Louisiana's Angola Prison offer an exception to this observation. There, the prisoners are shackled for their last walk. See H. Prejean, *Dead Man Walking: An Eyewitness Account of the Death Penalty in the United States* (New York: Random House, 1993).

4. Donald Cabana, who as warden allowed himself to get close to prisoners he executed, and indeed counted one of them as a personal friend, reports a similar experience. Cabana is unusual. Insightful and sensitive, he would not accommodate himself to the routine quality of modern executions. "There is nothing commonplace about walking a healthy young man to a room, strapping him into a chair, and coldly, methodically killing him. I knew after the first one that if it ever did become routine, if I found myself no longer haunted by doubt, then I would know the time had come for me to leave corrections behind." See D. A. Cabana, *Death at Midnight: The Confession of an Executioner* (Boston: Northeastern University Press, 1996), 17.

5. Bob McMaster, a Florida Department of Corrections public affairs officer has observed: "Our people are instructed not to become emotionally attached. . . . These people aren't on Death Row for jay-walking. It's not unheard of for inmates to devise escape plots that involve even the littlest things. You basically don't trust someone who is in jail for a murder. . . . If you do, you're a fool. Once they've killed someone in an illegal manner, they're capable of doing it again." See G. E. Goldhammer, *Dead End* (Brunswick, Me.: Biddle Publishing Company, 1994), 96. The logistics and emotional demands of running a death row reinforce these admonitions. In the words of Asst. Warden Ramsey of Alabama's Atmore Prison: "as soon as the cell is vacated, he's replaced by another inmate who needs us to take care of him. So we don't have time to sit around and say we miss a particular inmate. The longer you're here, the more you're able to accept that you're here to do a job. . . . We spend very little time on a personal basis with them. You have to subconsciously keep in mind who you're working around." (96, 113).

6. It appears that denial or even dissociation are common among correctional officials who must authorize executions. Nice people who profess moral scruples—some who even find executions "abhorrent to me personally"—have little or no trouble conforming their personal morals to the jobs as instruments of law. For them, personal contacts with the condemned may not give them pause but, instead, may convince them that they are good if not important people who have a job to do and the fortitude to do it. Here is a case in point:

With a reassuring pat on the shoulder I asked, "You doing alright, fella?"

With that, he turned to me and said, "Warden, I've told you for a long time not to worry about me. I told you I wasn't going to cause you any trouble, and I know I'm going to be fine when this is all over. But I've seen what this has been doing to you. You've always been straight with me, and I want you to promise that this won't make you leave here. They won't tell you so, but these guys need you and the people here who care something about them and try to treat them fair."

To hear that from a man who I would lead to his electrocution 15 minutes later was powerful experience.

Executions will never get any easier for me or anyone at Broad River. But that man's insight and his willingness to offer me a gesture of kindness—even in his own darkest hour—gave me a much needed measure of peace with myself. . . . [T]here is a limit to the number of times I intend to do this, but I can cope just a little better with doing what I must sometimes do.

It is hard to imagine a condemned prisoner who could be more accommodating. "Kill me, warden. I'll be good for you. And don't you stop what you are doing because others need you." One would think that it would be a nightmare to put such a prisoner to death, not a source of peace. See G. N. Martin, "A Warden's Reflections—Enforcing the Death Penalty with Competence, Compassion," *Corrections Today* 55 (4): 62 (July 1993).

7. R. F. Canan, "Burning at the Wire: The Execution of John Evans," in *Facing the Death Penalty: Essays on a Cruel and Unusual Punishment*, ed. M. L. Radelet (Philadelphia: Temple University Press, 1989), 74–75.

8. Johnson (n. 2), 80–88.

9. Though denial is the norm, there are exceptions. Cabana reports that Connie Evans, a prisoner whose execution Cabana oversaw as warden of Parchman State Prison, wanted to know the details of death by execution in the gas chamber. Uncomfortable and somewhat reluctant, Cabana passed along the information as well as the advice to breathe deeply in order to speed one's death. Evans, upon hearing this information, "crawled onto his bunk and curled up into a fetal position." This was days before his scheduled execution. One can only imagine the effect if the subject was discussed during the deathwatch. It is worth noting that Cabana and Evans had an unusual personal relationship, which may explain why they did not resort to denial. See Cabana (n. 4), 172.

10. Reverend Joseph B. Ingle, who has ministered to many condemned prisoners during their final hours, takes a similar approach. See J. B. Ingle, "Ministering to the Condemned: A Case Study," in *Facing the Death Penalty: Essays on a Cruel and Unusual Punishment*, ed. M. L. Radelet (Philadelphia: Temple University Press, 1989).

11. Johnson (n. 2), 85.

12. I have reviewed this literature at some length in Chapter 2. The notion that electrocution is a modern version of burning at the stake is cited in *The Case Against Capital Punishment* (pamphlet, Washington Research Project, 1971), 36.

13. See, for example, Cabana (n. 4), 175–176.

14. Johnson (n. 2), 87, 81.

15. Ingle (n. 10), 115.

16. A. Camus, "Reflections on the Guillotine," in *Resistance, Rebellion, and Death* (New York: Knopf, 1969).

17. As Prejean has observed, with respect to Angola's death house, "Music stirs emotions, and prison authorities want as little emotion as possible in this process." Prejean (n. 3), 36.

18. Johnson (n. 2), 89.

19. The key issue is walking to the chair more or less under one's own power. Some men are so afraid they keep their eyes closed, but as long as they keep on their feet—walking or led by the team—they are seen as dying with some dignity.

20. The disturbing effect on prisoners of tests of the electric chair was quite apparent in my study of Alabama's death row some years back, even though none of the prisoners I interviewed faced imminent execution. See Johnson (n. 2), 85. Cabana reports a moving encounter with a prisoner on the eve of his execution who was deeply affected by the testing of the electric chair:

"Did you test that thing last night?" he asked scornfully. I quickly responded that we had. "Jesus Christ," he thundered, "you actually tested the damned thing?" His face registered bewilderment and disbelief. The sergeant and another officer looked in on us, but I held my hand up and shook my head. Still refusing to sit down, Connie took a couple of steps to his right and leaned against the wall. "You're so fucking sure you'll get to kill me. I can't believe it, I mean, hell, I've still got a few days left. My lawyers are still working."

See Cabana (n. 4), 174.

21. Officers on Missouri's lethal injection team report a similar experience. "Standing down is very difficult mentally. Because you're so prepped for this thing, you see. I've found that when we go ahead and do the chore that we have to do, that you're not as depressed as you are when you stand down. The standing down just tears you up. You're so keyed to it. You're so tired." A last-minute stay can be stressful for the prisoner as well, who may finally feel ready to face his execution. Said a member of Missouri's execution team, "We got him within two hours of an execution one time, and when we got the stay, he was really hostile about it. He didn't want the stay. He was like us, you know. It

was a hell of a letdown for him. He wanted to go ahead and get this thing over with. So the next time we got him up there, he was ready to go without any problem. He was all hyped up and ready for it." S. Trombley, *The Execution Protocol: Inside America's Capital Punishment Industry* (New York: Anchor Books, 1993), 258–259. The experience appears to be a common one. See, generally, articles under the heading Special Focus—Managing Death Row, *Corrections Today* 55 (4): 55–96 (July 1993).

7

An Execution
and its Aftermath

As the team and administrators prepare to commence the killing routine that comprises the execution protocol, another group, the official witnesses, are also preparing themselves for their role in the execution. Drawn from the media and the public, the official witnesses are meant to be disinterested citizens in good standing drawn from a cross section of the state's population. As incarnations of Every Good and Decent Person, they are called upon to represent the community and testify to the propriety of the execution.

In the state under study, witnesses number between six and twelve for any given execution. For a regular citizen of the state to become a witness, he or she must ask to be present at an execution, sending a letter or filling out a form indicating their reasons. They must also submit to a criminal-records check and then be screened by the prison's public relations officer. In reviewing—as a corollary to my larger death-work study—applicants' stated reasons for volunteering to witness an execution, I found that witnesses are neither disinterested (most strongly support the death penalty) nor representative of the community at large (many work in law enforcement). They are, however, generally quite serious about the obligation they wish to shoulder. In the main, the community is well-served by its witnesses.

I reviewed the applications of thirty-five official witnesses (they were all accepted, but no reasons for acceptance were given). Of that group, eleven stated that moral considerations underlay their desire to witness an execution. Fully eight of these eleven wished to reinforce or reaffirm their belief in the justice of the death penalty and the rightness of the American criminal justice system. Two of these believers hoped to educate and deter delinquent youth with whom they came in contact in their work. (Curiously, one hoped to scare himself straight as well!) The remaining three of those concerned with moral issues sought to resolve their ambivalence about the death penalty. They wanted to see in the flesh this thing with which their consciences had wrestled, often for many years.

Another nine witnesses were motivated by concerns such as service and duty, seeing the experience as a civic obligation or as an opportunity for civic education they had missed. Seven others, police officers, saw attending an execution as an extension either of their general commitment to law enforcement or of their personal involvement with the case in question. Finally, several citizens, seven in all, were simply curious about what an execution was like. (In one man's peculiar view, an execution was a case study of democracy at work!) Only one person had a purely personal interest in serving as a witness. He had known the victims but gave no specific reason why he should attend their killer's execution.

In the main, the reasons for wanting to witness an execution were serious and proper. Some reasons, though, seemed strange and even silly. One ballroom dance instructor from a small town wanted to be a witness because she had time on her hands and relations in the area whom she hadn't visited for a spell! Such frivolous, even freakish, motives debase the execution process, but, fortunately, such considerations are in the minority.

For the first edition of this book, I served as an official witness at one execution and as a behind-the-scenes observer at another. In the latter instance, I was more or less appended to the execution team and permitted to observe and interact with them at all times during the deathwatch. I also exchanged a few words with the prisoner. Since then, I served yet again as an observer on the scene of an execution. Drawing on these experiences, in addition to research interviews, I am able to bear full and, I trust, authentic witness to the psychology of death work.

The experiences and reactions of the three condemned prisoners I observed did not differ in their essentials. To facilitate explication of these events, and so that I may draw more fully on my personal observations—both behind the scenes and as an official witness—I have created a composite portrait of a condemned prisoner's execution. The prisoner I have named Jones. I observed his last hours firsthand; I inferred the details of his walk to the chair, as viewed by official witnesses, from my interviews and from my prior experience as an official witness at another execution. Thus, my personal observations, supplemented by material from my research interviews, form the substance of the following account of Jones's demise. I hasten to add that though the composite character named Jones is fictitious, the dynamics of his execution are not.

WITNESS TO AN EXECUTION

At eight in the evening, about the time the prisoner is shaved in preparation for the execution, the witnesses were assembled. Eleven in all, we included three newspaper and two television reporters, a state trooper, two police officers, a magistrate, a businessman, and myself. We were picked up in the parking lot behind the main office of the Department of Corrections. There was nothing unusual or even memorable about any of this. It wasn't a dark and stormy night; no one emerged from the shadows to lead us to the prison gates.

Mundane considerations prevailed. The van sent for us was missing a few rows of seats, so there wasn't enough room for the group. Obliging prison officials volunteered their cars. Our rather ordinary cavalcade reached the prison only after getting lost. Once within the prison's walls, we were sequestered for some two hours in a bare and almost shabby administrative conference room. A public information officer was assigned to accompany us and answer our questions, but when we grilled him about the prisoner and the execution procedure the prisoner would shortly undergo, he confessed ignorance regarding the most basic points. Disgruntled at this and increasingly anxious, we made small talk and drank coffee. We didn't psych up as the execution team did, but we did tense up as the execution time approached.

At 10:40, roughly two and a half hours after we assembled and only twenty minutes before the execution was scheduled to occur, we were taken to the basement of the prison's administrative building, frisked, then led down an alley that ran along the outside of the building. We entered a neighboring cell block and were admitted to a vestibule adjoining the death chamber. Each of us signed a log, and we were then led to the witness area off to our right. To our left and around a corner, some thirty feet away, sat Jones in the condemned cell. He couldn't see us, but I'm quite certain he could hear us. It occurred to me that our arrival was a fateful reminder for the prisoner. The next group would be led by the warden, and it would be coming for him.

We entered the witness area, a room within the death chamber, and were escorted to our seats. Through the picture window filling the front wall of the witness room, we had a clear view of the electric chair, which was about twelve feet away and well-illuminated. A large, high-back, solid-oak structure with imposing black straps, the chair easily dominated the death chamber. The electric chair is larger than life, a paradox that no doubt derives from its sole purpose as an instrument of death. The warden had told me, "It's the biggest chair you'll ever see," and he was right. Behind the electric chair, on the back wall, was an open panel full of coils and lights; over the chair, two domed light fixtures were strung from the ceiling. Peeling paint hung from the ceiling and walls, which were stained from persistent water leaks. (The walls have since been painted, but the leaks remain.) A stark and lonely tableau, I assure you.

Two substantial officers—one a huge, hulking figure weighing some four hundred pounds, the other not much smaller—stood beside the electric chair. The message to the approaching inmate was clear. As one of these officers put it, "You got seven hundred or so pounds waiting for you at the chair, so don't go think about bucking." Each officer had his hands crossed at the lap and wore a forbiddingly blank expression. The witnesses gazed at them and the chair, absorbed by the scene, scribbling notes furiously. We did this, I suppose, as much to record the experience as to distract ourselves from the growing tension.

A correctional officer entered the witness room and announced a trial run of the machinery. Seconds later, lights flashed on the control panel behind the chair, as the officer had said they would, indicating that the chair was in working order. A white curtain, open for the test, separated the chair and the witness area. After the test, the curtain was drawn, allowing the officers to prepare the cap and mask that would be placed on the prisoner once he was secured in the chair. (It was thought that observing the staff preparing these paraphernalia would needlessly upset the witnesses. The impression the team wished to leave with the witnesses, at this point at least, was that executions simply happen.) The curtain was then reopened, to be left open until the execution was over. Then it would be closed to allow the officers to discreetly remove the prisoner's body.

Several high-level correctional officials were present in the death chamber, standing just outside the witness area. There were two regional administrators, the director of the Department of Corrections, and the warden. Also present were Jones's chaplain and lawyer. Other than the chaplain's black religious garb, subdued grey pinstripes and bland correctional uniforms prevailed. All parties were quite solemn.

I knew from my research that Jones was a man with a tragic past. Grossly abused at home, he went on to become grossly abusive of others. (His crime, committed while he was on drugs, was a gruesome murder of an elderly woman.) I was told he could not describe his life, from childhood on, without talking about fighting to defend his precarious sense of self—at home, in school, on the streets, in the prison yard. Belittled by life and choking with rage, he remained hungry to be noticed, even if notoriety was all he might hope for. Paradoxically, Jones the condemned prisoner had found his moment in the spotlight—though it was a dim and unflattering light cast before a small and unappreciative audience. "He'd pose for cameras in the chair—for the attention," I'd been told earlier that day by a member of the prison's psychological treatment unit. Yet the plain truth was that Jones had to endure one more losing confrontation, this time with the state. He won't be smiling, I thought, and there will be no cameras.

Virtually no one holds up well in the face of execution, and Jones was no exception. But Jones, like many other prisoners before him, did cope for a time, with the help of the outsiders the warden described as adjuncts to his team (see Chapter 6). In Jones's case, this group included two attorneys, a chaplain, and a personal counselor. Jones thought of his attorneys as allies and friends. The chaplain was "a presence, a spiritual safe harbor," there to help Jones discover that "he was a child of God, worthy of forgiveness." Jones's counselor, who had helped a number of other condemned men face their end, was known for her matter-of-fact, cut-and-dried approach. Her job was to help men get themselves through the emotional ordeal that lay ahead. Jones called her by her last name, mixing affection and respect. He also spoke by phone with a journalist covering his story, with whom he had become close. These sources provided an inside view of Jones's efforts to hold himself together in the face of his impending execution.

THE PRISONER'S DECLINE

The View from the Cell

Jones's decline began at the very outset of the deathwatch. In the words of his journalist friend,

> He was beyond eating. His last meal was the night before, maybe some fruit. He was nervous and didn't feel like eating. . . . He was a devout exerciser, doing hundreds of calisthenics each day.[1] He took care of his body. He needed his exercise to feel good, to feel alive. That last day, he didn't exercise. He tried, but he couldn't do more than a few push-ups. It was as though he felt his life draining out of him even then, hours before his execution.

Jones was very much affected by the countdown to death that occurs during the deathwatch period. The various procedures, especially the testing of the chair, forcefully brought home the reality of his impending execution. In the journalist's words,

> The countdown upset him. He knew the procedure, what to expect, but the experience was very hard for him. He could hear the testing of the chair, and it made him uncomfortable. He could hear it; he could smell it. It was like "they're getting ready to kill me." It made it all real. It made him depressed, saddened.

Later, Jones was horrified by the last-meal ritual, which struck him as barbaric and cruel. "He didn't even want to talk to the man who would ask him about his last meal."[2]

Earlier that afternoon, when his last appeal had been turned down, Jones had quite simply fallen apart. In the words of his personal counselor, who was with Jones until moments before his execution, "He panicked, cried, then went through denial, talking about a hopeless last-minute appeal." Jones pulled himself together after an hour or so but remained on the verge of tears throughout the ordeal of the deathwatch. His nervousness grew as the time of execution approached, with panic never far from the surface. As his counselor put it,

> He was revving, because he just wasn't prepared. It was like turning a record up, putting a 33 [rpm record] on a 45 [rpm] speed. His pitch went

up, too. And his body language was hyper. The eyes were really panicky; that's where I could really see it. He'd put real pressure on my hand now and again, and cry.

As his counselor made plain, Jones wasn't ready to die.

> My concern is that there was a lot of business that he didn't finish with himself. . . . He was trying in the end, making a hyper attempt to understand what was going to happen after he died. He was saying all the right words about an afterlife. The chaplain said, "He's got it." And my response was, "Down pat." He had it intellectually but not in his gut. Or he wouldn't have been that panicky; he would have been calmer.

Jones's belief in an afterlife, such as it was, provided him little comfort on the threshold of death.

Jones tried to distance himself from his situation by using gallows humor. "He did a mimic of himself being executed," said one of his supporters. "It was pretty graphic." What Jones thought of all this is unclear, but it proved too much for one of his attorneys, who insisted that he stop. "He wasn't doing it in bad taste," the journalist assured me. "It was his way of trying to trivialize the situation, which he really couldn't do." After he was shaved, he told his companions that he looked like a monk. Everybody kept running their hands over his head, as if physically helping him to suppress awareness of the awful significance of his bald pate. He described himself as a "lamb prepared for slaughter." To the dismay of those around him, more and more he was coming to look the part.

Physical contact, touching, was a vital part of the help Jones's supporters gave him. Jones's journalist friend remembered one scene in particular.

> There was a moment that was really moving. He was holding two people's hands, as well as a cup of coffee; someone had a hand on his knee, and another person had a hand on his shoulder. People were petting him, saying soothing things. He had the phone on his shoulder, and he said to me, "I can't even light a cigarette!" We laughed.

For a brief and fleeting moment, Jones felt protected. It was as if he felt his allies could keep him from being taken from the cell, could physically shield him from his executioners.

Yet signs of stress, of vulnerability, present at the outset of the deathwatch, became increasingly evident as the time of execution drew near. Here was a person who claimed never to be physically cold, who could sit in a chilly basement cell with nothing but a towel around his waist, proudly sporting his "pecan tan." That night, fully dressed, he shivered visibly. "The situation took the warmth and heat away from him, no matter how much we tried to help," observed one of his companions. Here, too, was a man who scrupulously cultivated the image that he was always in control. That night, the facade gave way. "What should I do?" he asked, plaintively. His supporters had no advice or comfort to give. Said one, "He was helpless, and he knew it. We knew it, too."

Jones was, however, unwilling to see himself as a pawn in a larger impersonal process; he struggled to keep the execution personal. "He felt the entire death penalty existed to get him," said his counselor. "He felt like the courts, the legislature, the law, death row, the prison guards, the execution squad—all were concentrating on getting him personally." The counselor felt, and communicated to Jones, that in an existential sense he was right.

It's ultimately personal because he's not dead; he has a mind and a heart and a psyche that are trying to live, even at that last moment. They [condemned prisoners] are live human beings, and life itself is stretching out of them. And the only way that you can accept dying in that way is to not let it be impersonal. That's a kind of death that is more unacceptable than going to that chair and being fried.

The problem is that the execution process is both out of the prisoners' control and, for the vast majority of them, overwhelming. The counselor acknowledged these hard facts. "The other side is that they are incredibly aware of the power controlling them. They're isolated in that death cell. In the end, they collapse from within."

Jones's last hours, even his last words, reflected his sense of helplessness and his final efforts to transcend it, to exert some personal control over his situation. Listen to the journalist's account of Jones at the end:

We talked about his life. It was almost as though he wanted to leave what was important about him with somebody; he wanted to leave bits and pieces of himself behind. He said, "I don't want to die and be a statistic. . . ." His last minutes were frantic. It was as though he was trying to articulate more things without knowing what to say. "Take care of yourself," he told me. He wanted to make sure I had somewhere to go after [the execution]. It was important for him to tell me to take care of myself and be with others. It made him feel useful, feel better, for a moment at least. His last words to me were spoken with a sense of urgency but no real emotion: "Don't forget my voice, don't forget me. . . . Celebrate the life you have."

Jones had little time left and, by all accounts, little life left in him at this juncture, but his words speak volumes about the human condition. Life is indeed personal and must be treasured as such for as long as one can.

Jones's last words bring to mind an observation by Czeslaw Milosz, from the aptly titled book *The Captive Mind*: "Probably only those things are worthwhile which can preserve their validity in the eyes of a man threatened with instant death."[3] By this hard criterion, Jones's effort, evident in his words, to preserve a sense of self in the face of its imminent annihilation was surely worthwhile. Yet, in the final analysis, his death was not personal, and he did not go to meet it as the person he was in life. Note that he did not refer in his last words to a life that *he* had had and could celebrate during its precious remaining minutes. No, for Jones, life as he had known it was over. He wished to leave a mark, to be a part of history, but only as he once was, not as he was then, a scared, shivering, emotionally numb creature on the edge of extinction.

The Executioners' Perspective

As is generally the case, the process of Jones's decay, and ultimately his collapse, was visible to the officers on the team. They saw Jones's nerves fray and his eyes redden with tears, heard his voice made hoarse by emotion. They saw—and saw through—his moments of bravado. One such moment occurred when Jones was being shaved for execution. During this solemn and intimidating procedure, he found the presence of mind to quip with the officer, telling him, "I'll meet you in heaven—if you get there." And asking, when the shaving procedure was completed, "What do I owe you for that, buddy?" The officer smiled. Jones didn't.

Each officer remarked on Jones's sadness. On a number of occasions, they agreed, he was holding back tears. He never made eye contact with anyone on the team. At one point, while he was being shaved, a clump of hair fell into his hands. Pensively, he sifted it through his fingers, then let it fall to the floor. He looked away, seemingly lost in thought, perhaps contemplating his mortality. In the shower after being shaved, Jones looked out at the officers and asked, "Why is everyone so sad?" No one responded. Later, the officers commented on this, claiming they weren't sad, just solemn. "That was a professional look," said one officer, "because no one enjoys putting a man to death." The implication, painfully obvious to the officers, was that the sadness Jones saw on their faces was really his own. As one officer put it, Jones was "falling apart from within." I learned later from Jones's companions that the officers were right. Jones was demoralized by this procedure and never really regained his composure.

Jones's sadness grew over time, sapping his strength. After the shaving procedure, he turned to putty in the officers' hands. In one officer's words,

> His expression became more subdued; his actions weren't as crisp as they had been. He was aware, but he wasn't alert. It's like when a doctor shoots you with novocaine—you just become number and number. . . . The man came to accept it, that this is gonna happen. He just let us do what we had to do to carry out the execution.

Jones's last request, for instance, made ten minutes before the execution, was turned down. Jones asked for water and a mint. The officers, their minds perhaps on the execution and not on service, told him that these things would adversely affect the body after execution. This exchange seems almost cruel in the retelling, but the officers spoke without malice, and Jones accepted their word without protest. Jones may not have been ready to die, but surely he was ready to be executed.

Minutes later, the warden arrived with the court order calling for the prisoner's execution. Jones stood erect before the warden, but the pose was strained. The warden, also showing strain, said in a kind tone, "I take no pleasure in carrying out this duty, son." Pausing, then marshaling a more official demeanor, he paraphrased the court order, which read like this:

> It is ordered and adjudged that the judgment pronounced and set forth in this order, entered herein on [a given date], sentencing the defendant to

death in the manner and by the authorities as provided by statute, shall be executed at this time.

The warden asked Jones if he had a last statement to make. Jones said he had none. (He had told one of his companions that the officials of the prison, including the team, meant nothing to him and that he would have nothing to say to them.) The door to the death cell was opened, and two officers entered, each taking one of Jones's elbows. Jones went limp. In the warden's words, "He was ready—he'd made up his mind that he was gonna go on in there and get it over with. He had already partially crossed over; he was just about gone already." Jones then "fell into the arms of the team." Guided by the officers, he proceeded down a short hallway leading to the death chamber. As he turned a corner and confronted the chair, Jones faltered once more, momentarily startled by the scene before him. At this point, still out of sight of the official witnesses, Jones was again physically supported by the officers, one of whom whispered in his ear, "Go out like a man." By some reckonings, he did.

THE EXECUTION

At 10:58, Jones entered the death chamber. He walked quickly and silently toward the chair, his escort of officers in tow. Three officers maintained contact with Jones at all times, offering him physical support. Two were stationed at his elbows; a third brought up the rear, holding Jones's back pockets. The officers waiting at the chair described the approaching Jones as "staring off in a trance, with no meaning in his stares. It was like he didn't want to think about it." His eyes were cast downward. His expression was glazed, but worry and apprehension were apparent in the tightly creased lines that ran across his forehead. He did not shake with nerves, nor did he crack under pressure. One could say, as did a fellow witness, "Anybody who writes anything will have to say he took it like a man." But a scared and defeated man, surely. His shaven head and haggard face added to the impression of vulnerability, even frailty.

Like some before him, Jones had threatened to stage a last stand. But that was lifetimes ago, on death row, with his fellow condemned to lean on. In the death house, alone, Jones joined the humble bunch and kept to the executioner's schedule. At the end, resistance of any kind seemed unthinkable. Like so many of those before him, Jones appeared to have given up on life before he died in the chair. His execution, like those of the men who preceded him, was largely a matter of procedure.

That procedure, set up to take life, had a life of its own. En route to the chair Jones stumbled slightly, as if the momentum of the event had overtaken him, causing him to lose control. Were he not held secure by the three officers, he might have fallen.[4] Were the routine to be broken in this or any other way, the officers believe, the prisoner might faint or panic or become violent, and have to be forcibly restrained. Perhaps as a precaution, when Jones reached the chair, he did not turn on his own but rather was turned, firmly but without malice, by the officers in his escort. Once Jones was seated, again with help, the officers strapped him in.

The execution team worked with machine precision. Like a disciplined swarm, they enveloped Jones, strapping and then buckling down his forearms, elbows, ankles, waist, and chest in a matter of seconds. Once his body was secured, with the electrode connected to Jones's exposed right leg, the two officers stationed behind the chair went to work. One of them attached the cap to the man's head, then connected the cap to an electrode located above the chair. The other secured the face mask. This was buckled behind the chair, so that Jones's head, like the rest of his body, was rendered immobile.

Only one officer on the team made eye contact with Jones (as he was affixing the face mask), and he came to regret it. The others attended to their tasks with a most narrow focus. Before the mask was secured, Jones asked if the electrocution would hurt. Several of the officers mumbled "no" or simply shook their heads, neither pausing nor looking up. Each officer left the death chamber after he finished his task. One officer, by assignment, stayed behind for a moment to check the straps. He mopped Jones's brow, then touched his hand in a gesture of farewell. This personal touch in the midst of an impersonal procedure was, in the warden's opinion, an attempt to help the officer himself live with the death penalty. The warden noted that it also by implication helped the team of which he was a part. "It's out of our hands," the gesture seemed to imply. "We're only doing our job."

During the brief procession to the electric chair, Jones was attended by a chaplain from a local church, not the prison. The chaplain, upset, leaned over Jones as he was being strapped in the chair. As the execution team worked feverishly to secure Jones's body, the chaplain put his forehead against Jones's, whispering urgently. The priest might have been praying, but I had the impression he was consoling Jones, perhaps assuring him that a forgiving God awaited him in the next life. If Jones heard the chaplain, I doubt that he comprehended his message. At least, he didn't seem comforted. Rather, he looked stricken and appeared to be in shock. Perhaps the priest's urgent ministrations betrayed his doubts that Jones could hold himself together. The chaplain then withdrew at the warden's request, allowing the officers to affix the mask.

The strapped and masked figure sat before us, utterly alone, waiting to be killed. The cap and mask dominated his face. The cap was nothing more than a sponge encased in a leather shell, topped with a metal receptacle for an electrode. Fashioned in 1979 in replica of a cap dating back to the turn of the century, it appeared decrepit, presumably from sitting in brine for a number of years. It resembled a cheap, ill-fitting toupee. "It don't fit like a normal hat," said the officer responsible for securing this piece of hardware to the prisoner, in a matter-of-fact tone, "it's for a person with no hair." The mask, also created in 1979 and modeled on a turn-of-the-century original, was made entirely of leather. Somehow it, too, looked well-worn, perhaps because it was burned in places—from saliva that had spilled from the mouths of some of the executed prisoners, then been brought to a boil by the heat of the electricity coursing through the chair and its appurtenances. The mask had two parts.

The bottom part covered the chin and mouth; the top, the eyes and lower forehead. Only the nose was exposed. The effect of the rigidly restrained body, together with the bizarre cap and the protruding nose, was nothing short of grotesque. To one member of the team, Jones looked like a hooded hawk—not a person but a constrained creature, poised, in this instance, for death.

A faceless figure breathed before us in a tragicomic trance, waiting for a blast of electricity that would extinguish his life. The internal dynamics of an electrocution are quite profound. As the electrician affiliated with the team made clear to anyone who would listen, in one swift and violent instant twenty-five hundred volts of electricity, at five to seven amps, shoot through the body, starting at the head, passing through the brain, then on to the heart and other internal organs, some of which explode, before the current comes to ground through the ankle. Jones presumably did not know the details, but the general picture is vividly impressed in the minds of all condemned prisoners facing death by electrocution.[5]

Endless, agonizing seconds passed. The execution team officers watched the clock, on the wall to the right of the chair, not Jones. They have been instructed to do this, as a "way to keep sane . . . to keep from thinking about it too much later." Men who only seconds before had focused their attention on the details of restraining the prisoner now let their minds wander from the grim business at hand; as one officer put it, "your mind goes a long ways away." The witnesses received no such instructions and sought no such escape; they sat transfixed on Jones, living with him, or so it felt, his last moments. His last act was to swallow, nervously, pathetically, his Adam's apple bobbing. I was struck by that simple movement then and can't forget it even now. It told me, as nothing else did, that in Jones's restrained body, behind that mask, lurked a fellow human being who, at some level, however primitive, knew or sensed himself to be moments from death.

Jones sat perfectly still for what seemed an eternity but was in fact no more than thirty seconds. Finally, the electricity hit him. His body stiffened spasmodically, though only briefly. A thin swirl of smoke trailed away from his head, then dissipated quickly. (People outside the witness room could hear crackling and burning; a faint smell of burned flesh lingered in the air, mildly nauseating some people.) The body remained taut, with the right foot raised slightly at the heel, seemingly frozen there. A brief pause, then another minute of shock. When it was over, the body was inert.

Three minutes passed while the officials let the body cool. (Immediately after the execution, I'm told, the body is too hot to touch and would blister anyone who did.) All eyes were riveted on the chair; I felt trapped in my witness seat, at once transfixed and yet eager for release. I can't recall any clear thoughts from this time. One of the officers later volunteered that he shared this experience of staring blankly at the execution scene. Laughing nervously, he said,

It's a long three minutes. It hits him and then you wait. The [current] goes on a couple of times. And you wait three minutes after the machine goes off; the doctor comes in and checks him. You just, you just, you just watch the whole thing. There's nothing really (pause) going through your mind.

Had Jones's mind been mercifully blank at the end? I hoped so.[6]

An officer walked up to the body, opened the shirt at chest level, then went to get the physician from an adjoining room. The physician listened for a heartbeat. Hearing none, he turned to the warden and said, "This man has expired." The warden, speaking to the director of corrections, solemnly intoned, "Mr. Director, the court order has been fulfilled." The curtain was then drawn, and the witnesses filed out. By one officer's reckoning, the execution had been "picture perfect"—no resistance, no complications.

The deathwatch team commenced its final duties. Approaching the chair, they found Jones's body frozen in an arched position, his right leg bent and rigid from the force of the electricity. The leg had received second-degree burns where the electrode touched the skin. Jones's head was facing upward, his eyes puffy and closed. This all looked quite grotesque to me, but the warden was of the opinion that Jones had died with a look of peace on his face. (The warden could speak comparatively on this matter. The inmate before Jones evidently had fared much worse. In the warden's words, "It looked like something terrible had reached in and snatched his soul right out through the mouth on his face, like his soul had been yanked from him.") Jones's inert body was lifted from the chair. This took several men, each now wearing protective rubber gloves to shield them from disease. (The officers feared AIDS, though there was no evidence Jones had had the dread disease. They speculated that germs would proliferate wildly in reaction to the heat generated by the electrocution.) The body was then placed on a gurney and wheeled into a nearby room to cool. Aptly, the room is known as the cooling room.

The team milled around the cooling room, congregating near the body. No one had specific duties at this point, and the mood was subdued.[7] No congratulations were exchanged here, though the feeling seemed to be one of a job done well. The officers were clearly relieved to be finished. For the doctor and his assistants, however, work was just beginning. They used sandbags to flatten Jones's right leg and otherwise prepared the corpse for the morgue. Their labors took some six or seven minutes. By the time they were finished, everyone was ready to go home.

THE MORNING AFTER

As the body was prepared for the morgue, the witnesses were led to the front door of the prison. On the way, we passed a number of cell blocks. We could hear the normal sounds of prison life, including the occasional catcall and lewd comment hurled at passersby. But no disturbance of any kind followed the execution. Small protests were going on outside the walls, we were told, but we could not hear them. Soon the media would be gone, and the protesters would disperse. Like the executioners, they would simply go home.

The prisoners, already home, had been indifferent to the proceedings, as they always are unless the condemned prisoner is a figure of some consequence in the convict community. Then there might be tension and maybe even a modest disturbance on a prison tier or two. But few convict luminaries are executed, and Jones was not one of them. Our escort officer offered a sad epitaph to Jones's life: "The inmates, they didn't care about this guy."

I couldn't help thinking they weren't alone in this. The executioners went home and went about their lives. Having taken life, they savored a bit of life themselves. They showered, ate, drank, made love, slept, then took a day or two off. For some, Jones's image lingered through the night. The man who met Jones's gaze kept picturing his eyes, haunted for a time by their vacant look. The men who strapped Jones in remembered what it was like to touch him at the end. They showered as soon as they got home, to wash off the feel and smell of death. (The smell, I learned, was faint but would persist for a few days, teasing the nostrils, causing a mild, lingering feeling of nausea.)

The warden sat up into the early morning hours, mulling over the events of the evening. It was his second night of troubled sleep.

> I didn't sleep well that night. I didn't sleep well the night before either. I'd sleep a bit, then wake up. When I think about this, it washes over you, it comes in a jumbled up mess of things: The job's over, it's been accomplished, nothing went wrong. And I think we're all under this little spyglass: If something goes wrong, your ass is gonna swing. And in so many words, we've been told that. Mess up an execution, or you don't get the man dead like you should get him dead, there'll be hell to pay. So there's a lot of pressure. Then there's the nightmare of having to fight the man into the chair. This has never happened, and it probably never will, but you worry. How would I explain all that? You want everything to go along fine, but here you're taking a man's life. How deep should you get into that, to ask that everything go along fine? Like I say, it comes in a jumbled up mess of things.

The warden, like his team, felt the pressure of getting the procedure right. Like them, he worried over likely and unlikely contingencies (see Chapter 6). The team was on display, to be sure, but the warden was the responsible party. He knew it, and the strain showed. The warden also felt some ambivalence about the death penalty, which he supports intellectually but about which he has emotional reservations. That is why he cannot wholeheartedly want "everything to go along fine." Executions can, indeed, evoke "a jumbled up mess of things."

It is the warden's impression that none of the men on the team were hurt by the experience of carrying out this or any other execution. In his words,

> It affects them, even if they don't let on, but they handle it. They're a strong bunch of men. They've come to terms with their conscience;

they've been able to not get lost in the right or wrong of the situation here. And the cohesion of the team is good. They're not gonna be hurt; it's not gonna leave any scars.

Several of the officers on the team seconded this view. Said one, in no uncertain terms, "Nobody has any problems from this." For the most part, these sanguine assessments are right. As dutiful agents of the law and loyal team members, the men understand and accept their roles as executioners. They "double," to borrow Robert Lifton's notion, developing a dehumanized work identity but retaining a humanized personal identity.[8] Quite simply, they carry out their jobs impersonally and go on with their personal lives as though nothing out of the ordinary had happened. They do not dwell on the right or wrong of executions, but instead concern themselves only with what is demanded of them as professionals with a job to do.

But problems would surface for some of the officers, I learned from my research, with the passage of time. One of the men had a recurring fear of being attacked by disgruntled cons seeking vengeance. When I spoke with him, there had been only rumors, but this officer remained alert and on guard: "You learn not to pay rumors no mind. You go in there and do your job and you try to have a contingency plan for what can happen out of the ordinary. You try to stick basically to what's happening now—keep control of that." Two other officers, perhaps sobered by the execution, spoke of limiting a person's tenure on the team, though the range bandied about, from five to twenty years, seemed pretty generous. One of these men estimated that he could count on putting somewhere in the neighborhood of twenty men to death over a twenty-year period, then he would step down. "Enough is enough," he said, without a trace of irony. The other man, in his fifth year on the team, felt ready to step down right then. He was the one who put the tenure cap at five years. "I think it's time for me to come off," he said somberly, though, as it turned out, he elected to stay on the team anyway.

Two officers worried about possible emotional problems in the wake of executions. One man, who assured me that he felt fine now, nevertheless harbored fears that a delayed guilt reaction might dog him in his declining years.

> Sometime I might wonder whether some day, after I retire, this here might come back and hit me in the face. Religious, like. When I'm an old man, ready to die, maybe this here will haunt me. I don't think it will, but it could. . . . I don't know how it will affect me in the future. Right now, I don't really think about it one way or the other.

As it happens, some executioners do in fact suffer delayed reactions, which may feature morbid dreams of men they have put to death.[9] I saw no value in pointing this out to the officer, however, though I did encourage him and his colleagues to seek help if they experienced difficulties.

The other officer, less fortunate, labored under the weight of substantial emotional problems. He traced his susceptibility to his role in the execution process: He was one of the two men who sat with the condemned at the end and then strapped him in the chair.

What I do, people don't wanna do that—physically have to touch this man after sitting with him. We all be with him [on our shifts], but most of the team don't actually have that much contact with him. But you be the one to sit with him his last few hours of his life and you have to walk him in and you strap him in—it takes a lot. And it's only a few others on the team that actually got to do that. So they really don't get that touch, get all their senses involved; they can more or less just cut theirselves off from what's happenin'. Like they don't have a great part in it.

On one occasion, a prisoner "made a special request for me to walk with him" to the death chamber. That was the officer's job, but the prisoner apparently didn't know that. The request, which implied a relationship and pulled the officer deeper into the process than he was prepared for, came as a shock. "I had to totally remove myself from being in it [the execution] to do this for the man." The officer, who described himself as devoid of emotions and even thoughts at this key juncture, operated on instinct: "I just got up and went on with it."

Interestingly, this officer's colleague on the deathwatch, who also sits with the prisoner until the end and then must strap the prisoner in the chair, reported no problems at all. None! Never a moment's afterthought! Even in the retelling, which loses some of the force of the original, this man's words suggest a profound level of denial:

> I don't think about it, you know. The man is executed, the body is gone, and I clean the place up and close the books out, and, hey, I go home and eat me a hearty meal. I just block it out, that's it. It all blocks out until the next time. . . . I say, "Hey, we got a job to do. We did the job. Let's go about our business, you know, go home." So that's the way I look at it, you know.

This same man could, when expedient, laugh and joke with a condemned prisoner during his last meal (see Chapter 6). It is perhaps not surprising that no prisoner has asked this man to escort him to his death.

Our troubled officer was less resilient than his colleague. He suffered an emotional numbness that, over time, came to affect his entire life. The cause of the problem, he explained in an extended exchange with me, was not being around death; it was taking part in a killing.

> I just cannot feel anything. And that was what bothered me. I thought that I would feel something, but I didn't feel anything. . . . When I was small, I guess about seven or eight, I used to spend time with my uncle and aunt. They ran a funeral home service, so death to me was nothing new, being around death. But the actual participation of killing a person—I hadn't experienced that. And I didn't feel anything. That was the thing that bothered me.
>
> *You know you should feel more but you don't, and that's what troubles you?*
>
> Yeah, 'cause you're supposed to feel something.

So somewhere along the line, you've shut down some faculties to get through this?

You better believe it.

Do you find this in other parts of your life? Less feeling than you would normally expect? Or is it just in this one area?

It's laying over my whole life.

So it seems to have started here and spread elsewhere?

Ever since I joined the team. Very seldom do I get upset or get upset to a point where I would feel my voice rise. I just shut everything down.

The officer fears that this emotional numbness, disquieting in itself, may portend deeper problems.

I don't want to wake up tomorrow and recognize that my mind is gone, because I figure the stress will come later. . . . There's nothing to protect you from that. If it do come, like it's something that I'll have to deal with for the rest of my life. You never know when you might wake in the middle of the night in a cold sweat and you lost your mind.

Do you have any hints that something is going on inside you that would get worse if you kept going?

The hint is that I haven't felt anything.

This man harbors a grievance against the prison for the inadequate psychological counseling available to him.[10] His first bone of contention is that counseling was forced on him, whether he liked it or not. He didn't, and neither did his colleagues on the team.

When I first began, we had one administrator who tried to make us go to a counseling session afterwards, far as debriefing, psychological support. You'll find a lot of resentment anytime it's not voluntary; it's not going to be that much of a help. First you gotta want help and accept help before you get it. If you just gonna like force it on him, you know, it's no good; you're defeating your own purpose.

He also resents the fact that help was offered after the fact, when it was too late for him to make an informed decision about the wisdom of his involvement in executions.

It's almost degrading for anyone to tell us to go see a psychologist after the fact. After the fact! If you want me to see one, I think you should let me see one before I do it. 'Cause if anything was gonna happen, it was gonna happen while I'm in the process of doing this. I need to be prepared to do this. I need to know if I'm able to do this. After the fact, what's done is done, and if I need help, I can ask for help or I can go get help. And if you can see that I do need help, then come ask me and then give me the opportunity to volunteer for it. But don't put it to me that, you know, "I must do this," 'cause I may feel that I'm all right. Maybe I don't want to think about it; I don't wanna even bother with it; I don't wanna think about this. I wanna go ahead on livin', you know.

Competent, voluntary mental health care offered prior to his joining the execution team—or at least prior to his participation in his first execution—might or might not have predicted or prevented this man's deadening of feelings. In any event, emotional numbness is now, for this man, a legacy of executions. That this reaction bears a striking resemblance, at least on the surface, to that of condemned prisoners during their final hours is perhaps not coincidental. For the condemned, who face a violent death, the muting of feelings, and perhaps of thoughts as well, appears to be a kind of anesthetic. To the extent that this officer's colleagues experience emotional numbness as a situation-specific corollary of their role as executioners, it may be a useful anesthetic for them as well. But for him, the result is a deep, abiding, and potentially disabling anxiety. He is, then, an unintended psychological casualty of the death penalty.

Whatever may be their personal reactions to carrying out executions, these undertakings have a way of making people contemplate the larger meaning of life and savor the privilege of living. Even our emotionally impaired officer can point to lessons about life he has learned from executions that offer hope for a better future.

I know death is my destiny. I find that now I can accept death. I won't look for it. But if it, you know, if it happens, I'd rather die than suffer. I try to enjoy life more. I try to get the full meaning out of life. I try to learn more, as far as, not so much as just about living, but just being a person.

Other execution team members, less hurt by their experience than this man, concur in these existential lessons. "Learned something about life? Yeah. Get ready. Prepare yourself." The officers laugh nervously when they say such things, but they speak with conviction.

Though people react differently to executions, some with blunted feelings, others with heightened anxiety, they have one thing in common: No one on the team was haunted by Jones's memory, nor did anyone grieve for him. "When I go home after one of these things," said one man, "I sleep like a rock." His may or may not be the sleep of the just, but one can only marvel at such a thing, and perhaps envy such a man.

EXECUTIONS AND AMERICAN SOCIETY

In the last few years, viewing executions has become a kind of cottage industry. Requests from citizens to attend executions as official witnesses appear to be at an all-time high. A sizeable and growing number of news reporters have come to cover this odd beat; they view anywhere from one to a handful of executions, then write reports for newspapers, magazines, radio, or television.

A number of television documentaries on executions have been produced. (For our purposes, the notable ones include "Fourteen Days in May," a BBC documentary detailing the execution of Edward Earl Jones at Mississippi's Parchman Prison under Warden Cabana; and "The Execution Protocol," focusing on the lethal injection protocol and execution team at Missouri's Potosi Correctional Center, based on the Trombley book by the same title.[11]) The gripping movie, *Dead Man Walking*, based on Sister Helen Prejean's best-selling book by the same name, introduced an enormous audience to the workings of the death house. Only a few years ago there was a concerted effort by several news channels to broadcast executions on television. This may one day come to pass. At least one legal scholar contends that there is "a First Amendment right of access to state executions" and argues forcefully that "the press must be allowed to televise executions."[12]

Television is the modern world's most powerful public medium, but it represents the world in a way that is oddly unreal. In the privacy of one's home, framed by the contours of one's television screen, one can see the whole world distilled neatly in electronic images. These images are often engaging but they are usually thematically disconnected; regularly, commercials are spliced between images that have little coherence to begin with. And always, television images are removed from their natural context—we are shown scenes of far-flung disasters, for example, with no appreciation of the larger social or cultural context in which they occurred or how they affected people's lives. Television images are held together by a common but extraneous format: entertainment. In the words of Neil Postman, "television has made entertainment itself the natural format for the representation of all experience." As construed by television, almost anything in the world can be entertaining and, thus, almost nothing can be terribly serious. In Postman's words,

> There is no murder so brutal, no earthquake so devastating, no political blunder so costly . . . that it cannot be erased from our minds by a newscaster saying, "Now . . . this." The newscaster means that you have thought long enough on the previous matter (approximately forty-five seconds), that you must not be morbidly preoccupied with it (let us say, for ninety seconds), and that you must now give your attention to another fragment of news or a commercial.[13]

Life in general, let alone the crises that make up the news, takes on an air of unreality for the viewing audience.

Television gives us life under glass, sterile and staged, delivered in brief, staccato bursts of imagery lacking substance. So it would be with executions, we must assume, not only due to the effects of television but also because modern bureaucratic executions are already sterile, staged events that bring with them a sense of unreality all their own. As Sister Helen Prejean has observed, comparing modern executions to their public counterparts in times past,

> Witnesses could see the flames lick the flesh. They could hear the cries of agony. But this death . . . with witnesses behind the square of Plexiglas

like that, it was like a framed scene, death in the movies, death in cellu-
loid, death under glass. There he was, saying his last words. There he was,
walking to the chair. There he was, being strapped in. Three clangs of the
switch. No smell of burning flesh (the Plexiglas shields witnesses from the
smell). No sight of his face (the mask conceals his face, his eyes). And
with his jaw strapped shut like that, he could not cry out.

"Who killed this man?" Prejean asks rhetorically. "Nobody," comes the re-
sounding answer, because "everybody can argue that he or she was just doing
a job," that the killing "is nothing personal."[14]

One would suppose that televised executions would be aired, initially, as
serious documentaries. The stories of the condemned, told in this format,
could well be compelling and even deeply moving. Soon, though, with executions occurring at a fairly regular clip, the novelty would wear off. Dreary
lives culminating in bloody crimes and routinized executions would become
old news. In all but the most notorious cases, documentaries would most likely
be replaced by short segments on some sort of crime show. Writing tongue-
in-cheek, my colleague Paul S. Leighton has adapted the situation of the lost
sailor introduced at the outset of this book to a twenty-first century scenario:

> One can imagine the sailor at the dawn of the new millennium returning
> from a tour of duty dictated by his temporary employment agency and
> checking on e-mail from friends washed up on other corners of the globe.
> He surfs the far reaches of the Internet and navigates through cyberspace
> to check out the latest promotional spin-offs from the "Cops" television
> show, then follows a link to information about an imminent execution.
> After reading a description of the crime and some statements from the
> victim's family, the cybernaut clicks on a button that turns the computer
> screen into a high-definition television set and programs his VCR to
> record the event. The monitor tunes in to the Criminal Justice Network
> (channel 237), and he sits back with a microwave espresso to watch the
> televised execution. "Ah, civilization!"[15]

But even these crime show segments would grow stale, since the execution
routine at the heart of each story would be sufficiently lifeless on its own that
it could never support an extended program of entertainment.[16] Eventually,
there would be only news clips of the final seconds of executions, which
would be mixed in with snapshots of other violence—car wrecks, murders—
typical of daily life. What are we to expect from the regular viewing of execution scenes on the news? A clue can be found in the reactions of people already
on the scene to view executions—official witnesses, brought in at the end of
the death work process to watch the execution, disconnected from its natural
context, as if they were viewing a news clip live.

The research to date on official witnesses has been limited to journalists.
We learn from a study conducted by a team combining psychiatric and psychological expertise that "journalists who witnessed an execution experienced
a high prevalence of dissociative symptoms"—symptoms that revealed that
they had to mentally or emotionally anesthetize or numb themselves to cope

with what they saw—"similar to that of people who endured a natural disaster."[17] (Perhaps we can think of an execution as an unnatural disaster.) Almost half or more of the sample of journalists in this study reported the following symptoms in the research questionnaire:

I felt distant from my own emotions	(53%)
Things around me seemed unreal or dreamlike	(53%)
I felt a sense of timelessness	(53%)
I felt estranged or detached from other people	(60%)
I tried to avoid thoughts or feelings about the execution	(53%)
I had a narrow focus of attention	(47%)[18]

Interviews carried out in conjunction with the survey revealed that these figures almost certainly underestimate the prevalence of dissociation in this group. "Some journalists who reported no dissociative symptoms in their questionnaires indicated that they may have been so dissociated as not to have *noticed* their symptoms"—an observation that may well apply to team officers who claim no problems whatsoever in the conduct of executions.[19]

The dissociative effects experienced by journalists, however, are almost certainly less pronounced than those experienced by regular citizens who serve as official witnesses at executions. Like executioners, journalists have a mission or purpose—in their case to record and report. These essentially dissociative activities shield them from stress or at least allow them to use denial as a coping strategy, either of which produce lower symptom scores. As one journalist put it, "You have to be almost robotic about the reporting," a tack similar to that taken by the execution team.[20] Similarly, another reporter states, "You have to detach yourself from it. . . . You can't say 'I'm going to come in here today and watch someone die.' You have to say, 'I'm covering a new story'"— that is, just doing my job.[21]

It is intriguing that many of the dissociative symptoms reported by the journalists revealed states of mind or emotion *actively* sought by members of the execution team, who are, in effect, trained to dissociate themselves from the killing business at hand. Members of the execution team *consciously strive* to be distant from their feelings, to be detached from people other than their teammates, and to avoid thoughts or feelings about the execution; they aim, perhaps struggle, to maintain a narrow focus of attention. When their narrow tasks are completed, they try to let their minds drift (perhaps in the timeless, dreamlike reverie reported by the journalists?) until the execution is over. From my observation of the team in action, I am reasonably certain that for them, events like the last meal and the last walk do take on an unreal or dreamlike quality, including a sensation of timelessness. I know they did for me. At junctures like this, one literally feels that the process has a life of its own, beyond human control; that one is but a spectator in an awful drama that will take its own course no matter what.

Dissociative symptoms were found to be more prevalent among television reporters than any other group of journalists.[22] As with executioners, dissociation may be an occupational hazard for television journalists; the television medium itself promotes dissociation. After all, reducing real-life flesh-and-blood events, many profoundly tragic, to disconnected images served up between commercials as nightly entertainment is a dissociative feat of some magnitude. We know from documentaries that when an execution is filmed by a television crew, the camera's very presence creates in the minds of the actual real-life participants a heightened sense of unreality, as if the event were a morbid piece of entertainment that could be called off at any moment. "Having the BBC people around was helpful" to people on the scene, struggling to deny or emotionally distance themselves from the tragedy unfolding around them, says attorney Clive Smith, "because they injected an air of total unreality. You kept waiting for someone to yell 'cut,' and that would be the end of the movie."[23] No one did, and Edward Earl Johnson, the subject of the film and Smith's client, went to his death in the gas chamber.

If Americans come to view "execution clips" as a regular feature of television news, it is likely that we, too, will experience dissociation. If so, the dissociative effects for us as the viewing audience are likely to be more pronounced than those of officials, witnesses, or even executioners because we do not have *any* buffering effects of job or peer support or even role to protect us. We will simply be exposed, over and over again, to acts of lethal violence disconnected from their meaningful context—the gradual death of the human spirit of the condemned as he moves from death row to the death-watch to the death chamber, ending in an ignominious last walk to his demise. Even more than those on the scene, we may eventually become inured to the violence of the death penalty, which will almost certainly seem entirely unremarkable over time. A seasoned Associated Press reporter tells us that at his first execution, he tried to imagine "what's going through the guy's mind," but that was troubling so he backed away: "Since then, I try not to get involved that way." Other than a botched execution, which he can still bring to mind, "the other seven or eight all sort of blend together. The more I saw, the easier it became."[24] This reporter observed electrocutions. Executions by lethal injection, the most common and most tame method in use today, may be easier still to observe without feeling or even a distinct memory. This desensitization to human tragedy is seemingly painless and even adaptive, but in reality "is itself dehumanizing and brutalizing," in the words of one of the authors of the execution witness study discussed previously. "Literally, it makes one brutish."[25] One can see an end point where virtually all involved become brutish—the executioners, the official witnesses, and the execution-viewing television public.

For the prisoners of death row, the effects of televised executions might produce a brand of dissociative trauma all its own. Television is far and away the number one pastime on the many death rows that permit the condemned to either have TV sets in their cells or to have access to TV sets in dayrooms. For many, maybe most, condemned prisoners, the television is nothing less than their emotional lifeline. States Mumia Abu-Jamal, himself a long-term resident of death row: "After months or years of noncontact visits, few phone calls, and ever decreasing communication with one's family and others, many inmates use TV as an umbilical cord, a psychological connection to the world they have lost. They depend on it, in the way that lonely people turn to TV for the illusion of companionship."[26] So powerful is the typical prisoner's attachment to the television that taking it from him is one of the worst punishments on the row. States Alabama's Warden Jones, "If you want to hurt a Death Row person right now, I mean really *cut him to the bone*, then go ahead and take the television out of his cell. It's just hell on Earth for him when you do that."[27] Against this backdrop, we must picture condemned men hunched over in front of tiny television sets—by regulation on many death rows, TV sets can have screens no bigger than five inches—peering at the executions of their neighbors, killed in many cases by officers known to the prisoners, all the while knowing full well that their day will one day come and they will be the ones in the camera's eye.

As things stand today, death row prisoners follow the news coverage of their own cases in the media with understandable interest. In the BBC's "Fourteen Days in May," Edward Earl Johnson is shown intently watching coverage of his case on the local news, including "person in the street" surveys about whether or not he should be executed. All the while, Johnson, absorbed in his television, was being filmed by the BBC camera crew! Here we see television feeding upon itself, perhaps leaving some condemned prisoners to wonder what it means that an unreal television life on death row only ends for them where real-life death begins—in the execution chamber, live on camera, for the whole world to see.

Some people claim that televising executions, and thereby exposing the violence, will lead to the abolition of the death penalty. It might, but the route would be circuitous. Whereas hiding executions, historically, may have undermined the efforts of abolitionists,[28] exposing them by way of television would probably have no dramatic effects on the sanction, largely because we can so readily become accustomed to televised executions as normal features of life. Certainly we will not abolish executions to spare prisoners the truly macabre experience of viewing the executions of their cell-block neighbors or of their compatriots on distant death rows. But world reaction to televised executions could be quite strong. America is already something of a pariah in the West because of the death penalty, which is widely viewed these days as a human rights violation rather than a legal sanction.[29] Were we to televise executions, I can't help but think that we would be seen as modern-day barbarians. One could imagine pressure from human rights groups and perhaps economic sanctions as well, such as levied against South Africa while it practiced apartheid.

There may be a curious parallel here to the abolition of lynching in the South, which was due in considerable part to negative news reports that helped turn public opinion against the South for maintaining this cruel cultural practice. Papers in the North and even in Europe ran articles highly critical of lynching, sometimes featuring photographs of large crowds, replete with smiling women and children, clearly entertained by it all. These reports made it apparent to the rest of the nation and much of the world that the South was a kind of primitive backwater, unworthy of tourism or other forms of invest-ment.[30] Though lynching remained quite popular with the general public in the South, the practice lost the support of the cultural elite—governors, news-paper editors, judges—and fairly quickly passed into history. Today, interna-tional pressure spurred by revulsion at televised executions might well move officials and other cultural elites to divorce themselves from the death penalty—to refuse to support the practice, and certainly to refuse to use it as a political selling point in our recurring wars on crime. Featured boldly on tele-vision for all the world to see, executions could become a profound embar-rassment for our country, even though many of us as individuals might still find them perversely entertaining.

NOTES

1. The execution team takes a mechanistic view of things like exercise in the death cell. Their only concern is whether a prisoner who exercises to remain calm will get himself sweaty and have to be dried off before he is placed in the electric chair.

2. I do not know how Jones expressed his feelings about the last meal. I do know that others have been repulsed by what they take to be the cruelty of this ritual. Former war-den Cabana reports the following exchange with a condemned prisoner in Mississippi, upon asking him what he wanted for his last meal: "'What am I supposed to want? I mean, what difference does it make?' His anger welled up as he passionately argued the futility of it all. 'It's like another little piece of the game, another bit of torture. Here, man, here's a steak and potato. Enjoy, 'cause in a couple of hours we're going to gas you.'" D. A. Cabana, *Death at Midnight: The Confession of an Executioner* (Boston: North-eastern University Press, 1996), 171.

3. C. Milosz, *The Captive Mind* (New York: Random House, 1981), quoted in R. Klein, "Molding a Cry and a Song," *Commonweal*, 15 January 1988.

4. The officers train for this eventuality, but they are more worried about last-minute resistance from the prisoner. One officer expressed this concern when he observed, "My position on the inmate was behind and to the left. That way, in case he started to struggle, I was to reach down and grab the hip pocket on his pants and pull up to take his balance away from him."

5. See R. Johnson, *Condemned to Die: Life under Sentence of Death* (Prospect Heights, Ill.: Waveland Press, 1989), esp. Chap. 5.

6. Some people who have had near-death experiences or who have been clinically dead for a short while have memories of their encounters with death. Their minds are not blank but instead alive with activity.

There is no pain or despair, grief, or overwhelming anxiety. . . . [M]ental activity at first became enhanced and accelerated, rising to a hundred-fold velocity and intensity. Then the individuals expe-rienced feelings of calm and profound acceptance. . . . This was followed in many cases by a sudden review of the victim's entire past. Finally the person facing the threat of death often heard heavenly music and had an experience of transcendental beauty.

See S. Grof and J. Halifax, *The Human Encounter with Death* (New York: E. P. Dutton, 1977), 132. It would seem to be just such a transcendent experience that Jones's counselor sought for him. The progressive deterioration of condemned prisoners like Jones does not suggest transcendence, however, but rather capitulation in the face of a uniquely arranged death. In this context, a blank mind, which allows the person to deny the impending violence of the execution, is perhaps the best one can hope for.

7. The lack of clear job roles at this point allowed one officer to avoid touching the dead body, which troubled him. Here is our exchange on this subject:

Does it bother you to start touching the dead body?

Yeah, just a little bit. See, what I usually do, I wear these gloves. I don't carry gloves. So, they go around and get him unstrapped and I run around finding my gloves. By the time I get back with a pair of gloves, it is all over. They got him on the stretcher.

You avoid it, huh?

Yeah, I avoid it.

8. See R. J. Lifton, *The Nazi Doctors: Medical Killing and the Psychology of Genocide* (New York: Basic Books, 1986), esp. Part 3, and R. Johnson, "Institutions and the Promotion of Violence," in *Violent Transactions: The Limits of Personality*, ed. A. Campbell and J. J. Gibbs (London: Basil Blackwell, 1986).

9. One retired Canadian executioner, John Robert Radclive, reported the following delayed reaction to carrying out executions:

I used to say to condemned persons as I beckoned with my hand, "Come with me." Now at night when I lie down, I start up with a roar as victim after victim comes up before me. I can see them on the trap, waiting a second before they face their Maker. They haunt me and taunt me until I am nearly crazy with an unearthly fear. I am two hundred times a murderer, but I won't kill another man.

See *Illinois Death Penalty Coalition Newsletter*, 16 June 1986, 3. For the traumatic reaction of a contemporary executioner, see I. Solotaroff, "The Last Face You'll Ever See," *Esquire* 124 (2): 98 (August, 1995). Others associated with executions, such as attending physicians, have reported traumatic after-effects as well. See A. H. Hussain and S. Tozman, "Psychiatry on Death Row," *Journal of Clinical Psychiatry* 39 (3): 183–188 (March 1978). Attorneys as reformers may pay a high price for their emotional involvement with the condemned. See, for example, G. E. Goldhammer, *Dead End* (Brunswick, Me.: Biddle Publishing Company, 1994).

10. Programs to "inoculate" execution team officers against stress or to help them manage the trauma of the experience are new in corrections, but early indications are that these programs can be helpful to officers and others associated with executions. See I. R. Payne, R. T. Pray, and L. F. Damis, "Utah Stress Education Program Helps Staff Deal With Executions," *Corrections Today* 52 (4): 162–166 (July 1990), and D. B. Vasques, "Trauma Treatment: Helping Prison Staff Handle the Stress of an Execution," *Corrections Today* 55 (4): 70–73 (July 1993).

11. There are others as well, including two by the title "Death at Midnight"—one produced by CBS's *48 Hours* and the other by a cable network.

12. See J. D. Bessler, "Televised Executions and the Constitution: Recognizing a First Amendment Right of Access to State Executions," *Federal Communications Law Journal* 45 (3): 355–435 (August 1993). Bessler also discusses an Eighth Amendment argument—that we should be able to directly ascertain whether the death penalty conforms with "evolving standards of decency" as they apply to punishment. One might further argue that effective access includes access to public executions, as in times past, in the public square. Advocates from different ends of the political spectrum weigh in on this subject. Some conservatives argue for execution in the town square, the better to deter criminals. Some liberals concur with this change in venue, but for the reason that it may shame us before the world. Of course, no one knows what these executions would be like, let alone what their effects would be. We do know that we cannot recreate the past. Life in general is more private these days, less public than when executions took place in our communities. A public execution in days past had a different resonance, in large measure because much of life was lived in public. Today, the notion of publicly displaying criminals, helpless and restrained, at the moment of their death, is almost literally unthinkable.

13. N. Postman, *Amusing Ourselves to Death: Public Discourse in the Age of Show Business* (New York: Penguin, 1986), 87, 99–100.

14. H. Prejean, *Dead Man Walking: An Eyewitness Account of the Death Penalty in the United States* (New York: Random House, 1993), 101.

15. P. S. Leighton, "Fear and Loathing in an Age of Show Business: Reflections on Televised Executions" (unpublished manuscript, March 1997).

16. I know of only one proposal to develop a crime show with a focus on the death penalty. Tentatively entitled "Death Row: True Stories" and proposed by SHO Entertainment as a half-hour show, the plan is to focus on a prisoner "currently on Death Row or executed in the past....[D]ramatic reenactments, personal interviews and news clips [will be used to] present a fresh, unbiased, informative, and ultimately revealing look from both sides of the bars." I am not aware of the status of this proposal, though in my view any such show would have a short run on television. See "The Executioner's Docudrama," *Harper's* 290 (740): 22 (May 1995).

17. A. Freinkel, C. Koopman, and S. Spiegel, "Dissociative Symptoms in Media Eyewitnesses of an Execution," *American Journal of Psychiatry* 151 (9): 1338 (September 1994).

18. Ibid., 1337.

19. Ibid., 1337.

20. C. Barnett, "Covering Executions," *American Journalism Review* 17 (May 1995): 28.

21. A. Radolf, "Executions," *Editor & Publisher* 122 (16): 95 (22 April 1989).

22. Freinkel, Koopman, and Spiegel (n. 17), 1337.

23. Goldhammer (n. 9), 121.

24. This reporter is quoted in Radolf (n. 21), 94.

25. Barnett (n. 20), 29, quoting D. Freinkel, one of the authors of the witness trauma study.

26. M. Abu-Jamal, *Live From Death Row* (Reading, Mass.: Addison-Wesley, 1995), 9.

27. Goldhammer (n. 9), 109.

28. This is made quite clear in the works of L. P. Masur, *Rites of Execution: Capital Punishment and the Transformation of American Culture, 1776–1865* (New York: Oxford University Press, 1989), and V. A. C. Gatrell, *The Hanging Tree: Execution and the English People 1770–1868* (Oxford: Oxford University Press, 1994), both discussed at some length in Part I of this book.

29. See W. A. Schabas, *The Death Penalty as Cruel Treatment and Torture: Capital Punishment Challenged in the World's Courts* (Boston: Northeastern University Press, 1995).

30. See S. E. Tolnay and E. M. Beck, *A Festival of Violence: An Analysis of Southern Lynchings, 1882–1930* (Urbana: University of Illinois Press, 1995), 246.

PART IV

Moral and Legal Considerations

The barbaric punishments condemned by history, "punishments which inflict torture, such as the rack, the thumbscrew, the iron boot, the stretching of limbs and the like," are, of course, "attended with acute pain and suffering." When we consider why they have been condemned, however, we realize that the pain involved is not the only reason. The true significance of these punishments is that they treat members of the human race as nonhumans, as objects to be toyed with and discarded. They are thus inconsistent with the fundamental premise of the [Eighth Amendment] Clause that even the vilest criminal remains a human being possessed of common human dignity.

SUPREME COURT JUSTICE WILLIAM J. BRENNAN

Until we stop determining that some human beings are not worthy of life itself, we will continue to warehouse those we think unworthy of really living.

LIFE SENTENCE PRISONER

8

A Modern
Instance of Torture

Thus far I have placed the death penalty in historical perspective (Part I), then examined in detail the nature and impact of death row confinement (Part II) and the modern execution process (Part III). With regard to modern executions, I have, on the one hand, examined the pivotal function served by confinement under sentence of death in preparing prisoners to play their part in the execution drill (Part II, especially Chapter 4). On the other, I have considered the parallel socialization process through which the staff, notably the deathwatch or execution team, are prepared to play their roles in confining and executing condemned prisoners (Part III). I now return to my claim, asserted at the beginning of the book, that death row confinement and the executions that are the fruits of such confinement are a form of torture. In this chapter, I defend that claim and examine its implications for the justice of the death penalty.

Death row confinement today is a two-stage process. There is death row proper, where prisoners may spend years of close confinement, and there is the deathwatch, a period of total confinement usually ending in execution. As recently as the 1950s, all death rows were run like deathwatches. This is not the case today, since some death rows have been liberalized. However, the social climate on death row remains essentially unchanged. Condemned prisoners today are still isolated, whether singly or as a group, and feel powerless and alone; they still feel vulnerable, sometimes starkly so, though executions remain for many prisoners a distant and perhaps even unlikely possibility.[1]

Once a prisoner reaches the deathwatch stage, the likelihood that he will be executed is high. At this juncture, the prisoner is warehoused for death by the very people who will be his executioners. He has experienced a long, lonely, and often debilitating wait on death row. Now, on death row or in another setting, usually designated the death house, he must endure the total and ultimately dehumanizing confinement that is the deathwatch. This is the condemned man who, in Camus's reckoning, suffers torturous confinement and dies twice under sentence of death. It is his confinement, culminating in the deathwatch and ending with his execution, that epitomizes death row confinement. This confinement-unto-death, I will argue, is a clear and complete case of torture.

DEFINING TORTURE

The term *torture* is sometimes used casually, and this has led some observers to see the word as devoid of meaning. Edward Peters was correct when he asserted that the word *torture* is often used in a purely figurative sense to describe "generalized emotion and suffering of any particularly extreme kind, from whatever cause." Professors periodically hear students refer to their exams as a form of torture; Peters gave an example of a social activist who decried poverty and its attendant frustrations as forms of torture. Given such loose usage, one might suppose that "everyone may now be accused of torturing everyone else, and therefore no one tortures anyone."[2] In a sense, then, the term has been gutted of meaning. But people readily distinguish between figurative and literal usage of words. When students (and others) are asked to give examples of torture, they do not cite final exams or general sources of unhappiness but instead describe gross acts of physical violence used to extract information or simply to inspire terror. Thus, torture is typically seen as raw physical violence deployed in service of ignoble goals. This is an imperfect definition, to be sure, but not a meaningless one.

Death row confinement is surely an awful experience, but it is hard to think of it as true torture. Even during the admittedly bleak deathwatch phase, there is no violence or brutality of any kind. Yet the notion that torture must involve overt physical violence, though simple and even compellingly clear, is needlessly narrow. Drawing on its first worldwide survey of torture, published in 1973, Amnesty International offered a broader definition: "Torture is the systematic and deliberate infliction of acute pain *in any form* by one person on another, or on a third person, in order to accomplish the purpose of the former against the will of the latter"[3] (emphasis added). By this definition, the pain of torture may take any form, be it physical, psychological, or both, and may serve any purpose, including an unconscious or unrecognized purpose. The spirit of the Amnesty definition was echoed in the United Nations Declaration against Torture, adopted unanimously in 1975. In this declaration, torture

> means any act by which severe pain or suffering, whether physical or
> mental, is intentionally inflicted by or at the instigation of a public official

on a person for such purposes as obtaining from him or a third person information or confession, punishing him for an act he has committed, or intimidating him or other persons.[4]

The specifying of public officials is an improvement over the Amnesty definition. As Peters's historical study made clear, torture "has always had as its essence its public character"; torture has always been the prerogative, legitimate or illegitimate, of public officials or their agents.[5] The UN definition of torture falls short, however, in excluding "pain or suffering arising only from, inherent in, or incidental to lawful sanctions."[6] This is a logical fallacy. Any punishment that requires torturous conditions for its administration, or in which such conditions occur incidental to its administration, is no longer a lawful punishment. Torture must be defined independently of law. To hold otherwise is to contend that anything can be done under color of law.

The same logical fallacy, in this instance in regard to restrictive conditions of confinement, underlies the Supreme Court decision in *Bell* v. *Wolfish*. This case reads, in pertinent part, as follows:

> A court must decide whether the disability is imposed for the purpose of punishment or whether it is but an incident of some other legitimate governmental purpose. . . . Absent a showing of an expressed intent to punish on the part of [correctional] officials, that determination generally will turn on "whether an alternative purpose to which [the restriction] may rationally be connected is assignable for it, and whether it appears excessive in relation to the alternative purpose assigned [to it]" [citations omitted]. . . . Ensuring security and order at the institution is a permissible nonpunitive objective, whether the facility houses pretrial detainees, convicted inmates, or both.[7]

The holding in *Wolfish* would seem to indicate that death row confinement, whether or not it meets independent criteria defining torture, may nevertheless be considered a reasonable restriction if it is imposed without expressly punitive intent.

Yet inmates do in fact experience the objectively harsh conditions of death row confinement as punishment, as the following observations by death row prisoners indicate:

- You know, they are hurting me over here waiting on death. That's the hurting part. Waiting on death. The real cruel and mean things what they done in here is keep you locked up waiting on death. Waiting on death. Every day go around, it come in your mind: "When all of this going to be over with?" That's how they really punish you. They know how they punishing you, they know how they hurting you. But just by putting that needle in or putting you in the electric chair or whatever, they not hurting you that way. If they do come, I'll probably be glad they fixing me up because I won't have to suffer days in that cell.[8]

- If they were to come to my cell and tell me I was going to be executed tomorrow, I would feel relieved, in a way. The waiting would be over. I would know what to expect. To me, the dying part is easy; it's the waiting and not knowing that's hard. . . . I have reached the point where I no longer really care. . . . They're killing me a little bit each day.[9]

In a perverse way, some condemned prisoners come to hunger for execution as an escape from the death-in-life they suffer on death row. When told of his last-minute commutation of sentence, Isodore Zimmerman responded with disbelief and then with despair.

■ I didn't believe it. What was more, I didn't care. For nine long months I'd been rehearsing my death, dying a little every day, dying a little more every night, while just up the hall from my cell they were killing men, thirteen of them. I knew my role as victim too well, knew it by heart, couldn't back down now. "I don't want clemency," I heard myself saying.[10]

Others "volunteer" for execution, dropping their appeals. Escape from death row is often a salient motive, and an increasingly common one as the threat of execution increases, adding greatly to the pressures of life on death row.[11]

That death row confinement is not in itself punishment, as implied in the *Wolfish* holding, is psychologically inconceivable, even if one can distinguish legalistically between intended and unintended suffering. This view is also legally suspect, at least according to holdings of the state supreme courts of California (*People* v. *Anderson*, 1972) and Massachusetts (*Commonwealth* v. *O'Neil*, 1975). These decisions examined the "total impact of capital punishment," emphasizing the "dehumanizing effects" of death row confinement and the resulting "psychological torture" produced by confinement under sentence of death (see, for example, *Anderson* at 892 and 894).[12] (In these cases, such key terms as *dehumanization* and *psychological torture* were used intuitively and not carefully defined, and conclusions were put forth as assertions rather than formal arguments with empirical support, which may explain why the holdings have not influenced higher courts.)

The emphasis on intent in *Wolfish* is, in any case, contradicted by developments in international human rights law with respect to "cruel treatment and torture," which in this body of case law includes both death row confinement (known as "the death row phenomenon") and execution. As Schabas's thorough assessment of this body of work makes clear, "Most cases on the subject of cruel punishment make no reference to intent."[13] As a result, "State action is unconstitutional if its consequence is to inflict unacceptable levels of cruelty, albeit that is not the intention of the organizers of the State action."[14] (As we shall see at the conclusion of this chapter, the U.S. Supreme Court is only just beginning to look at the death penalty in the light of the human rights holdings of international courts and tribunals.) Finally, even if the logical restrictions of *Wolfish* are accepted, death row confinement can be shown to be "excessive in relation to the alternative purpose assigned [to it]," because condemned prisoners can be confined more humanely than is now the case. That such reforms would make executions more difficult to carry out is existentially significant but legally irrelevant. No one ever promised that lawful executions would be easy.

If we put aside the question of whether or not torture can serve legal ends, the Amnesty and UN definitions of torture are useful as a starting point. In fact, these definitions or ones very like them are used to guide decisions by international tribunals considering human rights cases. They are unsatisfactory by themselves, however, because both hinge on the ambiguous notion of severity of pain and suffering. Punishment is, by definition, the intentional infliction of pain and suffering, and a serious crime, not to mention a heinous one, would seem as a matter of simple justice to warrant a severe punishment. Does this mean that we torture all serious offenders in the name of justice? More to the point, does this mean that we may inflict any pain we want on serious offenders and never cross the threshold of torture?

Distinguishing Torture from Punishment

We must distinguish torture from legitimate punishments that involve severe pain and suffering as well as from illegitimate punishments of great severity that do not constitute torture. Examples of the latter include isolated instances of guard brutality. A guard who beats up a prisoner inflicts severe pain and suffering, but this illegitimate violence is not, by itself, an instance of torture. For torture to have occurred, there must be a *pattern* of severely abusive treatment that is *deliberate* in that it is formally or informally sanctioned by persons in authority. In the words of the UN Declaration against Torture, there must be a series of encounters marked by "an aggravated and deliberate form of cruel, inhuman or degrading treatment or punishment."[15] Note that the intentions or aims of the individual guard or even the larger regime are irrelevant in establishing that torture has taken place. For example, the understanding on the scene might be that beatings serve a higher good, such as maintaining order or, more perversely, building character, and hence are not cruel. Still, regular, sanctioned campaigns of guard violence—which, however they are understood, are arguably *objectively* cruel and degrading, if not also inhuman—might well constitute torture because they meet the criteria as set forth in the UN declaration.

Distinguishing torture from severe but lawful punishments is more difficult, since such punishments are systematically and deliberately administered and inflict severe pain. To make this distinction, a more refined definition of torture is needed. I will arrive at this definition inductively, analyzing acts presently thought to constitute torture that, by social practice or custom, can be excluded from the category of severe but legitimate punishments (like lengthy prison sentences, which have never been classified by Amnesty or the UN as a form of torture) and logically distinguished from severe and illegitimate punishments short of torture (like sporadic guard violence, as mentioned above). My goal is to determine the underlying commonalities of the various forms of torture, and hence to identify the nature or essence of torture per se. I will then attempt to show that death row confinement, unlike regular confinement, is indeed an instance of torture.

What practices, then, qualify as torture, and what do they have in common? The Amnesty and UN definitions of torture encompass the ferocious physical violence of beatings and mutilations used systematically to inspire terror, as well as the suffering administered using thumbscrews and racks to facilitate interrogations. The catalog of gross physical abuses reported by Amnesty in its various reports on torture is chilling, both because of the cruelty of the methods and because of the routine and even cold-blooded way in which they are employed.

The Amnesty and UN definitions also encompass more subtle psychological forms of torture. Included, for instance, is the insidious psychological violence of brainwashing, a widely recognized form of torture in which various forms of psychological deprivation are used to inflict pain and suffering. Also included is ritual degradation, a lesser known form of psychological torture. Used on women by Spanish interrogators, ritual degradation has been described as pure psychological torture. Victims interviewed by an Amnesty International mission "told of sexual threats, including sterilization, of being made to walk naked in the police station, of being manhandled in front of male friends, and of insults that are (above all within the mores of Spanish society) so degrading as to be a form of psychological torture."[16] In this context, overt physical violence is superfluous. The psychological assault on the person is devastating, producing pain and suffering on an order normally associated with physical torture and never countenanced in law.

Cases of purely physical torture, moreover, are rare. In practice, physical and psychological abuse are often combined. Brainwashing, perhaps the twentieth-century version of the rack, is in many ways the paradigm of modern torture. I shall therefore use it as a case in point.

Brainwashing occurs in the context of a psychologically torturous regime of confinement, often accompanied by physical violence. Yet physical violence is not integral to brainwashing or to torture in general. Instead, as we have learned from Amnesty International, "gross acts of torture (such as electric shock, rape or tearing out fingernails) are situated within a coercive context of which such methods are *merely an extension*"[17] (emphasis added). The *method* of torture is often physical, in other words, but the *process* and the ultimate *goal* of torture are psychological. This is apparent from an analysis of the confinement conditions associated with brainwashing and, in less organized form, virtually all types of torture.[18]

The dominant features of the confinement regime associated with brainwashing are as follows:

1. *Total control:* "The prisoner's entire existence, down to the most intimate needs, is governed by strictly enforced rules that cover both waking and sleeping hours. The objectives are to keep the subject under constant psychological harassment and to drive home the lesson that his jailers are omnipotent and he is powerless." Where physical torture is used, it is an extreme and painful exercise of total control of the prisoner by his keepers.

2. *Isolation:* The person is "completely cut off from the outside world and receives only such information about his family and friends as his custodi-

ans see fit to give him." Persons may be isolated as a group, rather than singly, with individuals allowed varying degrees of interaction within their isolated world.

3. *Personal humiliation:* The prisoner is "deprived . . . of any previous claim to personal dignity or status." He is treated like a nonentity; in some cases, like an object or animal.

4. *Uncertainty:* The prisoner's fate is uncertain. What abuses await him and when will they occur? Will he live or die? The prisoner is made to feel anxious and afraid, even terrified. By some reckonings, uncertainty, which brings with it the raising and dashing of hopes, is often one of the more painful aspects of regimes of brainwashing.

5. *Physical debilitation and exhaustion:* The confinement regime is spartan, resulting in "loss of weight, strength, and stamina. Eventually the subject is so weakened that prolonged mental effort becomes increasingly difficult, if not impossible."[19]

Exposure to such conditions produces a syndrome marked by "dependency, debility, and dread," which culminates in dehumanization.[20] The goal of this confinement regime, and indeed of all forms of torture, whether explicit or not, is to "destroy the victim's personality, to break him down."[21] To "break" a person means, quite simply, "to destroy his humanity"[22]—that is, to literally dehumanize him, often completely. Once reduced to the status of something subhuman—an animal writhing in pain or an insensate object— the victim of torture is then used to further the torturer's ends. Under no lawful punishment can offenders be treated in this way, a point I shall return to later. Hence it is the literal dehumanization of individuals that distinguishes torture from punishment.

Death Row as Torturous Confinement

The death row regime, particularly during the crucial deathwatch period, incorporates many of the standard elements of torturous confinement. It features *total control* of basic life activities by essentially "omnipotent" keepers, who can neglect or abuse prisoners, sometimes at will, often with little or no accountability; *isolation* of condemned prisoners—either singly or as a group, for years on end and, increasingly, for a decade or more—from the larger prison and from the outside world, with only limited contact with other human beings in a carefully monitored and controlled environment; chronic *uncertainty* about one's fate—uncertainty which, like death row confinement itself, extends for years, leaving prisoners preoccupied about if and when they will be executed (a morbid reality brought home to them vividly by executions stayed at the final hour), and about what the experience of execution will be (troublingly, one way to eliminate much of this uncertainty is to give up one's appeals, which occurs with increasing frequency these days); a situation of *personal humiliation*, since the prisoners are, in effect, objects—mere "parcels" or "things," to quote Camus—stored for execution, itself an exercise in humiliation; and, in varying degrees, *personal deterioration*, if not debilitation and exhaustion, in the existentially spartan regime that is death row confinement. All of this occurs in the context of impoverished physical conditions. To be sure, the overall conditions of confinement on many death rows are less oppressive than the standard regime of confinement associated with brainwashing. In particular, though the control on death row is total, especially during the deathwatch, it is less intrusive than in brainwashing. Thus, harassment is standard fare during brainwashing, but is never a matter of policy on death row. Still, the psychological impact of death row confinement parallels that of brainwashing and other forms of psychological torture. Both death row prisoners and brainwashing victims are powerless, vulnerable, and alone. Both groups, moreover, share a common psychological fate: literal and often extensive dehumanization.

There is a basic difference between confinement during brainwashing and confinement on death row, and this difference accounts for a variance in emphasis in the two regimes and in the psychological reactions they produce. In brainwashing, psychological suffering is *systematically* inflicted and exploited to produce a result (such as a political confession). On death row, the suffering stems primarily from abandonment and neglect, and is not inflicted *expressly* because its effects are useful. Nevertheless, this suffering is known to exist, and is exploited because its effects *are* useful. The execution team recognizes the dehumanization process, watches it unfold, and knowingly benefits from it (see Chapters 6 and 7). For example, though condemned prisoners are not shaved prior to execution expressly to take their identities and make them more easily controllable, loss of identity and attendant malleability are the known results of that procedure, and nothing is done to counteract those useful effects. Likewise, prisoners are not placed in a barren death cell to further erode their capacity to resist, but this is the known effect of that procedure, and the procedure continues to be followed.

The execution team has inherited much of the routine by which it operates. The various procedures, distantly rooted in security or convenience, are perpetuated for the same reasons—security or convenience. The warden noted, for instance, that "it's not necessary to completely shave that head; all you need is a bald spot on the top." But it is easier to shave the entire head, in the manner of earlier executions. The warden similarly sees no purpose in moving the prisoner to the barren death cell after he has been shaved and showered.

> Why do we do that? You're taking him out of the cell that has been his home. You're putting him through two stages. And you're putting him in a stark, cold, tomblike cell. And every time you go for him, to read him the court order, he's standing at the bars in this desolate, ungodly place. That's how it appears to me. Why not let him out of his [regular] cell and let him have a seat? You've got the team all around him. Then I can go in and pull my chair up and say, "I got to read this here to you. . . ." There's not even a decent place to sit down in the death cell.

This procedure is maintained because it works. As one officer made clear, the death cell, being empty of any possessions, is perfectly secure. It is also a "straight shot" from there to the execution chamber, which further simplifies matters. Change, in any case, is seen as risky. "I don't dare change anything," observed the warden. "It works the way it is. I don't want to do anything that would upset things." If prisoners' identities go with their hair, or if their will is suffocated in a conveniently accessible storage cell that is also a tomb, those are unintended but accepted corollaries of conducting the business of death work as it has always been done.[23]

We have seen that brainwashing, in contrast, involves active, intentional, systematic abuse of subjects to establish control. Abuse is often artfully mixed with leniency, which cultivates dependency and hence enhances control of the prisoner. This process is a calculated invasion, and ultimately a usurpation, of the victim's personality. As Robert Lifton has noted, "penetration by the psychological forces of the environment into the inner emotions of the individual person is perhaps the outstanding psychiatric fact of thought reform," or brainwashing. The distinguishing characteristic of this procedure is manipulation marked, on the one hand, by "the fluctuation between assault and leniency," and, on the other, by "the requirements of confession and reeducation." It is Lifton's view that "the physical and emotional assaults" characteristic of this manipulation "bring about the symbolic death; leniency and the developing confession are the bridge between death and rebirth; the reeducation process, along with the final confession, create the rebirth experience." The person subjected to brainwashing feels helpless, vulnerable, and alone; he "dies to the world," in Lifton's fine phrase, and then is reborn in his captor's image.[24]

In brainwashing, control of even the smallest details of life is sought. Such control produces a profound dependency. This dependency, in conjunction with debility and fear, makes the person easier to manipulate in a systematic and sometimes elaborate way. In contrast, control and dependency on this order are avoided on death row. They would foster unwanted and, indeed, counterproductive relationships, relationships that would complicate rather than facilitate executions, which require nothing more from the prisoner than simple, passive compliance with the execution drill. (Some of the psychological penetration achieved by agents of brainwashing may also occur on death row as a result of external forces; for example, the interplay of the harshness of the environment together with the prospect of leniency offered by the appeals process—in the extreme, release to the free world, which happens on occasion—may produce a dependency comparable to that of "good guy–bad guy" relations with one's keepers, and would do so without any unwanted intimacy.) But aside from the difference in the degree of control directly exercised by their agents, brainwashing and death row share essentially the same basic confinement conditions, with essentially the same impact. Both dehumanize and both qualify as instances of torture.

DEHUMANIZATION

Since this argument hinges on the notion of dehumanization, let me detour briefly to define this term. Like *torture*, the term *dehumanization* has been used loosely, even in domestic and international human rights cases dealing with these subjects,[25] but I have something quite specific in mind when I invoke the concept.

Dehumanization as I use the term is not solely or even primarily a symbolic experience, as when one feels "dehumanized" because one has been treated in an impersonal or insulting or even demeaning manner. Rather, dehumanization entails the loss—in whole or in part, situationally or generally—of one's humanity. A dehumanized individual is in some sense dead as a person, either with respect to a segment of his behavior (such as his job) or more generally, such that his existence is more that of an object or automaton than that of a rational, sentient human being. Executioners and the condemned each suffer dehumanization, though of different types.

Human Nature Defined

To explore the ways in which humanity can be lost, one must specify what it means to be a person or human being. My claim, building on the work of my colleague Jeffrey Reiman, is that the essence of personhood or humanity is a sense of self that conveys the capacity and moral right to make choices and hence be self-determining.[26] Self-determination, in turn, both finds expression in and presupposes—that is, requires—some degree of (1) autonomy, defined as the capacity to influence one's environment and hence shape one's fate; (2) security, defined as the capacity to find or create stability in one's world and hence shelter oneself from harm; and (3) relatedness to others, defined as the capacity to feel for oneself and others and hence to have caring and constructive relationships. I shall examine each of these dimensions of self-determination to show how a sense of self both shapes and in turn is shaped by all three.

Scholars have variously seen each of the three dimensions of self-determination—autonomy, security, and relatedness to others—as the cornerstone of personhood. Autonomy, rooted in the use of reason, has been said to mark us as responsible moral beings rather than merely advanced or precocious animals. Accordingly, such classical philosophers as Socrates, as well as, more recently, Ernst Cassirer and Herbert Morris, have identified the capacity to reason, and hence to be responsible for ourselves, as the *sine qua non* of personhood.[27] In contrast, Abraham Maslow and others have seen security as the essential psychological precondition to the unfolding of human nature, observing that without stability and safety in one's world, self-determination would give way to determination by external forces.[28] Finally, John Dewey and others have seen relatedness to others—to things outside ourselves and, more specifically, to other people—as basic to our nature as social animals who exercise self-determination through self-defining transactions with the world.[29]

In addition, anthropologists and sociologists have demonstrated that each of these dimensions is central to human nature.[30] My point is not merely that each attribute is relevant to an understanding of human nature. Rather, I wish to argue that, *taken together*, they represent that which is distinctively human in the social and moral sense of the term.

To be self-determining, individuals must influence their environment, both the inner—their personal thoughts and feelings—and the outer—their interactions with others. This both presupposes and produces stability and hence safety, and establishes relationships with others in the social world. Autonomy, security, and relatedness to others thus develop in interaction with one another as individuals become persons. In Lewis Mumford's words,

> Each individual makes over the life-course of the species and achieves a character and becomes a person. The more fully he organizes his environment [autonomy], the more skillfully he associates in groups [security], the more constantly he draws on his social heritage [relatedness], the more does the person emerge from society as its fulfillment and perfection.

The process of becoming a person is never fully finished, Mumford asserted, as "man's nature is a self-surpassing and a self-transcending one."[31] We are emergent persons, in Mumford's reckoning, and this dynamism is central to our nature.

The distinctive dynamism of human nature derives from the ongoing interaction among the three dimensions of self-determination. Autonomy, security, and relatedness are interconnected at birth; helpless human infants can only gain control over their world, and be secure in it, through their relationships with their parents.[32] The continuing interrelatedness of these dimensions has been inversely confirmed by Hans Toch. Toch studied human breakdowns in confinement, looking at the experiences of hundreds of inmates in more than a dozen jails and prisons. He found that the absence of these dimensions—that is, impotence instead of autonomy, fear instead of security, and isolation instead of relatedness—interacted with one another so as to provoke "existential questions" that influenced "crises of every kind in every setting" and ultimately represented "universal motives" associated with human despair.[33] My own work with cotton mill workers suffering from terminal cases of brown lung extended Toch's analysis, uncovering the interplay of the same existential concerns among persons undergoing life-threatening crises.[34] Condemned prisoners, as well as victims of recognized forms of torture, also share these concerns. If no man is an island unto himself, neither is he merely autonomous or secure.

Persons of every known culture develop, in one form or another, a sense of self and self-determination. And though the potential is present at birth, these attributes are not birthrights. A sense of self and self-determination do not emerge automatically from the simple fact of our existence. Instead, as Reiman makes clear, the development of a sense of self and self-determination require the social institution of privacy.[35]

Privacy is honored in all cultures—is, indeed, a social and psychological universal.[36] As Barry Schwartz has noted, "some provision for removing oneself from interaction and observation must be built into every establishment." Moreover, each stage of personal development "has its own mode of privacy, which may be defined in terms of the ego's relationship to those from whom privacy is sought and the manner in which withdrawal is accomplished." It was first noted by Simmel that "human associations require a definite ratio of secrecy which merely changes its objects."[37]

Privacy confers and confirms selfhood and permits individual selves to become persons—that is, to negotiate their lives with some degree of autonomy, security, and relatedness to others. In effect, privacy constitutes a "social skin" that at once preserves the integrity of the individual as distinct from the external world and allows the individual to modulate his inner thoughts and feelings as well as his contacts with the outer world. An existential dialectic is at work here, featuring the interplay of privacy and society, self and person.[38]

Human Nature Defiled

As we have seen, to be a person is to have a sense of self and self-determination that set one apart from the rest of the world and relate one to that world at least partly on one's own terms. One develops and maintains these attributes through the social institution of privacy. Under this definition of personhood, dehumanization occurs in the absence of privacy and involves the loss of one's sense of self; one's capacity to make choices affecting either one's fate, one's security, or one's relationships with others; or all of these attributes. Partially dehumanized persons have lost some aspect of their personhood; for example, the capacity to make decisions that affect their (internal or external) environment or their relationships to other people. Fully dehumanized persons have lost all aspects of their personhood, becoming, for all intents and purposes, physical objects or automatons.

Just as dehumanization varies in degree, it varies also in scope, in its nature, and in the role played by individual choice or volition. Dehumanization may be situational in scope, affecting only a limited segment of one's life, or general in scope, affecting all or most facets of one's life. It may be symbolic in nature, limited to perceptual distortions of one's humanity, or literal, involving the actual suspension or loss of one's personhood. Finally, dehumanization may also involve an element of collusion under pressure, a conscious or unconscious relinquishing of one's humanity "to get by" or "to get the job done."

Now it is immediately obvious that punishment infringes on the personhood of the punished. Conviction and imprisonment, for example, necessarily reduce the prisoner's privacy. In the setting of prison, most of one's life falls under the ambit, if not the control, of a formal authority. Furthermore, the right to violate someone else's privacy and yet to remain inviolate oneself is integral to authority. But even prison authorities may violate a prisoner's privacy only with valid reason (primarily to maintain security) and with discretion (to minimize suffering).[39] Prisoners, though they have only a very limited legal right to privacy, are protected against "maliciously motivated searches"; moreover, intrusions of privacy that constitute "intentional harassment" are not to be "tolerated by a civilized society."[40] Still, imprisonment and the violations of privacy inherent in confinement threaten each prisoner's familiar sense of self and limit his capacity to make meaningful choices. (Guards, too, are imprisoned, as Lucien Lombardo has recently made clear,[41] insofar as they perform public roles that are narrowly defined by the prison organization and further limited by the conditions of imprisonment.)

The limitations on privacy in prison are quite real and substantial, but they lend themselves to overstatement. For example, it is simply untrue that

> the prison is, almost by definition, a place where the resident has lost his privacy, and his identity, and has become a number. Every day in every way, the prison reinforces the inmate's image of himself as that of something less than a human.[42]

In point of fact, neither inmates nor guards typically lose or relinquish their humanity in the context of regular confinement; they do not normally become faceless, stereotypical "cons" and "hacks." Regular prisoners generally have sufficient mobility, resources, and companionship to develop a familiar round of life and, in effect, carve out a niche for themselves within the prison.

It has long been known, for example, that prisons and mental hospitals, the typical total institutions discussed by Erving Goffman and other social scientists, offer sanctuaries to their inhabitants, places where the inmate or patient may "be his own man."[43] From an existential perspective, these niches provide privacy; they shield individuals from the particular pressures of prison life they find most noxious and allow them to live in ways that at least partially satisfy their personal preferences and needs.[44] By the same token, guards attempt to establish what might be termed "work niches" in which they can interact with inmates, exercise authority, and define goals in a way that is distinctly their own.[45] Prisons' inhabitants do periodically think and act collectively, the collective violence of riots being a tragic, though comparatively rare, case in point.[46] But the norm is for inmates and guards to live and work as individuals, not as role types—which is to say, as persons, not as dehumanized entities.

All this changes on death row, in particular during the deathwatch. Roles are sharply circumscribed. The daily work of death row guards makes them susceptible to situation-specific, symbolic dehumanization. They are cast in the anonymous role of agents of violence, for violence is inherent in their job. They are by definition agents not only of custody, which implies forceful restraint, but also of execution, which entails killing.

The role that death row guards play is necessarily marked by a substantial loss of individuality and choice. Their private feelings and sentiments—their very identities as individual officers, let alone as individual persons—are largely irrelevant. Others respond to them primarily, if not exclusively, in terms of their public roles. Autonomous, trusting relationships with prisoners are virtually precluded. Even superficially amicable relations with inmates are hard to establish. Still, even though prisoners complain about uncaring officers, some officers clearly do construe their role to include caring (see Chapter 4). The prisoners, however, usually cannot see beyond the guards' public role.

Role boundaries are pronounced during the deathwatch. The psychology of working the deathwatch is such that guards will actively embrace their role as agents of violence—will merge with and become what the job calls for—because this role is the one most readily offered them. During the execution process itself, of course, this is literally the only role available to them (see Part III).

Condemned prisoners, like their guards, are offered a dehumanized role, that of a subhuman creature, a thing that is an appropriate object of violence. This dehumanized identity is, at first, situation-specific and symbolic, involving prisoners' perceptions of their identity relative to the context of death row. As is true for the guards, such critical events on death row as execution rehearsals and, of course, actual executions of other prisoners, presumably intensify the prisoners' perceptions of their dehumanization. Gradually, each prisoner's identity becomes more generally and literally dehumanized. The prisoners come in reality to resemble the dehumanized creatures they are thought to be by their keepers and the larger society that has consigned them to the death chamber. On death row, Charles Cooley's famous dictum that "the imaginations which people have of one another are the solid facts of society" is given full play.[47]

Death row confinement features all the standard "mortifications, debasements, and profanations of self" identified by Goffman as potential sources of situation-specific and symbolic dehumanization among inmates of such total institutions as mental hospitals and prisons.[48] It entails, moreover, a profound loss of privacy. On death row proper, privacy is greatly reduced; during the deathwatch, surveillance is constant. The result is a daily round of life that negates any sense of self separate and apart from the environment. Prisoners become, in effect, mere extensions of the environment, items in the schedule, objects of custody. Those controlling the environment thus have achieved the distinctive psychological "penetration" that is at the heart of brainwashing and other forms of psychological torture.

Now, some events in the lives of the condemned, like visits with loved ones, do take place away from death row proper. Within these contexts, the condemned prisoners can resume a normal identity, such as that of husband, father, son, or friend. The difficulty in maintaining a normal individual identity, however, is that the inmate's "situation" on death row is quite pervasive, affecting nearly all aspects of his existence. As relationships with loved ones and others in the free world wane, and they typically do, the prisoner's entire world shrinks to fit the world of death row. This world, as we have noted, has a markedly barren underlife (see Part II). Existence there is public and exposed, and hence one's identity as a condemned man necessarily dominates.

As time passes and the prisoners' execution dates approach, the death row world and their identity as condemned prisoners naturally take on increasing weight. Supportive relations with counselors and other "outsiders" during the deathwatch may blunt this process, as we saw in Chapter 6, but, ultimately, when he takes his last walk, the prisoner is alone, in a psychological void. At this juncture, it is essentially, if not solely, in terms of his dehumanized prisoner role that he is defined by others and, it would seem from the accounts of those on the scene, by himself as well. If he knows anything at this juncture, he knows in his gut that "the death sentence is the ultimate rejection a society can impose," that there is "no other status . . . so demeaning and damaging as that of being formally condemned as unfit to live."[49]

The objective conditions of death row confinement reinforce the subjective identity of the condemned as a dehumanized entity. The condemned prisoners' actions are constrained by their dehumanized role. They spend virtually all their time in an environment that is, in fact, arranged to store them like objects and that limits their behavior accordingly. As a result, their very capacity to maintain an independent sense of self and to exercise self-determination is undermined. The prisoners' subjective identity, treated as the reality in the death row setting, is thus apt to become the objective reality over time. Persons perceived and treated as objects become, in part, if not in whole, exactly that.

Condemned prisoners thus typically suffer a more extensive and insidious form of dehumanization than their guards, literally losing their human attributes. The prisoners' dehumanization is a direct result of the guards'. For, whether intentionally or not, guards adopt a dehumanized view of themselves and the prisoners as an ego defense. This, in turn, enables them to participate in a confinement regime that defines and treats inmates as objects and eventually reduces them to objects. Object–object relations prevail during the deathwatch, and culminate in bureaucratically administered executions.

The link between the guards' dehumanization and the death work they perform is fairly straightforward. One can see how normal persons would readily, almost naturally, adopt a dehumanized and dehumanizing view of the prisoners and of themselves, within the death row setting, given the social forces at work on the row, especially during the deathwatch and execution procedure. To do so would not seem to require any special sort of personal background or disposition; to do otherwise would be to expose oneself to emotional pain and suffering. (As was the case for a death row major in Louisiana who told Sister Helen Prejean that, by getting to know the condemned prisoners, he'd discovered that "many of them are just little boys inside big men's bodies, little boys who never had much chance to grow up." For him, executions became moral and psychological ordeals.[50]) Organizations engaged in the business of violence must recruit and socialize their personnel to be dutiful agents or instruments of violence. In extreme cases, institutional arrangements foster in the staff the development of personality traits that allow guilt-free violence on the job. Almost any person can be trained to kill following a socialization process that emphasizes dehumanization of self and others. There is, sad to say, nothing inherently remarkable about this process or the people that are affected by it.[51]

The claim that prisoners suffer literal dehumanization as a direct result of their confinement under sentence of death is subject to question. Were not the prisoners dehumanized to begin with, as a result of their impoverished lives? To be sure, prisoners, particularly condemned prisoners, do not arrive at the penitentiary gates in the full bloom of their personhood. Condemned prisoners typically have prior records, and virtually all of them are products of bleak, brutal lives.[52] (There is evidence, in addition, that neurological and psychiatric impairments may be quite prevalent among this group.[53]) Yet, though many condemned prisoners are impaired or damaged human beings prior to their death row confinement, they are persons nonetheless. They generally have a fragile but sharply defined sense of self. Manipulation and violence, regrettably, are avenues to autonomy and security; both activities, and particularly violence, keep a dangerous and rejecting world at bay and allay doubts about one's potency and worth. These men hunger for relatedness to others, even as their abusive behavior precludes the stable ties on which loving and rewarding relationships are built.

Chronically violent men cope with life in immature and ultimately destructive ways, but they remain human beings, not dehumanized animals or monsters.[54] Sentenced to prison, they adapt to stress much as they did on the outside—by violence, bluster, and bluff; by strategic retreat and calculated relationships; above all, perhaps, by manipulation and deception. Under a death sentence, and particularly during the deathwatch, these tactics break down. Confined, vulnerable, alone, they are unable to muster the behavior that preserved self and self-determination in the free world and in the prison. As a result, dehumanization, the literal demise of personhood that is the product of torture, is a fact of life on death row.

THE BENEFITS OF TORTURE

Most familiar forms of torture are intentional, a fact recognized in the definitions of torture set forth earlier in this chapter, but as we have noted, intent is not required; torture need not be restricted to conscious, systematic, and purposeful brutality. That the brainwashing regime is carefully and elaborately calculated to make the victim do the bidding of his keepers while the death row regime serves no such explicitly understood purpose is irrelevant to whether or not the subjects of either regime experience torture. Standard instances of torture and death row confinement have in common an assault on defenseless persons that (1) causes them intense suffering through the imposition of a regimen of total control, whether this control is achieved through physical force, psychological coercion, or both; (2) violates their integrity as human beings by treating them as if they were mere animals or objects; and thus (3) damages or destroys the victims' humanity. Moreover, as with other forms of torture, death row confinement serves the ends of the torturer, even if unconsciously or unintentionally. For it cannot be denied that the dehumanized prisoner who goes passively to his death is easier to execute than the prisoner who, alive to his own feelings and hurts, struggles for freedom or, worse, protests his innocence or pleads for mercy.

If one is tempted to doubt the proposition that dehumanized and hence passive prisoners are comparatively easy to execute, one need only envision executions in which the prisoner behaves like a full human being—most likely, one in the throes of fear and despair. Surely such a prisoner would resist, maybe even panic and become violent. The execution team members I studied were alert to such a possibility. Indeed, their worst fear, one shared by the warden, was having to use force to get a man into the chair (see Chapter 7). That fear is well founded. Executions marred by such violence, though rare, are nightmares.

A case in point was the execution of one Leanderess Riley. Described as a "33-year-old, one-eyed, nearly deaf man" who weighed in for his execution at just over eighty pounds, he went kicking and screaming to his death in San Quentin's gas chamber.

> The next morning, a Friday, I went into the Holding Cell area about eight-thirty. The guard said Leanderess had slept for only fifteen minutes, around six o'clock. I offered to read from the Bible; he appeared to listen. I read from the Psalms, and parts of two hymns: "Rock of Ages" and "Abide with Me." Leanderess held up his hands, palms out, in a gesture for me to stop. He had not paid any noticeable attention at any time and had continued pacing around his tiny cell.
>
> He still had about an hour to live. I sat down outside his cell door. The guards talked about retirement, and whether the golf course would be too wet the next morning. At nine-fifty, Associate Warden Rigg and the doctors came in. I told Leanderess to say a prayer to himself, if he did not care to have me pray, and to relax in God's care. He did not seem to hear me. When the doctors started to approach his cell, he made a throaty, guttural growling sound. Frantically, at random, he picked up some of the old legal papers on his table and began passing them through the bars to the associate warden, as if they were appeals or writs. A guard unlocked his cell. He gripped the bars with both hands and began a long, shrieking cry. It was a bone-chilling wordless cry. The guards grabbed him, wrestled him violently away from the bars. The old shirt and trousers were stripped off. His flailing arms and legs were forced into the new white shirt and fresh blue denims. The guards needed all their strength to hold him while the doctor taped the end of the stethoscope in place.
>
> The deep-throated cry, alternately moaning and shrieking, continued. Leanderess had to be carried to the gas chamber, fighting, writhing all the way. As the witnesses watched in horror, the guards stuffed him into the chair. One guard threw his weight against the struggling little Negro while the other jerked the straps tight. They backed out, slammed the door on him.
>
> Leanderess didn't stop screaming or struggling. Associate Warden Rigg was about to signal for the dropping of the gas pellets when we all saw

Riley's small hands break free from the straps. He pulled at the other buckles, was about to free himself. The Associate Warden withheld his signal. San Quentin had never executed a man ranging wildly around the gas chamber. He ordered the guards to go in again and restrap the frenzied man. One of the guards said later he had to pinch the straps down so tightly the second time that he "was ashamed of himself."

Again the door was closed. Again Leanderess managed to free his small, thin-wristed right hand from the straps. Rigg gave the order to drop the pellets. Working furiously, Leanderess freed his left hand. The chest strap came off next. Still shrieking and moaning, he was working on the waist strap when the gas hit him. He put both hands over his face to hold it away. Then his hands fell, his head arched back. His eyes remained open. His heartbeat continued to register for two minutes, but his shrieking stopped and his head slowly drooped.[55]

The anxiety and guilt that that spectacle must have aroused in the executioners is not hard to imagine. A deathwatch officer termed Riley's demise "the nastiest execution we ever had." The warden, noted for his tough, pro–death penalty stance, elaborated. "The fact that the fellow is crying and baying like a dog . . . you just can't deal with it at that point. You've got to carry out the job at hand. . . . You feel sympathy for him, but you have to put those feelings aside."[56]

Executions of prisoners who meet their fate with dull-eyed resignation are, in comparison, almost easy. It is the dehumanized and hence compliant prisoner of whom observers like Camus and others speak when they state that "the rule is for the condemned to walk toward death passively, in a sort of dreary despondency," so that his death—and our execution—conforms to the etiquette of a dignified official killing.[57] Significantly, the same etiquette applies in other situations of torturous confinement and execution. Discussing the systematic dehumanization of concentration camp inmates, Terrence Des Pres observed:

This made it easier for the SS to do their job. It made mass murder less terrible to the murderers. . . . Inhibited by pity and guilt, the act of murder becomes harder to perform and results in greater psychic damage to the killer himself. If, on the other hand, the victim exhibits self-disgust; if he cannot lift his eyes for humiliation, or if lifted they show only emptiness—then his death may be administered with ease or even with the conviction that so much rotten tissue has been removed from life's body.[58]

On death rows, as in the death camps, killing is made easier by the dehumanization of the victims.[59]

Killing is also made easier by the dehumanization of the killers. Graeme Newman was correct when he maintained that "perfect authoritarian conditions," such as exist on death row, "provide the best possible situations for the ordinary man to turn into a torturer"—and, we might add, a killer.[60] Perfect authoritarian conditions, for Newman, comprise a clear-cut situation of dominance and submission combined with a neutralization of personal responsibility for authorized agents of violence. Under these conditions, the agents want to punish others and, as a result, embrace their role. They are "psyched up," as we saw in Chapter 6, and may even be disappointed should the execution be delayed or postponed. (Ironically, interruptions of the execution procedure are painful—one man said torturous—for the staff.) To act without guilt, the agents simply need support from their peers and permission from their superiors. As we have seen, however, dehumanization is fundamental to "perfect authoritarian conditions" and to the resulting desire to punish. Dehumanization of what I would term a situational and symbolic nature is necessary for those serving on the execution team, who are parties to both torture and killing. To the extent that the guards are dehumanized, their job is easier. Numb to their feelings and those of the ostensibly subhuman creatures in their custody, they are able to execute prisoners without moral qualms.[61]

The underlying function of death row confinement, then, is to facilitate executions by dehumanizing both the prisoners and, to a lesser degree, their executioners, making it easier for both to play their roles in the execution process. The confinement that produces these results is a form of torture. Indeed, the essence of torture is the death of the person—that is, his conversion into a subhuman object, a nonperson. Persons whose consciences have been muted by the official authorizations and routines that shape their work as well as by the dehumanization they too have sustained can then, without guilt, commit violence against that nonperson. Stated differently, the death penalty is simply a form of bureaucratically administered violence, a bureaucratization of death in which death row is an integral component. The executions that culminate this confinement are the work of "*instruments of authority* acting within stipulated routines on condemned prisoners rendered as *objects* to be stored and ultimately dispatched in the execution chamber"[62] (emphasis added).

THE LIMITS OF REFORM

Humane Death Rows

Though death row confinement serves a function that is essential to the death penalty as it is presently administered, it would seem to be a form of torture that can, in principle, be abolished. One can readily envision a humane death row. It would operate as a kind of high-security hospice with the objective of preparing "full-blooded human beings for a dignified death," whether death takes the form of "the physical death of execution" or "the civil death of extended death row confinement followed by life imprisonment." Such a setting would be staffed by mature, service-oriented correctional officers able to relate to condemned prisoners as persons in the process of dying at the hands of the state, a class of individuals analogous to and as deserving of humane care as terminally ill patients. A humane death row would be "characterized by custody that is not an end in itself, to be maximized at all costs, but by custody that is instead a means to maintain an ordered and secure milieu within which emotional support and personal relationships can develop." Visits would be encouraged, as would recreational activities and "programs of work or study that can take place in cells or in small groups." Also encouraged would be "self-help programs, preferably developed by and for the prisoners," which would be promoted as "collective adaptations to the stresses of death row confinement" and impending execution. The deathwatch, as the culmination of this process, might feature counseling aimed at helping the prisoner put his life in order and accept his demise. One might even find in all of this "a poetic justice in requiring the pariahs of death row to rehabilitate themselves" and prepare themselves for a fully human death.[63]

Members of the National Medical Association Section on Psychiatry and Behavioral Sciences have adopted a position statement that supports the claim that condemned prisoners have a right to care comparable to that afforded terminally ill patients. After calling for psychiatric interventions with death row prisoners that are designed to provide "the same type of psychotherapy that a terminally ill patient deserves, i.e., psychotherapy designed to work through the psychological issues everyone grapples with when knowingly facing death," they go on to state that "it is truly unfortunate that the same efforts and technology that ensure a swift, painless death [have] not been applied to the psychological being in an effort to make the execution emotionally painless."[64] Yet, in an execution, unlike with a terminal illness, death results from an intentional killing of an unwilling victim. At issue here, then, is not so much a humane death as a humane killing, which may well be a contradiction in terms, at least as humaneness and killing are understood in the modern world.

Be this as it may, the presumption underlying the concept of a humane death row is that even the worst offender retains some humanity that must be respected even as he is put to death. If a person deserves to die—if that is his just desert—then he should die as a human being, not as a dehumanized entity. This means, quite simply, that the condemned person has "a right to be treated as a human being until the moment of his death" so that he may have "the opportunity to prepare for and meet his death with the decency and dignity our laws demand for all human beings."[65] This has been asserted as a constitutional right. Pertinent here is the *Autry* case, which raised the issue of "the dignity due any person" facing imminent execution.[66] Also relevant is the *Harries* case, in which the court held that "a death-row inmate has an Eighth Amendment right to die with dignity." In *Harries*, that right was violated by "demeaning" and "degrading" conditions of confinement amounting to "wanton infliction of physical and psychological pain, which is anathema to the standards of decency that our society demands."[67]

The condemned prisoner thus has a right to humane confinement on death row, particularly during the deathwatch. No such death row exists in the real world, however, and one can readily understand why. A humane death row would preserve and indeed highlight the humanity of the condemned, and hence would complicate enormously the already difficult business of death work. Officials would be unable to ignore the hurt and loss they, as persons, would inflict on their prisoners, whom they would know to be full human beings. The prisoners, too, no longer dulled to their own feelings, might well suffer greatly. Executions would be traumatic events, the virtual antithesis of their current bureaucratic reality.

We get a glimpse of the effects of humane confinement on condemned prisoners and their executioners in the work of Donald A. Cabana, former warden of Mississippi's Parchman Prison. Cabana did not radically overhaul Parchman's death row or death house regime, so the lesson his work offers is a limited one. But he did introduce a genuine element of human concern in the running of these environments, and relaxed some key routines, particularly those relating to visits with loved ones during the deathwatch and especially on the eve of executions. The last meal was made into a family affair for those who had supportive families; at least one last meal, that of Edward Earl Johnson, was to a considerable degree a convivial and even congenial affair. Johnson's family ate with him, talked with him, sang to him, hugged him, and kissed him a warm goodbye. Certainly Johnson's last meal was a touching human affair to those present and to those who viewed it later—Johnson's execution was the subject of the BBC's "Fourteen Days in May," discussed earlier in the book. Though the humanitarian reforms at issue are objectively modest—Johnson had spent years on a solitary-confinement death row and most of his time in the death house was spent alone in his cell—they appear to have had substantial impact; such is the import of humanity when it is allowed to get a foothold in the death house. One measure of that success was the pain that came in the wake of Johnson's execution. According to Johnson's attorney, Clive Smith, some of the execution team "cried during the execution and resigned afterward in protest."[68] The execution had a traumatic impact on Smith and on Warden Cabana as well.

More significantly for our purposes, Cabana *radically* altered the human climate of death row for at least one inmate, Connie Ray Evans, whom Cabana befriended and who in turn came to see Cabana as a friend. The story of this execution is the story of the profound existential pains of executions carried out by and upon full-blooded human beings, which would become the norm if humane regimes of confinement on death row and in the death house became standard practice. The entire execution process was affected by the human relationship that bound warden and prisoner: Unlike most prisoners, Evans wanted to know the full facts about what awaited him in the death house, and by telling him, Cabana became more deeply involved in the killing process than would normally be the case and, indeed, more deeply than he wanted. Evans, almost certainly more than the average prisoner, took the last meal and final death chamber checks personally, as calculated affronts to his humanity that somehow his friend the warden should have been able to change. The most dramatic differences from the more typical execution routine were those that occurred as the final moments drew near. In the last moments, just before the last walk, warden and prisoner exchanged an extended and heartfelt hug. Warden Cabana, himself inside the gas chamber, watched Evans get strapped in the chair; he beheld a tearful figure, resigned but deathly afraid, shaking visibly even as the straps restrained him. At that point,

> Connie spoke quietly, haltingly. He wanted to whisper his final words to me privately, he said, and I leaned down so I could hear him. He thanks me for being his friend. I started to speak, but he asked me to wait, and then he told me softly, "From one Christian to another, I love you." I wanted to respond, but no words would come. Now I was the one in shock, shaken to my very soul.[69]

Cabana then touched the prisoner's arm, "gently squeezing for what seemed a very long time." Cabana sensed the prisoner's forgiveness for what he was about to do, and from that forgiveness Cabana drew the strength to, in his words, "fulfill my responsibilities." He then left the chamber and ordered it sealed, "even while realizing that some of myself remained inside."[70]

Cabana sums up the existential import of his experience with this observation: "There is a part of the warden that dies with his prisoner. Nobody else can suffer the intimacy of impending death, or experience the pitiable helplessness involved, in the same way as the warden and his condemned prisoner. Both are victims, unwilling captives of a human tragedy."[71]

Executions such as this one, in which the words *human* and *tragedy* are given full expression, could never become the standard. Such executions may well be the moral thing to do—if we are going to have executions, perhaps we all should suffer greatly in the process—but this is impractical if not also inhumane to the officials who carry out justice in our name. Cabana claims he could *never* carry out executions on a regular basis because for him they could never become routine—each would be unique, and uniquely painful. "I knew after the first one that if it ever did become routine, if I found myself no longer haunted by doubt, then I would know that the time had come for me to leave corrections behind."[72] Most wardens do not want to be haunted by doubt or, as Cabana makes clear, devastated emotionally. It is not hard to imagine why Cabana stands apart, and that the procedural norm is one of maintaining a safe emotional distance from the condemned, aided by the buffers provided by a bureaucratically administered and highly dehumanized execution protocol.

Closing Death Rows: Humaneness at a Safe Distance?

Rather than attempting to make death rows less dehumanizing, another avenue of reform would be simply to close them and confine condemned prisoners with regular maximum security prisoners, under conditions that are, at least relative to death row, arguably humane. Death rows, contrary to the views of those who run them, are not strictly necessary. Except for their sentences, condemned prisoners are not very different from typical prisoners. The vast majority of the condemned have criminal records that are no worse than those of other chronic felons, and a sizeable minority, in fact, have no prior record of felony convictions or imprisonments.[73] Moreover, condemned prisoners can expect to live behind bars for years awaiting execution, and this can be arranged more cheaply and more humanely in a regular prison than on death row. Thus, condemned prisoners are, at least for those years when their executions are not imminent, no more dangerous or desperate than other prisoners and, accordingly, could be managed in regular prisons.

This reform would free the condemned from the excessive restrictions and pressures of death row confinement. They would have greater opportunity to live in prison on their own terms and hence to prepare themselves for their deaths in a manner of their own choosing. Like virtually all other prisoners, they would no doubt be stressed by their confinement, but they need not be dehumanized. They would have a chance to live in prison—and, if need be, die in an execution chamber—as human beings. And they would come to the death house as strangers to those who must oversee the execution process, ostensibly sparing these officers and officials much of the grief borne by such figures as Cabana and his staff.

But how different would life in prison be from life on death row? The prisoners would still be condemned men, not regular convicts. Would this not set them apart from others in the prison community? Might they not live as pariahs, suffering a social isolation comparable to life on death row?

At present, we know little about the experience of living with a death sentence under conditions other than those of death row confinement. Currently, only a few states house condemned prisoners with the regular prison population. Maryland is one such state; their condemned prisoners number about fifteen.[74] An interview with one of them suggested that even within the relative freedoms of standard prison life, the condemned show a pattern of adjustment similar to that of death row prisoners. This prisoner spoke of a loneliness born of self-segregation, a heightened sense of helplessness and vulnerability, and a blunting of his feelings for himself and others. The researcher who conducted the interview summarized her impressions as follows:

> Life under sentence of death was a painful and solitary one for this condemned prisoner. He felt that none of the other prisoners could possibly understand his situation. He was not interested in people anyway, unless they had something to say that was relevant to his situation. He felt the need to protect himself and tried to live one day at a time, taking things as they came. Yet his life was marred by trauma, the trauma of living with the thought that he was marked for death by the very prison system that today housed and fed him but tomorrow might turn around and kill him.[75]

Another Maryland prisoner told me in no uncertain terms that he sees his keepers as executioners: "They could come and get me out of my cell and kill me any time." Though he knows intellectually that such a fate is technically impossible, he nevertheless feels vulnerable and alone. And if he ever is slated for execution, he will be taken from a deathwatch cell, not a regular prison cell. For the policy in Maryland and other states is to establish a deathwatch once executions become imminent, under the presumption that condemned prisoners will be desperate, and hence will require close custody for their secure containment.[76]

Here again, we see that torturous death row confinement conditions serve an essential function in the implementation of the death penalty. This function, moreover, cannot be served by other ostensibly more humane regimes of confinement, because the dehumanization that is at the heart of torturous confinement is essential to the bureaucratic administration of the death penalty. This reflects a paradox of bureaucratically administered violence; namely, that men must be dehumanized, dead as persons—that is, as moral beings—to play their roles as killers and victims. Death row produces the moral deaths necessary to carry out the physical killing of condemned prisoners.

This has been long known, though perhaps only vaguely appreciated, at least as it applies to the prisoners. Prisoners on death row are sometimes explicitly referred to as "dead men." The announcement "Dead man coming. Make way. Dead man coming" was a common warning to the living when a condemned man left the confines of death row and traveled, under heavy guard, through the prison. This macabre practice has ceased in most prisons.[77] Putting the unique experiences of Warden Cabana to one side, nothing has changed on any death row to alter the reality that the condemned are dead men whose bodies are being held for their executions—executions that will be carried out by men who, in the context of their roles as executioners, are perhaps as much marked by death as the prisoners themselves.

IMPLICATIONS

The death penalty, when preceded by long confinement and administered bureaucratically, dehumanizes both the agents and the recipients of this punishment and amounts to a form of torture. This raises two related moral arguments against the death penalty, one focusing on dehumanization, the other on torture. We will also examine, in closing, the complicating role of race.

By dehumanizing both the executioners and the victims, the death penalty violates a basic tenet of just punishment: that punishment be administered by and on persons in the name of the persons who make up the larger moral community. As Herbert Morris has made clear, a person, unlike an animal or object, has the capacity to choose and, moreover, has "a right to institutions that respect his choices." Furthermore, institutions have an obligation to cultivate the capacity for rational choice where it has not yet developed (for example, among children) or where it has been lost (for example, among the mentally ill). Since the capacity for choice cannot be abrogated or waived, the right to be treated as a person is a "natural, inalienable, and absolute right," violation of which "implies the denial of all moral rights and duties."[78] This analysis can be extended to other aspects of personhood. Thus, individuals have a right to institutions that respect their need for security and relatedness to others, denial of which would also "imply the denial of all moral rights and duties." It follows that even the worst offender must be treated within the justice system in a way that will either preserve or restore his personhood. Since only persons can choose to respect the actual or potential personhood of others, the justice system and the society it represents must also be composed of persons.

A justice system that engages in dehumanization hurts us all, making us accomplices to the devaluation of human life. It is perhaps with this thought in mind that Camus enjoined us to be "neither victims nor executioners."[79] As members of a society that inflicts the death penalty, we ignore his sage advice. We consent to executions and are made victims of the brutalization of the human spirit necessary to carry them out. We are a part of what Colin Turnbull eloquently termed "an ever widening circle of tragedy" that includes victims, criminals, those who authorize and implement death sentences, and, ultimately, the "society throughout, threatening our very understanding of the word humanity."[80] Our only genuinely humane alternative is to abolish the death penalty and devise less brutal punishments for our worst offenders, a topic I address in the next and final chapter of this book.

The second moral objection to the death penalty is simply that torture is inherently wrong. That the agents of torture are dehumanized along with the victims is irrelevant to this point. Even if executioners could torture and kill condemned prisoners while remaining autonomous and caring moral beings, torture would still be unjust. The goal of torture is never justice; torture seeks the destruction of the person, not his punishment. Camus's observation that the death penalty inflicts a "double death" and hence is an inherently excessive punishment is, in this context, not so much right or wrong as irrelevant. Some offenders, such as mass murderers, may well deserve a double death and more—and should receive it, presuming that pain commensurate with this notion of just desert could be administered equitably and without violating the personhood of the criminal. But condemned criminals are not tortured because this is what they deserve. They are tortured because the destruction of their person is useful to their torturers. It is the goal of destruction of the person that distinguishes torture from punishment and renders it gratuitous and hence immoral.

Fundamental reforms of death row conditions are unlikely to occur, or to endure, under a policy of regular execution of criminals. Thus today, and for the foreseeable future, the administration of the death penalty involves torture. Any justification of the death penalty must therefore also justify torturing condemned prisoners, not simply killing them. It is hard to envision such a justification. None can be found in the United States Constitution, for example, which expressly bans torture under the Eighth Amendment prohibition of "cruel and unusual punishments." Torturous confinement, which involves conditions at odds with the requirements of personhood, is by definition a flagrant violation of the legal standard of "minimal civilized measures of life's necessities,"[81] which, when met, is presumed to produce an "environment which does not result in [the prisoner's] degeneration or . . . threaten . . . his mental or physical well being."[82]

This is true, moreover, even though some offenders transcend their environment and, by virtue of strength of character, resist the threat of dehumanization inherent in the conditions of their confinement. It would be true even if many, perhaps even if most, offenders escaped dehumanization on death row. There are survivors of forced labor camps, prisoner-of-war camps, and even Nazi death camps who somehow emerged complete human beings. The Italian writer Primo Levi, for example, is a much heralded death camp survivor credited with having

> preserve[d] an extraordinary humanity. In the three books he has written about his time in Auschwitz and his return to Turin, Levi never gives way to bitterness or to easy feelings of victimization. His books are more than documentations of the atrocities man is capable of inventing; they are a study of the limits of being human.[83]

Levi and others like him are moving testimony to Fyodor Dostoyevski's dictum that "man is a creature that can get accustomed to anything" without changing his essential nature.[84] But these persons do not, by their survival, exonerate the prisons that confined them. Their confinement was inherently inhumane. It violated their personhood because it objectively denied prisoners a sense of self and self-determination. Their transcendent adjustment evokes awe, but to expect such accomplishments from the rest of us is unreasonable.

In making this claim, I am aware that the current procedure is to assess the humanity (or inhumanity) of confinement conditions primarily, if not exclusively, in terms of their impact on offenders. As Justice Brennan has stated, "In determining when prison conditions pass beyond legitimate punishment and become cruel and unusual, the 'touchstone is the effect upon the imprisoned.'"[85] This emphasis is mistaken, however, for two reasons. First, social scientists cannot provide impact or effect data of the kind the court presupposes. As Toch has cogently observed, effect, as understood by the Court, "assumes average impact (or impact on the average) that rarely occurs. Few 'effects' are cross-sectional, immediate, and 'purely out there,' because personal susceptibilities that intersect with environments are built up through personal histories."[86] Hence, the effects of prison conditions are almost always differential, varying with individual susceptibilities. Effects almost always vary, too, in the course of a given person's experience with punishment, which may promote adaptation, maladaptation, or simple stagnation.[87]

This raises a second point, alluded to above. One upshot of the natural diversity of the effects of punishment is that some people can adapt to any harm we might inflict in the name of justice, including even the worst forms of torture. And some situations—notably life-threatening ones—elicit a distinctively human transcendence, sometimes of heroic proportions, from at least a stalwart minority of individuals. Yet it is patently absurd to declare a punishment such as death row confinement to be humane simply because some or even many persons can endure it without losing their humanity in the process.

Moreover, those inmates who in fact preserve their personhood while confined awaiting execution do so, with rare exceptions, by protecting or sheltering it much as one would a helpless infant; they do not live in confinement as persons, but rather allow their selves to become dormant. On death row, even those who escape dehumanization tend merely to simulate personhood rather than to live fully as persons. Only after the confinement ordeal do those who physically survive confinement experience a reawakening of the self and a re-assertion of self-determination.[88]

A defining attribute in assessing the legal significance of death row confinement has been the focus on the length of that confinement and the attendant—and presumably cumulative—harms associated with such confinement.[89] Though we know from historical analysis that even short periods of confinement under sentence of death can be quite stressful and debilitating, it is certainly true that an attribute of the modern death penalty is extended confinement under sentence of death. In *Anderson*, the California death penalty case cited earlier in this chapter, the dehumanizing effects of death row were predicated on "lengthy imprisonment prior to execution during which the judicial and administrative procedures essential to due process of law are carried out."[90] International human rights cases have developed this line of analysis. Lords Scarman and Brightman, of the Judicial Committee of the Privy Council, have observed that

> It is no exaggeration . . . to say that the jurisprudence of the civilized world, much of which is derived from common law principles and the prohibition against cruel and unusual punishments in the English Bill of Rights, has recognized and acknowledged that prolonged delay in executing a sentence of death can make the punishment when it comes inhuman and degrading.[91]

Our Eighth Amendment is, of course, a descendant of the English Bill of Rights, and indeed was adopted, in the words of Justice Thurgood Marshall, with an explicit aim to "outlaw torture and other cruel punishments."[92]

Later decisions of the Judicial Committee of the Privy Council came to adopt the view that periods of confinement on death row of *five years or more*—short by American standards—constituted inhuman treatment. Ruling in a 1993 Jamaican case, this body held that "[I]n any case in which execution is to take place more than five years after sentence there will be strong grounds for believing that the delay is such as to constitute 'inhuman or degrading punishment or other treatment.'"[93] The underlying reason for this holding:

> There is an instinctive revulsion against the prospect of hanging a man after he has been held under sentence of death for many years. What gives rise to this instinctive revulsion? The answer can only be our humanity; we regard it as an inhuman act to keep a man facing the agony of execution over a long extended period of time.[94]

A similar result was reached by the Supreme Court of Zimbabwe in May 1993. The Jamaica and Zimbabwe rulings, in turn, were grounded in the *Soering* case, a 1989 ruling of the European Court of Human Rights, in which it was held that "extraditing an individual to the United States, where he would probably wait six to eight years between a death sentence and execution, violated the prohibition of 'inhuman and degrading punishment' set out in article 3 of the European Convention on Human Rights."[95]

The key issue is the *painful uncertainty* experienced by "a man facing the agony of execution over a long extended period of time." Schabas tells us that, "According to the *Medley* decision of 1890, uncertainty as to time of execution creates such mental anxiety that it amounts to a great increase in punishment." (Remember, uncertainty is a central ingredient of brainwashing and other forms of psychological torture.) In *Medley*, it was asserted that "[W]hen a prisoner sentenced by a court to death is confined in a penitentiary awaiting the execution of the sentence, one of the most horrible feelings to which he can be subjected during that time is the uncertainty during the whole of it . . . as to the precise time when his execution shall take place." In a recent Supreme Court case, *Lackey* v. *Texas*, Justice Stevens applied this line of argument, with the apparent support of the entire court: "If the Court accurately described the effect of uncertainty in *Medley*, which involved a period of four weeks . . . that description should apply with even greater force in the case of delays that last for many years." Such pain would be gratuitous in the case of a man on death row for an extended period—Lackey had been on death row for seventeen years at the time of his appeal—because, in the words of Justice Stevens, no such delays would have been possible at the time of the framing of the Constitution, "and thus the practice of the Framers would not justify a denial of petitioner's claim." In addition, stated Stevens, "after such an extended time, the acceptable state interest in retribution has arguably been satisfied by the severe punishment already inflicted" by extended confinement on death row, which thus serves no valid punitive purpose.[96]

Clarence Lackey's execution was stayed so that his habeus corpus petition could be reviewed by a lower court. Regrettably, Schabas informs us, "Lackey appears to have foundered in the lower courts, and it seems unlikely that the Supreme Court will address the merits of the death row phenomenon in that case."[97] But long stays on our death row are the norm, particularly if we adopt the emerging international standard of five years as an excessively long period of confinement under sentence of death. We can be reasonably certain that this issue will surface again for our Supreme Court to review. It may well be that we will one day conclude, in the words of David Pannick, that "A legalistic society will be unable to impose the death penalty without an unconstitutionally cruel delay, and hence it will be unable lawfully to impose the death penalty at all."[98]

That day would be here *now* if we faced squarely the arbitrariness and inequality in capital sentencing caused by racism, which results in discriminatory exposure to the cruel treatment that is the death row phenomenon. Arbitrariness and inequality are, in fact, *basic* to the international norm prohibiting cruel treatment and torture.

> It is as if the norm reads: "No one shall be subject to cruel, inhuman, degrading, arbitrary, and unequal punishment." This is because punishment is cruel when it serves no rational or logical purpose. In other

words, arbitrary punishment is also cruel punishment. The same applies to punishment that is unequal, because either it is overtly discriminatory or simply so capricious as to be incapable of consistent application.[99]

Violations of this human rights norm may be justified in the case of criminal law if the law serves a larger penological purpose or social end, which might outweigh the harm done by cruel punishment; but as we have seen, this is not true of the death penalty, which inflicts essentially purposeless pain and suffering.

Against this backdrop, it is chilling to review *McCleskey* v. *Kemp*, the main U.S. Supreme Court ruling with respect to race and capital punishment. In *McCleskey*, it was clearly established that murderers whose victims were white were much more likely to be sentenced to death than those whose victims were black. (Subsequent research on race and capital sentencing has only served to strengthen our confidence in these troubling findings.) The Supreme Court accepted this racist state of affairs not because they thought it was right but because they conceded "the impossibility of a death penalty system that was free of racism."[100] It is no small wonder that Mumia Abu-Jamal saw in *McCleskey* a modern-day variant of the *Dred Scott* decision of a century past. "Echoes of *Dred Scott* ring in today's *McCleskey* opinion," stated Abu-Jamal, "again noting the paucity of rights held by Africans in the land of the free." Quoting *Dred Scott*, Abu-Jamal makes the crucial point that blacks were then— and are arguably now, in the crucial matter of life and death punishments— seen by the U.S. Supreme Court "as beings of an inferior order, and altogether unfit to associate with the white race, either in social or political relations; and so far inferior, that they had no rights which the white man was bound to respect."[101] The sort of beings, we might suppose, around which one would develop and institutionalize a regime of torturous punishment.

SUMMARY

My focus has been on the entire "death row phenomenon," from regular death row confinement, through the deathwatch and, in many cases, only coming to an end in the death chamber. In America today, that process almost always takes more than five years, and brings with it not only painful uncertainty but all the attributes of torture, culminating in the dehumanization of the prisoner. This confinement violates any notion of humaneness or respect for persons one can adduce, and hence violates the Eighth Amendment to the U.S. Constitution, which bans "all punishments which do not comport with 'broad and idealistic concepts of dignity, civilized standards, humanity and decency.' "[102] As such, death row confinement "makes no measurable contribution to acceptable goals of punishment and hence is nothing more than the purposeless and needless infliction of pain and suffering."[103]

Nor, finally, is there any legal system in the modern world that countenances torture, even if it were distributed equally and fairly.[104] Even the philosopher Immanuel Kant, who maintained that "only execution would satisfy the requirements of legal justice" for murder, acknowledged that, to be just, "the death of the criminal must be kept entirely free of any maltreatment that would make an abomination of the humanity residing in the person suffering it."[105] The Supreme Court, in effect, endorsed this standard in *In re Kemmler*. The Court in *Kemmler*, decided in 1890, required that the death penalty, to comport with the Eighth Amendment, must result in "the mere extinguishment of life" and nothing more.[106] Torture or "a lingering death" were explicitly prohibited. Yet today, death row confinement followed by execution results in both torture and a protracted death, claiming first the person and then the body of the condemned. As the length of stays on death rows have increased, and will no doubt continue to increase over the coming years, the cruelty of the modern death penalty will become all the more apparent and egregious.

NOTES

1. In the 1980s, nearly half the condemned could expect to win appeals, gain clemency, or otherwise have their sentences changed. See J. Berger, "Living on Death Row in the 1980s," *Augustus* 10 (1): 11–14 (January 1987). Today, sentence reversals are less common.

2. E. Peters, *Torture* (Oxford: Basil Blackwell, 1985), 152, 154–155, 152.

3. *Amnesty International Report on Torture* (New York: Farrar, Straus & Giroux, 1975), 35.

4. *Torture in the Eighties: An Amnesty International Report* (London: Amnesty International, 1984), 13.

5. Peters (n. 2), 4.

6. *Torture in the Eighties* (n. 4).

7. Bell v. Wolfish, 441 U.S. 520, 60 L. Ed. 2d 447, 99 S. Ct. 1861, 483.

8. B. Jackson and D. Christian, *Death Row* (Boston: Beacon Press, 1980), 267.

9. Quoted in V. L. Streib, "Juveniles' Attitudes towards Their Impending Executions," in *Facing the Death Penalty: Essays on a Cruel and Unusual Punishment*, ed. M. L. Radelet (Philadelphia: Temple University Press, 1989), 45.

10. I. Zimmerman with F. Bond, *Punishment without Crime* (New York: Clarkson N. Potter, 1964), 97.

11. G. R. Strafer, "Volunteering for Execution: Competency, Voluntariness and the Propriety of Third-Party Intervention," *Journal of Criminal Law and Criminology* 74 (3): 889 (1983); R. Cordes, "Confronting Death: More Inmates Give Up Appeals in Capital Cases," *Trial* 30 (1): 11–12 (January 1994). See also W. A. Schabas, *The Death Penalty as Cruel Treatment and Torture: Capital Punishment Challenged in the World* (Boston: Northeastern University Press, 1995), 104, Note 36 at 238.

12. The citations for these cases are People v. Anderson, 6 Cal. 3d 628, 494, P.2d 880, 100 Cal. Rptr. 152, *cert. denied*, 406 U.S. 958 (1972), and Commonwealth v. O'Neal, 369 Mass. 242, 339 N.E.2d 676 (1975).

13. Schabas (n. 11), 51.

14. David Pannick, quoted by Schabas (n. 11), 51.

15. *Torture in the Eighties* (n. 4), 13.

16. *Report of the Amnesty International Mission to Spain* (London: Amnesty International, 1975), 9.

17. *Amnesty International Report on Torture* (n. 3), 52.

18. Note, for example, that Biderman's generic "Chart of Coercion" parallels closely the conditions of brainwashing. (See *Amnesty International Report on Torture* [n. 3], 53.) For a similar conceptualization of the elements of coercion, see also P. Watson, *War on the Mind: The Military Uses and Abuses of Psychology* (New York: Basic Books, 1978), esp. Table 25, 292–293.

19. A. Somit, "Brainwashing," *International Encyclopedia of the Social Sciences*, 18 vols. (New York: Macmillan and Free Press, 1968), 2:138–143.

20. A. D. Biderman, "Social–Psychological Needs and 'Involuntary' Behavior as Illustrated by Compliance in Interrogation," *Sociometry* 23 (2): 120–147 (June 1960). Quoted in *Amnesty International Report on Torture* (n. 3), 53.

21. I. K. Genefke, Medical Director of the International Rehabilitation and Research Center for Torture Victims, University Hospital, Copenhagen. Quoted in the *Washington Post*, 16 May 1983, A13.

22. *Amnesty International Report on Torture* (n. 3), 34.

23. In some states, only the crown of the condemned man's head is shaved. The psychological effect of this modified procedure has not been examined. It is likely that having a sizeable patch of hair shorn from one's head is as psychologically disfiguring as having the entire head shaved. After all, one's identity has to do not only with the presence of one's hair (for people who have hair) but also with the person's capacity to preserve its distinctive and presumptively flattering arrangement.

24. See R. J. Lifton, "Thought Reform: Psychological Steps in Death and Rebirth," in *Readings in Social Psychology*, ed. A. R. Lindesmith, A. L. Strauss, and N. K. Denzin, 2nd ed. (New York: Dryden Press, 1975), 275.

25. See, generally, Schabas (n. 11).

26. See J. H. Reiman, "Privacy, Intimacy, and Personhood," *Philosophy and Public Affairs* 6 (1): 26–44 (1976).

27. For an illuminating general discussion, see E. Cassirer, *An Essay on Man* (New York: Bantam Books, 1970).

28. See A. Maslow, *Eupsychian Management* (Homewood, Ill.: Irwin, 1966), and M. Rokeach, *The Open and Closed Mind: Investigations into the Nature of Belief Systems and Personality Systems* (New York: Basic Books, 1960).

29. See J. Dewey, *Human Nature and Conduct* (New York: Holt, 1922).

30. For a review of the pertinent literature, see B. Moore, Jr., *Injustice: The Social Bases of Obedience and Revolt* (New York: Pantheon, 1978).

31. L. Mumford, *The Condition of Man* (New York: Harcourt, Brace, 1944), 7.

32. W. Gaylin, "In the Beginning: Helpless and Dependent," in W. Gaylin et al., *Doing Good: The Limits of Benevolence* (New York: Pantheon, 1978).

33. H. Toch, *Men in Crisis: Human Breakdowns in Prison* (Chicago: Aldine, 1975), 24.

34. See R. Johnson, "Labored Breathing: Living with Brown Lung" (paper presented at the Annual Meeting of the American Society of Criminology, Fall 1982).

35. Reiman (n. 26), 26–44.

36. E. A. Hoebbels, *The Law of Primitive Man* (Cambridge, Mass.: Harvard University Press, 1954), 286–287.

37. See B. Schwartz, "The Social Psychology of Privacy," *American Journal of Sociology* 73 (1968): 741, 749.

38. E. Goffman, *Asylums* (New York: Doubleday, 1960), 319–320.

39. Schwartz (n. 37), 748.

40. See Hudson v. Palmer, 82 L. Ed. 2d 393 (1984), 404. The holding in *Hudson* reads as follows:

A right of privacy in traditional Fourth Amendment terms [prohibiting unreasonable searches and seizures] is fundamentally incompatible with the close and continual surveillance of inmates and their cells required to ensure institutional security and internal order. We believe that it is accepted by our society that "[l]oss of freedom of choice and privacy are inherent incidents of confinement." (Bell v. Wolfish, 441 U.S., 537)

Nevertheless, prisoners cannot be indiscriminately and gratuitously searched; searches that are not justified as security measures or that are otherwise malicious or intended to harass are impermissible. There is, in other words, some residual concern for privacy, even if it is not expressed in "Fourth Amendment terms." Moreover, Stevens, in dissent, quotes Burger (the author of the majority holding) to the effect that prisoners do have limited rights to privacy in contexts other than searches.

Inmates in jails, prisons, or mental institutions retain certain fundamental rights of privacy; they are not like animals in a zoo to be filmed and photographed at will by public or by media reporters, however "educational" the process may be for others. (Hudson, 413)

Thus, to claim that the *Hudson* holding amounts to a "declar[ation] that the prisoners are entitled to no measure of human dignity or individuality" and that prisoners are "to be little more than chattels" (421) is something of an exaggeration.

Nevertheless, flagrant violations of privacy such as occur in strip-searches and body-cavity searches, even when justified by security considerations, are poor correctional management practices. Respect for inmates' privacy may be incompatible with some notions of imprisonment, but we maintain such intrusive regimes in defiance of human needs and at great cost in terms of tension and conflict. The Court in *Hudson* would have been wiser to echo Schwartz's insightful observations about balancing the institutional need for security and order with respect for the privacy and dignity of convicts:

If highly efficient regimentation through mass processing and storage is inimical to the value of privacy, a measure of cost-efficiency may be candidly renounced in its favor. . . . While lessened surveillance places a great burden on trust, it may also build trust and obviate the tension and hostility that its absence entails. And while respect for an inmate's right concerning his own body and his own past may impede custody and security, it may also promote the dignity that would make them less necessary. . . . [Hence] expansion of the right to privacy may be in the interests of the prison as well as its prisoners.

See B. Schwartz, "Deprivation of Privacy as a 'Functional Prerequisite': The Case of Prison," *Journal of Criminal Law and Criminology* 63 (1972): 230.

41. L. X. Lombardo, *Guards Imprisoned: Correctional Officers at Work* 2/e (Cincinnati: Anderson, 1989).

42. R. Singer, "Privacy, Autonomy, and Dignity in the Prison: A Preliminary Inquiry Concerning Constitutional Aspects of the Degradation Process in Our Prisons," *Buffalo Law Review* 21 (1972): 669–670.

43. See Goffman (n. 38) and Schwartz (n. 37).

44. H. Toch, *Living in Prison: The Ecology of Survival* (New York: Free Press, 1977), and J. Hegel-Seymour, "Environmental Sanctuaries for Susceptible Prisoners," in *The Pains of Imprisonment*, ed. R. Johnson and H. Toch (Prospect Heights, Ill.: Waveland Press, 1988).

45. Lombardo (n. 41).

46. For an analysis of prison riots that examines how individual inmates and guards come to think of themselves as members of stereotypical collectivities and then turn to violence, see L. X. Lombardo, "Stress, Change and Collective Violence in Prison," in *The Pains of Imprisonment*, ed. R. Johnson and H. Toch (Prospect Heights, Ill.: Waveland Press, 1988).

47. C. H. Cooley, *Social Organization* (New York: Scribner's, 1909), 10.

48. Goffman (n. 38), esp. Chap. 1.

49. M. L. Radelet, M. Vandiver, and F. Berardo, "Families, Prisons, and Men with Death Sentences: The Human Impact of Structured Uncertainty," *Journal of Family Issues* 4 (4): 597 (December 1983).

50. H. Prejean, *Dead Man Walking: An Eyewitness Account of the Death Penalty in the United States* (New York: Random House, 1993), 180.

51. See R. Johnson, "Institutions and the Promotion of Violence," in *Violent Transactions: The Limits of Personality*, ed. A. Campbell and J. J. Gibbs (London: Basil Blackwell, 1986).

52. See R. Johnson, *Condemned to Die: Life under Sentence of Death* (Prospect Heights, Ill.: Waveland Press, 1989), esp. Chap. 2; H. Wisnie, *The Impulsive Personality* (New York: Plenum, 1977); and H. Toch, *Violent Men* (Cambridge, Mass.: Schenkman, 1980) and "The Management of Hostile Aggression: Seneca as Applied Social Psychologist," *American Psychologist* 38 (September 1983): 1022–1026.

53. See D. O. Lewis et al., "Psychiatric, Neurological, and Psychoeducational Characteristics of Fifteen Death Row Inmates in the United States," *American Journal of Psychiatry* 143 (7): 838–845 (July 1986). The fifteen death row inmates were "chosen for examination because of the imminence of their executions and not for evidence of neuropsychopathology." The examinations produced some rather startling findings:

All had histories of severe head injury, five had major neurological impairment, and seven others had other, less serious neurological problems. . . . Psychoeducational testing provided further evidence of CNS [central nervous system] dysfunction. Six subjects had schizophreniform psychoses antedating incarceration and two others were manic-depressive. (838)

Interestingly, none of these prisoners was "flamboyantly" psychotic; indeed, they consciously tried to mask their symptoms, evidently preferring to appear "bad" rather than "mad" (841). The researchers concluded that "many condemned individuals in this country probably suffer a multiplicity of hitherto unrecognized psychiatric and neurological disorders that are relevant to considerations of mitigation" (841–842) and may be unable to obtain, or to assist in, competent legal representation at trial (844).

54. Hugo Bedau has made a similar observation:

However dangerous, irrational, self-centered, stupid, or beyond improvement such a person may in fact be, these deficiencies do not overwhelm all capacity for moral agency. . . . No plausible empirical argument can support an alleged loss of moral agency in a convicted murderer as a result of the act of murder. . . . [T]he doctrine that certain persons, who had basic human rights prior to any criminal acts, forfeit or relinquish all those rights by such acts and thereby cease to be moral persons, receives no support from experience.

See H. A. Bedau, "Thinking of the Death Penalty as a Cruel and Unusual Punishment," *University of California, Davis, Law Review* 18 (4): 921 (Summer 1985).

55. Chaplain Byron Eschelman, in *Death Row Chaplain*, quoted in W. J. Bowers, *Executions in America* (Lexington: Lexington Books, 1974), 196–197.

56. M. A. Kroll, "Fraternity of Death," *I.E.* 7 (11): 20 (1984).

57. A. Camus, "Reflections on the Guillotine," in *Resistance, Rebellion, and Death* (New York: Knopf, 1969), 205. A number of wardens who oversaw executions in their time support Camus's observation. See C. T. Duffy with A. Hirshberg, *Eighty-Eight Men and Two Women* (New York: Doubleday, 1962); J. Sweat, "Anatomy of an Execution," *Nashville*, September 1979; and Kroll (n. 56), 20.

58. T. Des Pres, *The Survivor: An Anatomy of Life in the Death Camps* (New York: Pocket Books, 1977).

59. A dehumanized perception of one's victim may be all that is needed to kill at a distance. The fighter pilot drops bombs on victims who amount to faceless statistics and

consequently suffers little or no remorse. Killing at close range, particularly after extended contact, requires the actual dehumanization of the victims so that the illusion of their subhuman status is preserved and the killer does not have to confront the human consequences of his violence. See Johnson, "Institutions" (n. 51).

60. G. Newman, *The Punishment Response* (Philadelphia: Lippincott, 1978), 258.

61. H. Kelman, "Violence without Moral Restraint: Reflections on the Dehumanization of Victims and Victimizers," *Journal of Social Issues* 29 (4): 25–61 (1973).

62. Johnson, *Condemned to Die* (n. 52), 131.

63. See R. Johnson, "Life under Sentence of Death," in *The Pains of Imprisonment*, ed. R. Johnson and H. Toch (Prospect Heights, Ill.: Waveland Press, 1988), 142–144.

64. C. C. Bell, "Position Statement on the Role of the Psychiatrist in Evaluating and Treating 'Death Row' Inmates" (unpublished paper, adopted by the Psychiatry and Behavioral Sciences branch of the National Medical Association, prepared for the National Medical Association, March 1985).

65. C. Turnbull, "Death by Decree: An Anthropological Approach to Capital Punishment," *Natural History* 87 (1978): 56.

66. See Autry v. McKaskle, 727 F.2d. 358 (5th Cir.), 363.

67. See Groseclose *ex rel.* Harries v. Dutton, 594 F. Supp. 949 (1984), 962.

68. G. E. Goldhammer, *Dead End* (Brunswick, Me.: Biddle Publishing Company, 1994), 121.

69. D. A. Cabana, *Death at Midnight: The Confession of an Executioner* (Boston: Northeastern University Press, 1996), 15–16.

70. Ibid., 16.

71. Ibid., 16.

72. Ibid., 17.

73. Johnson, *Condemned to Die* (n. 52), and Jackson and Christian (n. 8).

74. Arkansas's condemned were allowed to mingle freely with regular prisoners at one juncture in the late sixties, during the moratorium on executions. They behaved well, though no research was done on their emotional or psychological reactions to the threat of execution, which was quite remote at that time. See T. Murton, "Treatment of Condemned Prisoners," *Crime and Delinquency* 15 (1969): 94–111.

75. J. Hoyle, personal communication following an interview with a condemned prisoner in Maryland State Penitentiary, 1984. I interviewed a Maryland Penitentiary inmate as recently as 1988 who described his life in the same terms.

76. Beverly Marabel, public relations officer, Maryland Department of Public Safety, personal communication, 1984 and 1989.

77. Condemned prisoners are still referred to as dead men in the Texas system and perhaps elsewhere as well. See J. R. Sorensen and J. W. Marquart, "Working the Dead," in *Facing the Death Penalty: Essays on a Cruel and Unusual Punishment*, ed. M. L. Radelet (Philadelphia: Temple University Press, 1989), 174.

78. H. Morris, "Persons and Punishment," in *Punishment and Rehabilitation*, ed. J. Murphy (Pacific Grove, Calif.: Wadsworth, 1973), 48, 50, 41.

79. A. Camus, "Neither Victims nor Executioners," *Liberation*, February 1960.

80. Turnball (n. 65).

81. Ruiz v. Estelle, 679 F.2d 1115 (5th Cir. 1982), *modified*, 688 F.2d 266 (5th Cir.).

82. Battle v. Anderson, 564 F.2d 388, 393 (10th Cir. 1977). See also Newman v. Alabama, 559 F.2d 283, 291 (5th Cir. 1975). Dehumanization as I have defined the term is essentially an existential concept, but it nevertheless encompasses the notion of degeneration as it has been defined by the courts.

83. V. Crapanzano, "Primo Levi: The Limits of Being Human," *Washington Post Book World*, 16 March 1986, 1. See P. Levi, *Survival in Auschwitz and The Reawakening: Two Memoirs* (New York: Summit, 1986) and *Moments of Reprieve* (New York: Summit, 1986). For a superb study of the phenomenon of preserving one's humanity in the death camps, see Des Pres (n. 58).

84. F. Dostoyevski, *House of the Dead* (New York: Dell, 1959), 34.

85. Rhodes v. Chapman, 452 U.S. 337, 69 L. Ed. 2d 59, 101 S. Ct. 2392, 80.

86. H. Toch, "The Role of the Expert on Prison Conditions: The Battle of the Footnotes in Rhodes v. Chapman," *Criminal Law Bulletin* 18 (1): 44 (January/February 1982).

87. See H. Toch and K. Adams, *Coping: Maladaptation in Prisons* (New Brunswick: Transaction Books, 1988).

88. See Levi, *Survival in Auschwitz* (n. 83).

89. See, for example, Johnson, "Life Under Sentence of Death" (n. 63), 129–145. Working with a limited statistical sample of confinement effects, this study does establish that stress reactions appear to increase over time, supporting the notion that lengthy death row confinement is distinctively stressful.

90. *People* v. *Anderson* (n. 12), 649, quoted in Schabas (n. 11), 107.

91. Dissent, *Riley* v. *Attorney General of Jamaica*, quoted in Schabas (n. 11), 97.

92. Marshall, in quoting the distinguished legal historian, Anthony Granucci. Quoted in Schabas (n. 11), 20–21.

93. *Pratt et al.* v. *Attorney General for Jamaica et al.*, quoted in Schabas (n. 11), 123.

94. Ibid., 123.

95. Schabas (n. 11), 3.

96. Ibid., 125.

97. Ibid., 125.

98. David Pannick, quoted in Schabas (n. 11), 98.

99. Schabas (n. 11), 57.

100. Ibid., 69.

101. M. Abu-Jamal, *Live From Death Row* (Reading, Mass.: Addison-Wesley, 1995), 39; also Abu-Jamal, quoting verbatim from Dred Scott v. Sanford 19 U.S. (How.) 393, 407, 15 L. Ed. 691 (1857).

102. Strafer (n. 11), 889.

103. Coker v. Georgia, 433 U.S. 584, 592 (1977).

104. J. H. Reiman, "Civilization and the Death Penalty: Answering van den Haag," *Philosophy and Public Affairs* 14 (2): 115–148 (Spring 1985).

105. I. Kant, "The Right to Punish," in *Punishment and Rehabilitation*, ed. J. Murphy (Pacific Grove, Calif.: Wadsworth, 1973), 36.

106. *In re* Kemmler, 136 U.S. at 447, 34 L. Ed. 519, 10 S. Ct. 930. Though *Kemmler* is, in important constitutional respects, an "antiquated authority" (see Justice Brennan's dissent in Glass v. Louisiana, 85 L. Ed. 2d, 517), this principle has endured.

9

Punishing Murderers

Choosing Life
Over Death

I n the last chapter I argued that the death penalty was a form of torture, a human rights violation rather than a valid criminal penalty. Seen in this way, one might ask, "Could it possibly matter that the American public supports the death penalty or that it is a legal sanction in this country?" After all, the public sometimes supports repressive practices, and the law can be used to promote or maintain a flagrantly unjust state of affairs. It is said that, were it put to a public vote, our Bill of Rights would likely be rejected out of hand by today's voters. Unjust laws, even obscenely unjust laws, have sometimes met with great popularity as well as the endorsement of even our highest courts. The Supreme Court's *Dred Scott* decision of 1857 is a telling case in point. A disgraceful decision, *Dred Scott* was celebrated in the South because it affirmed the view that slaves were mere property of their masters, no different from a mule or a horse. Following this, in the Supreme Court's *Plessy v Ferguson* case in 1896, discriminatory Jim Crow laws were upheld in an affirmation of the "separate but equal" treatment of the races.

These transparently unjust laws had an embarrassingly long and popular life in twentieth-century America, beginning around 1890 and only coming to a reluctant and somewhat tumultuous end with the emergence of the civil rights movement and the passage of the Civil Rights Act of 1964. During this shameful era, the Supreme Court endorsed the internment of Japanese-Americans for the duration of World War II, a decision (*Korematsu*, 1944) that lives on in a state of infamy on a par with Pearl Harbor, but which, in its day, produced no significant opposition from among the general public. Similarly,

Hitler cemented much of his power by passing discriminatory and unjust laws which were affirmed in the courts and supported by the many Germans who stood to gain at the expense of the Jews and others who were disenfranchised and later subjected to a campaign of extermination. Who took polls on these matters? What would one do with the results of such polls?

One day we in America may come to classify the death penalty as being among the grossly unjust practices supported in law and public opinion, but not now. International human rights norms have no binding effect on our society. When we as a nation sign international human rights declarations, we do so with specific provisos that exclude from consideration any practices, such as the death penalty, that are opposed in much of the world but supported by our legal system.[1] Today and for the foreseeable future, then, our society is committed to the death penalty. We need to understand that commitment, at least in part to see how we might move beyond the death penalty to sanctions less objectionable on the basis of human rights and at least arguably palatable to the American public.

RETRIBUTION AND THE DEATH PENALTY

Most Americans support the death penalty for the crime of murder. Public opinion polls tell us this in no uncertain terms. Since 1936, with but a brief interlude in the middle of the 1960s (when only 42% of those polled supported the sanction), 60% or more of the American public have stood behind executions as the right thing to do with murderers. Today, close to 80% of Americans support the death penalty for murderers. When specific murder scenarios are fashioned and respondents are asked to read them and then choose between execution, life in prison without parole, a prison term of a length specified by the respondent, or an alternative punishment of their choice, only 5% of the group refuse to use the death penalty under any circumstances. These are what might be termed hard-core abolitionists. Fully 95% of us, judging by this study, support the death penalty for at least some murderers.[2]

On the surface, most support for the death penalty is utilitarian. The threat of execution, many contend, scares potential killers straight and hence saves the innocent lives they would have taken. At a deeper, more visceral level, however, most people simply want murderers to be paid back for their crimes. When pressed, the average person will concede that deterrence, if it actually occurs, is gravy.[3] Many sense the weakness of the deterrence argument, which in fact receives little support in research, but that is not really important to them. Doubts about other aspects of the death penalty can be more prominent. According to one survey, close to 6 in 10 Americans worry about executing innocent people; about 5 in 10 are concerned about racism in the use of the death penalty as well as the excessive costs of this sanction; while only 4 in 10, though this is a considerable number, worry about failures of deterrence. These doubts may be troubling but they do not derail support for the death penalty (unless severe alternative prison sentences are convincingly available, a point I will develop later.)[4]

For most death penalty advocates, there is an abiding faith in the retributive justice meted out by the death penalty, following the simple but compelling formula: a life for a life. Justice can sometimes be a grisly, imperfect,
and even torturous business, the average citizen might concede, but justice
must be done. In general, opinions on the death penalty, for or against, reveal
more about one's ideological self-image than about one's thoughtfulness.[5] A
pro–death penalty stance often indicates a self-image of tough-minded prag-
matism, someone who sees himself (or herself) as having the fortitude, nerve,
and will to punish the guilty. (According to this line of analysis, the minority
who oppose the death penalty wish to advertise their compassionate, forgiving
natures.) Most death penalty supporters emphasize not the fine points of the
law, sociological findings on deterrence, or treatises on justice, but an essentially gut-level "belief that murderers deserve to die."[6] That condemned murderers should suffer in the process, even suffer greatly, is self-evident to many
of those who support the death penalty.

The popular view of justice as just deserts, though in some respects ill-in-
formed and even smugly self-righteous, has merit. Retribution means giving
criminals the punishment they deserve, and this is a sensible and just notion.
The virtues of retribution can easily be lost sight of, however, because retribution is generally tinged with revenge, and vengeance is considered a base motive that in turn debases any punishment with which it is associated. Yet
vengeance means more than a desire for retaliation; it also means "a reasser-
tion of human dignity or worth after injury or damage." Vengeance may be
primitive, but it is nevertheless a "form of moral outrage."[7] As a moral act and
not simply an eruption of passion, vengeance should not be dismissed out of
hand as barbaric or uncivilized. Indeed, one might say that retribution is, fundamentally, vengeance constrained by some notion of just deserts.

Retribution understood as constrained vengeance is not only just, it is also
humane. Unlike pure revenge, in which the criminal is devalued and thereby
made open game for any harm the victim or his representatives wish to inflict
on him, retribution, because it presupposes "the equality of persons,"[8] limits
punishment. Retribution thus treats criminal and victim alike as fellow human
beings of equal worth who have a score that must be settled fairly.

The just and humane aspects of retribution are lost, however, when we resort to the death penalty. The process by which we try, convict, sentence, confine, and ultimately execute condemned criminals has, when seen from the
condemned's vantage point, distinctly Kafkaesque qualities. These proceedings—some of which we examined closely in this book—are nothing short of
harrowing for those who must undergo them. Anthony Amsterdam's observations on this matter are, in my view, quite compelling.

First we bring men or women into court and put them through a trial for
their lives. They are expected to sit back quietly and observe decent
courtroom decorum throughout a proceeding whose purpose is systematically and deliberately to decide whether they should be killed. The jury
hears the evidence and votes; and you can always tell when a jury has
voted for death because they come back into court and they will not look

the defendant or defense counsel in the eyes. The judge pronounces sentence and the defendant is taken away to be held in a cell for two to six [or more] years, hoping that his appeals will succeed, not knowing what they are all about, but knowing that if they fail, he will be taken out and cinched down and put to death. . . . [He knows that] the people in prison . . . are holding him there helpless for the approaching slaughter; and that once the final order is given, they will truss him up and kill him, and that nobody in that vast surrounding machinery of public officials and servants of the law will raise a finger to save him.[9]

There is nothing just or humane about executions, if we understand these concepts to mean, at their roots, the showing of respect for the humanity of the person being punished. Rather, in executing a criminal, we treat him, in the words of Justice Brennan, "like an object to be toyed with and discarded."[10] One is led to hope against hope, with Amsterdam, that the death penalty is, appearances notwithstanding, a dying institution, and that it shall pass quickly and quietly from the current scene.

Opposition to punishments that treat a person like an object—and that thus harm us by assaulting our humanity—has a long and venerable lineage in philosophy. Plato once observed, for example, that, ideally, "judgment by sentence of law is never inflicted for harm's sake. Its normal effect is one of two; it makes him that suffers it a better man, or failing that, less of a wretch."[11] Perhaps even more to the point, he also stated, "We ought not to repay injustice with injustice or to do harm to any man, no matter what we may have suffered from him."[12] The pain of punishment, as distinct from gratuitous suffering, must engage the offender as a person and offer a moral lesson in the process.[13] Thus, to be humane, punishment must be not only civilized, conforming to some notion of a fair measure of pain or loss, but also civilizing, offering at least the possibility of personal reform.[14]

Some methods of execution are more civilized than others, and there have been progressive efforts to limit and even eliminate the physical pain caused by execution (see Part I). The assumption, widely shared among legal authorities though less popular with the average citizen, is that the penalty is solely the loss of life, and hence any pain attendant to the taking of life should be minimized or avoided altogether. The use of a lethal injection, complete with a battery of anesthetics, represents the most recent effort to civilize executions. Were this method shown to be painless (we have noted that some anesthesiologists contest this), and, further, were its reliable administration combined with a humane confinement regime, one might argue that the death penalty extinguished life and nothing more, in accord with the demands of the Supreme Court. Such executions would exact a heavy psychological toll on executioners, however, and perhaps on the prisoners as well, because, as we have seen (in Chapter 8), killing and dying do not come easily to full human beings. Still, one might maintain that such executions were civilized.

But not civilizing. Given our current understanding of human nature and the finality of death, the death penalty, however it is administered, can never be civilizing. If, as science seems to indicate, death is the termination of all experience, then execution cannot offer the criminal the experience of his just deserts,[15] and it is the experience of one's just deserts that alone holds out the prospect of reform and marks a sanction as humane. (Even the proper anticipation of one's just deserts is eliminated by the dehumanization inherent in modern executions.) Hence, there can be no such thing as a humane execution in the modern world—only executions that are more or less smoothly and painlessly orchestrated by the state.

The Finality of Death

In taking this stand, I am mindful of the fact that Plato envisioned executions in his *Republic*. He saw crime as a kind of disease that contaminated and tortured its host. Execution would release serious and incurable criminals from their earthly bondage; the oblivion of death was presumed to be humane because it made the offender "less of a wretch."[16] The French historian Phillippe Aries has noted that other notions of death prevalent before the twentieth century, particularly those associated with a personal God and a congenial afterlife, made a foreseen death desirable. Here, too, execution might be conceived as a blessing of sorts, allowing criminals to reform themselves by coming to terms with their Maker and experiencing an exemplary afterlife in His care. The views of Robert Bellarmine, a seventeenth-century Jesuit, are instructive. For him, Aries reported,

> the condemned man was actually rehabilitated by his suffering and his repentance. His piety transformed his execution into an expiation, and his death became a good death, better than many others. "When they have begun to depart from mortal life," Bellarmine wrote almost admiringly of condemned criminals, "they begin to live in immortal bliss."[17]

On some occasions, offenders were permitted to confess and receive absolution on the scaffold, virtually ensuring their salvation.[18]

One can readily see how executions in this context could partake of a public and even celebratory nature, with religious and other officials prominently involved (see Chapter 1). The tortures of the condemned, often serving as the centerpiece of the execution, were thought to provide the time and the motivation for the prisoner's repentance. "The more the condemned was tortured on his way to release from this life," Samuel Edgerton observed, "the more penance he was privileged to offer up for possible redemption." The ceremony would be brought to a satisfying close when the "brave but penitent" criminal renounced his evil ways and died "like a stoic Christian martyr."[19] In this fashion, offenders would at once secure forgiveness for their sins and clear of guilt the community they had compromised in God's eyes. Finally, everyone would take comfort in the fact that God was the ultimate authority. He would take responsibility for the proceedings, which after all occurred in His name, and could be expected to ameliorate any earthly injustices in the next life.[20]

To be sure, the masses did not attend executions to watch criminals ascend blissfully into heaven. And it is safe to assume that many prisoners, captives of terror, had their doubts as well—it is entirely plausible, as Gatrell suggests, that the confessors and even the crowd were more comforted by the scaffold ritual than were the poor condemned.[21] (For everyone but the condemned, the whole enterprise was a painless confirmation of cherished beliefs; for the prisoner, the reluctant sacrificial object, agony and doubt would almost certainly be the order of the day.) Most common folk saw the condemned as bound for an eternity of punishment and were happy to see them go. For much of premodern history, "it was commonly believed that the criminal about to be executed was a diabolical creature who had already gone to hell. Under the circumstances, all spiritual consolation was seen as useless and forbidden, if not sacrilegious."[22] But the actual fate of the condemned was always ambiguous. Was the church or the populace right? And how would one know?

The meaning of the condemned's suffering on the scaffold was unclear. Their suffering could be considered a form of penance. Certainly this was implied by the presence of a confessor on the scaffold, who in some cases used religious icons to help the prisoners control their terror by subjugating it to religious belief, ideally achieving a kind of spiritual anesthesia that would allow the prisoners to better endure their final agonies in a manner consistent with the execution ritual.[23] The criminals' suffering could also be considered a harbinger of what awaited them in the hereafter, as many citizens believed, confirming strongly held popular beliefs about the essentially retributive nature of the afterlife.

In any event, a symbolic struggle was waged on the scaffold between the devil (personified by the executioner) and God (variously represented by a visible confessor and invisible angels). The executioner, "frequently recruited from the swarthy races" because this would make "his appearance on the scaffold all the more devilish," was supposed to look like an agent of Satan; his victim, though generally reviled in life, was at this time of utter vulnerability "a pitiable soul struggling for salvation."[24] No one could know in advance how this struggle would end. Furthermore, there was often room for doubt about the accuracy of the verdict. (Criminal procedure was still comparatively crude and self-serving, with evidence often obtained through ordeals or torture.) In this vein, the prisoners' suffering might serve to shed light on their guilt or innocence as well.

And certainly death, always mysterious, might reveal something about itself to the viewing audience. Death was ever-present in the Middle Ages, and it is possible, as Gatrell suggests, that the crowd might hope to find in the scaffold ritual a means to symbolically control death, to tame and take charge of that which so cruelly controlled their daily lives.[25] As noted in Chapter 1, strange and mysterious happenings, including miraculous cures of the sick, were thought possible on the scaffold. For all these reasons, people watched executions closely, with a curiosity that was both morbid (literally) and almost insatiable.

The scaffold, then, was nothing less than a grand stage on which was prominently displayed for all to see a

spectacle of sufferings truly endured; there one could decipher crime and innocence, the past and the future, the here below and the eternal. It was a moment of truth that all the spectators questioned: each word, each cry, the duration of the agony, the resisting body, the life that clung desperately to it, all this constituted a sign.[26]

The communal nature of life in premodern times, together with the typical citizen's deep religious beliefs about an afterlife, meant that death was never "a solitary venture," to quote Aries, but rather had worldly and otherworldly implications for the community.[27] The arranged death of an execution, in particular, involved the community as a whole as well as the separate souls of its members—hence the preoccupation with signs. Church bells tolling the advent of an execution tolled for everyone.

Things are, of course, profoundly different today. In the West, at least, we live in a secular, individualistic age. A preoccupation with signs from God is likely to be regarded now as a symptom of mental illness or a bid for entry into a religious cult. Today, condemned criminals are neither believed to be possessed by demons nor considered the confident recipients of a guaranteed afterlife. (Some major religions still promise an afterlife, but many Christian theologians now view "the idea of an afterlife [as] clearly an embarrassment to modern thinking.") Death no longer has any universally accepted communal or transcendental meaning; in many quarters it is regarded simply as the end of individual life as we know it. Some religious leaders acknowledge this quite bluntly: "Dead is dead," Rabbi Terry Bard, director of pastoral services at Boston's Beth Israel Hospital, has stated.[28] It is increasingly hard to sustain the belief that death is not an end to this life but instead the beginning of a life hereafter in the arms of a personal God. "In recent times," as Barrington Moore has noted, "a fairly large number of educated people [has] come to realize that there is not and cannot be any source of moral authority except human beings themselves."[29] Like Camus's stranger, some of us have concluded that we would be wise to lay our "heart[s] open to the benign indifference of the universe," acknowledging that we are ultimately alone in this world and that life ends with death.[30] Others, we learn from Norman Podhoretz, choose to serve and praise the concept of God—the spiritual ideal of goodness—"by cherishing life on this Earth to the very end and by refusing to curse it" even as death encroaches.[31] Still others see God embodied, or at least presaged, in the workings of nature and the maturing of human reason; death, ever final for the individual, punctuates the gradual but inexorable perfection of the species.[32]

For many thoughtful people, at least, today's God, if they believe one to exist at all, has been shorn of personal attributes and evicted from a personal hereafter. These ideas have been slow in coming to human consciousness and even slower in gaining popular acceptance. But the evidence from science is compelling. "For modern science," McDannell and Lang tell us, "the mind is a function of the brain rather than an independent, spiritual entity. There is no soul to survive physical death. When the body dies, and with it the brain, the mind and its personality also vanish." This materialist view of life, they assure us, "is implied in the entire range of disciplines dealing with the human being: biology, medicine, psychology, and psychiatry."[33] Whether or not these ideas gain popular acceptance is ultimately irrelevant (though there can be little doubt that these notions have worked their way into our culture, sowing doubt about immortality and making death an evermore fearful prospect). The objective finality of death alters drastically the nature of death as a punishment, and this is the case independent of how we may come to grips with this fact individually or as a society or, indeed, however much we may deny this reality. As a result, neither the spiritual significance nor the justice of a life in the hereafter can be plausibly invoked to defend the death penalty. Gone are executions that are genuine rituals. Gone are spiritual defenses of the death penalty.

Punishments, including the death penalty, should respect the criminal's personhood.[34] In the previous chapter, I took the liberty of defining a person as an individual with a sense of self and a capacity for self-determination based on and expressed as autonomy, security, and relatedness to others. An afterlife negates the finality of death; hence, a person's self and capacity for self-determination can be regarded as continuing after death. Death as a punishment, therefore, does not inherently violate a criminal's personhood. One enters the hereafter as a soul (self) separate and distinct from other souls (selves). One's fate there is a product of prior autonomous choices, including any choice to repent, even if made as one mounts the scaffold. In the hereafter, one can find security in relatedness to God as well as to God's other creatures. One can knowingly forfeit these benefits—for example, by refusing to repent—but this is something one chooses, and hence one suffers the consequences of this choice as a person.[35] Once the notion of an afterlife is relinquished, however, the penalty of death can no longer be seen as a punishment that respects the criminal's personhood. Instead of offering a moral lesson to the offender, the death penalty then simply terminates all moral discourse with him.

To be sure, popular beliefs in a personal God and an afterlife persist in the modern world. Public opinion polls indicate that such beliefs are alive and well among the laity if not among their religious leaders, with as many as 81% of the public claiming to believe in heaven and immortality.[36] This is perhaps to be expected. For one thing, such beliefs are still the conventional view, the scientific rendering the minority position; people readily make the conventional selection in public opinion surveys, even if this is not their actual view or if they harbor doubts about the view they are espousing in conformity with others. A belief in heaven is also, of course, a great comfort. (It is interesting to note that belief in the death penalty is also the conventional view, and one that may offer false comfort as well.) We yearn to be immortal, as Ernest Becker reminds us, and for the common man this desire is "the basic motive for . . . religion."[37] We also yearn to be happy, to feel good about ourselves, to know that we are special and unique and that things will always be so. Unfortunately, the wish to live on in the hereafter as always-evolving, ever-improving, and perpetually-cherished souls in the embrace of a kind and forgiving God is, as Sigmund Freud made clear, profoundly self-serving and hence deeply suspect as a basis for religion:

We say to ourselves: it would be very nice if there were a God, who was both creator of the world and a benevolent providence, if there were a moral order and a future life, but at the same time it is very odd that this is all just as we should wish it ourselves. And it would be still odder if our poor ignorant enslaved ancestors had succeeded in solving all these difficult riddles of the universe.[38]

Such wishes, however devoutly they may be embraced, are no substitute for a solid bedrock of religious faith. Death is the acid test of faith, and our response to death reveals the poverty of our faith. For, sad to say, belief and comfort come hard nowadays, and it is difficult indeed "to die with the peaceful resignation of a true believer."[39] Our image of heaven has become vague, blurry, as if we really don't want to be pressed on the matter. Even ministers who profess belief are either silent or evasive when asked to describe heaven. "[I]n a curious way, heaven is AWOL," states Biema. "To reverse the words of the old spiritual: Everybody's goin' to heaven, just ain't talkin' 'bout it. The silence is such that it sometimes seems heaven might as well not be there."[40] The implication is that belief in heaven and an afterlife is broad but not deep; that we can believe it in the abstract—when polled, or at the funerals of others—where a comforting ritual supports it. But not so easily in relation to our own deaths on an everyday basis, where we are on our own.

Knowing death to be final—or at the very least, sensing and fearing, even dreading, its finality—we hide from death. We prefer the sudden death, a death that strikes without warning and is over so swiftly that it seems not even to happen to the person at all. (By contrast, during much of human history, and particularly the Middle Ages, a sudden death was thought to rob persons of the chance to die with dignity and prepare themselves for a peaceful afterlife. As Aries has observed, "In this world that was so familiar with death, a sudden death was a vile and ugly death; it was frightening; it seemed a strange and monstrous thing that nobody dared talk about."[41]) When death threatens to linger in the modern world, we relegate the dying to hospitals and nursing homes, far from the ebb and flow of contemporary life.[42] Our heroes no longer die nobly for a good cause, then go on to receive their just deserts from their Maker in a pleasing hereafter. They merely survive adversity—often to bear witness to evil, always to celebrate life.[43]

Faced with the ugly prospect of the finality of death, we have become a death-denying culture, perhaps even inaugurating a death-denying era. Hence, according to our own cultural values, capital punishment today is both cruel (because it forces the offender to confront his mortality) and unusual (because it radically departs from our normal denial of the reality of death). It is also perversely arrogant. For it is unconscionable to take the lives of individuals who might have been able, even if only in some small way, to make up for the wrongs they have caused. In a world without an afterlife, Camus maintained, "a right to live, which allows a chance to make amends, is the natural right of every man, even the worst man."[44] In taking the lives of criminals, we reduce them to pieces of meat—inert bodies; so much decaying matter—when the *persons* could have been punished in life and, potentially at least, reclaimed by society or at least allowed to make some reparation to society. Whether or not criminals are reclaimed through punishment, and whether or not they use that punishment as a means to make amends or merely make their way through a life in prison, our evolving standards of decency—as seen in how we as a society understand and deal with death—can be said to have changed sufficiently to render the death penalty no longer permissible under the Eighth Amendment prohibition of cruel and unusual punishments.[45]

Then why so much current enthusiasm for the death penalty? Desperate, last-ditch crime control measures like the death penalty may have a special appeal today. More than at any other time in recent memory, we fear crime and distrust our justice system, which we view as ineffectual and lax.[46] Feeling helplessly at the mercy of criminals, many of us want to punish at least some of them as forcefully as we can. If nothing else, we want a potent and hence reassuring symbol of a tough-minded approach to crime. The death penalty fills the bill quite handily.[47]

On a deeper level, popular support for the death penalty is, in part, a product of the modern denial of death. We talk tough on the subject of death, I fear, because we do not know what we are talking about. Executions are nothing more than an abstraction for us, insofar as we have, through our denial, reduced death itself to an abstraction that is, in Aries's words, "invisible and unreal."[48] Our current bureaucratic execution procedure in itself denies the reality of death inherent in executions, revealing the moral bankruptcy of the modern death penalty, a sanction we use but cannot look squarely in the face and call our own.[49] (Even televising executions will not make them visible in the sense Aries has in mind or change their essential death-denying nature; television will only heighten the unreality of executions and help us further dissociate ourselves from this violence.) Instead, perversely, we try to make the dehumanization of the condemned prisoner seem decent and humane: "He felt nothing; he was dead to the world before we took his life." Executions masquerade as morally neutral events—as tactical moves in a war on crime, not as face-to-face killings of other human beings. All of this is but a tragic charade that masks the inhumanity of the death penalty.

A CIVIL DEATH PENALTY

If we reject death as a legitimate sanction, what punishment do we use instead? More to the point, how do we decide what punishment fits the crime of murder, particularly the premeditated and often heinous murders that people think of when they call for the death penalty? What do we do with the "monsters" who commit monstrous crimes?

Murderers treat their victims "like objects to be toyed with and discarded," if I may transpose Justice Brennan's fine phrase, but murderers are reprehensible people and we as a society must not fashion our punishments after their acts. Murderers must be paid back for what they have done to their victims, but this must be done justly and properly, showing due regard for their inherent human dignity.[50] (At the heart of the Eighth Amendment ban on cruel and unusual punishments is the prohibition of punishments that deny the inherent dignity of human beings.[51]) Like other criminals, murderers must be punished as persons in a way that is commensurate with the harm they have caused. Thus, their punishment must approximate death and yet treat them as full human beings.

This means lengthy prison terms for murderers, including, for our worst murderers, true life sentences without possibility of parole. When we sentence criminals to prison we suspend their civil lives, rendering them civilly dead until they are deemed worthy of return to the society of the living.[52] A civil death entails the loss of one's freedom and of the attendant benefits of civil life in the free world. Civil death should not be confused with moral death, the dehumanization suffered by the condemned. During their confinement, regular prisoners do not suffer a moral death. They remain persons, even if their circumstances are impoverished and they suffer great privations. They are still individuals (of admittedly low status), and they are afforded a degree of autonomy (by prison officials and within their society of captives), security (usually by virtue of the staff's policing and human-service roles), and relatedness to others (selected fellow prisoners and staff, as well as loved ones who write or visit). Prison life may not be much of a life, but it is a life nonetheless.

How much time behind bars, how much of a civil death, is enough punishment for the crime of murder? At what point does a prison term inflict suffering commensurate with a murderer's crime? The answer varies. The context in which the crime occurred, for example, is a critical factor in assessing punishment. In sentencing, judges currently take into account some specific contextual factors such as duress or the presence or absence of explicit prior intent. But rarely considered are more general, often crucial social factors, such as those relating to poverty and brutality. Psychiatrist Willard Gaylin has reminded us that the impoverished lives of violent men typically give rise to a host of mitigating factors that should be, but presently are not, taken into account in assessing their just punishment.[53]

Individual sensibilities also come into play. Pain is a subjective experience. It would be futile, in my view, to attempt to precisely and systematically calibrate the pains of punishment, at least in part because of the substantial variations in sensitivity to suffering one can expect to find, first among victims, whose degree of suffering would determine the punishment, and second, among offenders, who are to suffer commensurately. Nevertheless, what constitutes even a gross notion of sufficient pain for any given crime will depend on the capacity of the person inflicting or authorizing punishment to empathize with the criminal and hence to have at least a primitive sense of when the criminal has or will have suffered his just deserts.

This presents a serious problem in the case of murder. Though murderers are people, too, many of us have no empathy for them. Some of us, for instance, see murderers as so many anonymous crime statistics. For others, murderers are monsters, animals, or psychopaths. These jaundiced views, moreover, are not restricted to an uninformed and vindictive segment of the populace. Walter Berns, a scholar and advocate of the death penalty, openly mocked Supreme Court Justice Brennan for contending that "even the vilest criminal remains a human being possessed of human dignity." It was only a decade or so back that the chief justice of Georgia's Supreme Court likened murderers to mad dogs, a characterization that must have deeply unsettled the one hundred or so condemned prisoners housed (kenneled?) on Georgia's death row and subject to his rulings on their appeals. Similarly, an editorialist in Alabama described execution as "an act approaching judicial euthanasia," a merciful gesture putting brutish criminals out of their (our?) misery. William Raspberry, a syndicated columnist, summed up this point of view when he observed that "it is possible for a criminal to commit acts so heinous as to place himself outside the category of human, to render him subject to extermination as one might exterminate a mad dog, without consideration of how the animal came to contract rabies in the first place."[54] Never mind that the "rabies" may have originated in an abusive home, during the criminal's impressionable years.[55] Or that it may have been the predictable result of harsh and inequitable social conditions (like poverty) that we as a society permit to exist because of the benefits we reap from them (such as cheap labor to do menial tasks for our convenience).[56] Or that it may have reflected neurological impairments produced by genetic anomalies, physical abuse, or inadequate diet (especially during the prenatal period).[57]

If we are unable to empathize with murderers, unable to feel for them, we cannot develop a sense of their lives and their suffering and hence cannot determine when they have suffered enough. In fact, in the absence of empathy, there is no limit to the pain one can inflict, since by definition the pain affects individuals for whom one feels nothing and who one naturally assumes feel nothing themselves. Thus, we imagine we are dealing with cold-blooded felons who are impervious to normal hurts and hence must be punished according to a scale of suffering far in excess of what we would apply to ourselves or others like us. We may even believe that no punishment is really adequate. This may explain how we can bandy about prison terms of five, ten, twenty, forty, or (in states like Texas) literally hundreds or thousands of years as though they were civilized, even soft, penalties.

Perhaps a way out of this dilemma is to relate prison sentences to our own life experiences. Four years in prison, for instance, sounds like a snap, a travesty of justice in the case of murder. But imagine spending the whole of your high school years, including summers, separated from your loved ones and confined for the greater part of each day to a cage. Ten years behind bars would equal your entire twenties. A thirty- or forty-year sentence would equal the entire life of the average American who is middle-aged. A natural-life sentence or true life sentence comes close to obliterating any life at all. Though a true life sentence falls short of execution, surely no criminal deserves a harsher fate than this.

The vast majority of murderers can point to a host of mitigating circumstances in their lives (though, as noted above, only some are currently recognized in law). For them, serving sentences of roughly ten to fifteen years would probably be sufficient punishment. (This is approximately the average sentence murderers serve today, and their recidivism rates after release from prison are reassuringly low.) Some are more culpable and would no doubt deserve longer sentences; a few might marshall such an impressive array of mitigating circumstances that they would warrant shorter terms of confinement. Our worst murderers, those seeming monsters we presently consign to the death chamber because their actions are thought to place them beyond the bounds of human decency, would of course be subject to lengthy prison terms, including a natural or true life sentence without possibility of parole.

In fact, lengthy incarceration alternatives are presently available to the courts in sentencing offenders. Forty-five states and the District of Columbia offer life with no possibility of parole for at least twenty-five years.[58] Of these jurisdictions, thirty-two states and the federal government offer life with no possibility of parole at any time—what I have called a true life sentence. These sentences have proven credible. In California, which has had life without parole for some time, "no prisoner sentenced to life without parole has been released in 25 years."[59] Comparable evidence of what is sometimes called "truth in sentencing" is available for other jurisdictions as well, notably Louisiana, South Dakota, and Connecticut. Unfortunately, most Americans, including many jurors in capital cases, know little about these harsh alternatives to the death penalty. The typical citizen, according to one survey, is "poorly informed about the likely sentences which capital murderers would receive if not given the death penalty. Only 4% believed that those sentenced to life for first degree murder would be imprisoned for the rest of their lives."[60] Ignorance breeds skepticism, which undermines faith in the justice system and leads many citizens, again including jurors, to doubt the integrity of these sanctions. "Even when asked how long someone with a life without parole sentence would serve, only 11% believed that such a person would never be released."[61]

Yet people *can* be informed that stiff sentences will be carried out according to the letter of the law. When citizens are armed with accurate information, polls reveal that support for capital punishment drops dramatically. When the alternative to execution is life without parole, support for the death penalty falls below 50%; when life without parole is combined with compensation for the loved ones of the victim, support for the death penalty drops to a mere 41%, the lowest level of support on record since 1936. Polls reinforcing this conclusion have been conducted in California, Florida, Georgia, Kentucky, Minnesota, Nebraska, New York, Oklahoma, Virginia, and West Virginia. Popular support for life without parole, moreover, with or without restitution, appears to be growing.[62]

Under our alternative sanction—at the heart of which is a life without parole or true life sentence—the offender is slated to spend the remaining years of his life in prison. Though courts do mete out true life sentences with some regularity, as we have seen, this sentence is not recognized as being, in fact, a kind of death penalty. To be sure, true life prisoners remain physically alive and in the company of other convicts and guards; they are treated as human beings and remain members, however marginal, of the human community. They can forge a life of sorts behind bars, but a limited life steeped in suffering, for at a profoundly human level they experience a permanent civil death, the death of freedom. The prison is their cemetery, a six-by-nine-foot cell their tomb. Interred in the name of justice, they are consigned to mark the passage of their lives in the prison's peculiar dead time, which serves no larger human purpose and yields few rewards. In effect, they give their civil lives in return for the natural lives they have taken. Yet they can, through their suffering, atone for their crimes. And they can make amends, in small but meaningful ways, by living decently in the prison community. They might, for example, establish a modest career of service to others built around the work and remedial opportunities available within the prison's walls. (To the extent that such careers are paid, or that we decide as a matter of policy to offer lifers paid work, any money made by these inmates can and should be used as restitution to the families of victims.) A true life sentence, then, can and should serve as both a practical and a moral alternative to the death penalty. It is a civilized—and potentially civilizing—application of retributive justice in the extreme case of premeditated murder in the absence of mitigating circumstances.

OBSTACLES TO REFORM

Economic Objections

One objection to this proposal is the price tag. We've all heard about the cost of new prison construction, which can run in the neighborhood of sixty thousand to one hundred thousand dollars per cell, and about per capita confinement costs of anywhere from fifteen thousand to fifty thousand dollars a year.[63] True life sentences would presumably cost a fortune in new cell construction and in the cumulative cost of confining individuals for forty or more years each, depending on how long the prisoners live, on average. With factors such as inflation and unexpected costs figured in, the tab could reach a million or more dollars per life-term prisoner. If nothing else, taxpayers are apt to see executions as humane.

But the actual cost of true life sentences would fall considerably short of these estimates and are less than the cost of executions. We will not have to build new cells expressly for true life prisoners. (Or at least not many new cells. At present we execute about fifty prisoners a year out of a total prison population of more than a million. Even if the execution rate were to double over the coming years, executions would free few cells for other prisoners.) Today's condemned prisoners would be confined under any sentencing scheme, whether on death rows or in standard maximum security prisons. Where crowding is a problem, less serious offenders can be released to make room for murderers, a policy that seems eminently sensible. (It has been long known that a sizeable minority of prisoners, such as nonviolent property and public-order offenders, could be safely sentenced to community-based sanctions. These include such restrictive programs as intensive probation, electronic monitoring, and house arrest.[64]) Moreover, the true or actual out-of-pocket cost of confining any given prisoner in an existing prison may be as low as ten to fifteen thousand dollars a year.[65] Higher estimates of per prisoner costs incorrectly attribute to individuals the prisons' overhead expenses—that is, the fixed costs of running prisons, independent of who and how many people are in them. Such estimates also overlook one unique economic aspect of the confinement of life-sentence prisoners: "Most lifers tend to be employed, sooner or later, on productive jobs, which may eliminate the cost of keeping them altogether."[66] (As noted above, those wages can be used to underwrite restitution programs.)

A true life term, then, calculated as a forty-year sentence of imprisonment, would directly cost taxpayers some four hundred thousand to six hundred thousand dollars per prisoner in states like New York and California (perhaps less in other states). These estimates are necessarily imperfect: Inflation would, of course, push the cost up, and cost-defraying labor by the prisoners would lower it. Though high, and perhaps becoming considerably higher over time, these figures compare quite favorably with the estimated cost of death sentences, which are nothing short of astronomical. Death sentences, appearances to the contrary, are elaborate enterprises. They require complicated trials, lengthy appeals, years of special custodial housing for the condemned, and carefully arranged executions. It is unclear how much of these costs represent specific out-of-pocket expenses, but what is clear is that a single execution costs millions of dollars. I am aware of no cost study in which an execution costs less than two million dollars, and no study in which a true life prison term costs even half that much.[67] There are, to be sure, no bargain punishments for murder. Neither life sentences nor death sentences come cheaply, though life sentences are considerably cheaper than death sentences.

Beyond the matter of cost, some people will balk at the idea of a true life sentence because they don't believe prison is punishment. They refuse to subsidize the lives of luxury that country club prisons are presumed to afford their inmates. This cynical but widely held view is seriously misleading. A prison joke has it that the country club prison is much like the Loch Ness monster: There have been sporadic citizen sightings but no scientific confirmations. On closer examination, one cannot fail to note that our "country club" prisons permit no heterosexual contact, issue nondescript clothing or sharply limit prisoners' choice of civilian attire, and serve meager portions of poor food in noisy mess halls (well named) filled with dangerous guests who occasionally resort to violence when they are unhappy with the cuisine. The accommodations feature iron bars or steel doors, bare furniture, dim lighting, and poor ventilation. Guards control the inmates' daily movements. Like country clubs, prisons are costly to operate, but unlike country clubs, little of the money is spent on convict sustenance, let alone on amenities. For instance, in New York, a state noted for its progressive penal system, a prisoner's meal bill comes to but a few dollars a day.[68] Some country club! In point of fact, prisons are impoverished environments. A lifetime in prison is a lifetime of suffering and privation.

Public Safety Questions

Other objections to this proposal relate to public safety. After all, dead prisoners pose no threats, whereas life-term prisoners are at least potential dangers to the community. For all intents and purposes, however, prisoners serving true life sentences are punished and incapacitated for life. Maximum security prison walls, in contrast to the notoriously permeable fences that enclose medium and minimum security prisons, virtually assure that society has nothing more to fear from these prisoners. Of course, convicts sometimes escape from maximum security prisons (and have from at least one death row). The rate of such escapes, however, is quite low. Even less common are escapes from prison that are accompanied by violent crimes against the public. As Ernst van den Haag has reminded us, prisons are costly, in the main, "because they are too secure."[69]

Nor are life prisoners a special threat to other prisoners or to guards. Thorsten Sellin long ago established, and the relevant statistics today bear him out, that "prison homicides are not usually committed by prisoners serving [life] sentences for capital murder and that such persons . . . pose no special threat to the safety of their fellow men."[70] If paroled, these prisoners, again, pose no special threat to others. The same holds true for formerly condemned prisoners. Indeed, when the sentences of condemned prisoners are reduced to life terms (not true life terms, usually following court decisions) and some of these prisoners are paroled, they have "recidivism rates as low as or lower than those of other offenders."[71]

Most lifers are good prisoners. Those who are troublesome can be segregated from the main prison population. (Secure systems of custodial segregation can be mobilized in the rare instances when long-termers are persistently violent.[72]) The notion that lifers typically are unmanageable prisoners—that they have nothing to lose and hence disobey prison rules, harming and even killing others in the prison world with seeming impunity—would appear to be a practical stumbling block to my proposal, were it not completely without foundation.

As a group, lifers simply do not rebel, nor do they make life miserable or dangerous for their keepers or fellow prisoners. Paradoxically, lifers are usually compliant prisoners. Why? Quite simply, because prison becomes their home. To make the most of a bad situation, they try to get through each day in prison with as little trouble as possible. More than other prisoners, who from the lifers' point of view are essentially impetuous tourists, lifers have a vested interest in the stability and integrity of the prison. Lifers and other long-termers "are not necessarily more *accepting* of their situation than short-term prisoners, [but] they appear to more fully realize the need to *coexist* with correctional authorities within the confines of the institution." One might say that they have "'wised up' to the exigencies of the situation."[73]

In my experience, many American prison wardens privately concur with these observations, though I am aware of no systematic research on their perceptions of lifers. Some have spoken out on the matter. Leo Lalonde, of the

Michigan Department of Corrections, has remarked, with respect to prisoners serving life without parole: "After a few years, lifers become your better prisoners. They tend to adjust and just do their time. They tend to be a calming influence on the younger kids, and we have more problems with people serving short terms."[74] Essentially the same observations have been made about "true lifers" by Thomas Coughlin, former Commissioner of the New York State Department of Correctional Services.[75] The findings of a survey of Australian prison wardens supports these claims: "The replies of 64 wardens showed overwhelmingly that, as a group, long-term inmates are not a management problem. On the contrary, they are a stabilizing influence in the institution."[76]

Perhaps more to the point, a number of empirical studies support the claim that lifers are less likely to break prison rules than the average inmate. (Sometimes the differences in infraction rates are statistically insignificant, but I am aware of no instance in which long-termers were found to break rules more often than other prisoners.) Alabama prison officials report that "life-without-parole inmates commit 50% fewer disciplinary offenses per capita than all other types of inmates combined."[77] In a rigorous study conducted in several maximum security prisons in New York, Timothy Flanagan concluded that "the infraction rates of long-term inmates are significantly lower than the rates for short-term prisoners." This was true, moreover, "even in the early years of confinement," when the long-term prisoners could be expected to be angry and resentful about their sentences. Furthermore, "the types of infractions committed by long-term and short-term prisoners tend to be similar," though the data did indicate "that the infractions committed by long-term inmates may be somewhat more serious in nature" than those committed by short-termers.[78]

Lifers are defined in this body of research as including (1) prisoners serving long sentences that are technically not life terms (a person sentenced to fifty-six years, for instance, might not be officially termed a lifer), (2) prisoners sentenced to life terms who are eligible for parole, and (3) prisoners serving true life sentences who are ineligible for parole. Long-termers and lifers eligible for parole are usually released after ten to twenty years of imprisonment, though in a growing number of states today, lifers serve twenty-five years or more.[79] This raises a pertinent question. Are true lifers, whose sentences are counted in decades rather than in years and who presumably expect to die behind bars, more desperate and hence more disruptive than others serving lengthy terms? Only one study of this question has been conducted to date. The conclusion: True life sentence prisoners do in fact commit more rule infractions than other long-termers, but they still are less troublesome than the typical prisoner.[80]

That lifers are decent prisoners would count for little if life sentences were to deter fewer potential murderers than does the death penalty. If would-be murderers are less afraid of life sentences than of death sentences and hence are less likely to be deterred from violence, we might wish to execute at least some murderers for the greater good of deterring others and hence preserving the innocent lives of their prospective victims. Yet here we have another paradox. Life sentences may well be a better deterrent than death sentences.

There are no data bearing directly on this point, because deterrence studies compare death sentences with all other sentences for murder, not specifically with life sentences. But the logic is compelling. Criminals tend to be present-centered; they live for today and let tomorrow take care of itself.[81] Executions may be notable when they occur, but they take place long after the crime, are over quickly, and may fade from memory after but a brief period of time. Life sentences are less dramatic than death sentences, to be sure, but they are experienced in the present and last well into the future. Life sentences envelop the prisoner. By virtue of their persuasiveness, they also impinge on the other convicts, who observe at close range—and often with great apprehension—the melancholy fate of lifers.[82] Unlike executed prisoners, who are dead, gone, and soon forgotten by their fellows, lifers stand as tangible, enduring, flesh-and-blood testaments to the wages of violent crime.

Moral Objections

A final objection to this proposal is that it does not really represent an improvement at all, but rather will do more harm than good. This objection takes two forms, the first being that life in prison is worse than death. This claim was originally advanced by the nineteenth-century philosopher John Stuart Mill, who saw the life sentence prisoner as immured "in a living tomb," which Mill took to be a uniquely degrading punishment that was worse than "the short pang of a rapid death."[83] A modern advocate of this position is Jacques Barzun. Those who would abolish the death penalty, Barzun has observed,

> speak of the sanctity of life, but have no concern for its quality. . . . They read without a qualm, indeed they read with rejoicing, the hideous irony of "Killer Gets Life"; they sigh with relief instead of horror. They do not see and suffer the cell, the drill, the clothes, the stench, the food; they do not feel the sexual racking of young and old bodies, the hateful promiscuity, the insane monotony, the mass degradation, the impotent hatred. . . . Quite of another mind, the abolitionists point with pride to the "model prisoners" that murderers often turn out to be. As if a model prisoner were not, first, a contradiction in terms, and second, an exemplar of what a free society should not want.[84]

Yet it is precisely because prison offers more than either an empty tomb or a life of polluted human community that model prisoners can and do emerge from its midst. (Whether this was true or not in Mill's time is unclear. On the other hand, not all executions in Mill's day produced a rapid death.) Barzun might well "choose death without hesitation" rather than suffer a life in prison,[85] but the vast majority of prisoners he would have us kill surely would not. Like Barzun, some of them talk about being better off dead, but unlike him, they discover that a hallmark of a free society is its willingness to spare their lives and allow them a place in the prison community. Some of these prisoners also come to delight in the simple esthetic pleasures of living. As one lifer housed near death row reluctantly admitted, "Living above the electric chair has a way of giving new meaning to clichés about the joy of beholding the natural beauty of a sunrise."[86]

Some penologists, particularly those working during the late nineteenth and early twentieth centuries, thought of the prison as an inherently destructive environment. They presumed that lifers deteriorated as a matter of course amid the monotony and degradation that surrounded them. Accordingly, respected men like William Tallack thought of "absolute life imprisonment . . . not so much as a substitute for capital punishment, [but] as a slower and more disadvantageous method of inflicting it."[87] Such conclusions are clearly wrong. Research does not support claims about the deterioration of lifers.[88] (Interestingly, lifers tend to be a healthy lot; they have a slightly greater life expectancy than comparable people in the free world.[89]) Dying in prison, moreover, is not the same as being executed there. We all die, but few of us are killed in *any* way, let alone being executed by the state.

Some early wardens also reinforced the image of the deteriorating lifer. Warden Lawes of Sing Sing, for example, noted that some 10 percent of lifers were declared insane during their tenure in prison.[90] Lawes failed to note that, at that time, commitment to a mental asylum required little more than a history of self-injury and that such confinement meant doing easier time than was possible in the prison. One must also remember that the condemned prisoners in Lawes's time were confined in what he termed "wire-caged traps" on a death row known as "the slaughterhouse." There, Lawes believed, no prisoner was assured of his sanity (see Chapter 3).

A second form of moral objection to the proposed reform consists of concern about potential abuses of the true life sentence. Is it not possible that true life sentences will be used in addition to, and not instead of, the death penalty? The result would be a growing population of lifers even while executions continue. There is also the possibility that true life sentences will be used for less extreme crimes than murder; indeed, evidence from Alabama indicates that most offenders sentenced to life without parole in that state had committed unspecified "crimes against property" rather than homicide.[91] In addition, because due-process protections are less substantial when the penalty is life in prison rather than death, some true life sentences will be handed down arbitrarily.[92] It is hard to prevent such misadventures; they are the product of political and legal factors rather than moral analysis. But it is worth emphasizing that the essence of this proposal is that a true life sentence, with or without restitution, should be the most severe punishment a civilized society can inflict upon its criminals, and that it should be used with great caution and care. Accordingly, this sanction should be limited to cases of premeditated, aggravated murder, and those cases should be adjudicated using high standards of due process. To do less would be to mete out sentences that are both arbitrary and excessive, serving no valid penological objective.[93]

Conclusion

A true life sentence is an awesome sanction but, unlike a death sentence, it need not destroy the prisoner or result in an irreversible miscarriage of justice. (Innocent people have been executed in the past, including the recent past; there is no reason to suppose that such tragedies will not recur as long as the death penalty remains in force.[94]) Though painful, a life sentence can be borne with dignity. It can also be changed, if and when authorities deem it appropriate. New evidence may alter a verdict or indicate a lesser sentence; substantial and enduring changes of character may, in extraordinary cases, permit a few prisoners to be resurrected—for example, through special pardons. New evidence is only rarely discovered, of course, and pardons are even harder to come by. But at least with true life sentences, avenues of mercy and redress remain open to us in our search for justice.

Now some will claim that all of this is well and good but that the loss of a civil life is never commensurate with the loss of an actual life. They will contend that murderers, at least the worst ones, deserve to die in payment for the lives they have taken. I am willing to concede that point, but not its corollary: that we must execute some murderers. As things stand today and for the foreseeable future, we cannot execute prisoners without also torturing them, which is always unjust. And even if reforms were to enable us to execute people justly, pitting fully human executioners against fully human prisoners, I would urge that we refrain from such an undertaking. The suffering that would attend such executions would be awful and, in a very real sense, gratuitous. For the loss of one's civil life is punishment enough for any murderer, even though some or even many murderers may deserve to die. Partial justice is justice enough here. Once again, I must fall back on the wisdom of Albert Camus. Like Camus, I find it better to be wrong without killing fellow human beings than to be right in the cold stillness of the death house.

NOTES

1. See W. A. Schabas, *The Death Penalty as Cruel Treatment and Torture: Capital Punishment Challenged in the World's Courts* (Boston: Northeastern University Press, 1996), esp. Chap. 2.

2. A. M. Durham, H. P. Elrod, and P. T. Kinkade, "Public Support for the Death Penalty: Beyond Gallup," *Justice Quarterly* 13 (4): 726 (December 1996). See also R. M. Bohm and R. E. Vogel, "A Comparison of Factors Associated with Uninformed and Informed Death Penalty Opinions," *Journal of Criminal Justice* 22 (1994): 124–143.

3. Deterrence is the main reason most people cite in support of the death penalty. When presented with evidence that the death penalty does not deter, or may not deter, opinions are largely unchanged. This implies that retribution or revenge were all along the main reasons for advocating the death penalty. See P. Ellsworth and L. Ross, "Public Opinion and Capital Punishment: A Close Examination of the Views of Abolitionists and Retentionists," *Crime and Delinquency* 29 (1): 116–169 (1983), and P. Harris, "Oversimplification and Error in Public Opinion Surveys on Capital Punishment," *Justice Quarterly* 3 (4):

429–455 (December 1986). For an interesting discussion on the import of public opinion regarding the death penalty, see J. O. Finckenauer, "Public Support for the Death Penalty: Retribution as Just Deserts or Retribution as Revenge?" *Justice Quarterly* 5 (1): 81–100 (March 1988).

4. See R. C. Dieter, "Sentencing for Life: Americans Embrace Alternatives to the Death Penalty" (unpublished paper, April 1993, available from the Death Penalty Information Center, 1606 20th Street NW, Washington, D.C. 20009 or on the Internet at http://www.essential.org/dpic).

5. Ellsworth and Ross (n. 3), 116.

6. Ibid., 168.

7. B. Moore, Jr., *Injustice: the Social Bases of Obedience and Revolt* (New York: Sharpe, 1978), 17. "All acts of vengeance," claim Pietro Marongiu and Graeme Newman, "arise from an elementary sense of injustice" that vengeance is meant to ameliorate. See P. Marongiu and G. Newman, *Vengeance: The Fight against Injustice* (Totowa, N.J.: Rowman & Littlefield, 1987), 9. Marongiu and Newman have provided an interesting and insightful analysis of the evolution of revenge, from an almost unfettered, instinctual act of individual violence against one's enemies to a social and morally restrained act of punishment or retribution orchestrated by the state. Finckenauer (n. 3) has taken a different view of this matter from that of Moore or Marongiu and Newman, arguing that offenders should pay back society (retribution as just deserts), rather than society's demanding the chance to pay back the offender (retribution as revenge). For Finckenauer, retribution as revenge is not a proper basis for punishment. However, as long as society demands a retributive punishment that accords with the principle of proportionality (an eye for an eye) rather than simply giving vent to indiscriminate rage, it is hard to see how this is bloodthirsty, excessive, or otherwise illegitimate.

8. J. H. Reiman, "Civilization and the Death Penalty: Answering van den Haag," *Philosophy and Public Affairs* 14 (2): 121 (Spring 1985).

9. A. G. Amsterdam, "Capital Punishment," in *The Death Penalty in America*, ed. H. A. Bedau (Oxford: Oxford University Press, 1982), 347.

10. Furman v. Georgia, 92 S. Ct. 2726, 368.

11. Plato, *Laws*, 854.

12. Plato, *Crito*, 10.49.

13. See H. Morris, "Persons and Punishment," in *Punishment and Rehabilitation*, ed. J. Murphy (Pacific Grove, Calif.: Wadsworth, 1973) and "A Paternalisitic Theory of Punishment," *American Philosophical Quarterly* 18 (4): 263–271 (October 1981); and J. Hampton, "The Moral Education Theory of Punishment," *Philosophy and Public Affairs* 13 (3): 208–238 (1984).

14. The notion that punishments should be both civilized and civilizing was first developed by Reiman in "Civilization and the Death Penalty" (n. 8). His point of reference, particularly for determining what constitutes a civilizing punishment, is the society administering the punishment. My point of reference is the offender, the person being punished.

15. See M. E. Gale, "Retribution, Punishment and Death," *University of California, Davis, Law Review* 18 (4): 973–1035 (1985). Retribution, according to Gale,

keeps the individual offender at the center of the institution of punishment. The consequences that make punishment legitimate must occur in the life of the individual offender. There is no other way in which the offender can experience "just deserts.". . . Yet, if at the instant of the infliction of the punishment the offender is rendered forever unable to appreciate the justness of her punishment, much if not all of its moral force is lost. (1028)

Elsewhere Gale stated,

Retribution itself has a moral content inconsistent with final punishments. . . . Retribution appeals to nothing more than the stark right to continue to exist, to experience the pain, duration, and conse-

quence of punishment. These characteristics describe all punishments except those that extinguish consciousness and life itself. (1030)

Note that an afterlife would make death acceptable as a punishment on retributive grounds, because offenders would experience their just deserts after death.

16. See Plato, *Laws*, esp. Books 5 and 9.

17. P. Aries, *The Hour of Our Death* (New York: Vintage, 1982), 308.

18. S. Y. Edgerton, Jr., *Pictures and Punishment: Art and Criminal Prosecution during the Florentine Renaissance* (Ithaca, N.Y.: Cornell University Press, 1985), 181.

19. Ibid., 15, 198.

20. The unjustly executed were virtually guaranteed salvation: "Such a case of mistaken execution, which so horrifies us today, would, in the pure Christian logic of the Middle Ages, have been considered the highest form of justice" (Ibid., 16).

21. See V. A. C. Gatrell, *The Hanging Tree: Execution and the English People 1770–1868* (Oxford: Oxford University Press, 1994), 382.

22. Aries (n. 17), 308.

23. The aim of the confessor, like that of the counselor and, presumably, the priest associated with Jones's execution, was to help the prisoner transcend the grim realities of the scaffold and dwell instead on the promise of life after death (see Chapter 7).

Confessors might also have helpers, usually brothers from religious orders. Noteworthy are the scaffold labors of the brothers of Santa Maria della Croce al Tempio, a confraternity formed in 1343 out of concern "about the lack of interest on the part of public officials in the spiritual needs of prisoners of death" (Edgerton [n. 18], 179). These brothers developed the tavoletta, a religious painting, or "devotional image," that was held before the gaze of the condemned as he made his way to the scaffold and awaited his demise. Equipped with a handle and featuring the image of Christ crucified on one side and a secular execution scene on the other, the tavoletta reinforced the link between pain on earth as penance and redemption in heaven as one's reward for renouncing sin.

The brothers produced a manual on the proper ways to use the tavoletta to comfort the condemned. In Edgerton's words,

The brothers were instructed to hold the tavoletta directly before the face of the victim, blocking as much as possible his field of vision. This was especially important as the afflitto [afflicted one, a euphemism for condemned prisoner] approached the scaffold and the instruments of his imminent death. Sometimes the frame at the sides of the picture was considerably widened in order to ensure that the afflitto would not inadvertently see the executioner and suddenly lose his nerve. (180)

The brothers were also admonished "to stand a little back" from the executioner, yet keep the devotional image within easy view of the condemned (180).

The purpose of the tavoletta was to provide "a kind of visual narcotic to numb the fear and pain of the condemned criminal during his terrible journey to the scaffold" (172). By many accounts, the condemned were indeed comforted. "The devotional image succeeds best," we are told, "when it manages to lift the viewer from consciousness of the sensate world to a transcendental feeling of spiritual ecstasy" (173). The use of the tavoletta "represents one of the earliest acts of recognition that the condemned criminal remains a fellow human being deserving of charity no matter how heinous his crime" (219).

24. Edgerton (n. 18), 135.

25. Gatrell (n. 21), 80–89.

26. M. Foucault, *Discipline and Punish: The Birth of the Prison* (New York: Pantheon, 1977), 46.

27. Aries (n. 17), 604. This was particularly true in the Middle Ages, when people "lived collectively in infinite numbers of groups, orders, associations, brotherhoods. . . . If a man was condemned to be executed, fellow members accompanied him to the scaffold." See

B. W. Tuchman, *A Distant Mirror: The Calamitous 14th Century* (New York: Knopf, 1978), 39–40. The presence of one's fellows must have been immensely supportive to the condemned, since, as we have seen, those outside the criminal's immediate world would normally reject him as a damned soul en route to perdition who had had the temerity to jeopardize the spiritual well-being of the larger community. See Aries (n. 17).

28. K. L. Woodward, "Heaven," *Newsweek*, 27 March 1989, 55, 54.

29. Moore (n. 7), 434.

30. A. Camus, "Reflections on the Guillotine," in *Resistance, Rebellion, and Death* (New York: Knopf, 1969).

31. N. Podhoretz, "Do Not Go Gentle into the Night," *Washington Post*, Op Ed Section, 18 March 1986, A19.

32. Phillip Scribner has advanced a fascinating "naturalistic argument for the existence of God." He has shown, to my satisfaction at least, that "given a world of objects in space like our own, the existence of a perfect being is necessary." This perfect being is not a personal God, however, nor can this God be said to be the creator of this world, or for that matter, a world hereafter. See P. Scribner, "A New Proof for the Existence of God" (paper delivered at a Philosophy Department symposium at The American University, 25 February 1986. This work is still evolving; the most recent version—now a paper in three parts—was revised in 1993).

33. C. McDannell and B. Lang, *Heaven: A History* (New Haven: Yale University Press, 1988), 325.

34. Morris (n. 13).

35. These themes appear to be particularly clear in eighteenth- and nineteenth-century versions of heaven, which feature a place that is a continuation of our present existence in some describable form, that offers new experiences over time to persons who are conscious of those experiences, and in which relatedness to God is the central and all-encompassing dynamic. In such a heaven, "The growth of the soul after death . . . requires the self-conscious spirit to make choices and to participate actively in the various levels of after-death experience." McDannell and Lang (n. 33), 350.

36. Morris (n. 13), 53.

37. E. Becker, *Escape from Evil* (New York: Free Press, 1975), 4.

38. S. Freud, *The Future of an Illusion* (New York: Doubleday, 1957), 57–58.

39. Podhoretz (n. 31), A19. The near-dead and the once-dead (who have revived after being clinically dead for a brief period) sometimes report transcendent experiences, which they take to be incontrovertible evidence of a life after death. They no longer hide from death because they no longer fear its finality. Unfortunately, what is at work here is almost certainly a profound form of denial that is fed by both biological and psychological processes. A more plausible view of this phenomenon, in Pfister's words, is that it is "a brilliant victory of wishful thought over dreadful fact and illusion over reality." Quoted in S. Grof and J. Halifax, *The Human Encounter with Death* (New York: Dutton, 1977), esp. 144.

40. D. B. Biema, "Does Heaven Exist?" *Time Magazine*, 24 March 1997, 73.

41. Aries (n. 17), 11.

42. See E. Kübler-Ross, *On Death and Dying* (New York: Macmillan, 1969), and E. Kübler-Ross, *Death: The Final Stage of Growth* (Englewood Cliffs, N.J.: Prentice-Hall, 1975).

43. See T. Des Pres, *The Survivor: An Anatomy of Life in the Death Camps* (New York: Pocket Books, 1977), and C. Lasch, *The Minimal Self: Psychic Survival in Troubled Times* (New York: Norton, 1984).

44. Camus (n. 30), 221.

45. The Eighth Amendment prohibition of cruel and unusual punishments "must draw its meaning from the evolving standards of decency that mark the progress of a maturing society." See Trop v. Dulles, 78 S. Ct. 590 (1958) (Plurality opinion).

46. J. Gorecki, *Capital Punishment: Criminal Law and Social Evolution* (New York: Columbia University Press, 1983).

47. Given the comparatively rare use of the death penalty today, the message this sanction sends is mainly a symbolic one. See F. E. Zimring and G. Hawkins, *Capital Punishment and the American Agenda* (New York: Cambridge University Press, 1986). At least one pair of anthropologists finds a magical component to this symbolization. See E. D. Purdum and J. A. Paredes, "Rituals of Death" in *Facing the Death Penalty: Essays on a Cruel and Unusual Punishment*, ed. M. L. Radelet (Philadelphia: Temple University Press, 1989).

48. Aries (n. 17), 599.

49. As Lofland has noted, modern execution procedures have a "concealment dramaturgics" that give them "a definite death-denying quality." See H. Bleackley and J. Lofland, *State Executions Viewed Historically and Sociologically* (Montclair, N.J.: Patterson Smith, 1977), 321.

50. As mentioned earlier, beliefs about the nature of crime and the existence of an afterlife may at other times have made executions proper punishments that were commensurate with some crimes. Those times have passed. Today, killing criminals, even our worst criminals, does most certainly treat them "like objects to be toyed with and discarded."

51. As Strafer has cogently noted, the Eighth Amendment ban "applies to all punishments which do not comport with 'broad and idealistic concepts of dignity, civilized standards, humanity and decency'" (citations omitted). See G. R. Strafer, "Volunteering for Execution: Competency, Voluntariness and the Propriety of Third-Party Intervention," *Journal of Criminal Law and Criminology* 74 (3): 889 (1983).

52. Interestingly, prisoners, until fairly recently, were viewed as the legal equivalent of dead men. They were *civilites mortuus*, and their estates, if they had any, were managed like those of dead men.

53. W. Gaylin, "In the Beginning," in W. Gaylin et al., *Doing Good: The Limits of Benevolence* (New York: Pantheon, 1978), 33–34. It is true, as an anonymous reviewer has reminded me, that Lockett v. Ohio, 438 U.S. 586 (1978) and related cases require that all "relevant" mitigating factors must be considered at a capital sentencing. The difficulty is in establishing the relevance of broad social forces in the minds of jurors. Being raised in a poor and brutal home is a case in point. People from such environments are hurt and hostile because of their maltreatment. Some express their hostility in criminal violence; others develop mental health problems; still others react in a mix of ways. A few transcend the brutality in their lives and go on to be healthy, decent citizens. Yet the fact remains that most violent offenders have been maimed by the neglect and abuse that have pervaded their lives, and this should be counted as a mitigating factor even though some, perhaps even many, other people treated in this way do not turn to criminal violence. Convincing a jury of this, however, is another matter altogether.

54. See R. Johnson, *Condemned to Die: Life under Sentence of Death* (Prospect Heights, Ill.: Waveland Press, 1989), 25.

55. The link between abuse during the formative years and impulsive violence later in life is widely supported. See, for example, H. Wisnie, *The Impulsive Personality* (New York: Plenum, 1977).

56. See J. H. Reiman, *The Rich Get Richer and the Poor Get Prison*, 4th ed. (Boston: Allyn and Bacon, 1995), and J. H. Reiman and S. Headlee, "Marxism and Criminal Justice Policy," *Crime and Delinquency* 27 (1): 24–47 (1981).

57. See, for example, D.O. Lewis et al., "Psychiatric, Neurological, and Psycho-educational Characteristics of Fifteen Death Row Inmates in the United States," *American Journal of Psychiatry* 143 (7): 838–845 (July 1986). This research has been expanded to include

the neurological effects of neglect, which like those of abuse can result in disinhibitions that allow for profound outbursts of violence. The latest developments in this area, which relate to a wide sample of violent offenders not limited to death row inmates, have been thoughtfully examined in M. Gladwell, "Crime and Science: Damaged," *The New Yorker*, 24 February and 3 March 1997, 132.

58. Dieter (n. 4), 2.

59. Ibid., 3.

60. Ibid., 6.

61. Ibid., 6.

62. Ibid., 6–9.

63. See, for example, D. McDonald and B. J. Berstein, *The Price of Punishment: Public Spending for Corrections in New York* (Boulder: Westview Press, 1980), and R. J. Lauen, *Community-Managed Corrections* (Laurel, Md.: American Correctional Association, 1988), esp. Chap. 4.

64. See B. R. McCarthy, *Intermediate Punishments; Home Supervision, Home Confinement and Electronic Surveillance* (Monsey, N.Y.: Criminal Justice Press, 1987), and R. A. Ball, C. R. Huff, and J. R. Lilly, *House Arrest and Correctional Policy: Doing Time at Home* (Beverly Hills, Calif.: Sage, 1988).

65. J. P. Conrad, personal communication during Conrad's tenure as a Research Fellow at the National Institute of Justice, when he had access to the relevant figures, 1986. (I have adjusted these figures for inflation.) See also *The Corrections Yearbook*, 1996 (South Salem, N. Y.: Criminal Justice Institute, 1996), for daily consignment cost estimates that range from $25.00 to $107.00 a day, with an average daily cost of $53.85 or just under $20,000 per inmate per year.

66. J. P. Conrad, personal communication, 1986.

67. The Death Penalty Information Center provides the following financial information on the death penalty:

- The most comprehensive study in the country found that the death penalty costs North Carolina $2.16 million per execution *over* the costs of a non–death penalty murder case with a sentence of imprisonment for life.

- The death penalty costs California $90 million annually beyond the ordinary costs of the justice system—$78 million of that total is incurred at the trial level.

- Florida spent an estimated $57 million on the death penalty from 1973 to 1988 to achieve eighteen executions—that is an average of $3.2 million per execution.

- In Texas, a death penalty case costs an average of $2.3 million, about three times the cost of imprisoning someone in a single cell at the highest security level for forty years.

The highest bill is for capital trials, not appeals or associated confinement. This means that efforts to limit capital appeals will not result in much savings though they will almost certainly increase the number of wrongfully executed persons. See "Financial Facts About the Death Penalty" available from the Death Penalty Information Center (DPIC) via the Internet: http://www/essential.org/dpic. See also, R. C. Dieter, "Millions Misspent: What Politicians Don't Say About the High Costs of the Death Penalty" (1994) also available from the DPIC at the same Internet address; and Comment, "The Cost of Taking a Life: Dollars and Sense of the Death Penalty," *University of California, Davis, Law Review* 18 (4): 1221–1273 (1985). Costly trials and appeals are the price we must pay if we wish to administer the legal proceedings attendant to the death penalty in a way that shows due respect for the value of life. See E. Nathanson, *An Eye for an Eye* (Totowa, N.J.: Rowman & Littlefield, 1977), 37–40.

68. In New York as recently as 1980, approximately 80 percent of the spending for state prisons went to staff salaries and fringe benefits, with $1.83 per day allocated for inmate

meals. See McDonald and Berstein (n. 63). In 1996, New York spent $2.51 per day to feed each inmate. The national average for 1996 was $3.57. See *The Corrections Yearbook, 1996: Adult Corrections* (South Salem, N.Y.: Criminal Justice Institute, 1996), 69.

69. E. van den Haag, "Prisons Cost Too Much Because They Are Too Secure," *Corrections Magazine* 6 (2): 39–42 (1980).

70. Sellin's observations hold for regular life-term prisoners (as distinct from true life-term prisoners) who have been released on parole. See T. Sellin, *The Penalty of Death* (Beverly Hills, Calif.: Sage, 1982), 120. This finding has been confirmed for English lifers released on parole. See J. B. Coker and J. P. Martin, *Licensed to Live* (London: Basil Blackwell, 1985).

71. A number of studies support this claim. The pertinent literature is discussed in J. R. Sorensen and J. W. Marquart, "Working the Dead," in *Facing the Death Penalty: Essays on a Cruel and Unusual Punishment*, ed. M. L. Radelet (Philadelphia: Temple University Press, 1989), 171.

72. In the entire New York State penal system, one of the largest in the nation, only one long-termer is so unmanageable as to require special isolation. See F. Butterfield, "A Boy Who Killed Coldly Is Now a 'Prison Monster,'" *New York Times*, 22 March 1989, A1 and B5. See also Butterfield's book on this inmate (Willie Bosket), *All God's Children: The Bosket Family and the American Tradition of Violence* (New York: Knopf, 1995).

73. T. J. Flanagan, "Time Served and Institutional Misconduct: Patterns of Involvement in Disciplinary Infractions among Long-Term and Short-Term Inmates," *Journal of Criminal Justice* 8 (6): 364, 365 (1980). [Italics in original.] See, generally, T. J. Flanagan, ed., *Long-Term Imprisonment: Policy, Science, and Correctional Practice* (Thousand Oaks, Calif.: Sage, 1995).

74. Quoted in Dieter, "Sentencing for Life" (n. 4), 15.

75. Ibid., 24 (Note 67).

76. G. Wardlaw, "Are Long-Term Prisoners a Management Problem in Australian Prisons?" *Australian and New Zealand Journal of Criminology* 13 (1): 9 (1980).

77. Quoted in Dieter, "Sentencing for Life" (n. 4), 15. See, generally, J. Wright, "Life-without-Parole: An Alternative to Death or Not Much of a Life at All?" *Vanderbilt Law Review* 43 (1990): 529–568.

78. Flanagan, "Time Served and Institutional Misconduct" (n. 73), 365, 357, 363.

79. See CONtact, "Lifers," *Corrections Compendium* 5 (10): 1–5 (1981). For a systematic treatment of statistics and trends as they relate to lifers, see Flanagan, *Long-Term Imprisonment* (n. 73).

80. H. E. Williamson and J. K. Thomas, "Prison Misconduct among Life-without-Parole Inmates" (paper presented at the American Academy of Criminal Justice Sciences, Spring 1984).

81. For a review of the pertinent literature, see R. Johnson, *Hard Time: Understanding and Reforming the Prison*, 2nd ed. (Belmont: Wadsworth, 1996), esp. Chap. 4.

82. S. Cohen and L. Taylor, *Psychological Survival: The Experience of Long Term Imprisonment* (New York: Pantheon, 1972).

83. John Stuart Mill, quoted in L. S. Sheleff, *Ultimate Penalties: Capital Punishment, Life Imprisonment, Physical Torture* (Columbus: Ohio State University Press, 1987), 60.

84. J. Barzun, "In Favor of Capital Punishment," *American Scholar* 31 (2): 189 (Spring 1962).

85. Ibid., 189.

86. J. E. Hopkins, "My Life above Virginia's Electric Chair," *Washington Post*, 30 June 1985, G2.

87. William Tallack, quoted in Sheleff (n. 83), 62.

88. A critical review of this literature is provided in T. Flanagan, "Lifers and Long-Termers: Doing Big Time," in *The Pains of Imprisonment*, ed. R. Johnson and H. Toch (Prospect Heights, Ill.: Waveland Press, 1988). See generally, Flanagan, *Long-Term Imprisonment* (n. 73).

89. See J. S. Wormith, "The Controversy over the Effects of Long-Term Incarceration," *Canadian Journal of Criminology* 26 (4): 423–437 (October 1984). Research on geriatric American prisoners, the vast majority of them lifers, revealed that

many of the experiences associated with aging in open society including retirement, loss of spouse, and financial insecurity were not present and that traditional physical and emotional deterioration resulting from work and stress was absent. Inmates appeared and reported feeling younger than their chronological age. (431)

Lifers also tend to have better mental health than regular prisoners and to be generally better adjusted to confinement than other prisoners (431–432).

90. Warden Lewis Lawes, quoted in Sheleff (n. 83), 71.

91. J. P. Conrad, "Research and Development in Corrections," *Federal Probation* 48 (2): 59–62 (June 1984).

92. See Sheleff (n. 83).

93. For a thorough and thoughtful discussion of the legal and penological ramifications of true life sentences, see J. Wright, Note: "Life without Parole: An Alternative to Death or Not Much of a Life At All?" *Vanderbilt Law Review* 43 (1990): 529.

94. H. A. Bedau and M. L. Radelet, "Miscarriages of Justice in Potentially Capital Cases," *Stanford Law Review* 40 (1): 21–179 (November 1987). See, generally, M. L. Radelet, H. A. Bedau, and C. E. Putnam, *In Spite of Innocence: Erroneous Convictions in Capital Cases* (Boston: Northeastern University Press, 1992).

Index

Abu-Jamal, Mumia, 92, 100–101, 106, 187–188, 223
African-Americans
  lynchings of, 6, 7–8, 32–37, 56n. 34
  modern executions of, 7, 23n. 17
  in post-Civil War America, 6, 22n. 14, 31–33
  public executions of, 37–40
  violent crime by, 6–7, 23nn. 17, 23
  See also Racism
Alabama, 86, 100, 125, 150
American Correctional Association (ACA), 83
Amnesty International (AI)
  on brainwashing, 200–201
  on Oklahoma's death row, 22n. 4, 80–81, 83
  torture defined by, 196, 199–200
Amsterdam, Anthony, 232–233
Anderson, People v., 221
Aries, Philippe, 38, 234, 236, 238, 239
Arkansas, 228n. 74
Attorneys, 149–150, 154, 170
Auto-da-fés, 15–16
Autry v. *McKaskle*, 214

Bardaman, James K., 33
Bard, Terry, 236

Barfield, Velma, 86
Barnes, H. E., 44
Barzun, Jacques, 247
Becker, Ernest, 237
Bedau, Hugo, 227n. 54
Beheading, 16–17
Bellarmine, Robert, 234
Bell v. *Wolfish*, 197, 198
Berns, Walter, 143, 240–241
Blackmun, Harry A., 6
Bradley, Grubbs v., 89n. 50
Bragg, Willie Mae, 39
Brainwashing, 200–201, 202, 203
Brasfield, Philip, 94
Breaking on the wheel, 14, 26n. 69
Brennan, William J., 45, 46, 193, 220, 233
Bronstein, Alvin, 94
Bundy, Ted, 42
Bureaucratic procedures
  executions as, 9, 40–43, 129, 139, 141n. 16, 202–203
  written specifications for, 77–79, 134

Cabana, Donald, 93, 109, 126
  on guards, 103, 118n. 42, 141n. 18
  on warden/condemned prisoner relationship, 140n. 12, 141n. 21, 164n. 4, 165nn. 9, 20, 189n. 2, 215–216

257

Cameron, James, 36
Camus, A., 52, 64, 156, 212, 219, 238, 249
Capital punishment. *See* Death penalty
Carroll, John, 75–76
Cassirer, Ernst, 204
Ceremony. *See* Public executions
Chaney v. *Heckler*, 46
Chaplains, 149, 154, 170
Chessman, Caryl, 50–52, 95
Chesterton, G. K., 121
Chiles, Lawton, xii
Christian, D., 94–95, 99
Civilization
  death penalty and, 3–4, 53–55, 233–234, 250n. 15
  of punishment, 53–55, 233, 250n. 14
Class, socioeconomic, 7
  emancipation of slaves and, 32–33
  public executions and, 28, 29, 30, 34–35, 55nn. 3, 14
Condemned prisoners, xv, 227n. 53
  counseling of, 154, 170–172, 173, 209, 214
  dehumanization of, 8, 93, 155–158, 193, 208–209, 210, 220–221
  deterioration of, 89n. 50, 104–106, 107, 116n. 11, 171–175, 202
  execution team and, 143–149
  guards and, 109–114, 117n. 21
  last meal for, 152, 171, 189n. 2
  likelihood of execution of, 195–196, 224n. 1
  loneliness of, 98–101
  powerlessness of, 95–98, 173
  in regular incarceration, 217–218, 228n. 74
  resistance by, 83, 143, 175
  television for, 187–188
  visits with, 99–101, 115, 146, 149, 208
  vulnerability of, 65, 101–104, 172
  women, 86–87
Confessors, 15, 235, 251n. 23
Cooley, Charles, 208
Correctional officers. *See* Guards
Cost
  death penalty, 231, 244, 254n. 67
  life sentences, 243–244, 254n. 68
Coughlin, Thomas, 246
Counseling
  during deathwatch, 154, 170–172, 173, 209, 214
  for executioners, 182–183
Crime, 147
  murder, 231–232, 239–243

  rape, 34, 57n. 50
  violent, 6–7, 23nn. 17, 23
  white-collar, 7

Davies, N., 28
Dead Man Walking, 184
Death
  changing view of, 234–239
  civil, 240, 242–243
  as defining death row, 92–93, 106–108
  finality of, 54, 236–239
Death penalty
  civilization and, 3–4, 53–55, 233–234, 250n. 15
  class and race bias in, 6–8, 23nn. 19, 23, 57n. 50, 222–223, 231
  costs of, 231, 244, 254n. 67
  as deterrent, 231, 249n. 3
  moral arguments against, 218–222
  public support for, 6, 231–232, 242
  as retribution, 231–234, 250nn. 7, 15
  as torture, 64, 219, 223–224
  See also Executions
Death row, 61–87, 92–116, 195
  abolishing, 216–218, 228n. 74
  brainwashing compared to, 200–201, 202–203
  current conditions on, 70–74, 89n. 46
  as defined by death, 92–93, 106–108
  deterioration on, 89n. 50, 104–106, 107, 116n. 11, 202
  effect of executions on, 114–116
  history of, 64–70
  human services provided on, 113–114, 117n. 21
  lack of privacy in, 94–95
  length of time on, 221–222, 223, 224, 229n. 89
  loneliness during, 98–101
  modern high-tech, 80–84
  number of prisoners on, xv
  powerlessness during, 95–98
  racism on, 106–107
  reforms of, 74–80, 84–85, 93, 96–98, 110, 213–218
  as torture, 201–203
  visitors to, 99–101, 115, 208
  vulnerability during, 101–104
  women on, 86–87
  See also Deathwatch
Death sentence inmates (DSIs). *See* Condemned prisoners
Deathwatch, 93, 142–163, 195–196, 214
  behind-the-scenes preparations during, 158–162

counseling during, 154, 170–172, 173, 209, 214
defined, 126
final hours of, 151–158
prisoner/execution team relationship during, 143–149
visits during, 146, 149
Deathwatch team. *See* Execution team
Dehumanization, 8, 204–210
benefits of, 210–213, 227n. 59
of concentration camp inmates, 212, 220
of condemned prisoners, 8, 93, 155–158, 193, 208–209, 210, 220–221
of death penalty, 218–219
defined, 204, 228n. 82
of executioners, 8
of guards, 207–208, 209
of modern executions, 47–53
resistance to, 220–221
with torture, 201, 202–203
Denial, 107, 149, 152, 155, 171
by executioners, 147, 164n. 6, 165n. 9, 181
of death, 238–239
Denno, D. W., 44
Dernley, Syd, 41, 45
Des Pres, Terrence, 212
Deterioration
on death row, 89n. 50, 104–106, 107, 116n. 11, 202
during deathwatch, 171–175
of prisoners, 205, 248
Deterrent
death penalty as, 231, 249n. 3
life sentences as, 246–247
Dewey, John, 204
Disemboweling, 14, 16
Dissociation. *See* Emotions
Dixon, Asbury, 38, 54
Dostoyevski, Fyodor, 220
Draco, 53
Drawing and quartering, 14
Dred Scott decision, 223, 230
Dutton, Harries v., 73–74, 89n. 50, 95, 106, 107, 214

Edgerton, Samuel, 234
Eighth Amendment, 190n. 12, 221, 239–240, 253nn. 45, 51
death row and, 89n. 50, 214, 219, 223, 224
execution methods and, 44, 45, 46
Electric chair, 1, 38–39, 139, 154
botched executions in, xii, 45

execution process in, 44–45, 175–178
number of executions by, xv, 43
testing, 158–159, 165n. 20
Emotions
of executioners, 180–183
guards' detachment from, 145–147, 164nn. 4-6
of witnesses, 185–187
See also Deterioration
Encyclopedia Judaica, 10
England
death row confinement in, 65–67, 87n. 9
early modern executions in, 16–18, 21, 25n. 63
Escapes, 78, 110, 245
Eschelman, Byron, 47
Evans, Connie Ray, 118n. 42, 165nn. 9, 20, 215–216
Evans, John, III, 149–150
Executioners
as craftsmen, 20
dehumanization of, 8
professionalism of, 129
variations in role of, 125–127
See also Execution team; Guards
Executioner's Song (Mailer), 123, 124
Execution Protocol, The (Trombley), 139
Executions
aftermath of, 114–116, 178–183
botched, xii, 39–40, 45, 46, 128–129, 140n. 15, 162
as bureaucratic procedures, 9, 40–43, 129, 139, 141n. 16, 202–203
dehumanization and, 47–53
history of, 8–21, 27–47
of innocent people, 5–6, 7, 231, 251n. 20
isolation of, 9, 30–31, 40–43
last-minute appeals before, 161–162, 165n. 21
media and, 67–68, 88n. 27, 183–189, 190n. 12, 191n. 16, 239
methods, xv, 43-47, 155. *See also* specific methods
procedure for, 175–178
public. *See* Public executions
statistics on recent, xiv-xv, 43–44
as violence, 9–10, 20–21
See also Death penalty
Execution team, 126–139
botched executions and, 128–129, 140n. 15
condemned prisoner's relationship with, 143–149

Execution team, 126–139 *(continued)*
  dehumanization and, 180, 202–203
  division of labor on, 132–133
  doubts about death penalty among, 130
  final duties of, 178
  group cohesiveness of, 134–138, 139,
    141n. 29
  outsiders' cooperation with, 149–151
  performance under pressure by,
    162–163
  preparations by, 158–162
  psychological aftermath for, 179–183,
    190nn. 9-10
  selection for, 114, 131–132, 141n. 17
  training of, 133–134, 141n. 18
  See also Executioners

Fear
  condemned prisoners, 65, 104
  guards, 110–113
Ferguson, Plessy v., 230
Fierro v. *Gomez*, 46
Final statements, 11, 13–14, 17, 19, 38,
    88n. 27, 175
Firing squad, xv, 43, 123, 124
Flanagan, Timothy, 246
Florida, xii, 72–73, 86, 100, 125
"Fourteen Days in May," 188, 215
Fourth Amendment, 226n. 40
Francis, Willie, 39–40, 47
French Revolution, 26n. 65
Freud, Sigmund, 237–238

Gallows, 10, 21
Garrison, William Lloyd, 32
Gas chamber, xv, 43, 45–46, 48–49,
    165n. 9
Gatrell, V. A. C., 66, 234, 235
Gaylin, Willard, 240
Germany, 19–20
Gilmore, Gary, xiv, 123–124, 139n. 2
Gilmore, Mikal, 124, 139n. 2
Glass v. *Louisiana*, 45
Goffman, Erving, 207, 208
Gomez, Fierro v., 46
Greece, ancient, 11–12, 24n. 33, 53
Grubbs v. *Bradley*, 89n. 50
Guards
  on death row, 102, 103, 109–114
  dehumanization of, 207–208, 209
  human services actions of, 113–114,
    117n. 21
  selected for execution team, 114,
    131–132, 141n. 17
  training of, 103
  See also Executioners

Guillotine, 24n. 41, 26n. 65

Halifax Gibbet, 24n. 41
Halleck, Seymour, 107
Hanging, xv, 2, 9, 17, 30–31, 43, 45. *See
    also* Lynchings
Harries v. *Dutton*, 73–74, 89n. 50, 95, 106,
    107, 214
Harwood, Joseph, 66
Hebrews, ancient, 10–11, 24n. 32
Heckler, Chaney v., 46
Hemlock, 53, 60n. 112
Herrera, Leonel, 5
Hillman, Harold, 44–45
Hobbes, Thomas, 143
Holland, 19, 20, 21
Holliday, Billie, 35
Holt, Sam, 33–34
Hudson v. *Palmer*, 226n. 40
Hughes, Langston, 35
Hugo, Victor, 1
Humaneness
  of death row, 213–216
  of execution methods, 40–41, 43–47
  of work of execution team, 129,
    130–131, 141n. 16
Humor, 108, 119n. 63, 159, 160, 172

Incarceration, regular, 53, 217-218, 228n.
    74. *See also* Life sentences
Indiana, 5
Innocent people
  executions of, 5–6, 7, 231, 251n. 20
  lynchings of, 34, 57n. 48
Inquisition, 15–16
Institutional operating procedures (IOPs),
    77–79, 134
Isolation
  with brainwashing, 200–201
  on death row, 96, 99
  of executions, 9, 30–31, 40–43
  of execution team, 137–138
  See also Solitary confinement

Jackson, B., 94–95, 99
Jackson, Jesse, 7
Jacobs, Jesse Dewayne, 6
Johnson, Edward Earl, 187, 188, 215
Jones, Charlie, 93, 141n. 16
Jones, Sam, 121, 125–126
Journalists, as witnesses, 185–187
Judicial Committee of the Privy Council,
    221
Just deserts, 232, 234, 250nn. 7, 15.
    See also Retribution
Juveniles, 4, 5

Kant, Immanuel, 224
Kemmler, In re, 224, 229n. 106
Kemp, McCleskey v., 223

Lackey v. *Texas,* 222
Lalonde, Leo, 245–246
Lang, B., 236
Last meal, 152, 171, 189n. 2
Lawes, Lewis, 68, 69, 248
Leighton, Paul S., 185
Lesy, Michael, 62
Lethal injection, xv, 1, 43, 43–44, 46–47, 139
Levine, Stephen, 62
Levi, Primo, 220
Life sentences, 249
    behavior of prisoners with, 245–247, 248, 256n. 89
    cost of, 243–244, 254n. 68
    as deterrent, 246–247
    moral objections to, 247–248
    for murder, 239–243
    public safety objections to, 245–247
    See also Incarceration, regular
Lifton, Robert, 180, 203
Lombardo, Lucien, 207
Louisiana, 38, 39–40, 89n. 46, 96, 164n. 3
Lynchings, 6, 7–8, 32–37, 56nn. 34, 39, 188–189

McCleskey v. *Kemp,* 223
McDannell, C., 236
McKaskle, Autry v., 214
McMaster, Bob, 164n. 5
Mailer, Norman, 123, 124
Marshall, Thurgood, 221
Maryland, 217–218
Maslow, Abraham, 204
Masur, L. P., 28, 29
Media
    executions portrayed in, 67–68
    executions on television, 183–189, 190n. 12, 191n. 16, 239
    lynching accounts in, 188–189
Medina, Pedro, xii
Medley, In re, 84, 222
Mentally ill, on death row, 106, 118n. 52
Mentally retarded, execution of, 5
Mill, John Stuart, 247
Milosz, Czeslaw, 173
Mississippi, 38–39, 125
Missouri, 139
Morris, Herbert, 204, 218
Mumford, Lewis, 205
Murder
    death penalty for, 231–232

life sentences for, 239–243
Music, 67, 156

National Medical Association Section on Psychiatry and Behavioral Sciences, 214
Newgate Prison, 65–67, 87n. 9
Newman, Graeme, 18, 63n. 25, 212
Nuremberg Prison, 12–13, 65

Offenders. *See* Condemned prisoners
Oklahoma, 80–84, 86, 93

Pain, 44-47, 52. *See also* Dehumanization
Palmer, Hudson v., 226n. 40
Pannick, David, 222
"Peepers", 72, 89n. 46
People v. *Anderson,* 221
Peters, E., 196, 197
Plato, 233, 234
Plessy v. *Ferguson,* 230
Podhoretz, Norman, 236
Powerlessness, of condemned prisoners, 95–98, 173
Prejean, Helen, 42, 62, 184–185, 209
Privacy, 94–95, 205–207, 226n. 40
Public executions, 9, 234–236
    in America, 27–30, 31–40
    crowds at, 29–30, 55n. 14, 56n. 19
    in early modern times, 16–20, 26n. 65
    in Middle Ages, 12–16
    socioeconomic class and, 28, 29, 30, 34–35, 55nn. 3, 4
    stonings as, 10–12
    violence of, 8–10, 20–21
    See also Lynchings
Punishment
    civilization of, 53–55, 233, 250n. 14
    death row confinement as, 197–198
    vs. torture, 199–201, 219

Racism
    in administration of death penalty, 4, 6–7, 23n. 19, 57n. 50, 222–223, 231
    on death row, 106–107
    in post-Civil War America, 6, 22n. 14, 32–33, 37, 58n. 65
Radclive, John Robert, 190n. 9
Radelet, M. L., 7, 111
Rape, execution for, 34, 57n. 50
Raspberry, William, 241
Reiman, Jeffrey, 204
Retribution, death penalty as, 231–234, 250nn. 7, 15
Rideau, W., 106
Riley, Leanderess, 211–212

Ritual. *See* Public executions
Rome, 12, 60n. 111

San Quentin, 95, 96, 102–103
Santa Maria della Croce al Tempio, 251n. 23
Sartre, J.-P., 98
Scaffold. *See* Hanging
Scapegoating, 28–29
Schabas, W. A., 198, 222
Schwart, Barry, 206
Sellin, Thorsten, 245
Shackles, 143, 164n. 3
Shaving procedure, 153, 174, 202, 225n. 23
Sing Sing, 68–70, 248
Smith, Clive, 187, 215
Socrates, 53, 204
Solitary confinement, 65–66, 75, 82, 84, 87n. 9, 96–97
Solon, 53
South
    lynchings in, 32–37, 56n. 34
    public executions in, 37–40
Spierenburg, Petrus, 19
Stevens, John Paul, 222
Stoning, 10–12, 24nn. 32, 33
Suicide, 66, 69, 88n. 32, 94, 124, 157
Sutton, Willie, 23n. 19

Tallack, William, 248
Tavoletta, 251n. 23
Television
    for condemned prisoners, 187–188
    executions on, 183–189, 190n. 12, 191n. 16, 239
Tennessee, 73–74, 85, 89n. 50
Texas, 6, 74–75, 85, 86–87
Texas, Lackey v., 222
Thompson, Jim, 39
Toch, Hans, 205, 220
Torture, 8, 20
    benefits of, 210–213
    death penalty as, 64, 219, 223–224
    death row as, 201–203
    defined, 196–199

dehumanization, with, 201, 202–203
vs. punishment, 199–201
Trombley, Steve, 139
Tuchman, Barbara, 13
Turnbull, Colin, 103, 219
Turner, Willie, 85

United Nations Declaration against Torture, 196–197, 199–200
United Nations Universal Declaration of Human Rights, 83

van den Haag, Ernst, 245
Vengeance, 232, 250n. 7
Victims, race of, 6–7
Violence
    acceptance of, 8–10, 20–21
    civilization and, 53
    of guards, 101–102, 103
    torture and, 196, 199
Violent crime, racism and, 6–7, 23nn. 17, 23
Visits
    on death row, 99–101, 115, 208
    during deathwatch, 146, 149
Vulnerability
    of condemned prisoners, 65, 101–104, 172
    of guards, 110–113

Wardens, 126, 138, 140nn. 9, 12, 141n. 21, 174–175, 179
Watson, Tom, 33
Weber, Max, 44
Welcome to Hell (Arriens), 98
Wikberg, R., 106
Williams, Renwick, 17–18, 65
Witnesses, 41, 42, 58n. 79, 167–168
    journalists as, 58n. 79, 185–187
    observations of, 169–171
Wolfish, Bell v., 197, 198
Women, xv, 86–87
Wouters, Hendrina, 19, 21, 54

Zimmerman, Isodore, 198